ORSON WELLES

portfolio

ORSON WELLES PORTFOLIO

Sketches and Drawings from the Welles Estate

ISBN: 9781789090321

Published by Titan Books
A division of Titan Publishing Group Ltd.
144 Southwark St.
London
SE1 0UP

www.TitanBooks.com

First edition: February 2019
2 4 6 8 10 9 7 5 3 1

Did you enjoy this book? We love to hear from our readers.
Please e-mail us at: readerfeedback@titanemail.com or write to Reader Feedback at the above address.

To receive advance information, news, competitions, and exclusive offers online, please sign up for the Titan newsletter on our website.

A CIP catalogue record for this title is available from the British Library.

Printed and bound in China.

ORSON WELLES
portfolio

SKETCHES AND DRAWINGS
FROM THE WELLES ESTATE

SIMON BRAUND

FOREWORD BY MARK COUSINS

TITAN BOOKS

CONTENTS

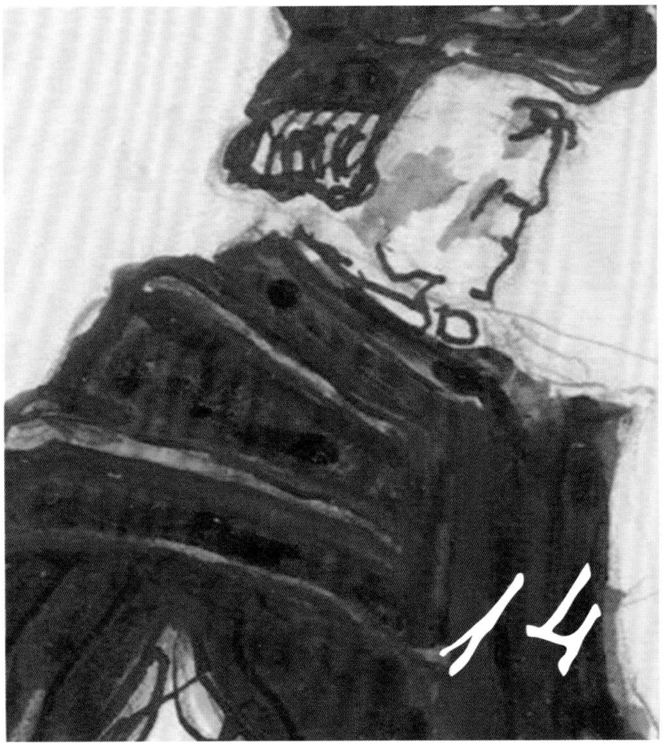

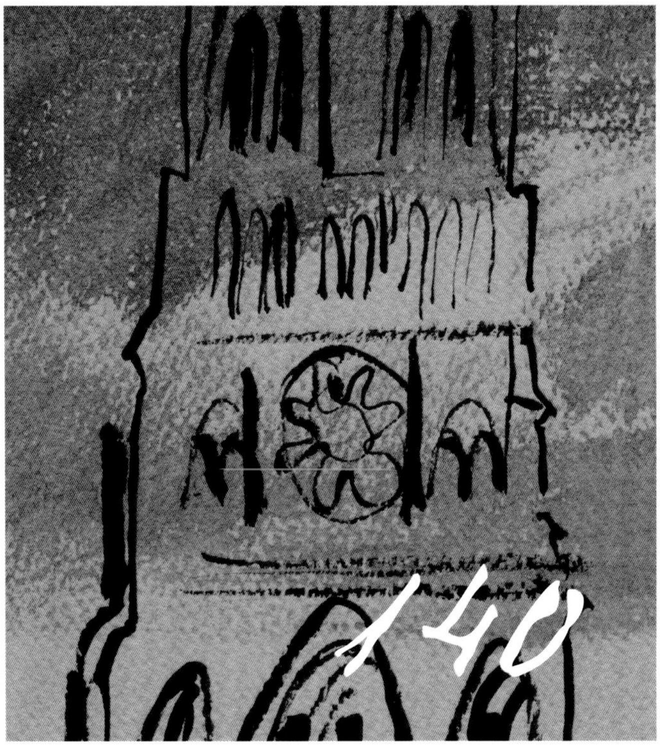

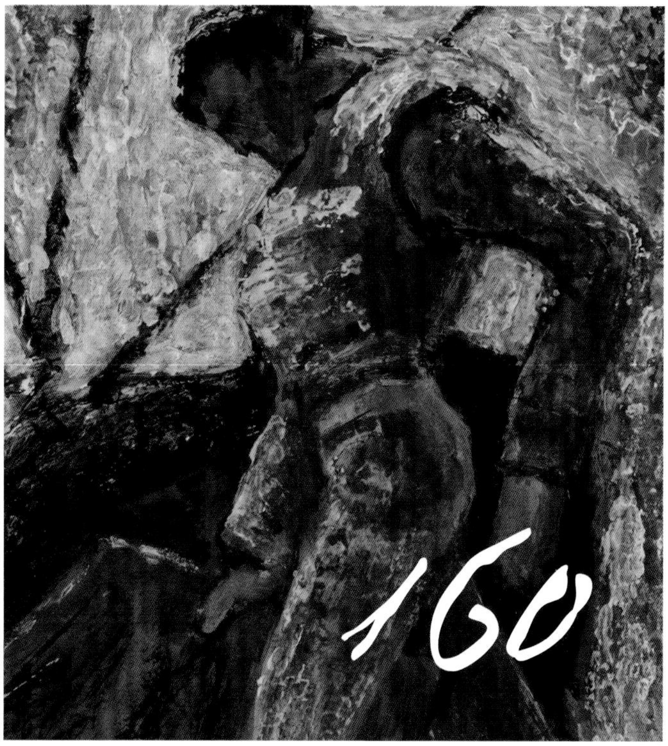
160

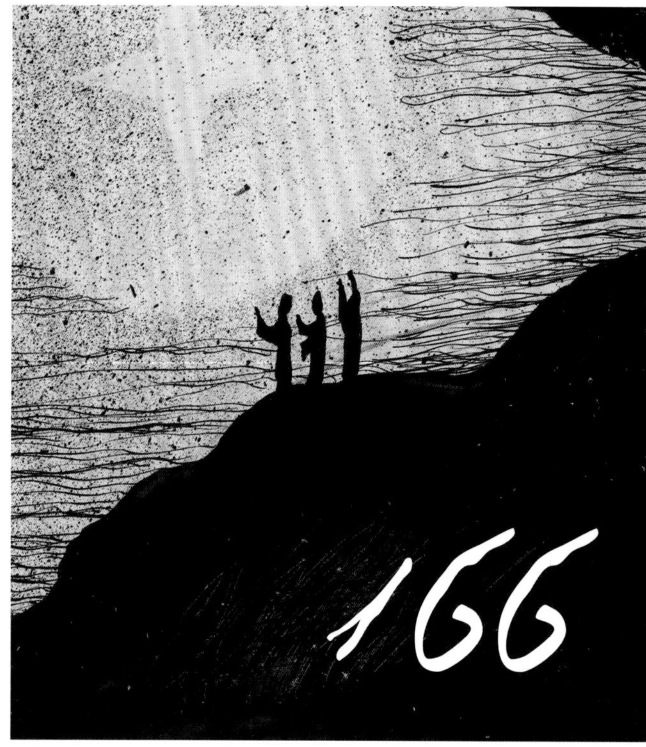
166

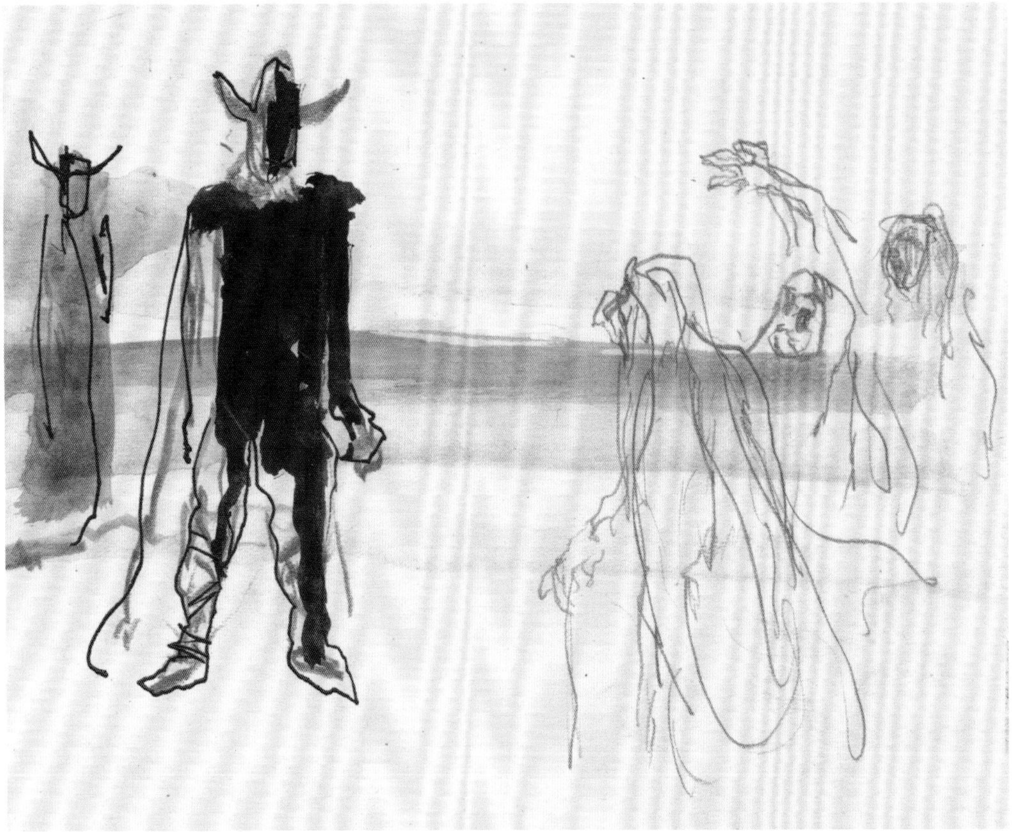

FOREWORD

BY MARK COUSINS

Orson Welles was one of the great image-makers of the twentieth century, but even more so than we realised. His films were prominent and public, but also, as we can see between these covers, private, familial, romantic, theatrical, apologetic, drunken, playful and exasperated.

This book presents another Orson, stripped of his sound track, his spoken voice, one of the best and most distinctive things about him. And yet he's still interesting. Still he gives us expressive gowns, noses and buildings. Still we see a lust for life and its codicil.

The films of some old moviemakers, like Cecil B De Mille, are dated now, but the work of Welles will never be because he hitched a ride to the wild horses, the bucking broncos of progressive politics and erotic discovery. He was more learned than many of the people he knew, this movie Nietzsche, this swaggering, sometimes effete giant, and yet you spent a night with him at your peril. Few could out-carouse him, and you couldn't get a word in edgeways.

He's gone now, of course, but his art isn't. The films are a click away. The drawings are a page away. Turn the page.

INTRODUCTION
AN INTERVIEW WITH BEATRICE WELLES

Given his genius in other areas, do you feel your father is underrated as an artist?

Beatrice Welles: Oh, definitely. I always have. He was so much more than a great filmmaker, much more important than people realize. He was really one of the most interesting men of the twentieth century: the very first American independent filmmaker – which people are finally recognizing him for – and a great artist as well. When you look at his art, you realize why so many of his movies, so many of the images he achieved on screen, look like paintings. It takes your breath away, what he did with light and shadow.

He did study painting briefly.

BW: Yes, he did, at the Chicago Art Institute. [After graduating from the Todd School for Boys in 1931, Welles studied art with Russian-born painter and theater designer Boris Anisfeld.] So much has been written about him you almost want to throw up. (laughs) But so little of it has been about his art. Which is crazy. He *was* an artist, that's how he started, he was a painter. He wasn't a film director trying to be a painter, he was a painter first.

What are your earliest memories of him painting and sketching? Did you pester him to draw things for you when you were little?

BW: I'm not sure I ever pestered him, but he would draw cartoons of us, of my mother and I, all the time. There's one sketch he did of himself, a caricature with a cigar in his mouth, that I remember very well. He'd done a picture of me – I've no idea what happened to it, you lose things when you live like a gypsy – so I asked him if he'd do one of himself for me. But really, my first memories of his drawings were the Christmas cards he made every year.

Judging by the number of cards he made, and the time and effort he lavished on them, Christmas was a major event in the Welles household.

BW: Christmas was the biggest day of the year! Birthdays weren't celebrated at all because his mother died [May 10, 1924] four days after his ninth birthday. So, at Christmas he made up for the fact that we really didn't celebrate anything else. I'm an American and I was twenty-one before I'd even *heard* of Thanksgiving! People think of my father as this very cosmopolitan person – which of course he was – but at heart he was an American. So it's extraordinary that I'd never heard of Thanksgiving. It wasn't just that we didn't celebrate it, he never even told me about it. I didn't go to school; everything I learned came from him, so everything was about Christmas. And he made it magical. I believed I heard Santa Claus and his reindeer landing on the roof, all of that stuff. It was just wonderful.

Were all the cards hand-made?

BW: Every single one.

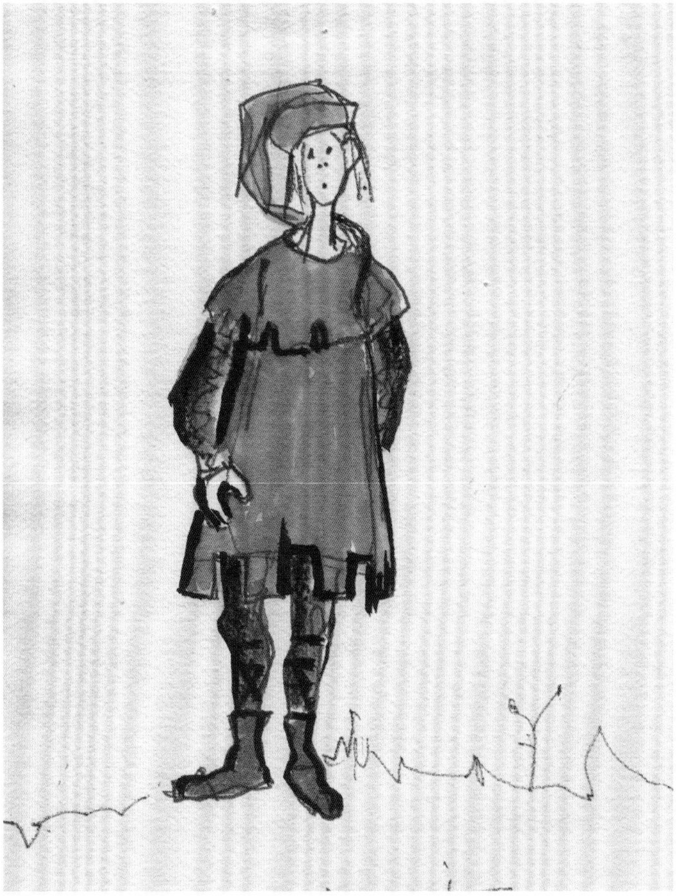

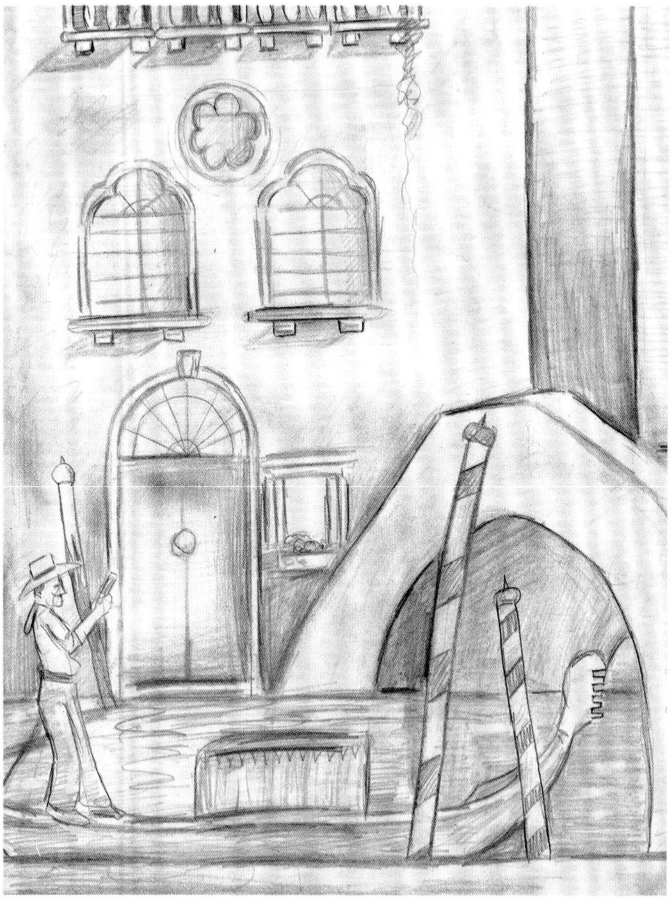

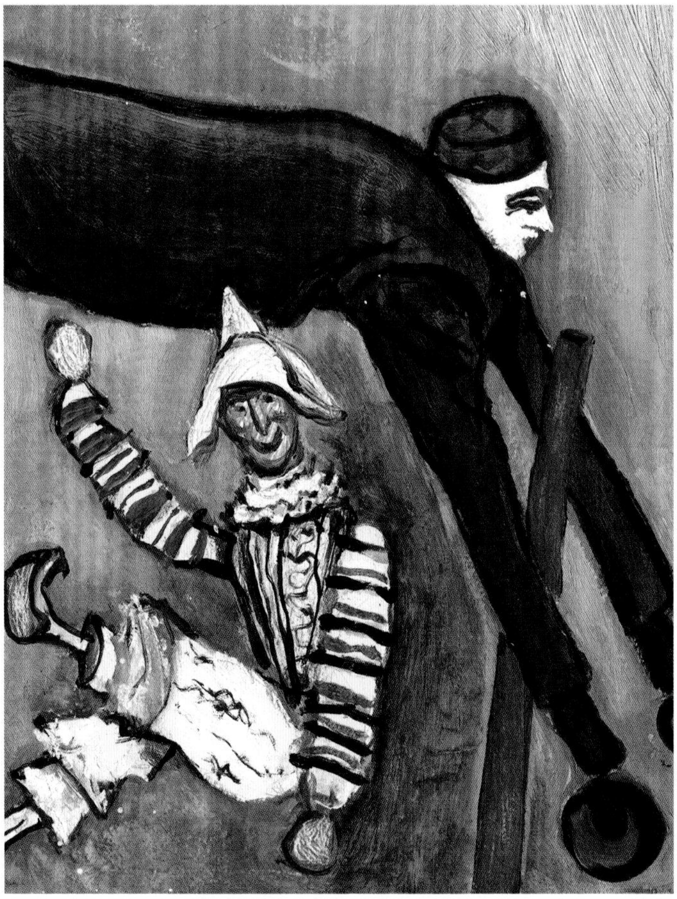

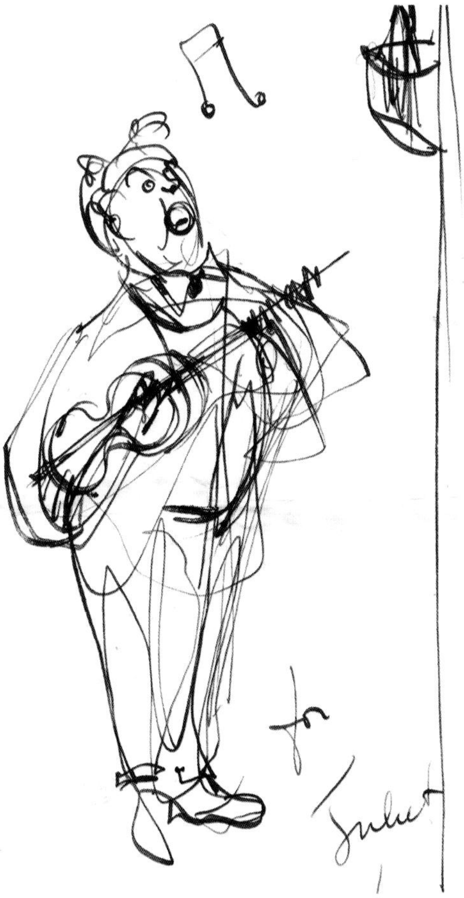
for Juliet

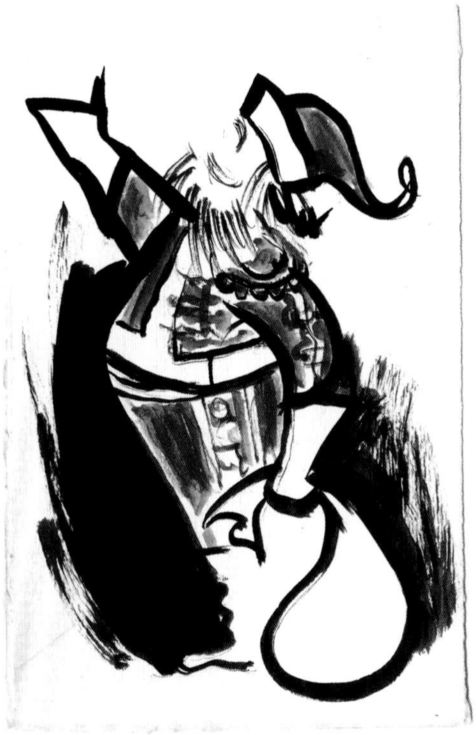

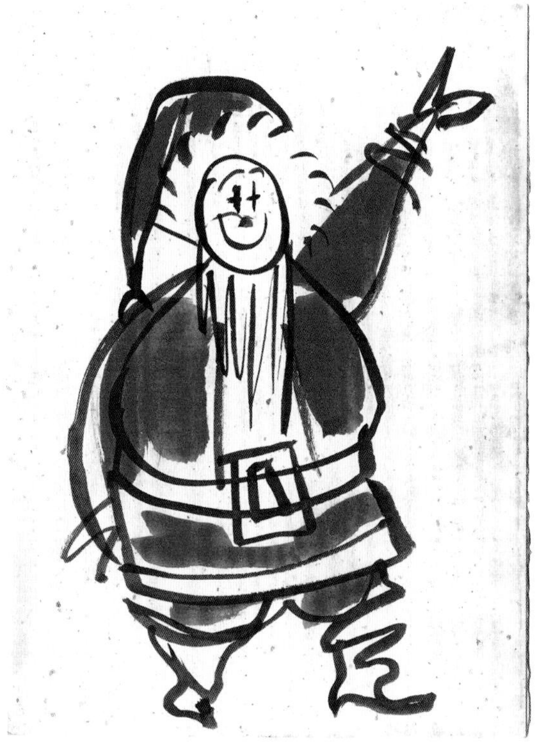

And were they just for family or for friends as well?

BW: I think he made cards for friends when I was smaller and he had more time. The first Christmas after I was born he went to an awful lot of trouble to make a cut-out frame for a baby photograph of me to send to all his friends. He didn't just send a photograph with 'Love from Orson, Paola and Beatrice' written on the back. The next year it was a picture of the three of us. In the beginning – and I mean when I was a tiny little girl – he would send them to his dear friends, like Joe Cotten and Lennie Lyons and [Roger] 'Skipper' Hill, but after that the Christmas cards were just for us. Every gift from him had a hand-painted Christmas card on it, and he'd give us so many gifts that they'd literally spill out of the room. (laughs)

He seemed very fond of depicting Santa Claus somewhat the worse for wear.

BW: Drunk! (laughs) Yes, he had a lot of fun with that. It's because in the old days you always left something out for Santa Claus. His story to me, when I still believed in Santa Claus, was that everyone left him a glass of wine or a glass of whiskey. It was never Santa Claus's fault that he got drunk, it was all these people leaving booze out for him.

Would you forgive people for detecting an element of self-portrait in them?

BW: Of course I'd forgive them. (laughs) But I don't think there is. I see more of Falstaff in them than I see of my father. Then again, you can see a lot of Falstaff in my father.

The countless drawings and sketches he did suggest he was constantly, almost absent-mindedly at times, recording visually what was going on around him.

BW: He was, partly because he wrote so many letters. If we were out somewhere and he didn't have a typewriter, meaning he had to write letters in long-hand, I can guarantee he'd have included drawings of something he'd seen and was trying to describe. The two went hand-in-hand for him.

He kept an illustrated journal when he was seventeen and traveling around Ireland, but did he keep one later in life?

BW: My father kept a journal for a while; I think he wrote one regularly until just before *Citizen Kane*, but it didn't really last. I think he was too busy chasing women, but that was my father. (laughs) What he found more interesting was to write to his guardian, [Maurice] 'Dadda' Bernstein, and to his old headmaster, Skipper Hill. And it was easier for him to draw something for them than to try to describe it in words. So yes, he did sketch and draw profusely in those letters – which are more-or-less his autobiography.

Do you have memories of him painting?

BW: I have one very vivid memory. We were living in Italy at the time. It was after we came back from Hong Kong, so I must have been about four years old, and we were at my mother's house on the Mediterranean, north of Rome. He was always in the garden painting. One day he got up to go do something and I went running over to his easel and stuffed the paints in my mouth. (laughs) I had to be rushed to hospital to have my stomach pumped.

Do you know what he was painting at the time?

BW: I have no idea, I was only four! I think it was one that stayed at that house, which went to my mother's sister. But that's where I remember him painting the most, in the garden in Fregene. He would sketch and draw very quickly, but he took time with his paintings, because they were something he would return to. He would leave everything out and go back to it the next day. I remember being just fascinated by his paints. He was a very messy painter; all the tubes were open and squeezed out and the paint and the colors were everywhere. I don't know how he even knew what was what, but for me it was like a candy store.

ABOVE: Christmas cards front; originals scanned for publication

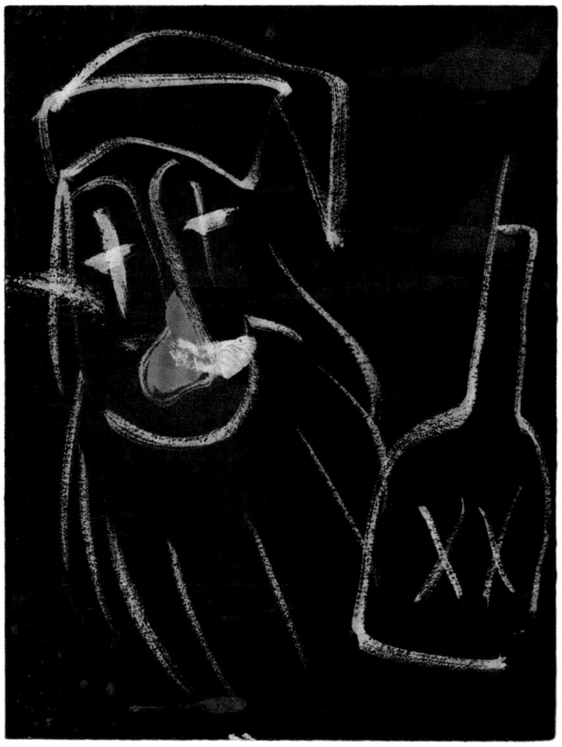

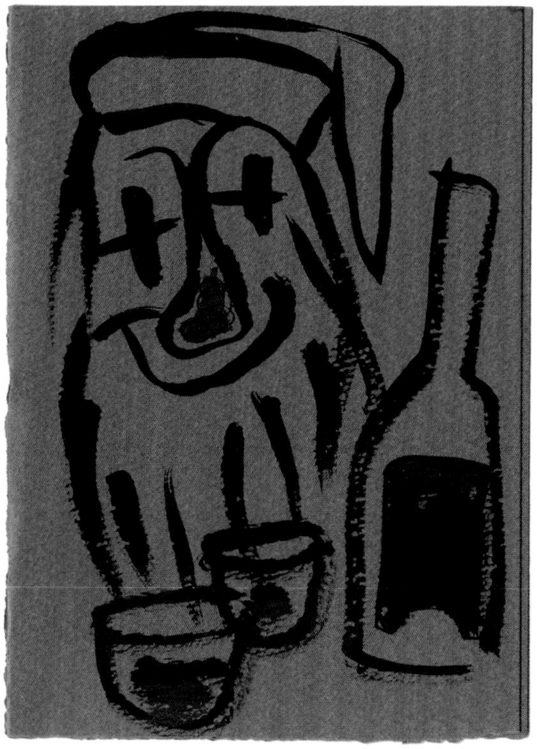

Theater and film are intensely collaborative processes, whereas painting is very much the opposite. What role did painting play in his life that his other pursuits didn't, or couldn't, satisfy?

BW: I think he tended to paint when he was sad.

When he was generally sad, or sad over something specific?

BW: I think it depends. One of the few paintings of his that I have is called Abolishment, and it's the one he did just after they threw him off *Touch of Evil.*

Some very complex emotions there, obviously.

BW: Yes, I think it's an angry painting. And I know he painted it directly after he'd been removed from the film. My mother told me he came back from the studio on the day they told him, 'That's it, you're not finishing your movie,' and the next day he was in the garden painting. He always painted in the garden. It was his favorite place.

He must have been devastated.

BW: He was. *Touch of Evil* was going to be his comeback. He firmly believed that. He was back. The studio had accepted him, he'd rented a house in Beverly Hills, he had a new wife who he adored – he adored my mother, and he adored me. From the time I was two years old we were inseparable. So, in a way, the timing was lucky for him. If he hadn't had us, I don't know what he'd have done.

Perhaps his most famous unfinished film was Don Quixote, *a project he poured his heart into for years. No surprise that there's a painting associated with that, too.*

BW: No, it isn't a surprise. Of course, it happened many times throughout his career that he thought he'd be able to make a film and then couldn't. But *Don Quixote* was one of the greatest sorrows of his life. He was obsessed with Quixote as a character, and the movie he tried to make would've been extraordinary; I saw so many bits and pieces of it over the years. And it wasn't like *Touch of Evil*, where they just said, 'It's over. You're out.' [The problem with] *Don Quixote* was always lack of money.

Did he paint the picture when he finally realized – or admitted to himself – that the film was never going to get finished?

BW: I don't think he did, because it took a long, long time for him to admit that. (laughs) My father was pretty determined. Most of the things he did, he'd been working on for many years. He'd had *The Other Side of the Wind* in mind since 1962. I mean, the beginnings of *Kane* were in a play he wrote about John Brown [*Marching Song*] while he was still at school. So, I don't really know when he did the Don Quixote painting, but it must've been at some point when he was depressed over wanting to get the film finished and not being able to. That melancholy really comes through.

Another painting that you own is the very dramatic one of the matador.

BW: Yes, a lot of people just love the matador. I've never had a great attachment to it.

Is that because of the subject matter?

BW: Not at all. I used to go to the bullfights with my father – and I'm an animal activist! Seriously, one of my best friends is Alex Pacheco, the co-founder of PETA. I'm the biggest animal lover, and so was my father. But when it came to bullfighting, it was a whole other thing. I can't defend it in any way, but he loved it. And he knew all the bullfighters, they were his friends. That's why his ashes are buried in Spain at Antonio Ordóñez's ranch; Antonio was one of his best friends.

ABOVE: Christmas cards front; originals scanned for publication

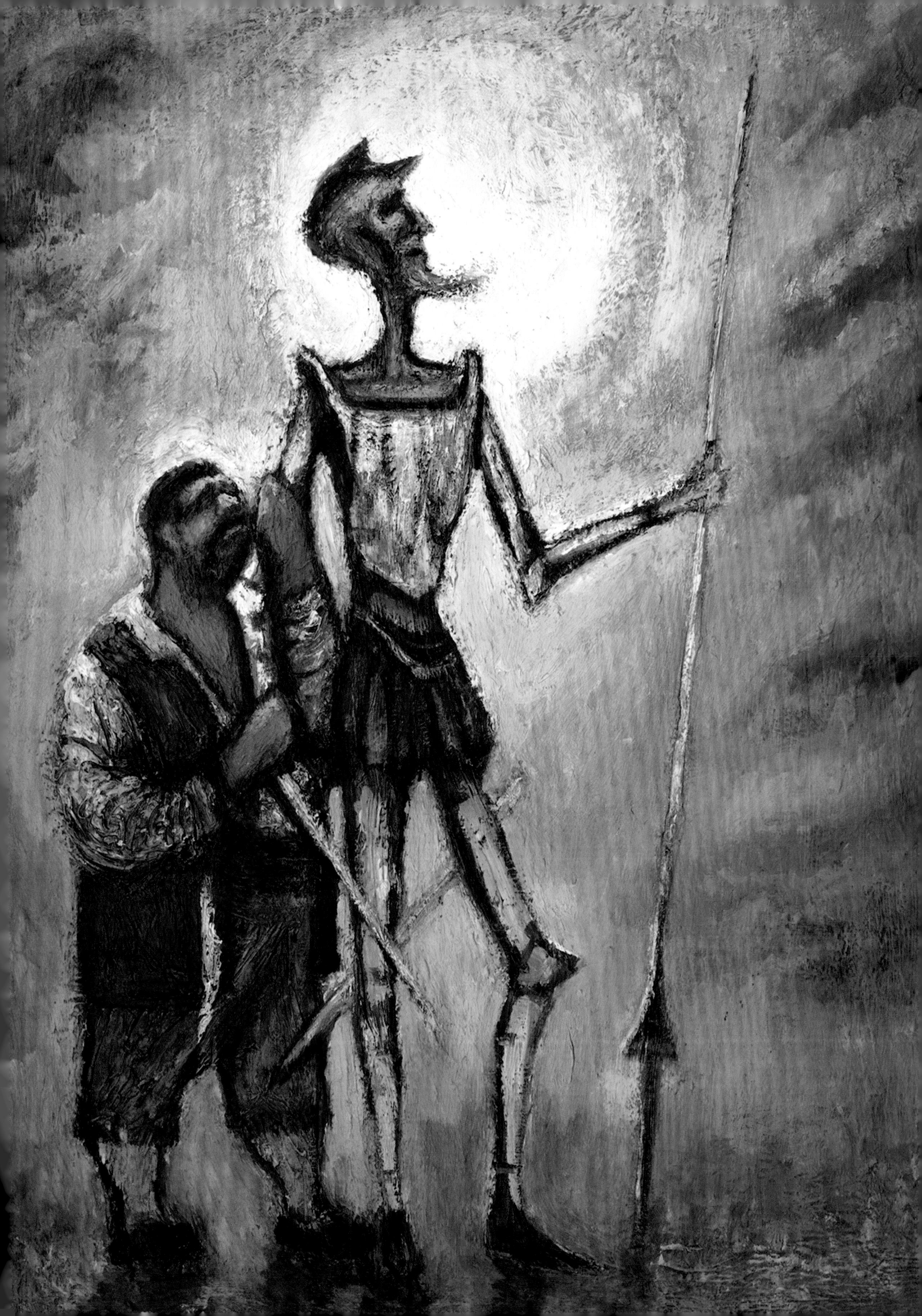

Is the painting of Ordóñez?

BW: I don't think so. I don't think it's of anyone specific. If it is, I don't recognize them, and I think I would, because it was done while we were living in Spain and he would take me to all the fights.

How old were you when he started to take you?

BW: I don't know why, but seven was the magic year. When I was seven he decided he had someone to go to the bullfights with him. My mother used to go with him but she hated it, (laughs) so as soon as I was seven, it was just me and my father.

He spent some time in Seville when he was seventeen.

BW: Yes, after he'd been to Morocco.

And he actually tried his hand in the corrida *– or at the amateur fights at least.*

BW: He did, he was so young. He called himself 'The American.' Isn't that original? (laughs) I would say to him, 'Really, daddy. That's the best you could think of, calling yourself The American.' Maybe it was the crowds who named him that.

It's still an incredibly brave thing to do. Did he ever talk about it?

BW: He admitted he wasn't very good. He was a far better spectator than he was a matador. He was actually fascinated by the bulls. I don't know if you've ever been near a Spanish fighting bull, but they are the scariest animals you can imagine. Nothing comes close. They are just pure power, a machine that's bred to kill. I remember one year when we went to Pamplona for the running of the bulls. My parents had some friends who lived on one of the streets the bulls ran through, so we went up there early in the morning. And my father knew everything. The real aficionados who knew him and who are still alive say he knew much more about bullfighting than Hemingway.

I'm so glad that bullfighting is dying out, but it's still extraordinary in a way. And my father was fascinated by it, and when he was fascinated by something he had to learn everything that there was to learn.

You were obviously extraordinarily close to your father when you were young.

BW: Well, I was born when he was forty years old. He didn't get to spend a lot of time with my two older half-sisters [Christopher Welles Feder and Rebecca Welles Manning], because he was busy making movies. He had a lot more time for me. (laughs) I was the lucky one. I never went to school; I was just with him and my mother wherever they went. If they went out to dinner, I went with them. I was never left at home with the nanny. We traveled the world, we lived everywhere. We were always at this hotel or that hotel: London, Rome, Paris, Spain, it was just constant. And I loved it! I mean, room service when you're a little kid, it's a dream come true. If he was working he'd either drag me to the set or into the editing room with him. Wherever he went, he wanted me with him. I was his shadow.

In a delightful instance of art imitating life, when he played Falstaff in Chimes at Midnight*, you were cast as his page.*

BW: It was his favorite film, so it's lovely to have been in his favorite film. And it was such fun, even though it was *freezing* cold.

He designed the costumes for Chimes at Midnight*, and a lot of the drawings have survived. Do you have any of you in character?*

BW: I don't have any, not one! And I was there when he was drawing them. I wish I knew if the ones of me still exist. Sandro [Alessandro Tasca, the film's executive producer] picked up everything after the film; my father would've just left them somewhere. And thank god Sandro gave them to the University of Michigan. [As overseer of her father's estate, Beatrice donated a treasure trove of previously unseen material to the University of Michigan in 2017.]

Did he make a point of introducing you to art on your travels by taking you to galleries and museums?

BW: Oh yes, we were always going to museums. We went to the Louvre and the Prado I don't know how many times.

Were there any artists he particularly admired?

BW: There are the obvious ones, da Vinci and Michelangelo, and I do remember when he and I were in Paris once there was a Cézanne exhibition that he was very keen to take me to, so I know he loved Cézanne. But if there was a painting he particularly loved, we'd talk more about the painting than about who painted it.

I know he admired Picasso, but he wasn't a huge fan. I don't think he thought he was as great as everyone else did. Picasso did come to lunch once when we were living in Madrid. I remember sitting in his lap. I thought he was a very nice little old man.

Of all your father's artwork, which means the most to you?

BW: Don Quixote. Without a doubt.

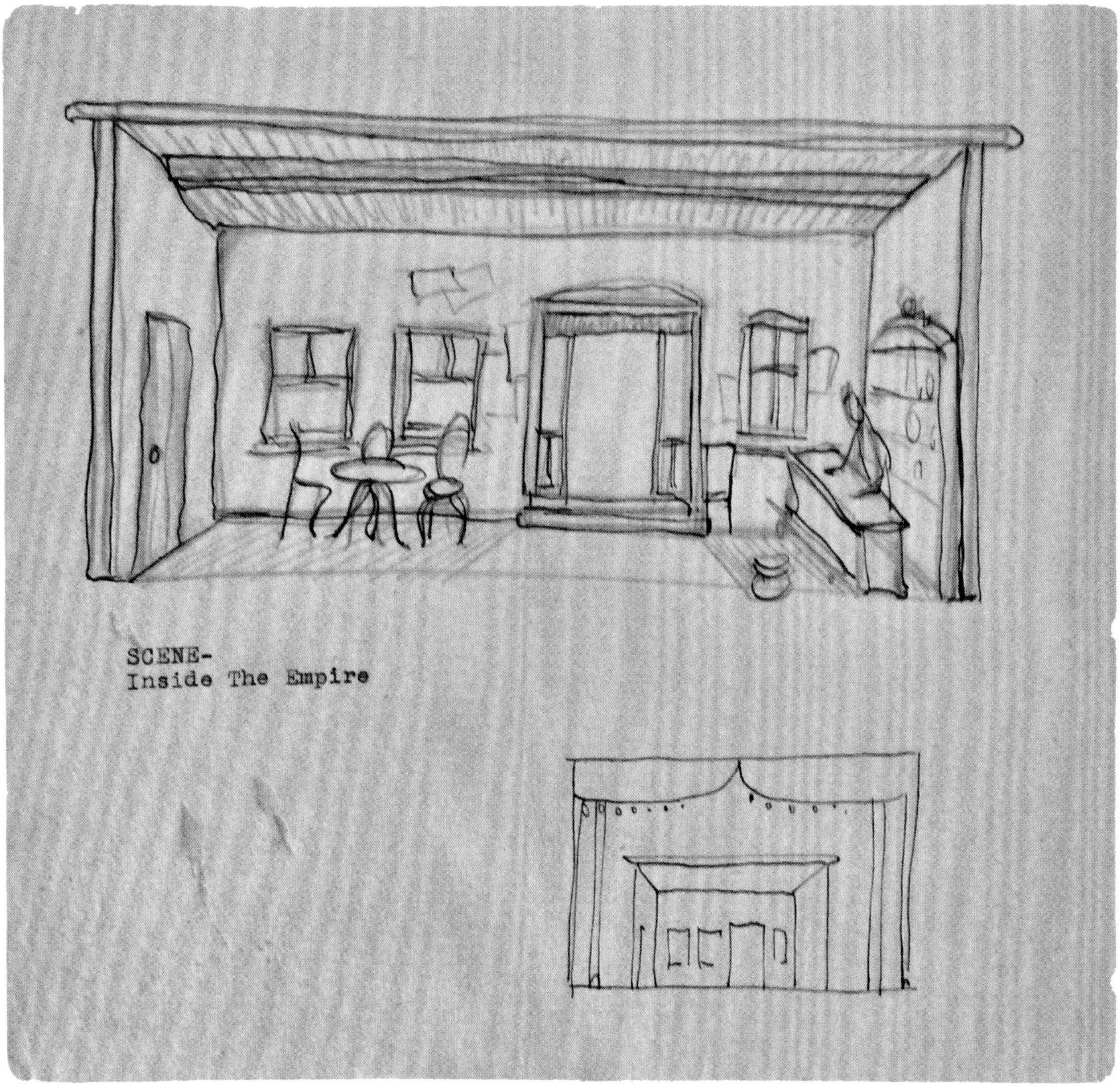

MARCHING SONG

What grabs most people about Welles's first effort as a playwright, a portrait of abolitionist John Brown, written when he was sixteen, is its narrative device: that of a journalist attempting to evaluate a man's life from various, often conflicting, sources. It does have a familiar ring to it. But let's not get carried away. The seeds of an artist's great works can always be found in their past, if that's what you're looking for.

What is arguably more remarkable is the maturity the play shows, a grasp of character and structure befitting a far more seasoned dramatist. Welles was generous enough to credit Todd School headmaster Roger Hill as co-writer, but by Hill's own admission he contributed only the first draft of the first act, 'Just enough to start our tireless boy off,' he recalled. 'And, more importantly, *send* him off. Out of my hair.'

That maturity is borne out in the set designs and their accompanying notes. The drawings have confidence and clarity; the stage directions are forthright, technically savvy and concise. In tandem, they represent the work of a director who has a crystal-clear vision and the skill to express it. They also show ingenuity and imagination – a town hall meeting seen in shadows on a wall; closed stage curtains acting as a magic lantern screen.

More remarkable still is that these notes and sketches were done effectively on spec. Although it attracted some interest from theatrical agents, *Marching Song* was never produced in its entirety, and never in any form by Welles. A heavily truncated version, performed by the Todd Troupers, was staged in 1950 by Hascy Tarbox, the arch-rival of Welles's adolescence and Hill's son-in-law. Welles's reaction went unrecorded.

ABOVE: Set design; scan supplied for publication

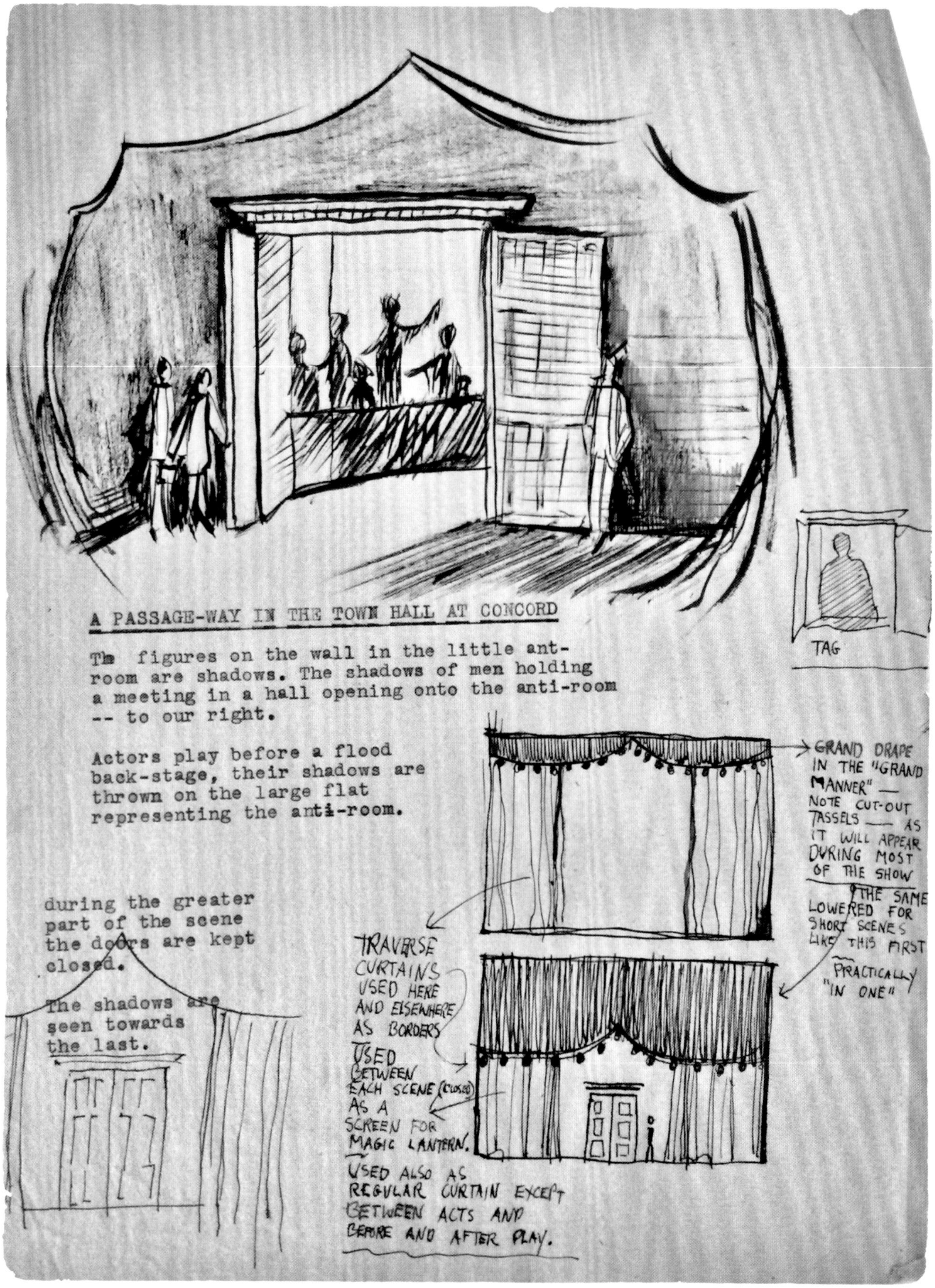

ABOVE: Set design; scan supplied for publication

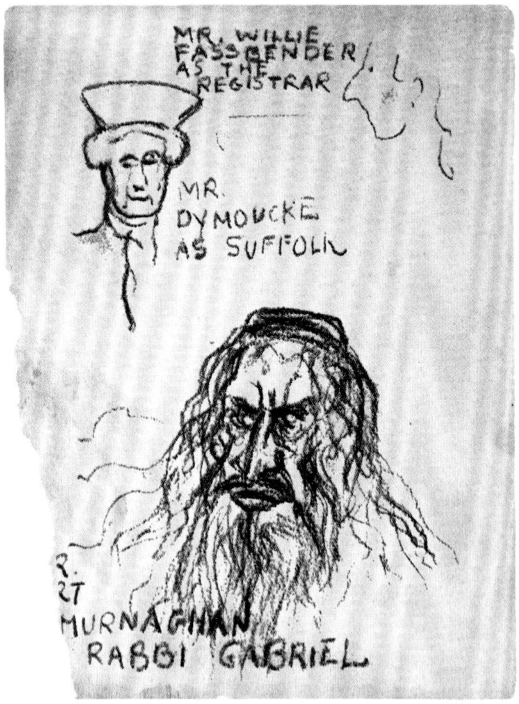

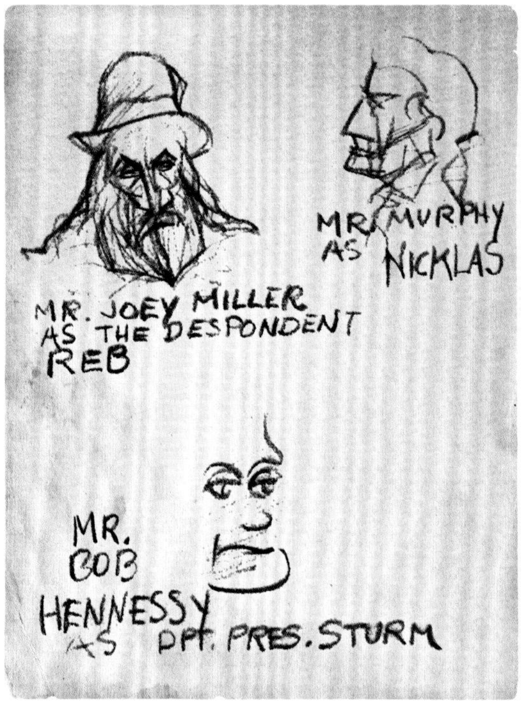

JEW SÜSS

Of the hundreds, if not thousands, of sketches and drawings Orson Welles dashed off throughout his life, for no other purpose than to record what was going on around him, few are as noteworthy as these.

Vividly rendered in pencil on what must once have been pristine white paper, now yellowed with age, they depict actors in costume and makeup for a 1931 production of the play *Jew Süss* at the Gate Theatre in Dublin. They are not the finest of Welles's impromptu doodles, nor the worst. And although they clearly reflect both the mores of the time and how the performers actually looked, the stereotypical Semitic features are unseemly at best by today's standards. Their significance lies in the fact that *Jew Süss* marked Welles's professional stage debut and the dawning of his extraordinary career.

In 1931, after touring rural Ireland for a month, in blissful thrall to the country's bounteous charm and powerful mythology, the seventeen-year-old Orson Welles pitched up in Dublin. Just fifteen years on from the Easter Uprising, raffish and imposing, the city presented a sobering, and at first demoralizing, rebuke to the rural hospitality he'd so far enjoyed.

To combat what he described as 'The despairing, ready-for-the-river anguish one experiences when unknown and alone in a big city,' he dove headfirst into Dublin's thriving cultural scene, at the heart of which was the redoubtable Abbey Theatre, then still under the directorship of William Butler Yeats.

Disappointed to find the Abbey Players away on tour, Welles had to content himself with the mothership's more avant-garde offshoot, the Gate Theatre, a diminutive hive of creative activity presided over by its visionary founders, Hilton Edwards and Micheál MacLiammóir.

Welles was not especially impressed with what he saw at the Gate, but it proved an auspicious evening nevertheless. Shortly afterwards he engineered a meeting with Edwards and, with preamble sufficient only to inflate his acting experience, asked him for a job. No doubt taken aback, but impressed with the brash young American, Edwards offered him a minor role (on amateur wages) in the Gate's pending production of *Jew Süss*, an adaptation by Ashley Dukes and Paul Kornfeld of German-Jewish author Lion Feuchtwanger's novel (not to be confused with the loathsome 1940 Nazi propaganda film of the same name). Somewhat underwhelmed by the prospect, Welles perked up considerably when he was invited instead to join the company on a more permanent basis. 'Stand back John Barrymore, Gordon Craig and John Clayton,' he wrote in his diary. 'Your day has passed, a new glory glows in the East. I am a professional!!!' He neglected to inform his journal that most of his professional duties at the Gate involved the kind of behind-the-scenes manual labor Barrymore would have slit his throat rather than submit to. Still, had he known what was around the corner, Welles might have deemed the word 'professional' worthy of more than the mere six underscores he gave it.

Fortuitously for him, Edwards and MacLiammóir were in a spot. Having committed to the production of *Jew Süss*, they found themselves without a suitable actor for the part of Duke Karl Alexander, arguably the more challenging of the play's two leading roles. Although a full thirty-five years younger than the character, Welles was among those given an opportunity to audition – an opportunity he repaid, according to MacLiammóir, with 'an astonishing performance. Wrong from beginning to end but with all the qualities of fine acting tearing their way through a chaos of inexperience.' Edwards, apparently, spent the entire time in 'silent guffaws,' proclaiming Welles's efforts 'bloody awful.' Of course, any misgivings over entrusting a pivotal role to such a raw recruit were simply steamrollered by Welles's gargantuan charisma and armor-plated self-belief. And he was, of course, a sensation, showered with critical plaudits from the press and earning curtain call after ecstatic curtain call every night.

Not surprisingly, the intoxicating rush of such adulation, the purest and most uncritical he would ever receive, went straight to his head; he wasn't just a professional, he was a star. If the Irish adventure had been intended by Welles's guardians as a diversion from his foolish ambitions to pursue a career in the theater, it achieved precisely the opposite, serving instead to focus them with burning intensity. There was no looking back now.

ABOVE: Playbill; photo supplied for publication

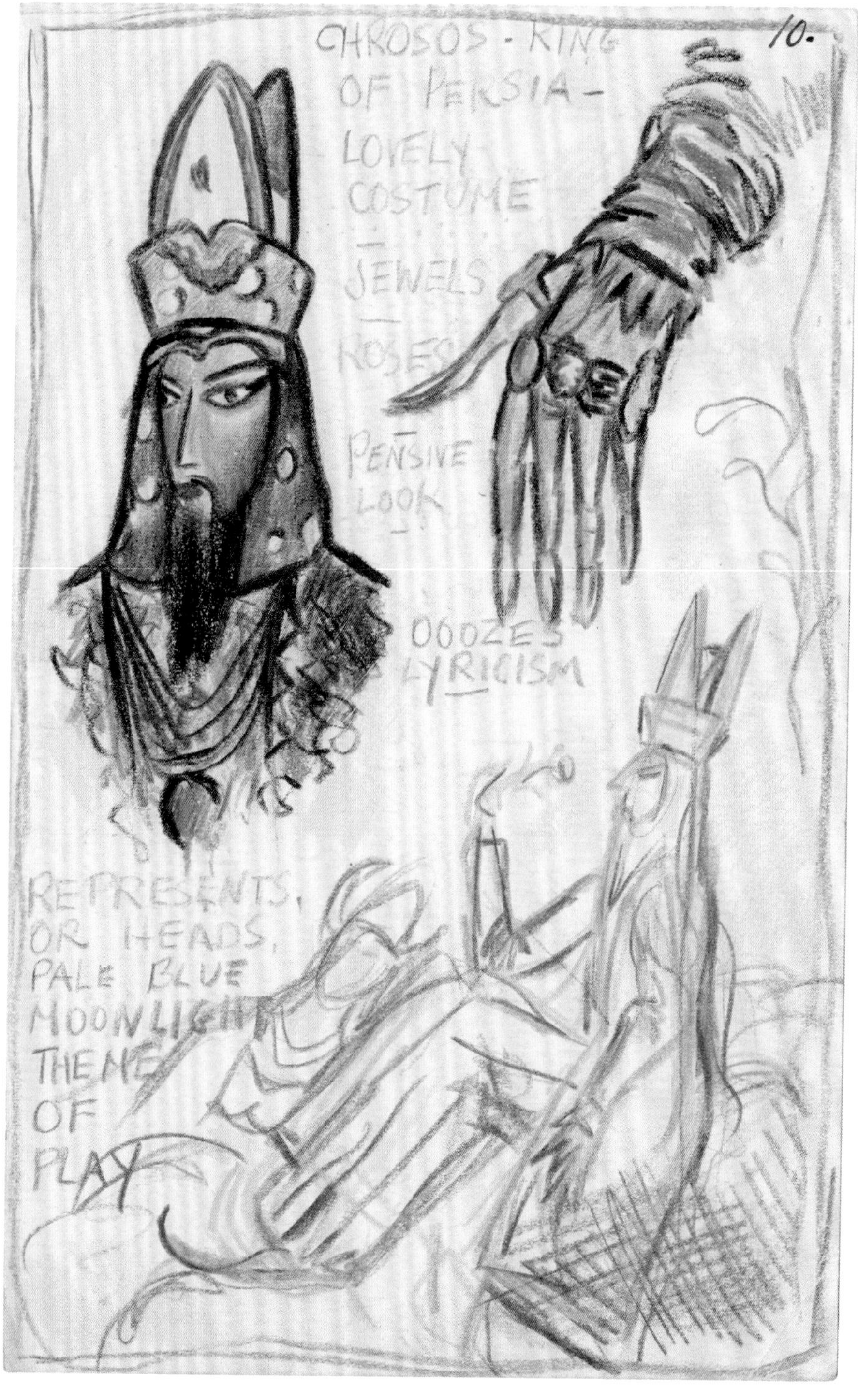

MOGU OF THE DESERT

These colorful drawings, depicting Chosroes (misspelt 'Chrosos' by Welles), the King of Persia, are designs for the Gate Theatre's short-lived 1932 production of *Mogu of the Desert*, a relatively obscure work by Irish poet and dramatist Padraic Colum. Whether they were officially sanctioned by Hilton Edwards, the play's director, is unclear; they might simply be the seventeen-year-old Welles reveling in the Arabian Nights splendor of his costume. If they were commissioned by Edwards – and it seems probable, given the Gate's emphasis on multi-tasking – they are almost certainly Welles's first professional costume designs.

The full-face image on the left can also be considered, at a stretch, an early self-portrait, albeit a flattering one. Welles was notoriously self-conscious about his small nose and is obviously indulging in wishful thinking here. Defunct when it came to the actual production. His appearance on stage, according to the Gate's co-director Micheál MacLiammóir (who was credited with the play's overall design), called for 'several pounds of nose putty.' He also notes, with some amusement, 'a white turban at least two and a half feet in diameter, and three-inch fingernails of peacock-blue and silver,' which suggests that Welles did indeed design his own outfits, even though we are cruelly denied the pantomime headgear in the drawings.

ABOVE: Costume design; scan supplied for publication

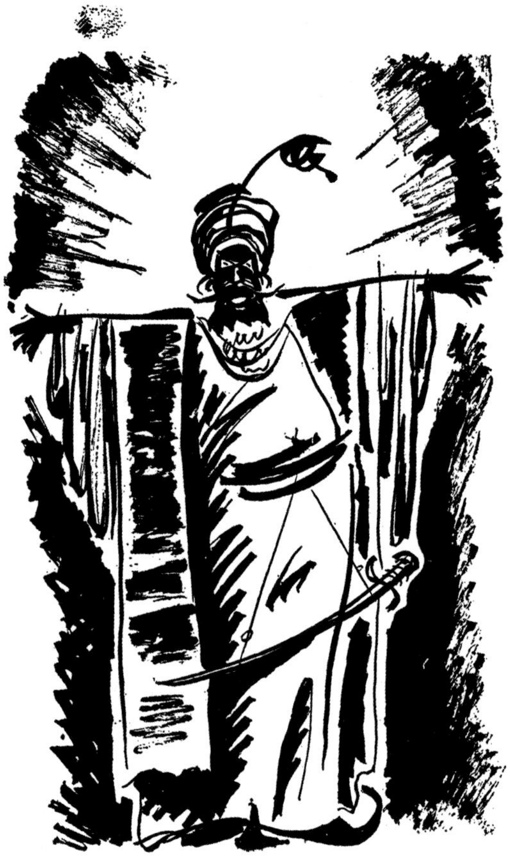

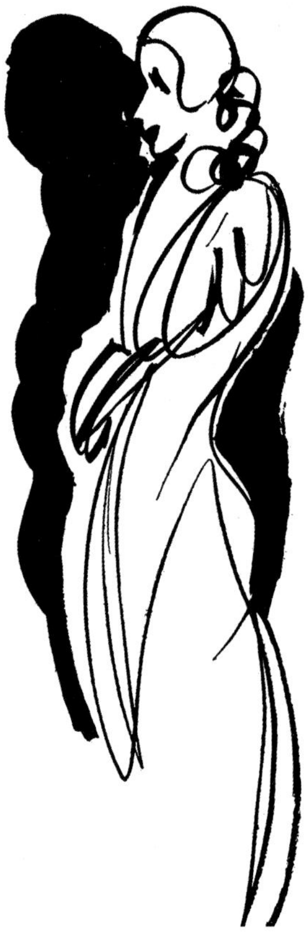

EVERYBODY'S SHAKESPEARE

Everybody's Shakespeare was a book project concocted by Welles and Todd School Headmaster Roger Hill, affectionately known to Welles and the many others whose lives he touched as 'Skipper'.

The book was Skipper's idea, a ploy to distract Welles from the failure of his first play, *Marching Song*, to find a producer. Focusing on three plays, *Twelfth Night*, *Julius Caesar* and *The Merchant of Venice*, the objective was a three-volume handbook for schoolteachers keen to introduce children to the Bard without the dead hand of academic study. With the emphasis firmly on performance rather than laborious dissection, Skipper would edit and do the research; Welles would supply the text and the all-important illustrations.

Welles began work in the spring of 1933 aboard the American Export Lines freighter *Exermont* bound for Morocco, the plan being that he would write and draw while touring the country. Equipped with pen and ink, and laden with volumes of Elizabethan drama though he was, it's hard to tell how much he got done while in North Africa. If Welles's own account is to be believed – and those words are chosen with care – most of his time in Morocco was spent in astonishing exploits, many of them while enjoying the lavish hospitality of Berber warrior-chieftain Thami El-Glaoui, Lord of the Atlas and Pasha of Marrakech.

It's more likely that Welles drew the illustrations for *Everybody's Shakespeare* on his return to America, chained metaphorically to the drawing board by Hill in a makeshift Chicago studio. But where's the fun in that? Much more rewarding to imagine him sketching away while reclining on silken cushions in the opulent surroundings of the Pasha's palace, or the isolated splendor of his mountain fastness, sipping mint tea, a bowl of sweetmeats at his elbow, the air perfumed with all manner of exotic, probably illicit, substances. Even if it isn't true, it's very much, you feel, how Welles would have wanted it.

Wherever he did the work, it is, naturally, superb. His opening paragraph sets the tone: 'Shakespeare said everything. Brain to belly; every mood and minute of a man's season. His language is starlight and fireflies and the sun and moon. He wrote it with tears and blood and beer, and his words march like heart-beats.'

Thereafter, Welles's stage directions are a marvel. Written with youthful bombast and breathtaking self-assurance, they are provocative and inventive, brimming with vitality and dramatic possibilities. And they are enlivened immeasurably by Welles's more than 400 illustrations, which are far more than the doodles in the margin they might have been. Ranging from the briefest of brushstrokes to finely detailed vignettes, they are instructive and often charmingly playful. Only a selection are featured here.

Hill's introduction is titled On Studying Shakespeare's Plays, to which the response is, '*Don't!* Read them. *Enjoy them.* Act them.' At the top of the page is a drawing of a book (the First Folio?) with a devil's tail, chasing a bunch of academics from the scene. At the bottom, the book, now sporting a halo, takes a curtain call with a troupe of actors. With attitude like that, it's no wonder *Everybody's Shakespeare* remained a classroom favorite decades after its publication.

ABOVE: ***The Merchant of Venice*** **illustrations;** ***Everybody's Shakespeare*** **scanned for publication**

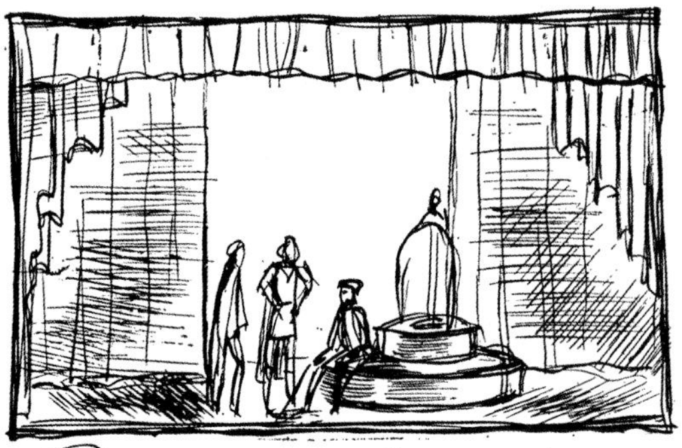

Some sky - Some drapes and a well for Antonio to sit on

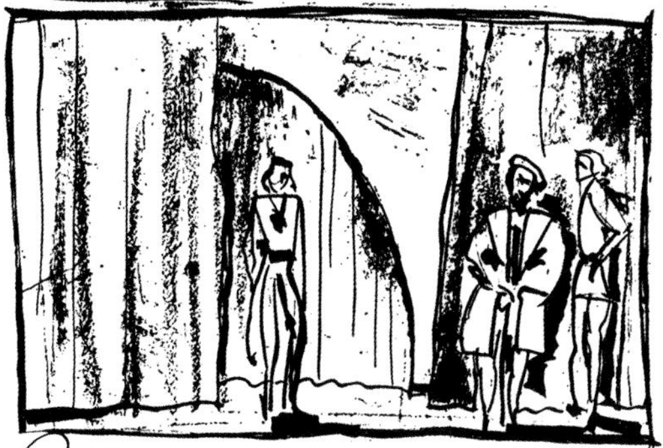

Curtain and the suggestion of an arch cut out of beaver-board for an extremely small stage

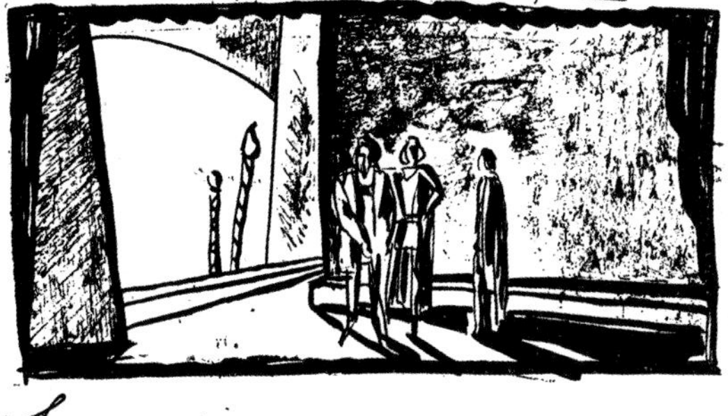

Two flats angled against a glowing sky - Poles in the distance and in the foreground a long ledge for sitting

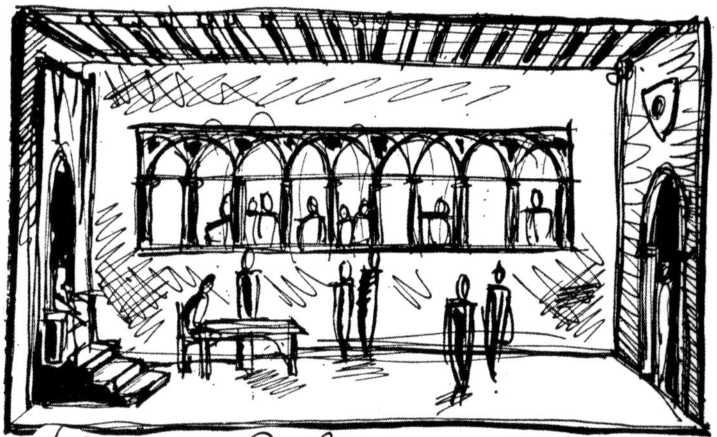

Note - Crowd looking in at windows

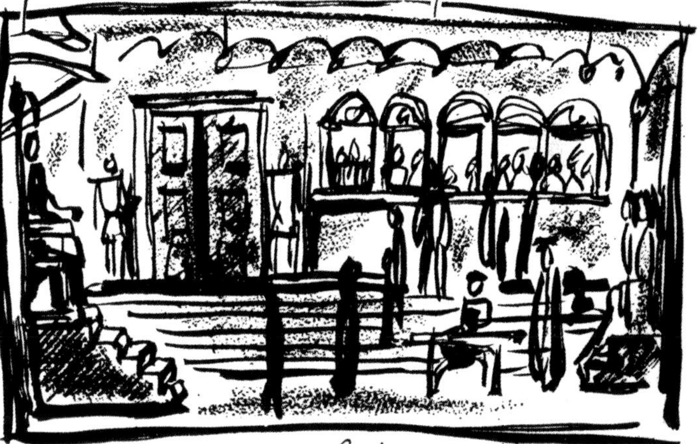

Same idea with Magnifico's throne and a center entrance with steps

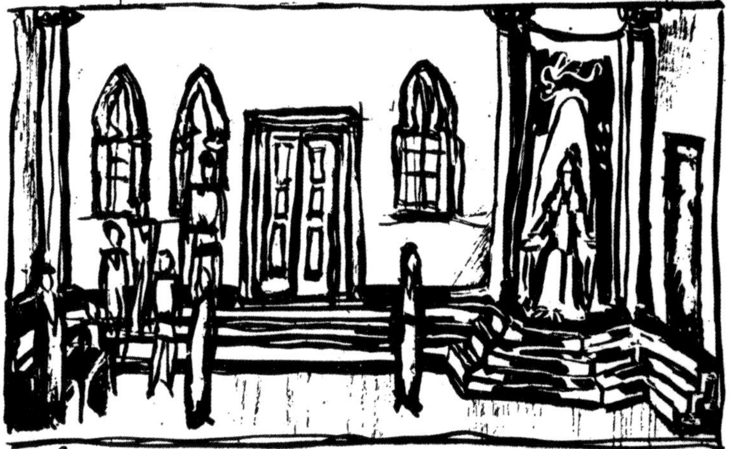

The Duke in a very dominant position

ABOVE: *The Merchant of Venice* illustrations; *Everybody's Shakespeare* scanned for publication

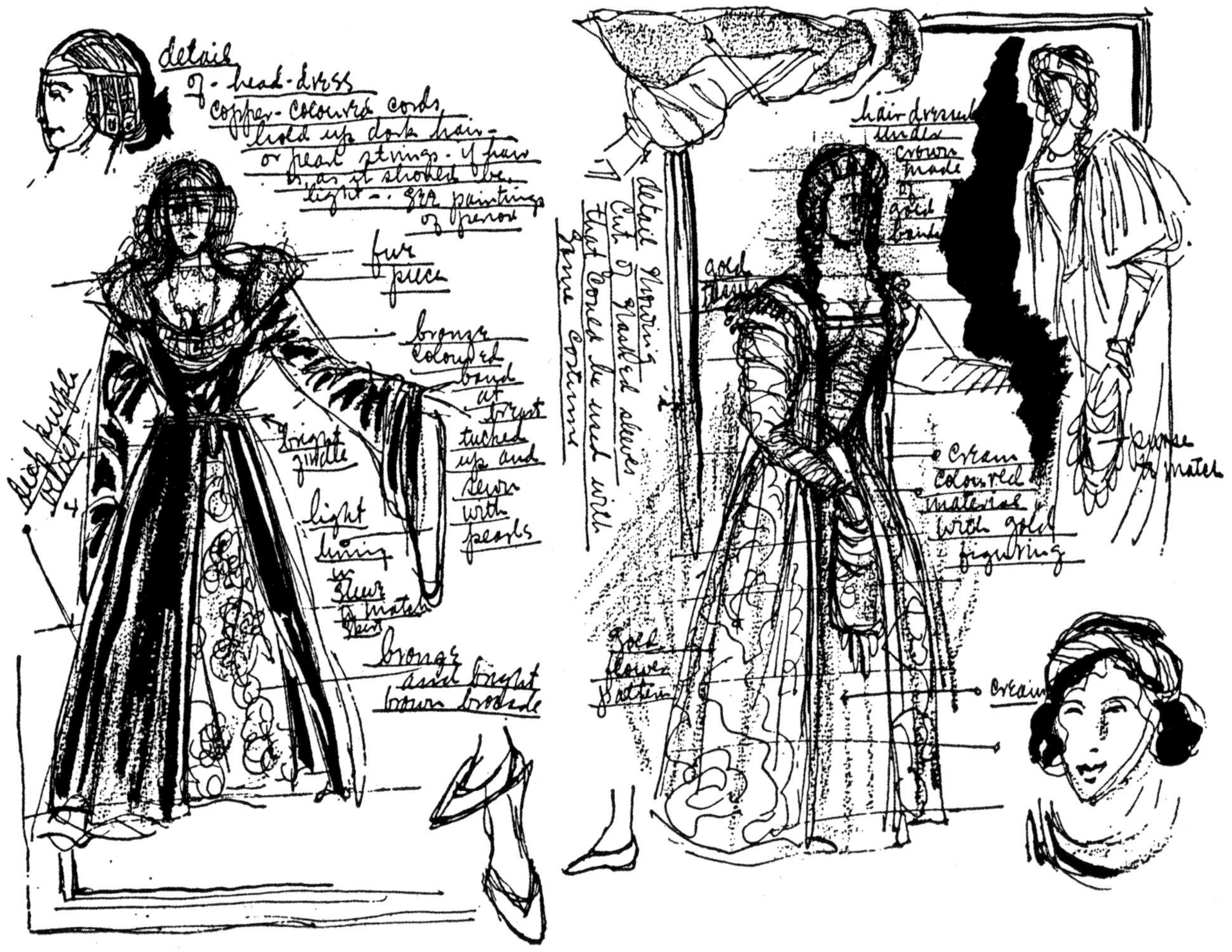

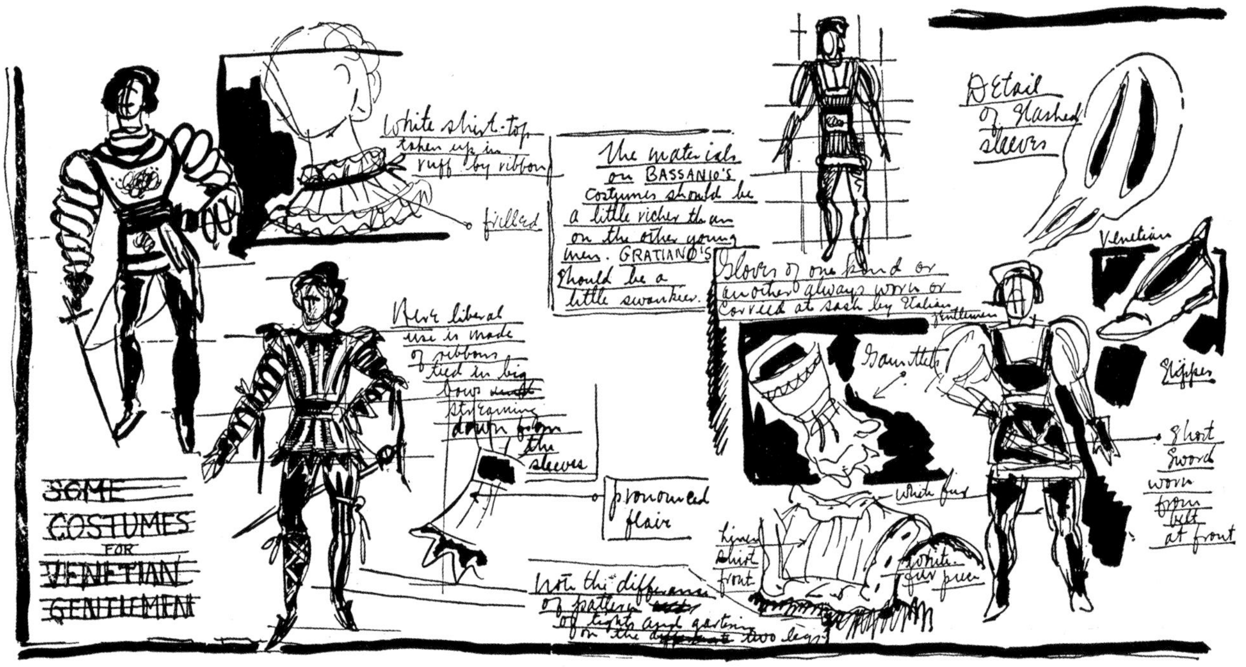

ABOVE: *The Merchant of Venice* illustrations; *Everybody's Shakespeare* scanned for publication

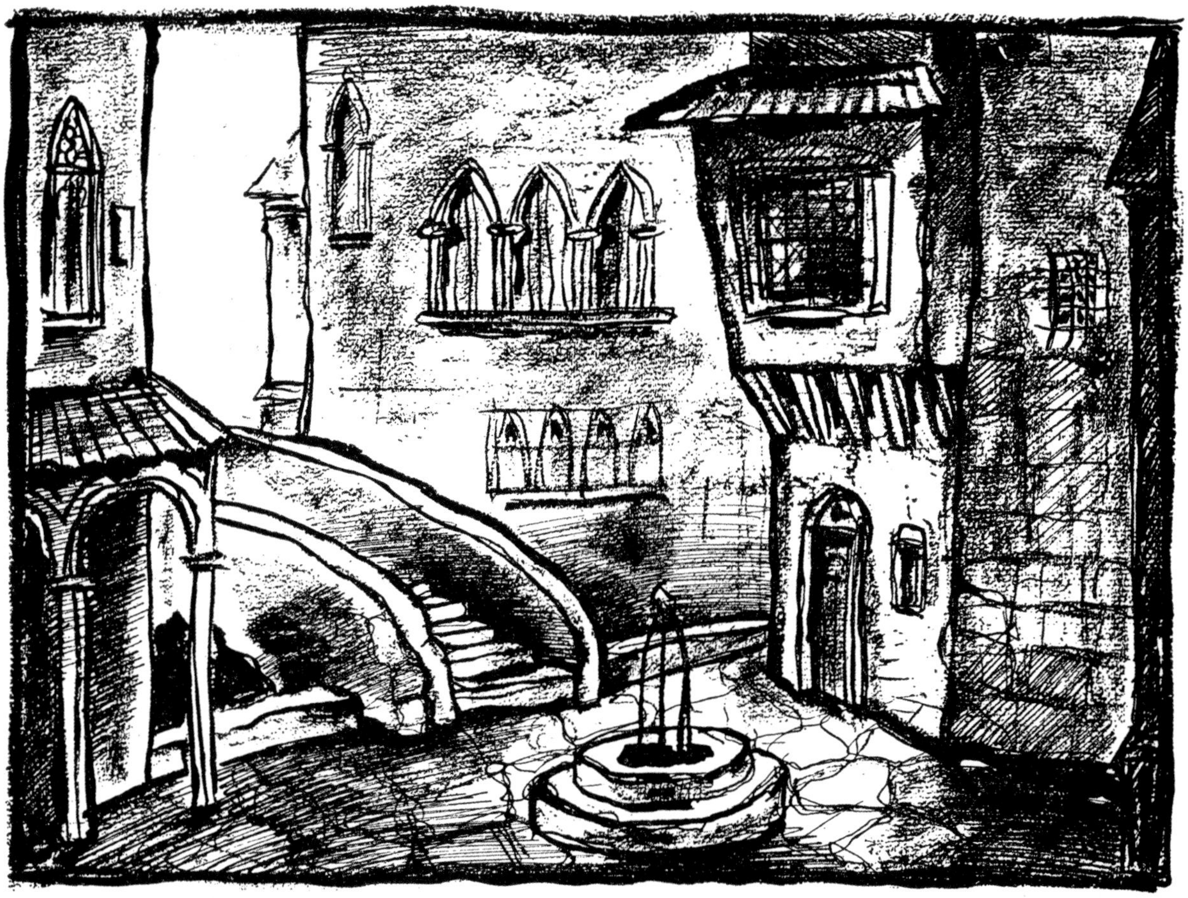

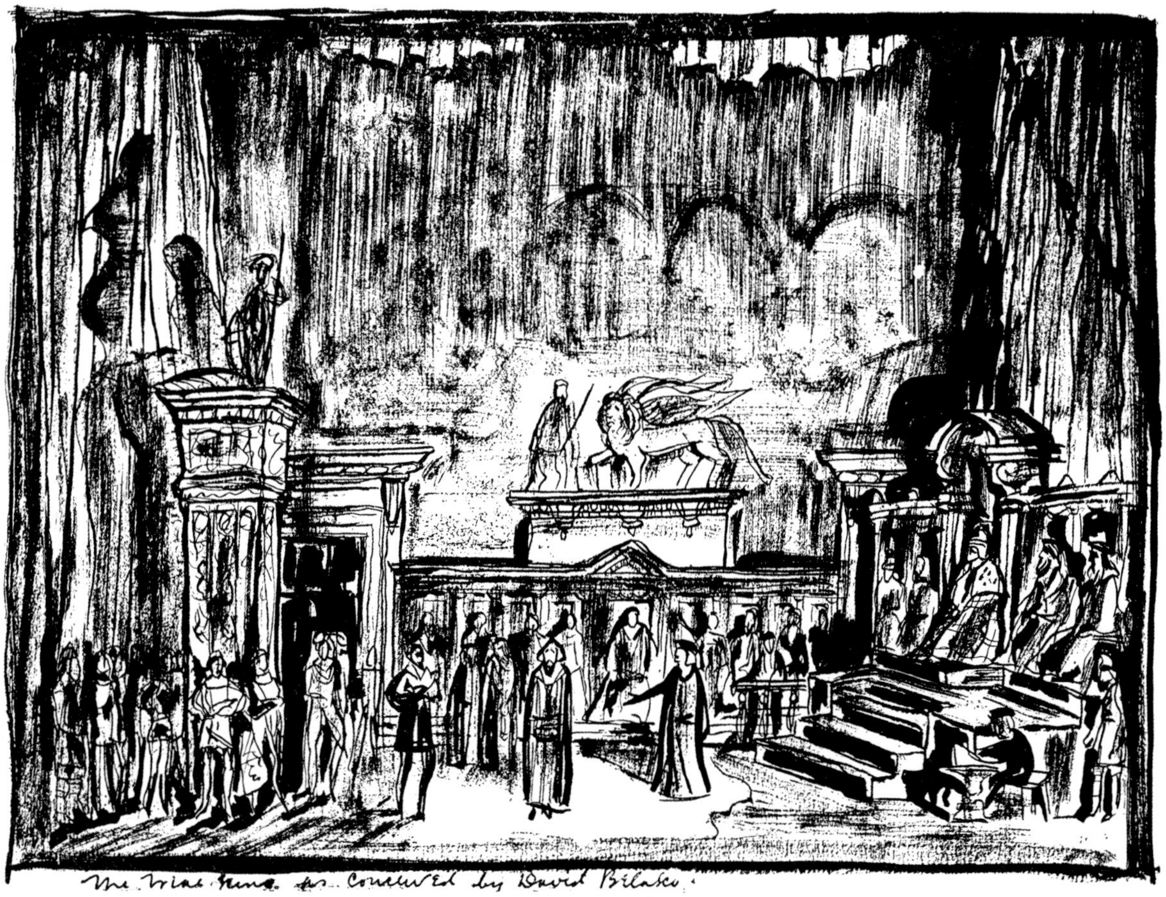

The Trial Scene as Conceived by David Belasco.

ABOVE: *The Merchant of Venice* illustrations; *Everybody's Shakespeare* scanned for publication

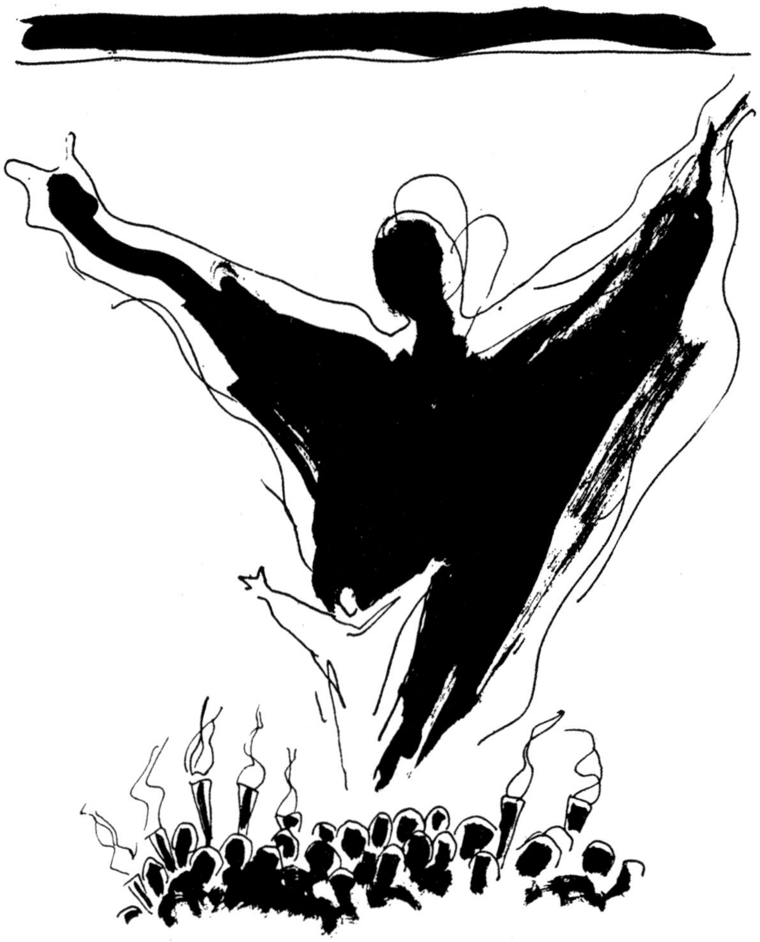

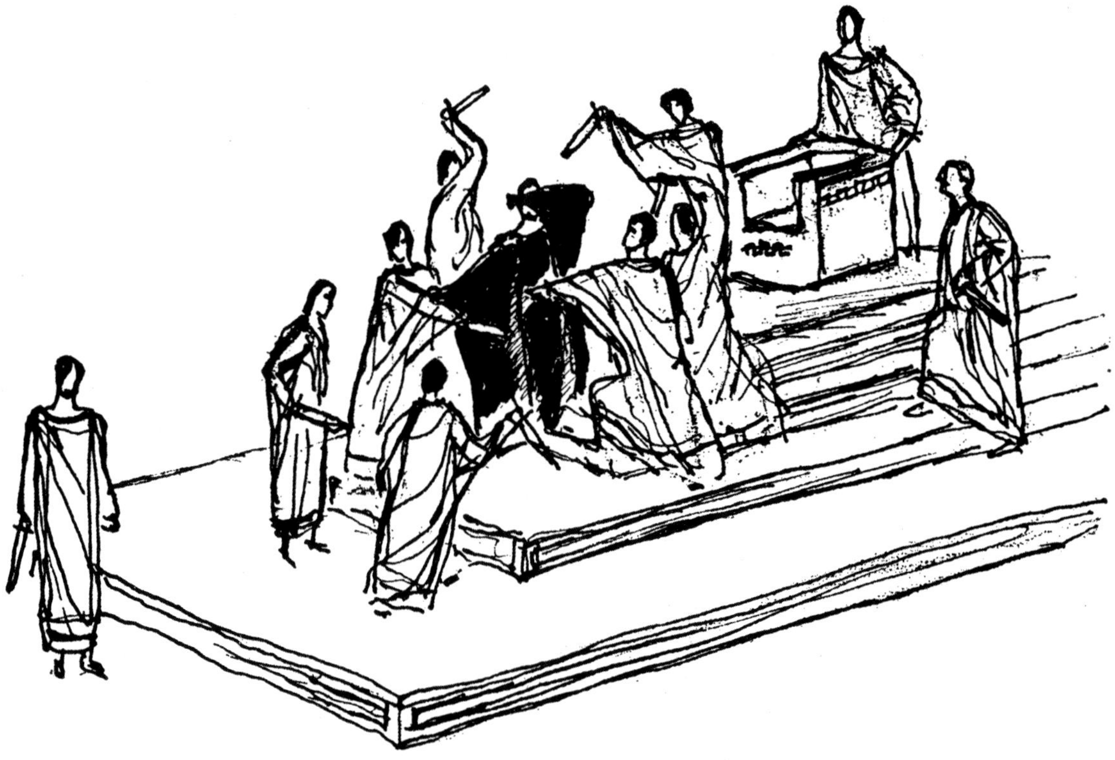

ABOVE: *Julius Caesar* illustrations; *Everybody's Shakespeare* scanned for publication

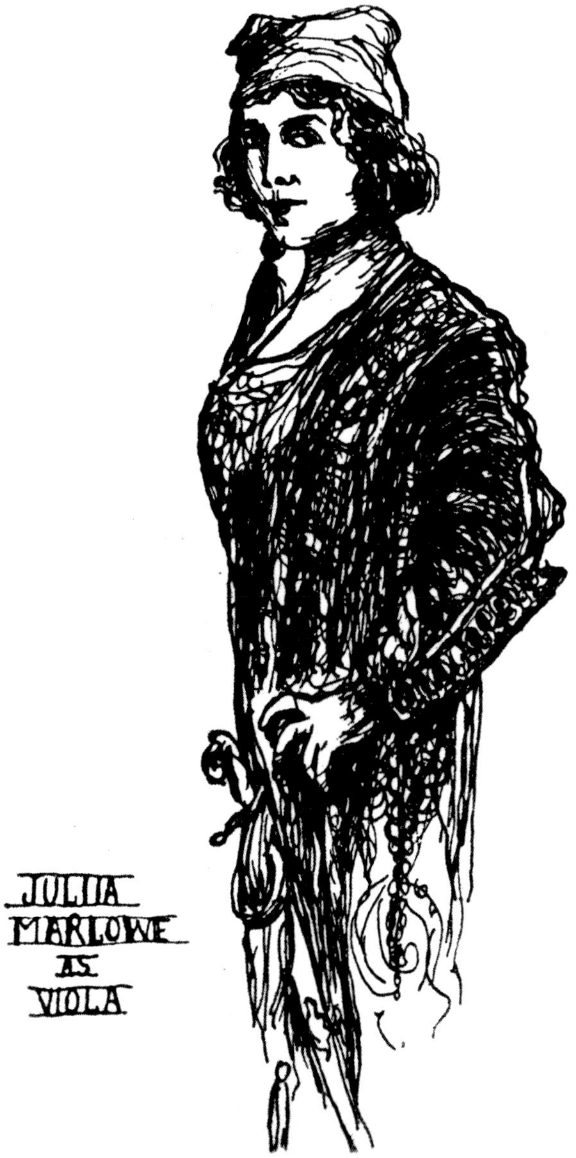

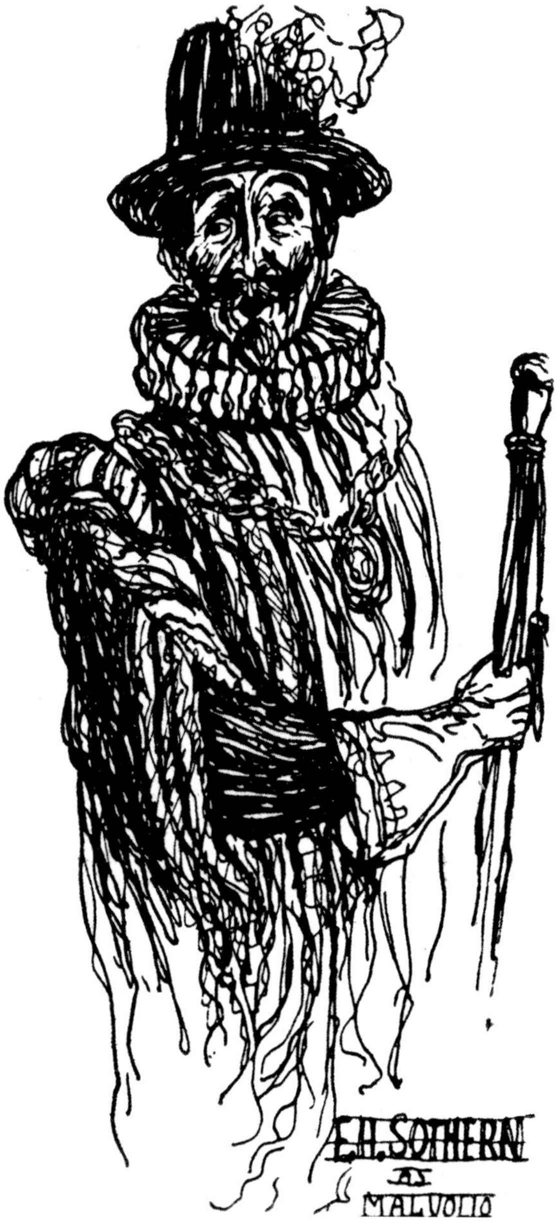

ABOVE: *Twelfth Night* illustrations; *Everybody's Shakespeare* scanned for publication

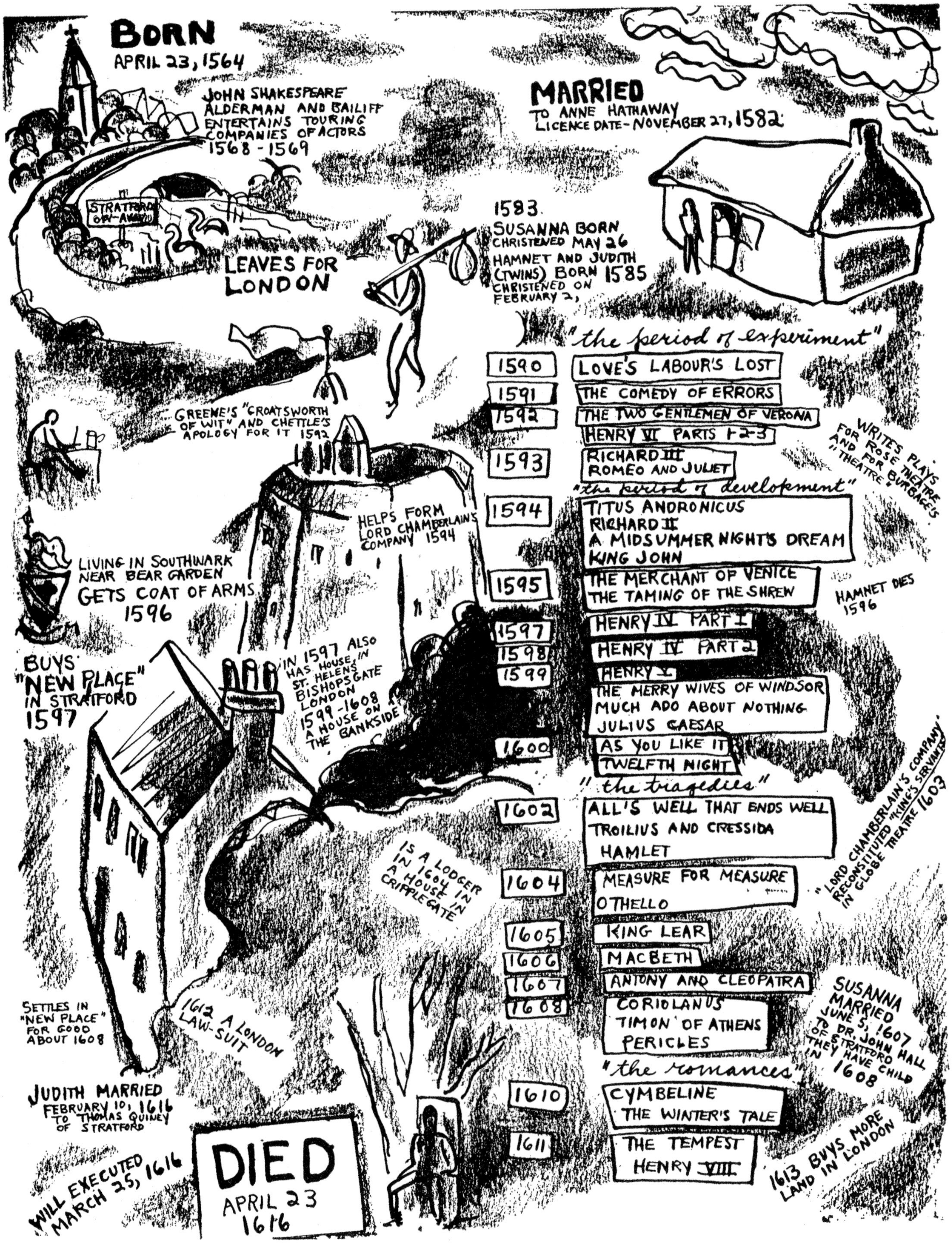

ABOVE: Introduction illustration; *Everybody's Shakespeare* scanned for publication

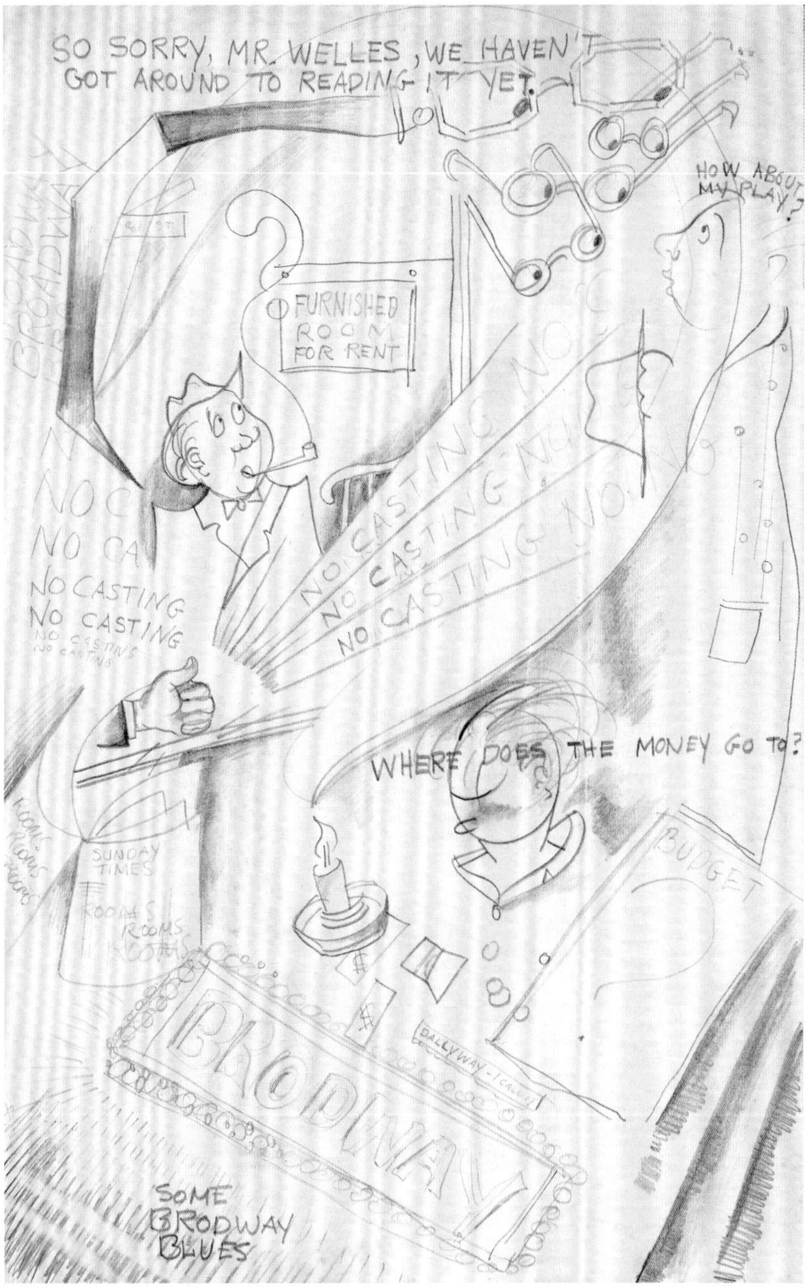

ABOVE: Some Broadway Blues; scan supplied for publication

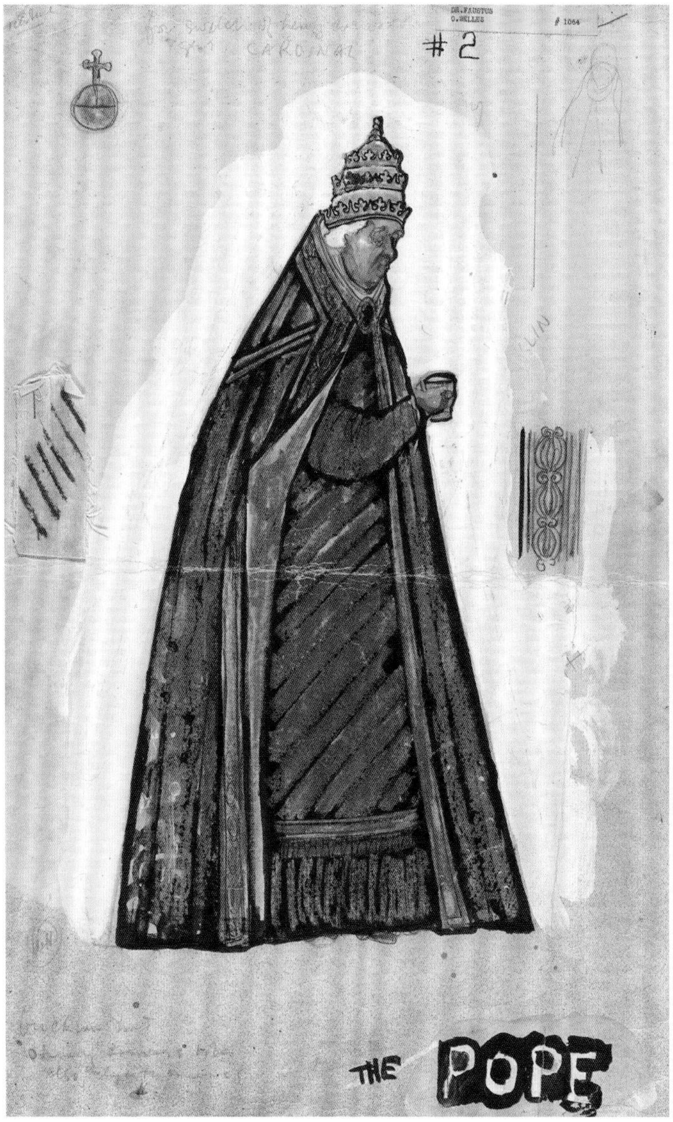

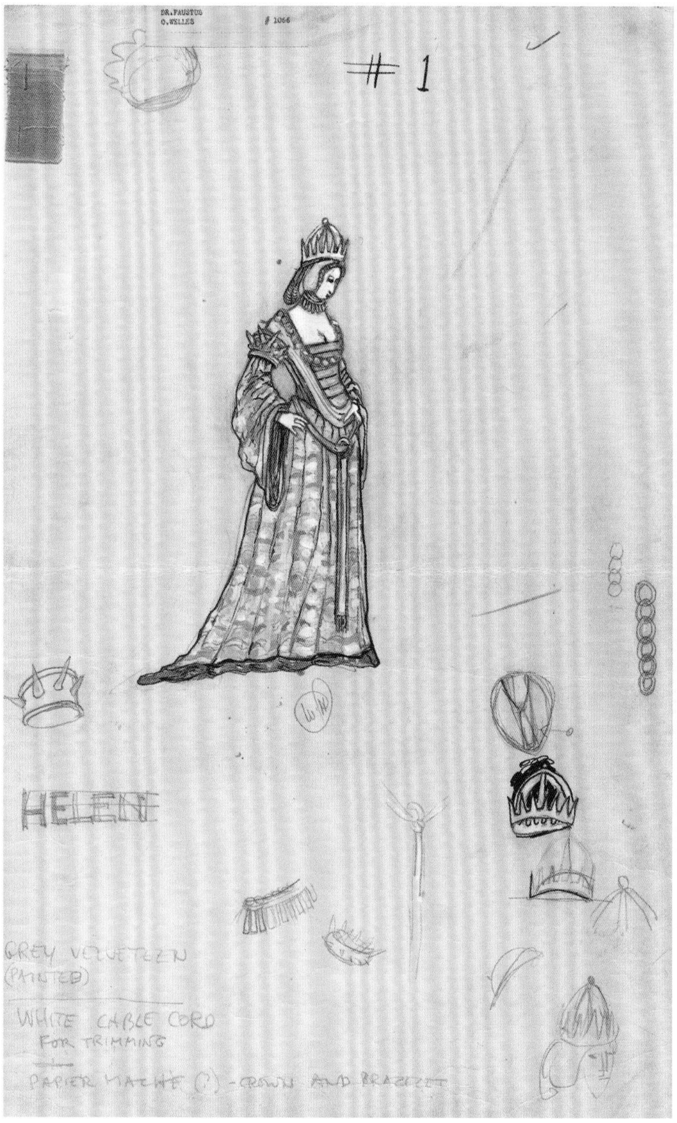

FAUSTUS

Opening on January 8, 1937 at the Maxine Elliott's Theater in New York, *Faustus* (as it was billed; a staging of Christopher Marlowe's *Doctor Faustus*) was the third of four plays Welles produced for the Federal Theater Project, a New Deal initiative set up to fund and revitalize live theater during the Great Depression. He had previously helmed the legendary 'Voodoo' *Macbeth* and the largely forgotten *Horse Eats Hat*, a bizarre adaptation of the classic French farce *The Italian Straw Hat*.

Just twenty-one years old at the time, Welles not only cast himself in the title role of Marlowe's masterpiece, but assumed hands-on creative control of virtually every aspect of the production, a herculean task he performed with customary gusto, sweeping cast and crew along with him.

Overshadowed in the popular imagination by the 'Voodoo' *Macbeth* and Welles's audacious take on *Julius Caesar* it may be, but *Faustus* was nevertheless a landmark in American theater, boasting revolutionary lighting, electronic amplification, a stage honeycombed with trapdoors and state-of-the-art special effects that included a monstrous thunder drum, capable of summoning the bowel-quaking dread of damnation with the faintest tap of a hammer.

'Our aim is to create on modern spectators an effect corresponding to the effect in 1589 when the play was new,' Welles told journalist Helen Ormsbee. 'We want to rouse the same magical feeling, but we use modern methods. I think Marlowe would be delighted.'

Welles's superb drawings and sketches for the production are ample evidence that had he not possessed genius as a director, he could have made a good living as a costume designer.

Ranging from brief thumbnails to vibrant full-color images, they positively leap off the page. In *Orson Welles: The Road to Xanadu*, the first installment of his outstanding three-volume biography of Welles, Simon Callow describes them, with enviable pith, as 'Skillful and witty, [giving], as the best costume designs do, vivid intimations of character.'

ABOVE: Costume designs; scans sourced from The Library of Congress

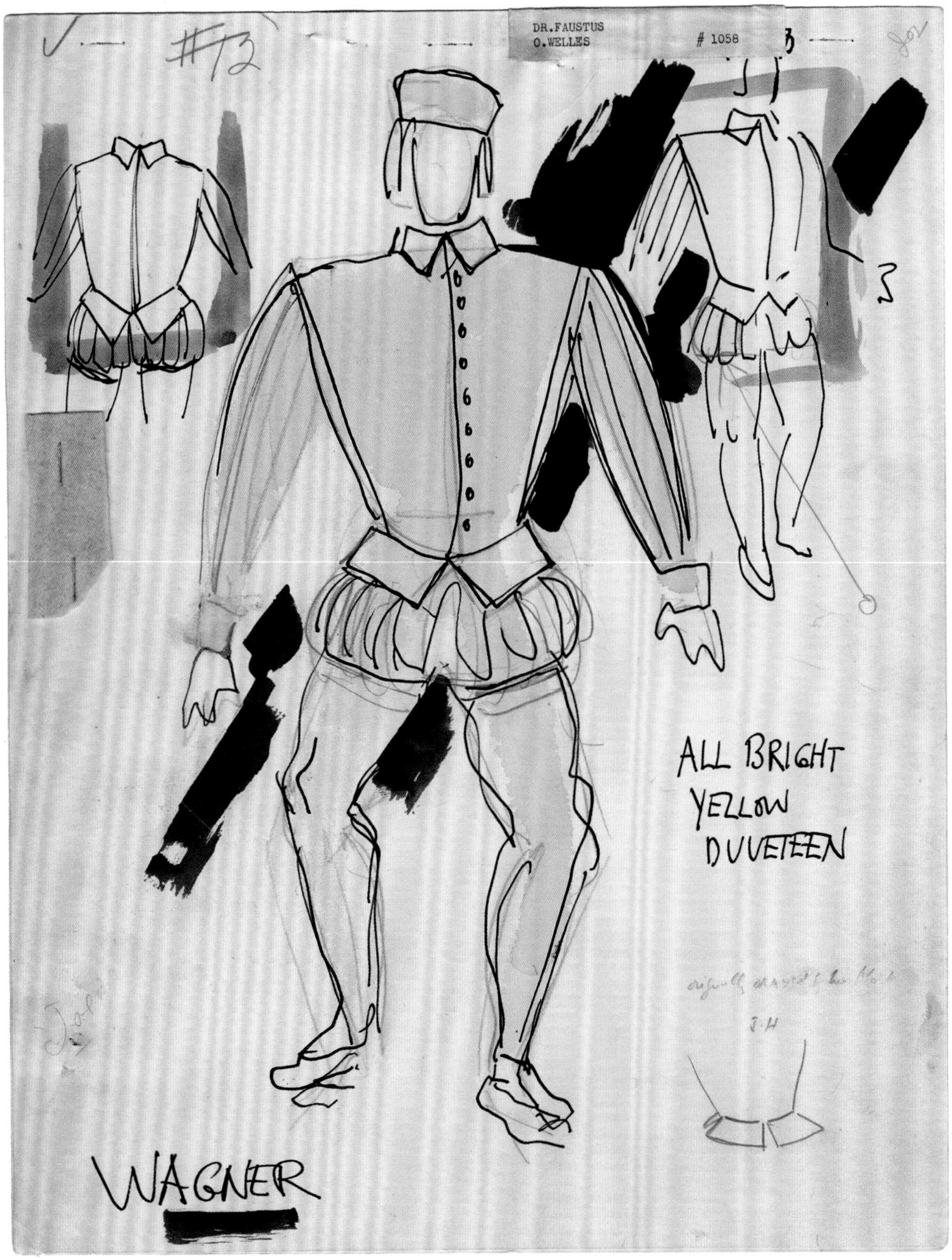

The drawings for Cornelius, one of the two scholars who tutor Faustus in the art of magic, are awash in fascinating detail – the high-wound turban with its suggestion of the Orient (in the text he is German); his frailty revealed in a pair of walking sticks; the sleeve – and indeed inner sleeve – of his robe, 'much torn and patched,' evidently the sleeve/inner sleeve of a man fallen on hard times. A note on the rich red Jester's costume (worn in the play by veteran Vaudevillian Harry McKee) brings attention to the bunching at the back of the tunic. Another of Cornelius has urgent instructions for the wardrobe mistress: 'whole costume dyed-down and streaked-looking.' Even minor characters get the full treatment. A jolly-looking Vintner, who appears briefly in one scene, and a lowly Horse Carrier are both meticulously attired, right down to the Vintner's buttons and contrasting 'fly'.

In preparation for *Faustus*, Welles dispatched his wife Virginia and his leading lady Paula Laurence to the New York Public Library on research expeditions, basing his designs on what they came up with. What he came up with was conventionally Elizabethan, but no less impressive for that; audiences would have to wait another nine months to have their minds blown by his modern-dress rendition of *Julius Caesar.*

The costumes themselves were created by wardrobe mistress Beverly Juno, an ex-showgirl with a game leg who was fond of a drink. Photographs of the production (including a magnificent one of Welles, captured in a column of light, grasping his cape to his body in imitation of Rodin's statue of Balzac) show that Ms. Juno did a fine job. But it's Welles's drawings that carry the essence of the production. With swatches of fabric still attached, scrawled notes in Welles's own hand – humanized by terrible handwriting and bad spelling ('duveteen' for duvetyn) – they have a vigor and vitality that faded stills in a dog-eared playbill could never hope to capture.

ABOVE: Costume design; scan sourced from The Library of Congress

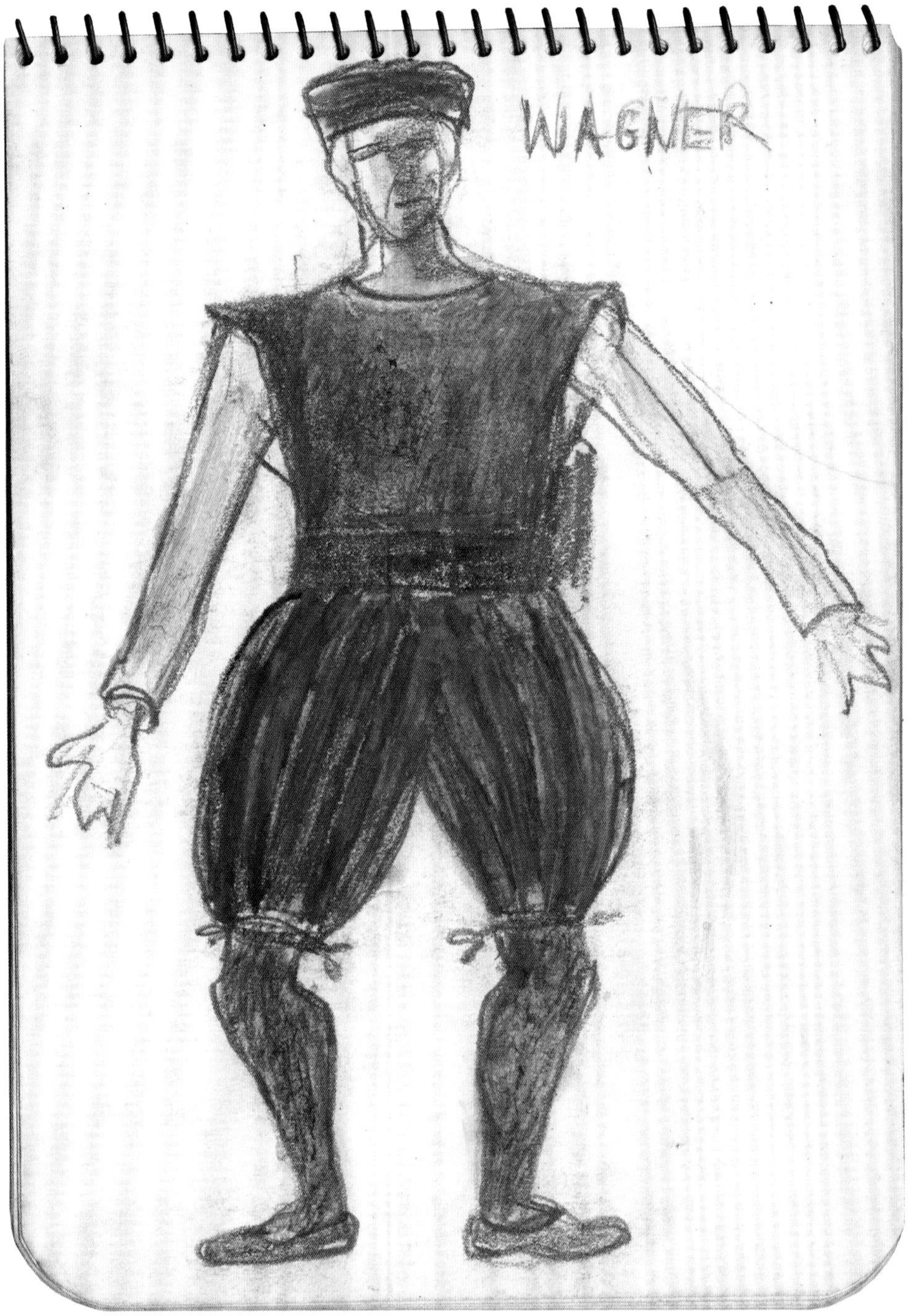

ABOVE: Costume design; scan supplied for publication

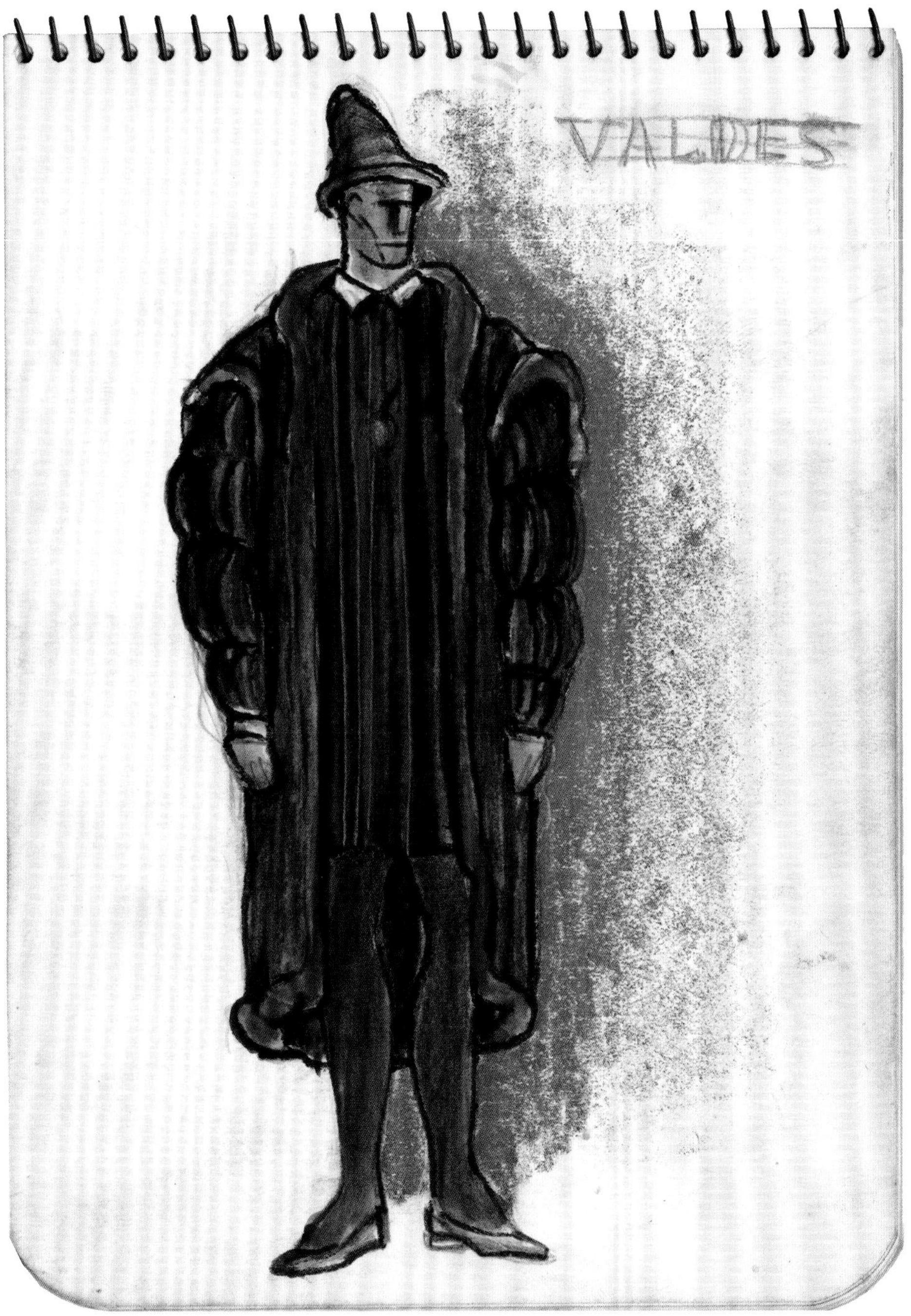

ABOVE: Costume design; scan supplied for publication

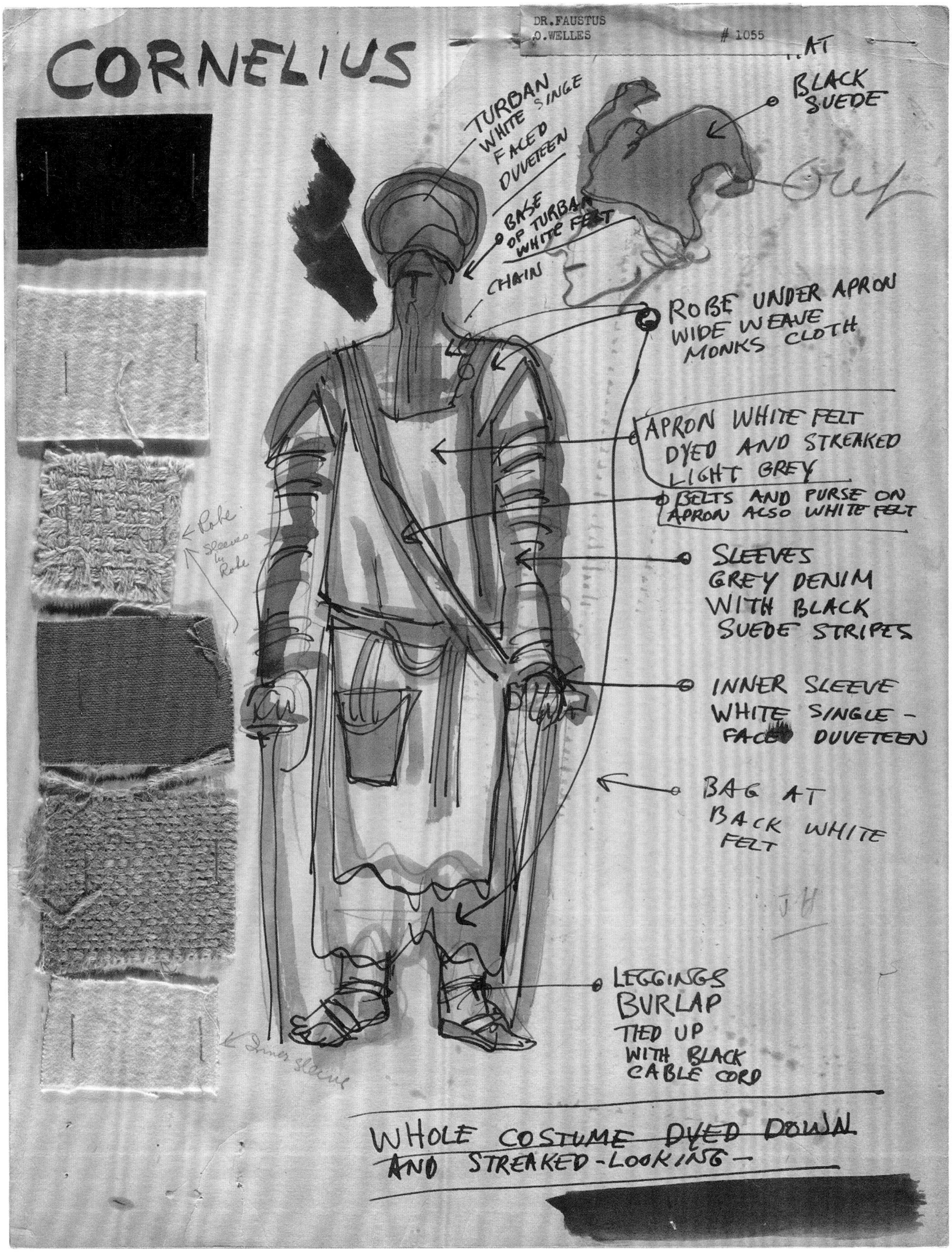

ABOVE: Costume design; scan sourced from The Library of Congress

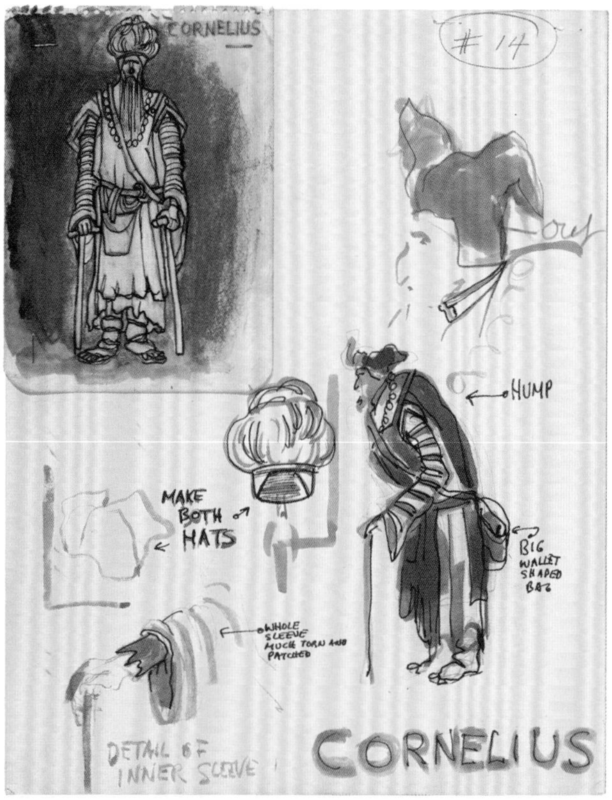

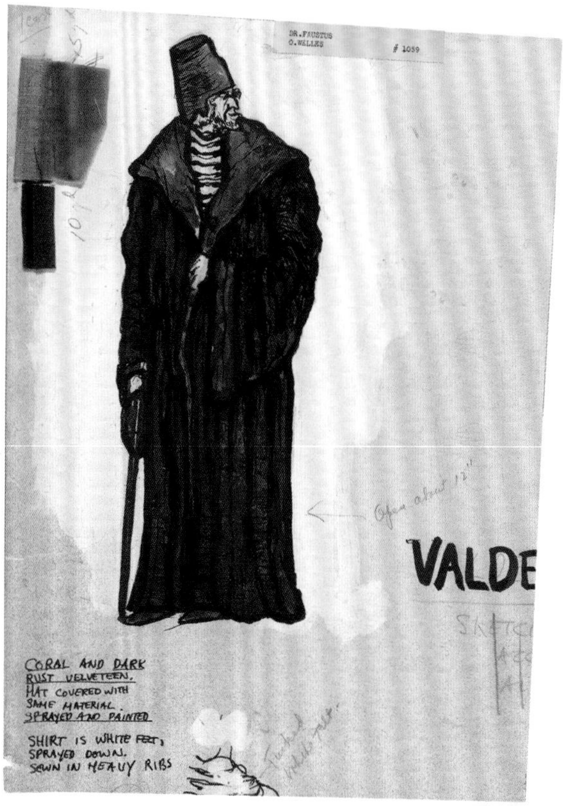

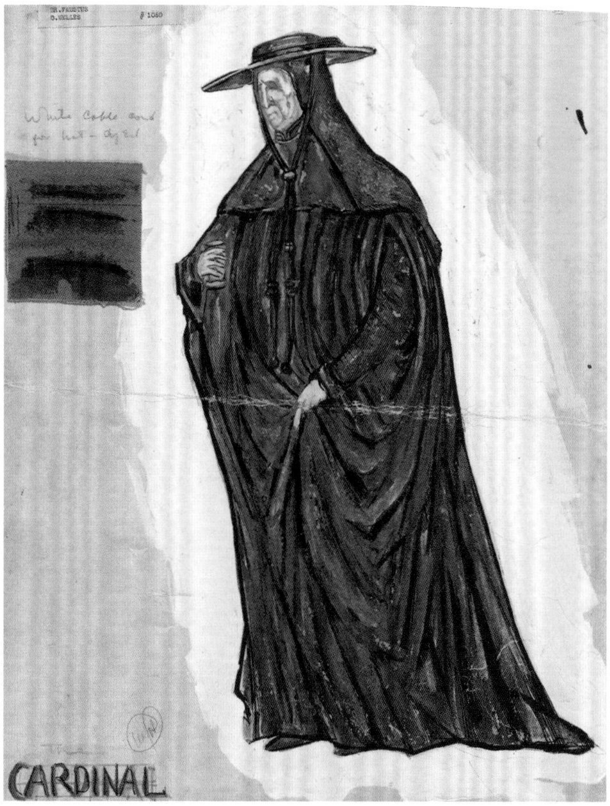

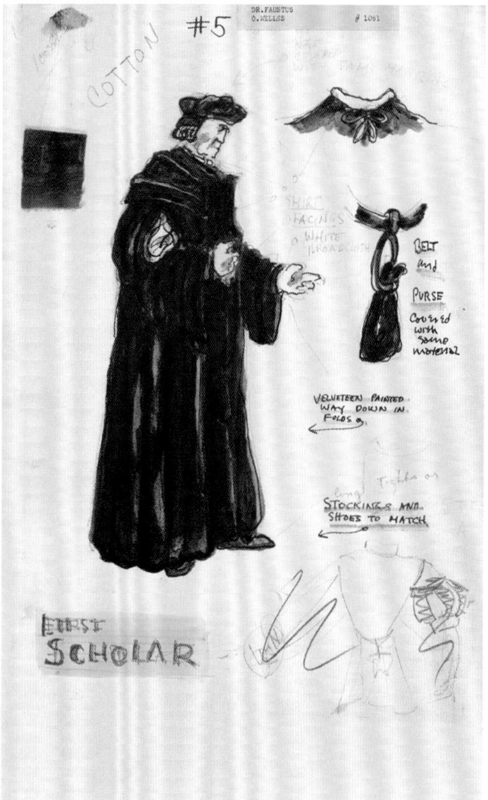

ABOVE: Costume designs; scans sourced from The Library of Congress

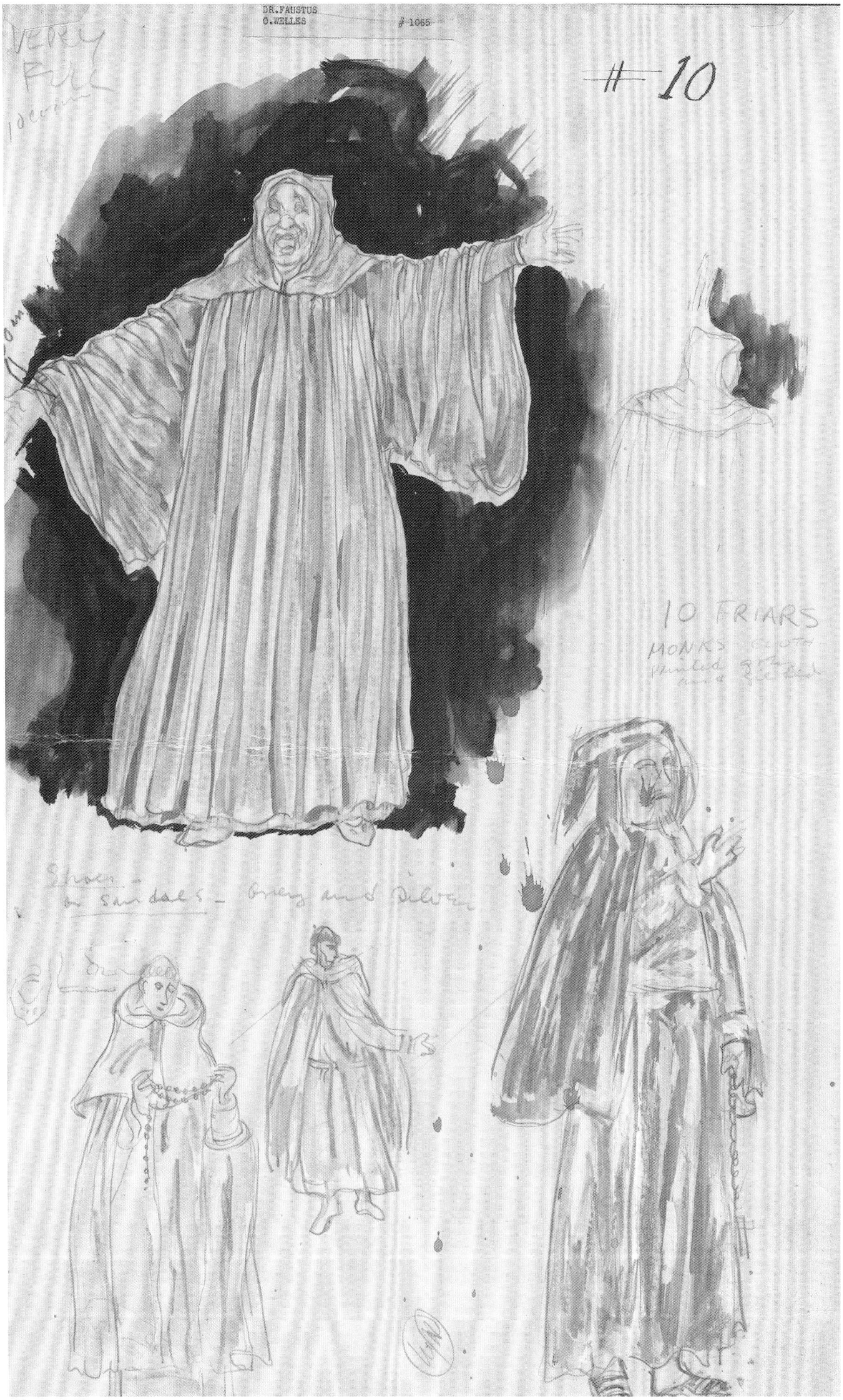

ABOVE: Costume design; scan sourced from The Library of Congress

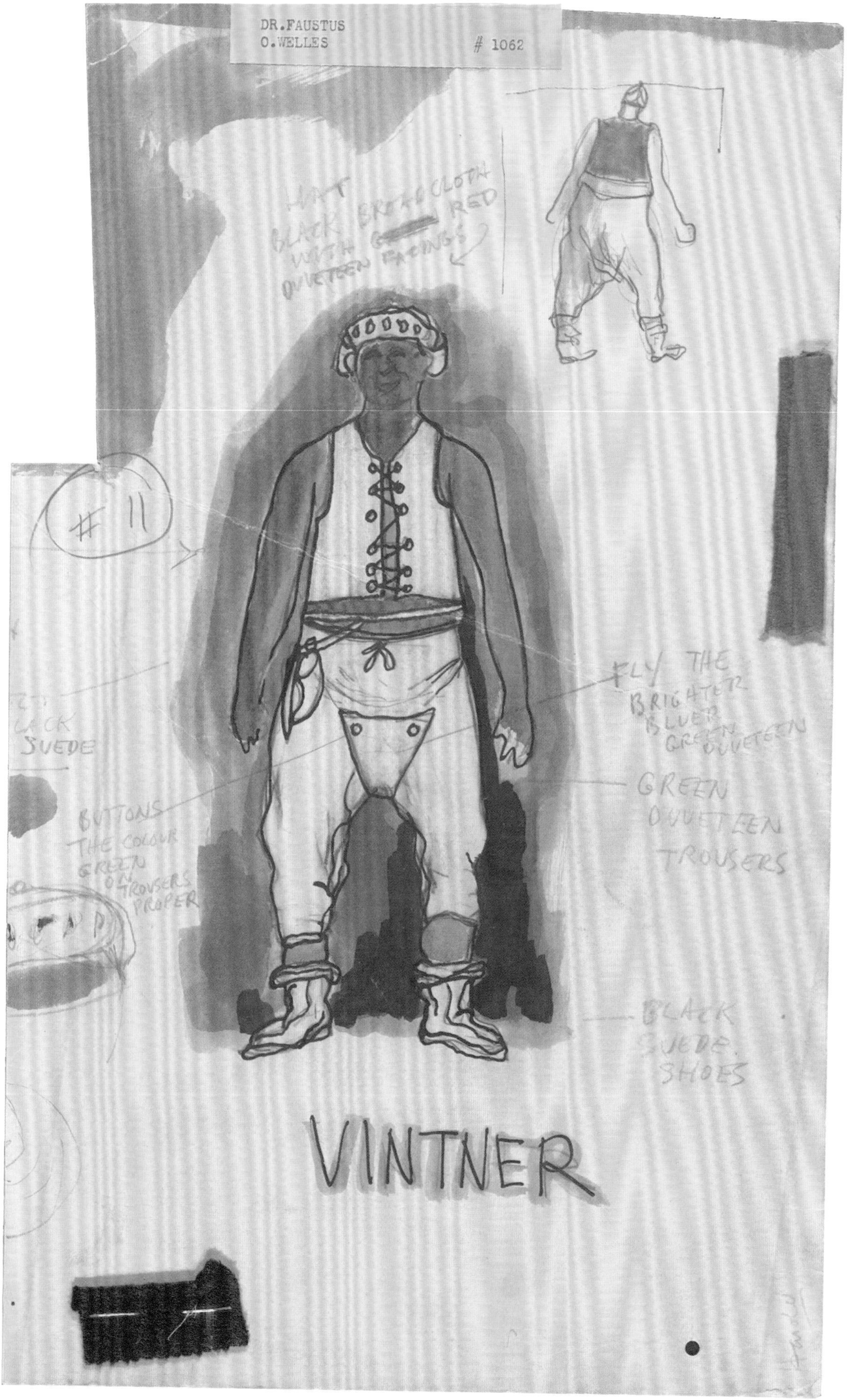

ABOVE: Costume design; scan sourced from The Library of Congress

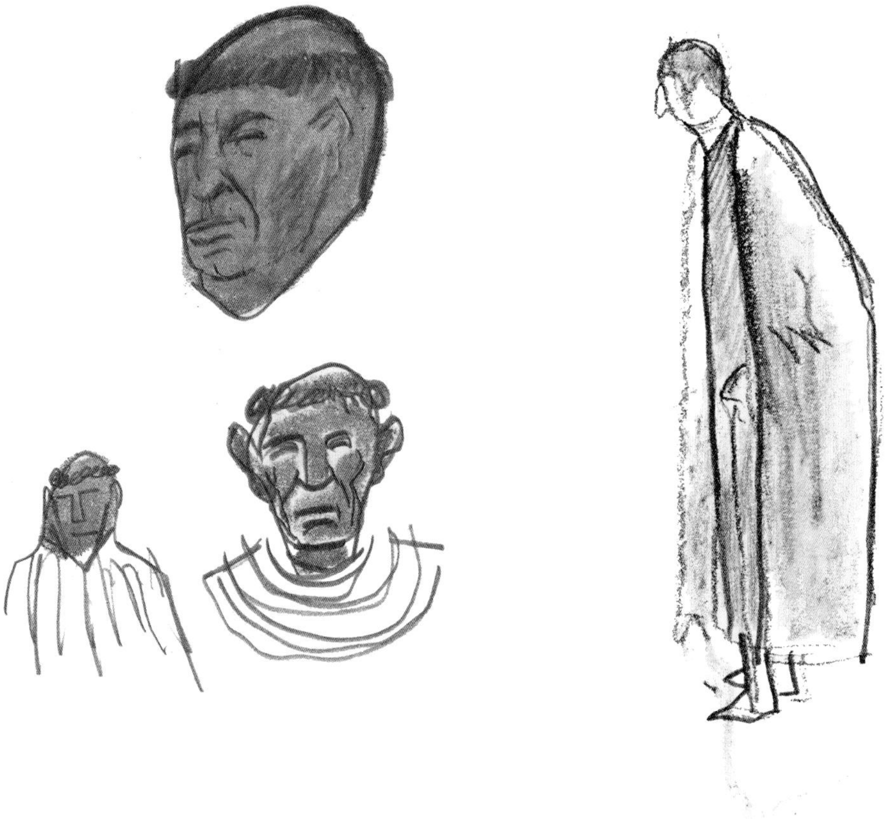

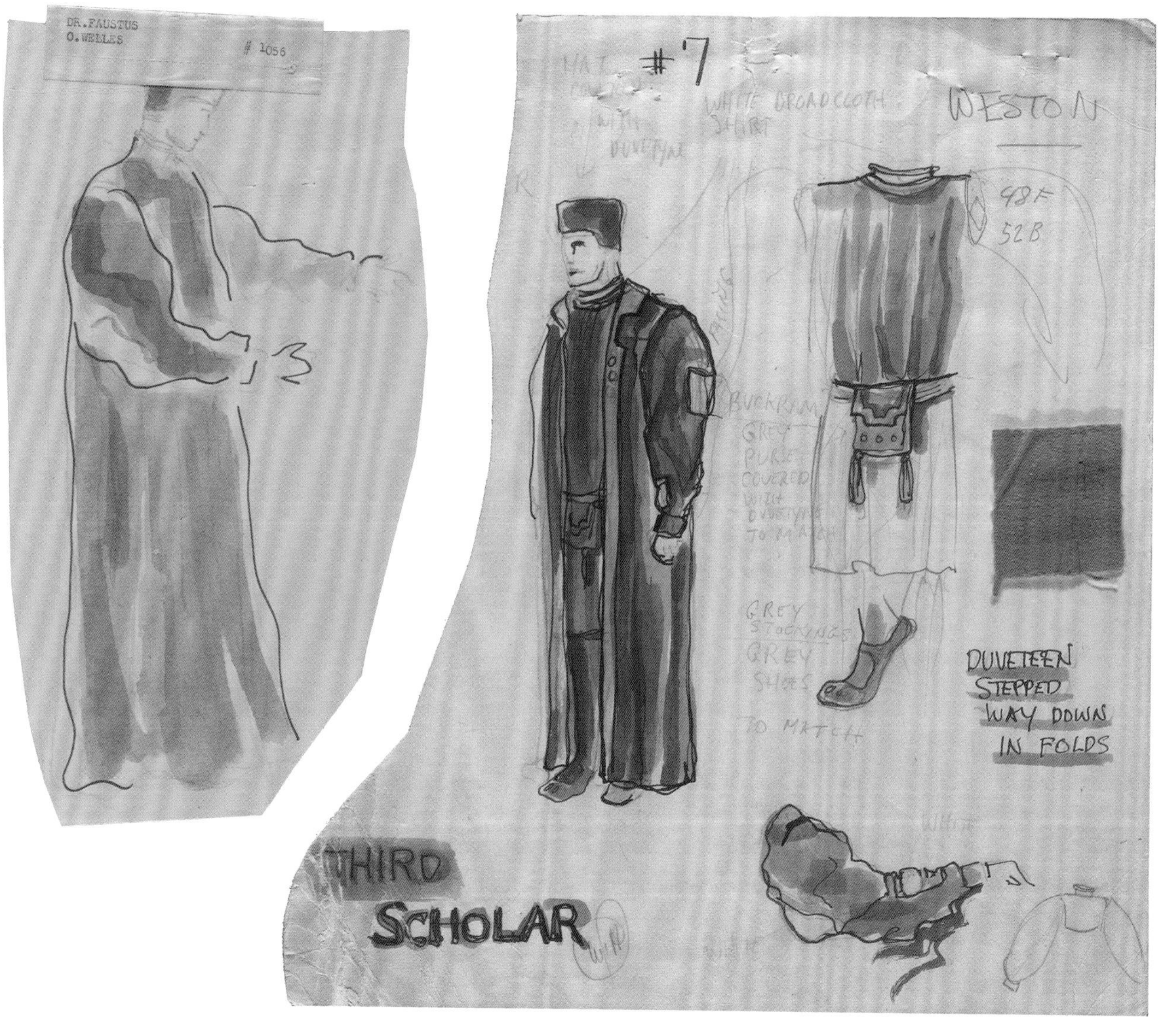

TOP: Character sketches; scans supplied for publication

ABOVE: Costume designs; scans sourced from The Library of Congress

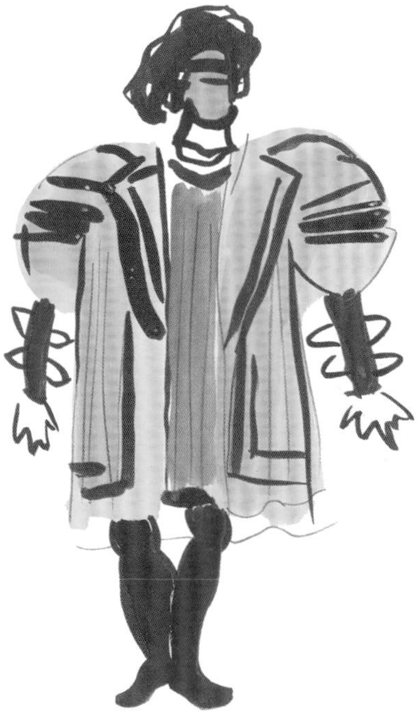

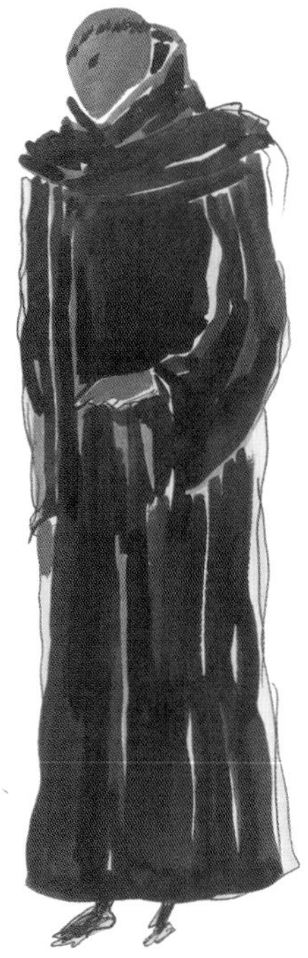

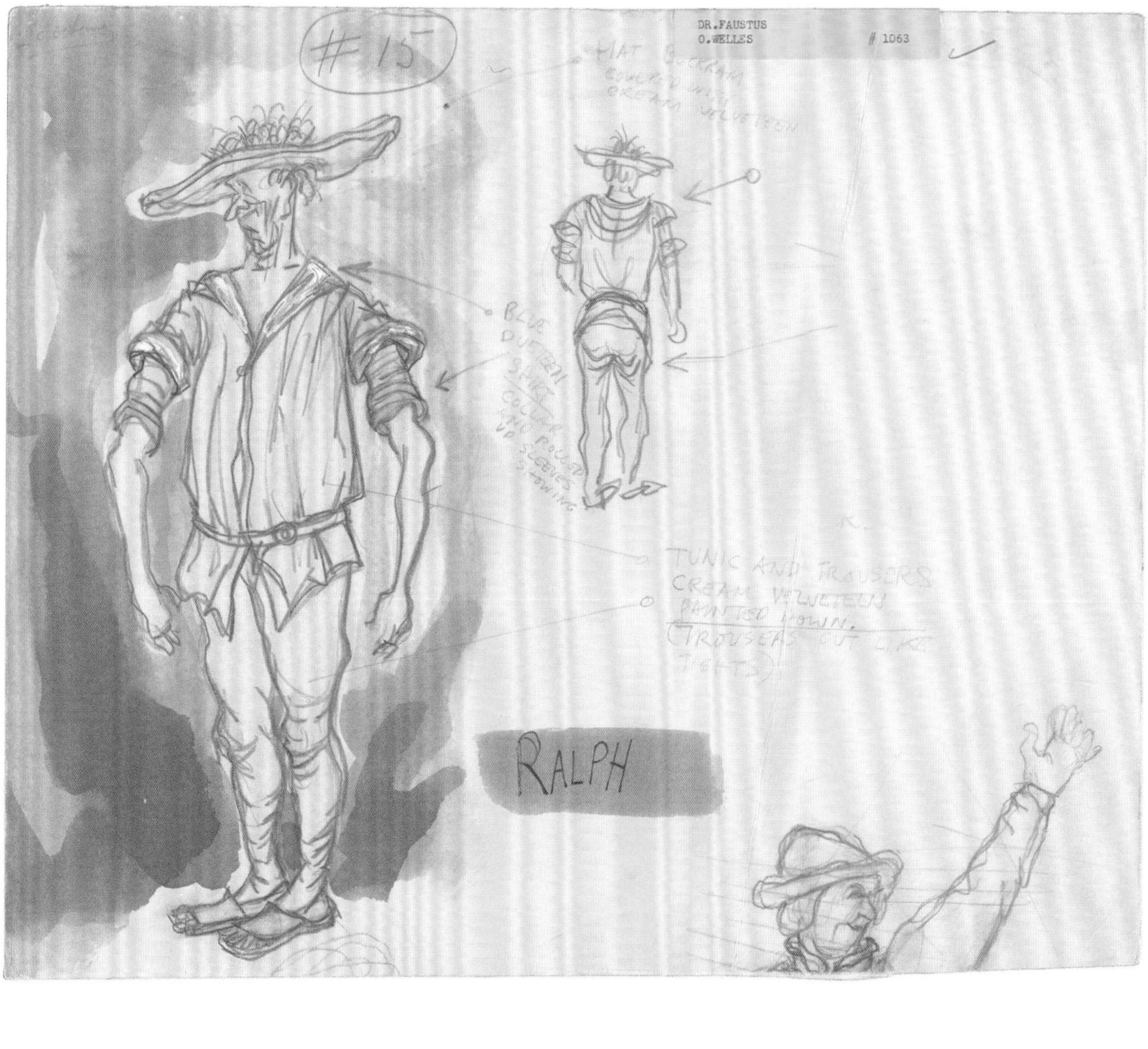

ABOVE: Costume designs; scans sourced from The Library of Congress

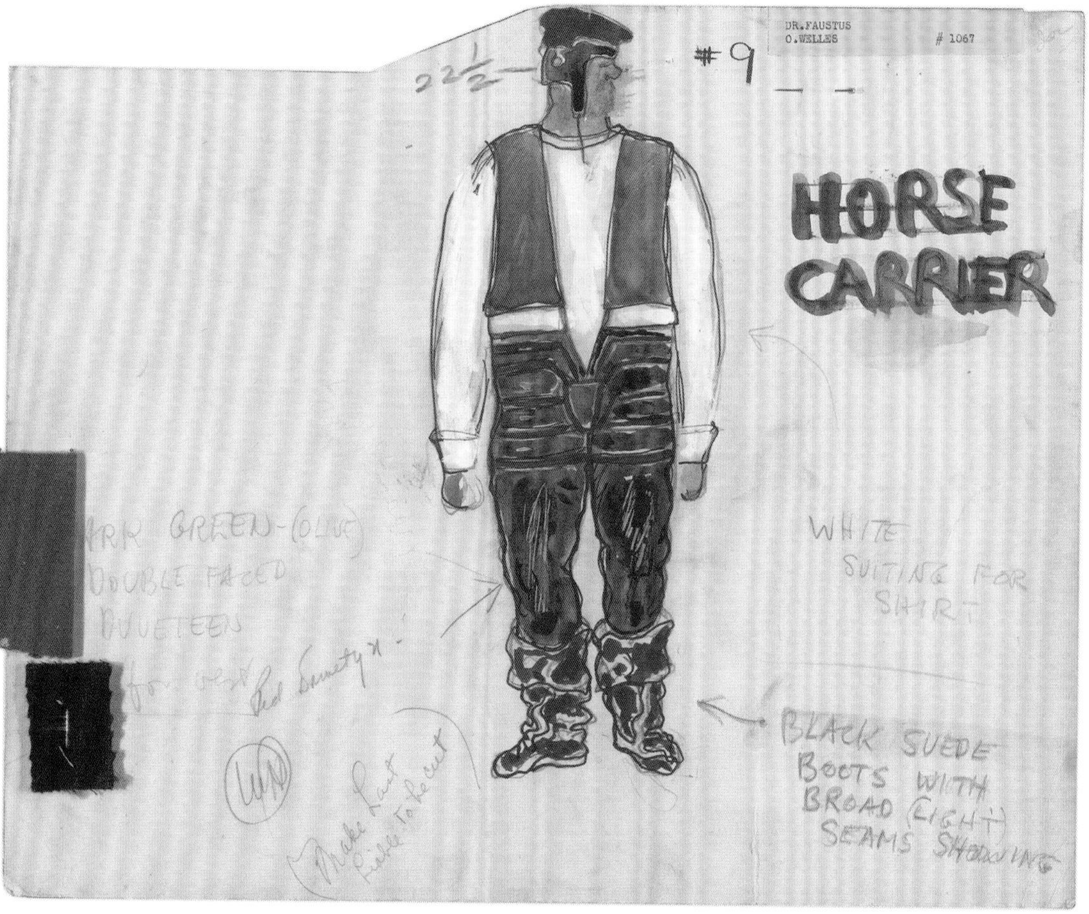

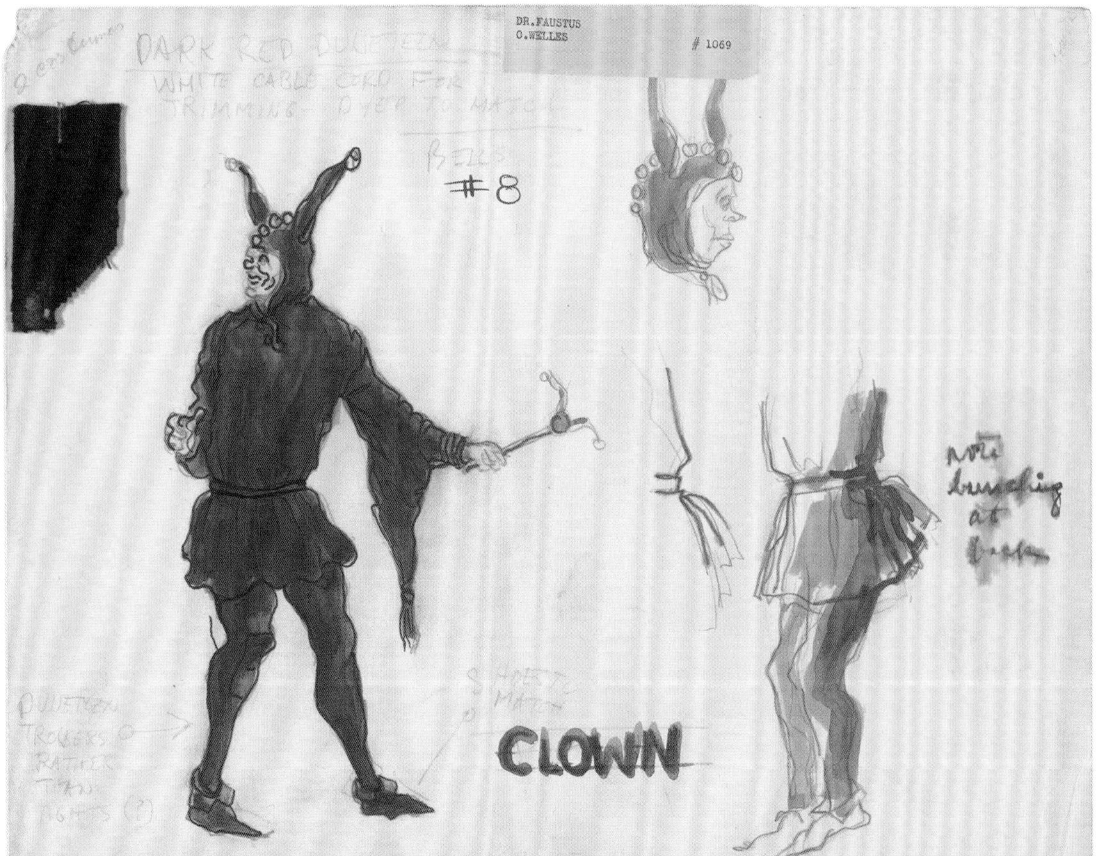

ABOVE: Costume designs; scans sourced from The Library of Congress

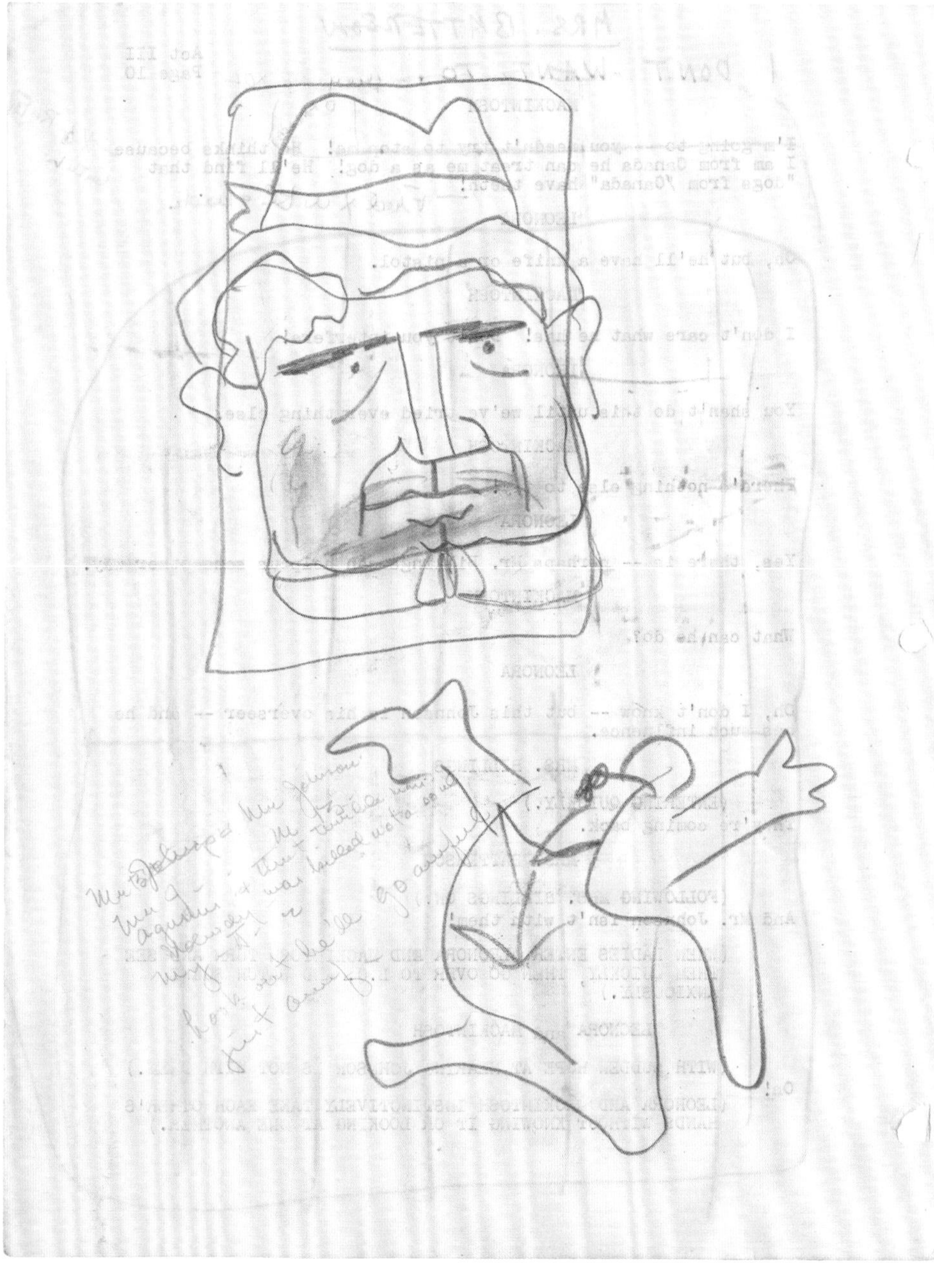

TOO MUCH JOHNSON

The Mercury Theater, founded in 1937 by Welles and John Houseman, stakes its claim to history as a hotbed of artistic upheaval, the crucible of innovation in which the American theater was reborn. Its legend rests on a handful of great works, audacious interpretations of *Macbeth, Doctor Faustus* and *Julius Caesar* for the stage and the infamous *The War of the Worlds* for the airwaves. As with all legends, there is rather more to it than that.

The Mercury had its share of failures and fiascos, and *Too Much Johnson* was both. It was also, literally, a farce. Written in 1894 by William Gillette and revolving, as farces often do, around marital infidelity and mistaken identity, it was showing its age by the time Welles and co. got their hands on it. Even so, Welles's solution to its creaking bones was radical even by his standards. The first act exposition was, he decided, boring, so out it went. In its place, he proposed a short film. This was to be based on the silent comedies of Charlie Chaplin, Buster Keaton and the Keystone Cops, complete with pratfalls, stunts and frantic chase scenes. That all this was wildly at odds with Gillette's verbally dexterous play was incidental. As ever, once Welles sank his teeth into a concept, he was a dog with a bone.

Starring Mercury stalwarts Joseph Cotten, Ruth Ford and Mary Wickes, the film was shot at breakneck speed on the streets of Lower Manhattan and at a Hudson River quarry, dressed with palm trees to resemble Cuba, the setting for the play's second and third acts.

Again, the rough sketches that survive from the production seem a fragile hook on which to hang a tale. But as with *Jew Süss*, their significance far outweighs their lack of sophistication.

ABOVE: Sketches on back of script page; scan supplied for publication

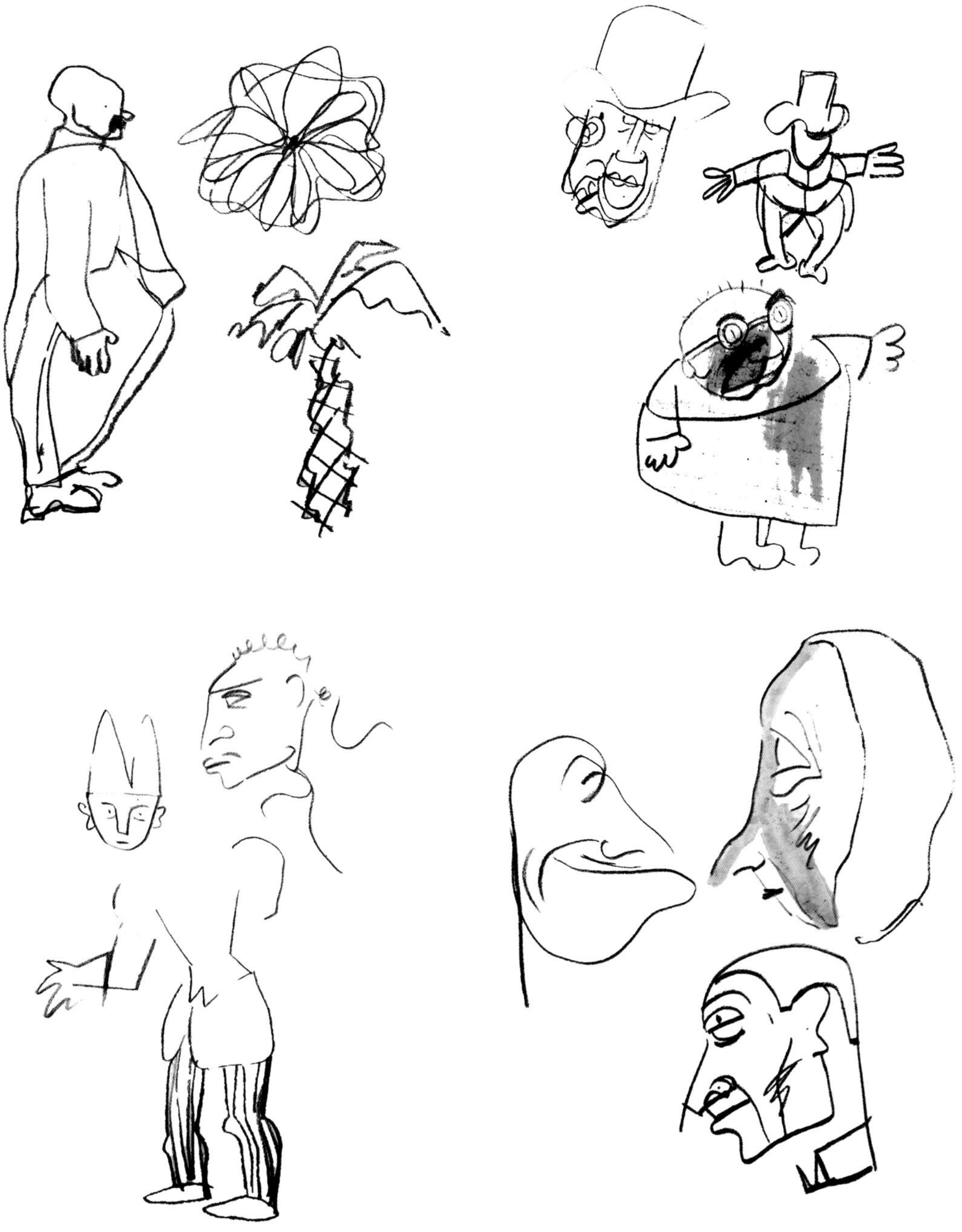

Welles had previous experience with film, but *Too Much Johnson* was his first brush with true cinema. And it was love at first sight. The shoot had been a ball, pitting him against disgruntled cops, irate passers-by and a bona fide hurricane that threatened to blow his sets flat, but it was the editing process that captured his imagination. Houseman, appalled at the production's spiraling cost, recalled visiting Welles's suite at the St. Regis and wading knee-deep through a sea of highly flammable nitrate stock, his collaborator bent oblivious over his Moviola.

The fun came to an abrupt end when it was discovered that Paramount owned the film rights to the play and would be demanding a hefty fee if it was shown in a Broadway theater. That was not an immediate concern since it was due an out-of-town tryout at the Stony Creek Theater in Connecticut in August 1938. The problem there was a projection booth that had not been fireproofed. The film could not be shown at any cost, meaning the cast had a single day to learn and rehearse the scenes Welles had cut to make way for it.

That a small-town Connecticut audience took to throwing things at the stage is an indication of how shambolic the results were. The only possible consolation was that Paramount would not be collecting a penny. *Too Much Johnson* never made it to Broadway.

Welles was devastated and took to his bed, convinced he was dying. He never finished work on the *Johnson* footage, which, when properly edited, was intended to open each of the play's three acts.

The film went unseen into storage, but is now available on the American National Film Preservation Foundation website.

ABOVE: Sketches on back of script pages; scans supplied for publication

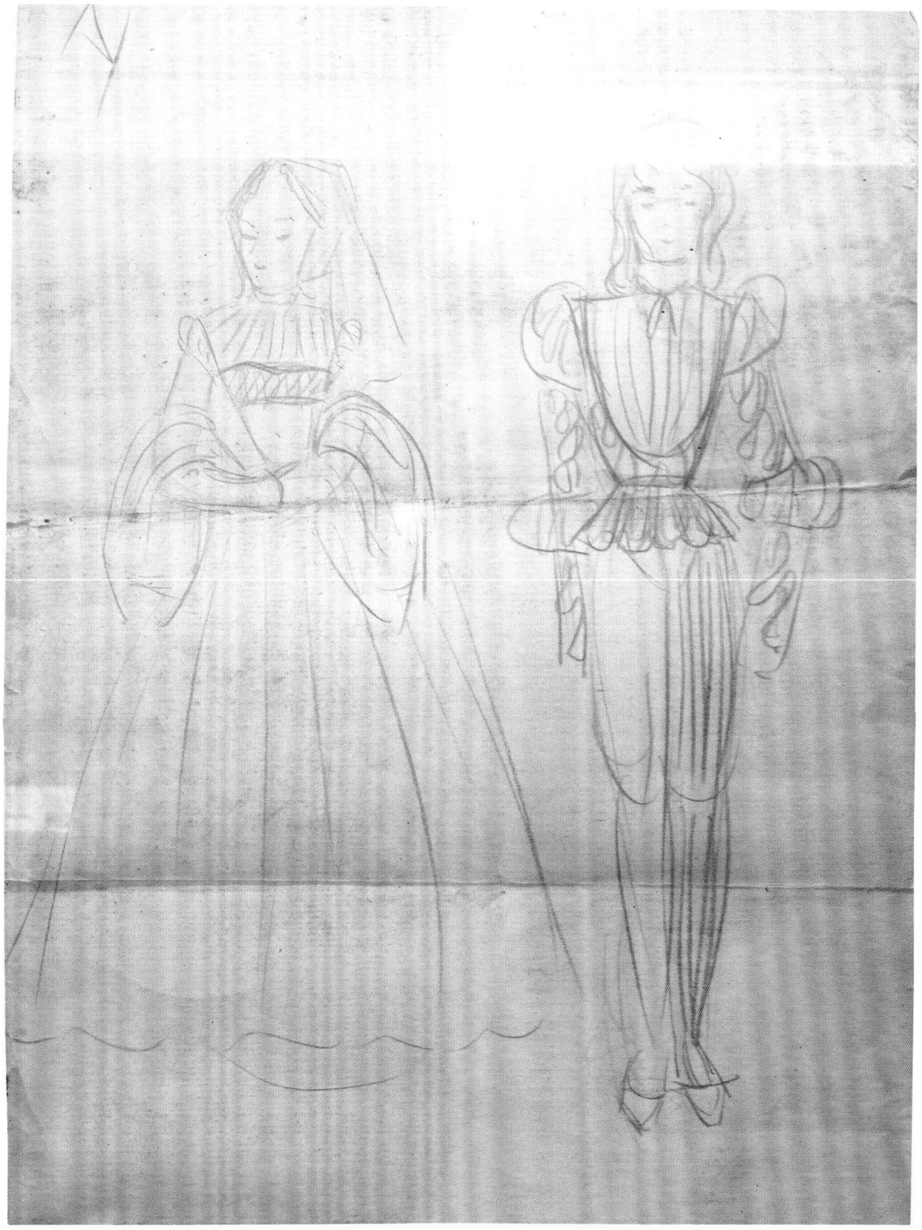

FIVE KINGS

Announced with much fanfare at a lunch to celebrate Shakespeare's birthday, *Five Kings* was Welles and the Mercury Theater's most ambitious endeavor to date. A typically daring adaptation of five history plays (*Henry IV Part*s *1* and *2*, *Henry V*, *Henry VI* and *Richard III*), it was to be the theatrical event of its age, a Shakespearean extravaganza of unrivaled magnitude. It was a disaster from start to finish.

Rehearsals began long before there was a finished script to rehearse, a ridiculous situation made worse by Welles's habit of arriving – if he arrived at all – chronically late, ill-prepared and invariably hungover. His behavior throughout the rehearsal process was, by all accounts, atrocious: when his Mercury partner John Houseman refused to postpone the play's opening, he threw a telephone at him. On another occasion he accused Houseman, hysterically, of trying to poison him when dry ice found its way into Falstaff's tankard in imitation of mulled wine.

On opening night (February 27, 1939), the audience in the front row had to take cover when the revolving stage, speeding out of control, began flinging pieces of scenery at them. The performance ran four-and-a-half hours, by which time the auditorium was empty save for die-hard fans.

Welles tried valiantly to bring the behemoth to heel, but it defeated even him. The production fared no better – worse, in fact – in Boston and Philadelphia, where the revolving set refused to budge and had to be cranked, torturously slowly this time, by a gang of audibly cursing stage hands. With dwindling ticket sales, poor notices and funding from the Theater Guild, the project's sponsor, exhausted, Welles finally threw in the towel, abandoning all hopes of returning the show to Broadway.

Five Kings was not a total loss. Welles revived it in 1960 at the Gate Theatre in Dublin, and it formed the blueprint for 1965's *Chimes at Midnight*, ranked by many, Welles included, among his finest films.

ABOVE: Costume designs; photo supplied for publication

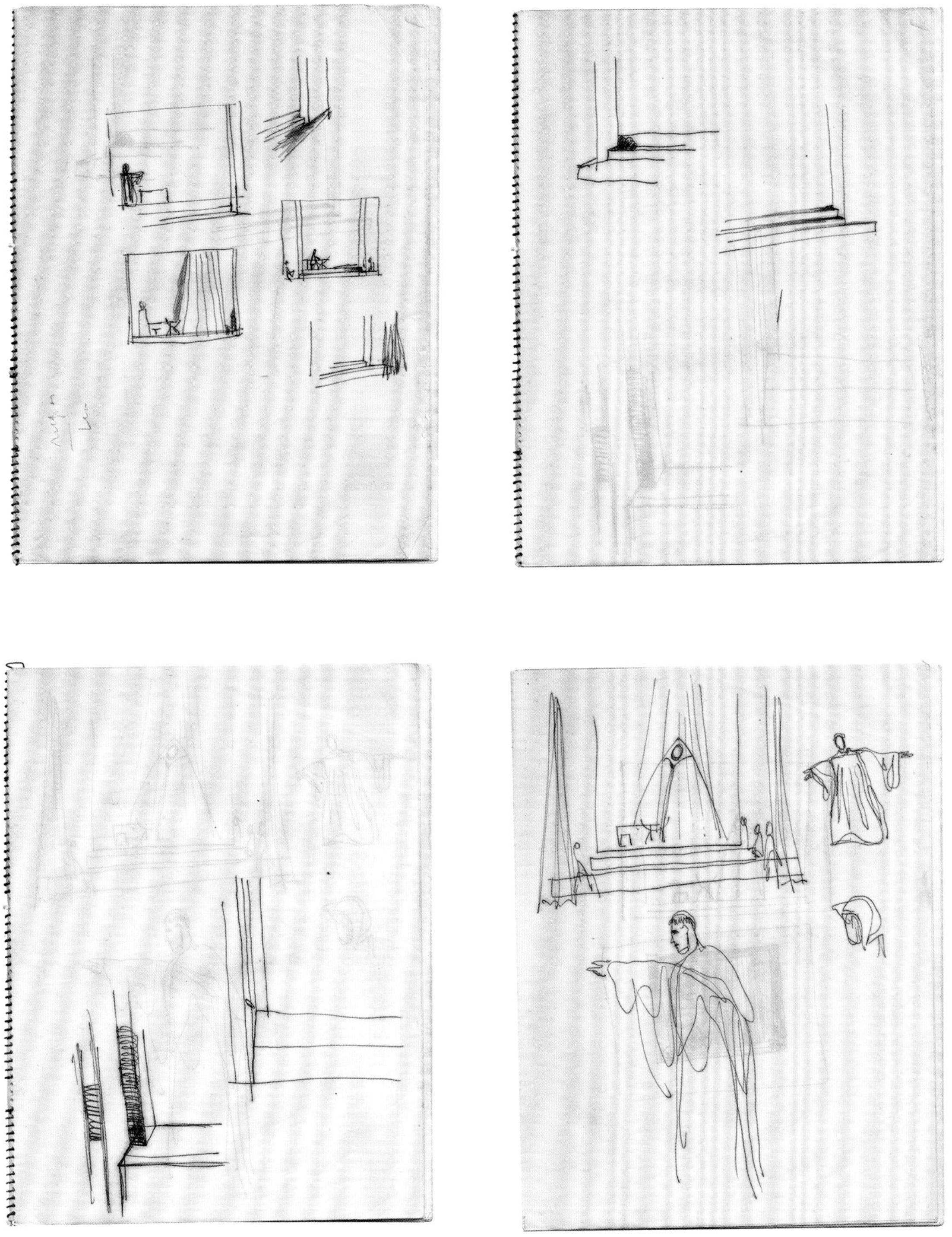

THE BLESSED AND THE DAMNED

In the spring of 1951, while struggling to get *Othello* finished and mulling over a screen version of *Ulysses*, Welles concluded that his life was not nearly complicated enough and embarked on a brand-new theater project. It was to comprise a pair of one-act plays, both penned by him and staged, in English, at the Edouard VII Theater in Paris.

The plays were titled *The Unthinking Lobster*, a broad satire on Hollywood, and *Time Runs*, a Danté-infused retread of *Doctor Faustus* – 'An old legend in a new mixture,' according to Welles's hand-scrawled title page. They would be presented under the blanket banner of *The Blessed and the Damned*, and their announcement caused an uproar. Such would be the demand for tickets, gushed one local rag, that special flights would be laid on from London and Rome to accommodate the expectant hordes. Duke Ellington was recruited to write the music, and a then-unknown Eartha Kitt was cast, at the last moment, as Helen of Troy.

Welles wrote and directed a short film called *The Miracle of St. Anne* to accompany the opening scene of *The Unthinking Lobster*, a poke at Hollywood's penchant for biblical epics. Sadly, it hasn't survived, and the sketches by Welles

ABOVE: Staging and character notes; originals scanned for publication

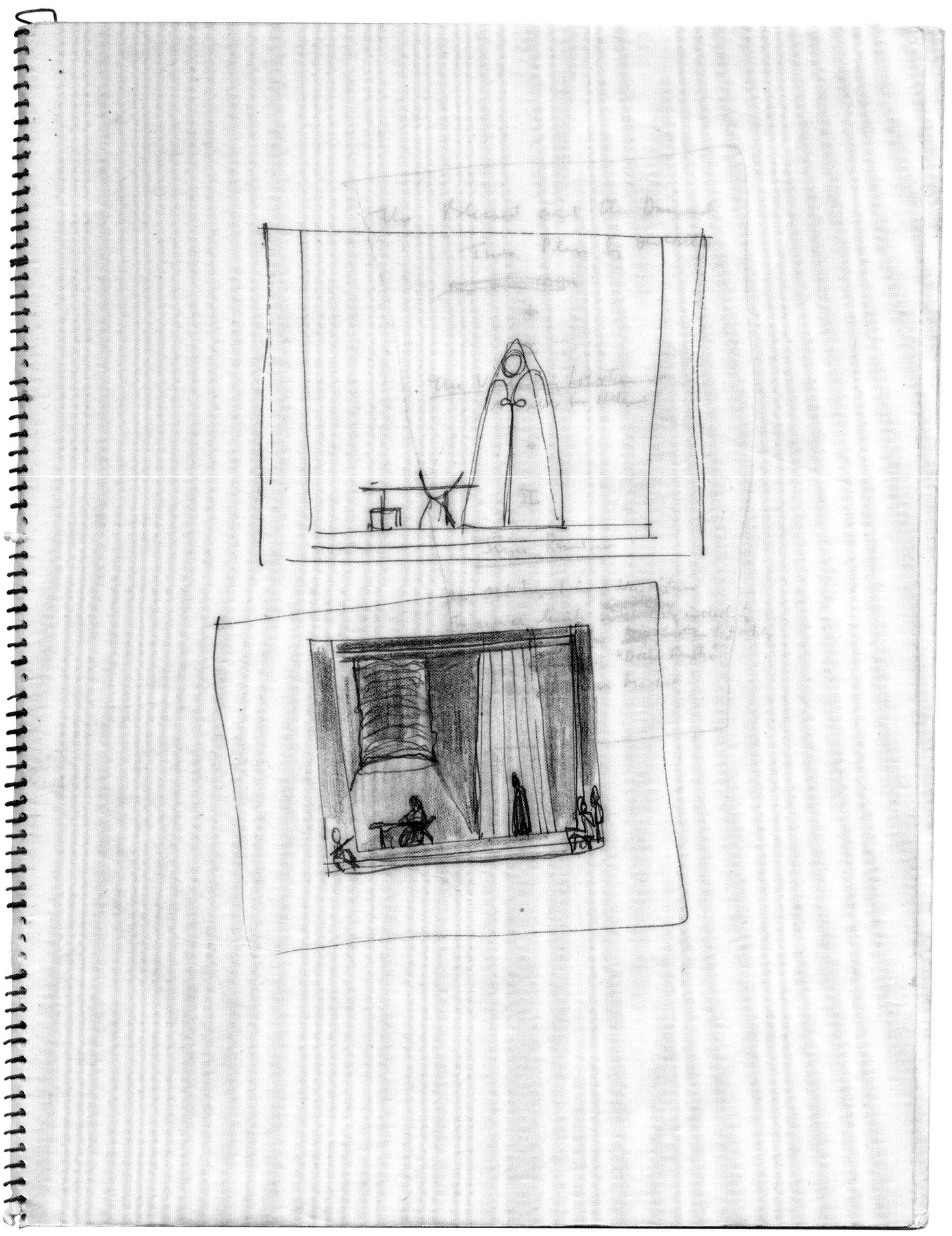

that have all relate to *Time Runs*.

After myriad technical difficulties, not helped by Welles's erratic rehearsal schedule, *The Blessed and the Damned* opened at the Edouard VII in June 1951. Despite the fanfare, the event was a disappointment. Kitt received ten curtain calls, but overall the reviews were mixed. Of the two, *Time Runs* was pronounced the better play ('*The Unthinking Lobster* becomes a satire of Orson Welles doing a satire of Hollywood,' wrote Art Buchwald in the *International Herald Tribune*), but neither found much favor with the local audience. Needless to say, the much-vaunted special flights never left the ground.

After the show closed in Paris, as much a victim of the language barrier as anything else, Welles took a modified version of *The Unthinking Lobster* on a tour of Germany. He had plans to turn it into a feature film, but, preoccupied as he was with *Othello*, it never materialized.

ABOVE: Staging and character notes; original scanned for publication

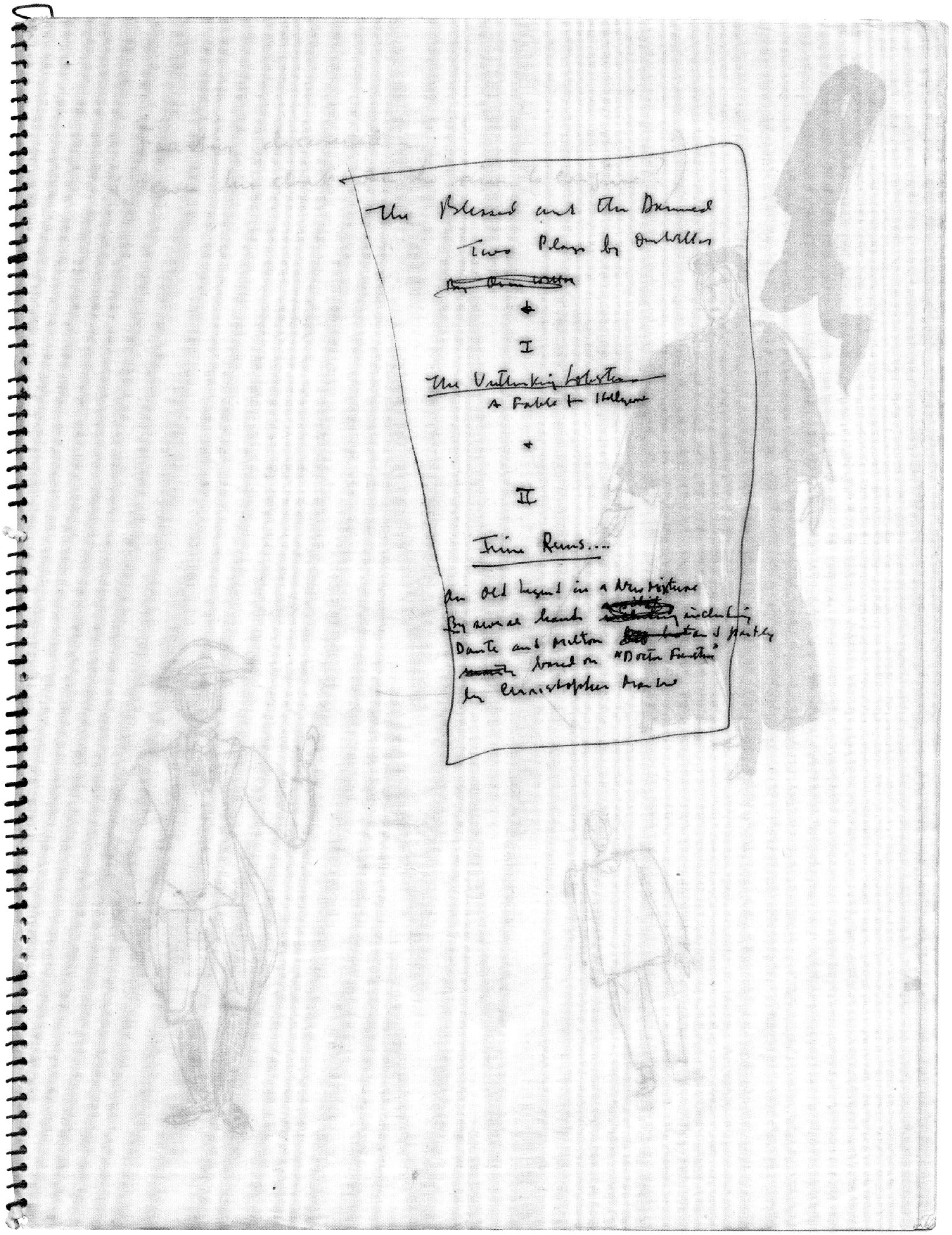

ABOVE: Staging and character notes; original scanned for publication

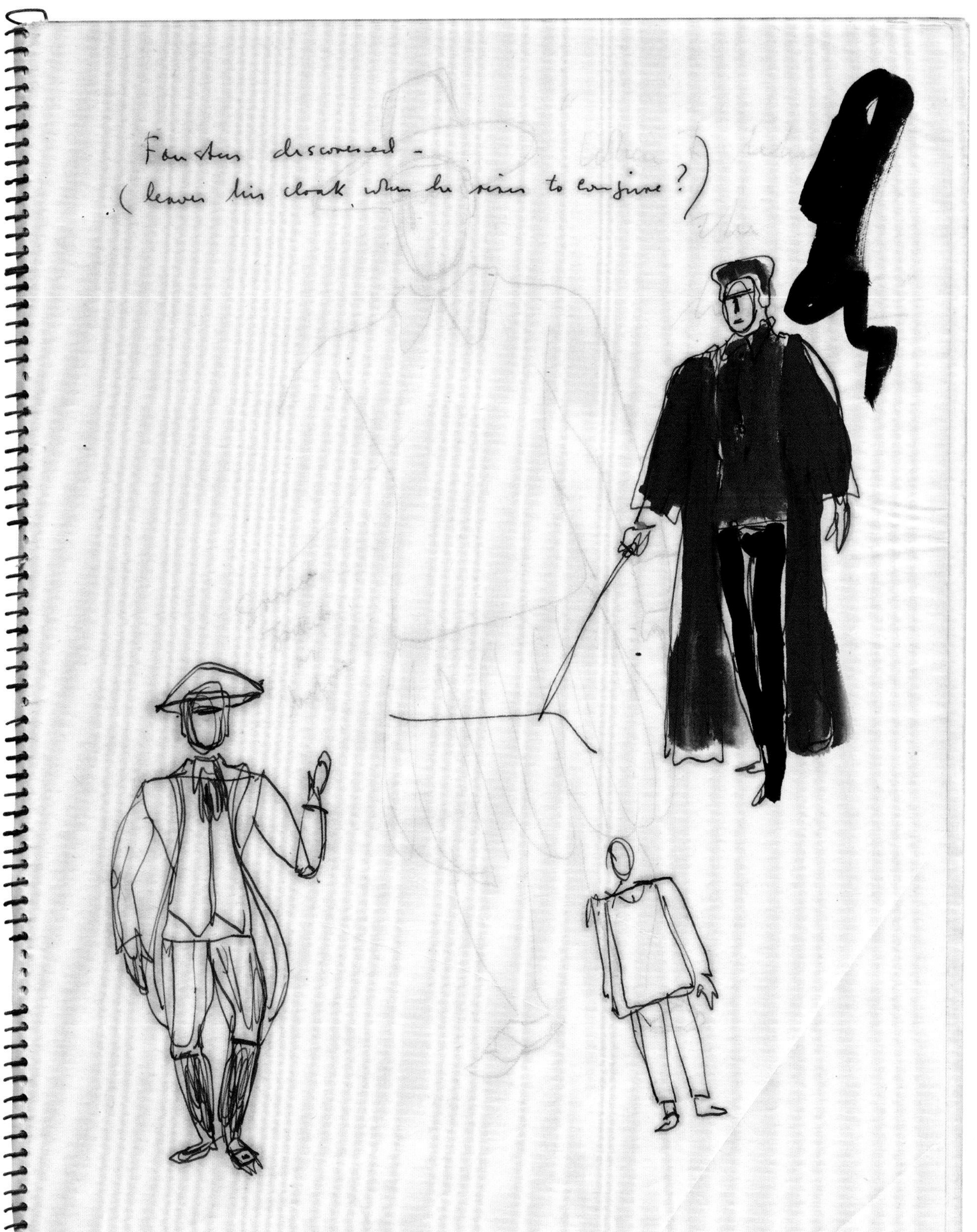

ABOVE: Staging and character notes; original scanned for publication

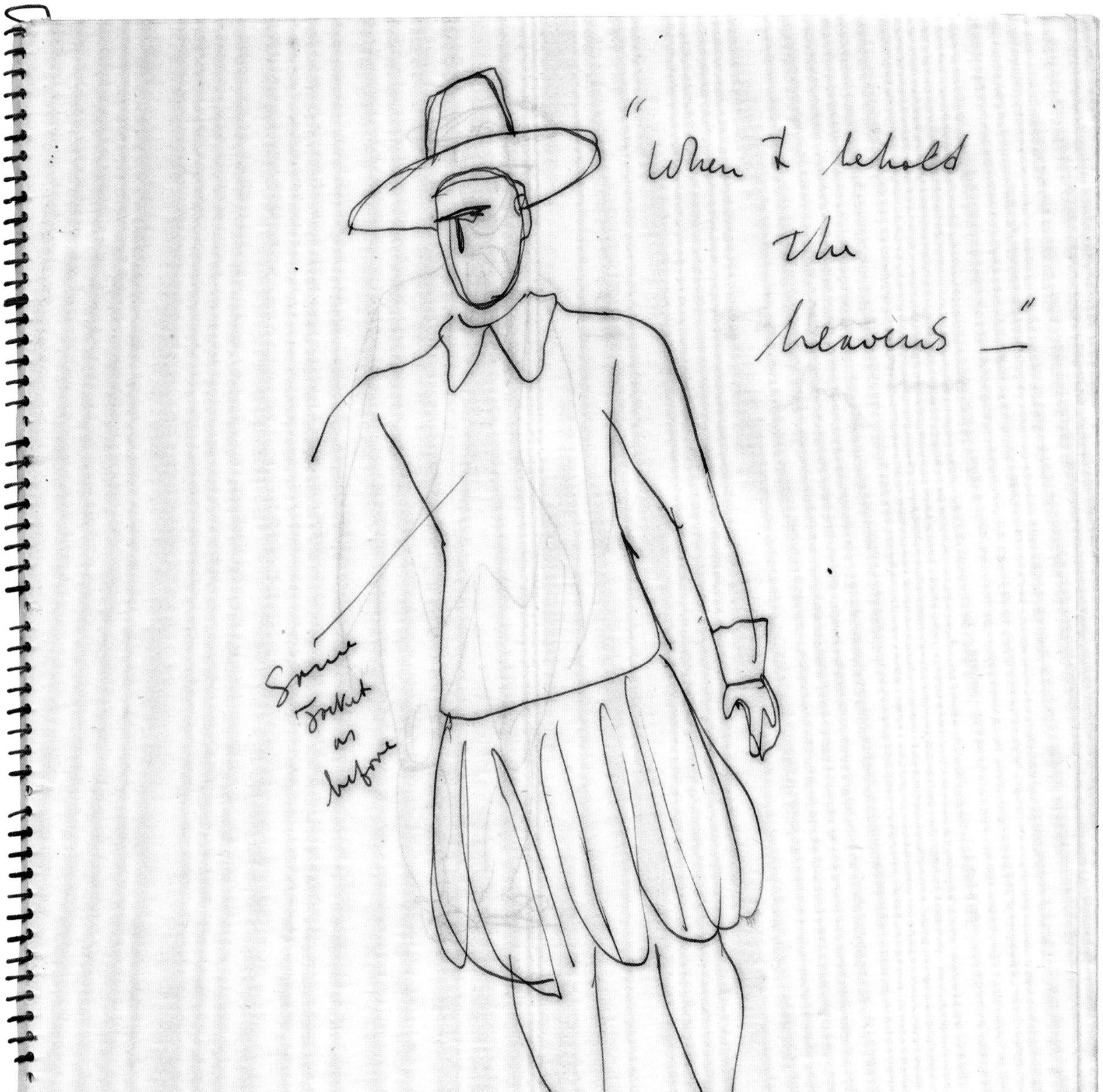

ABOVE: Staging and character notes; original scanned for publication

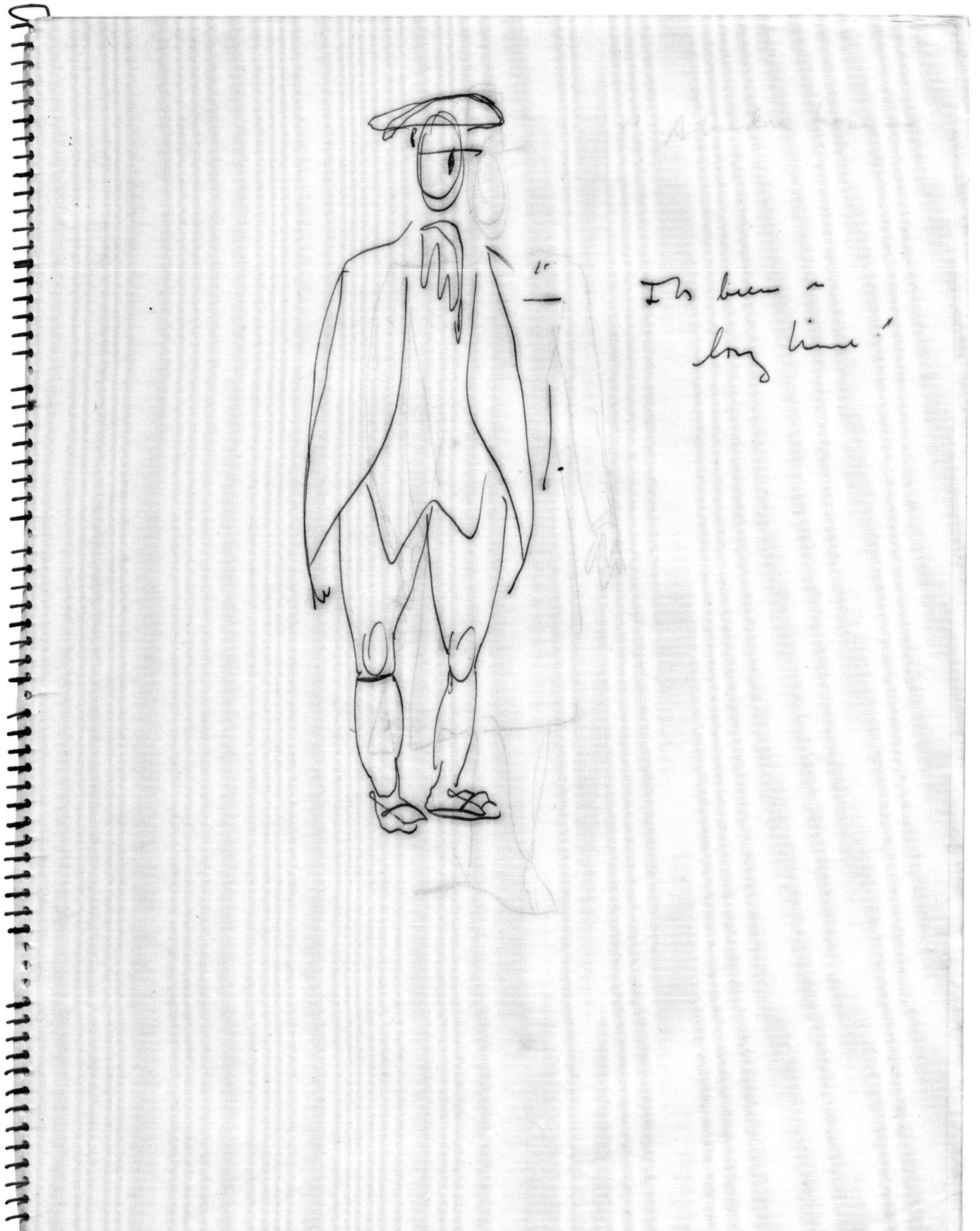

ABOVE: Staging and character notes; original scanned for publication

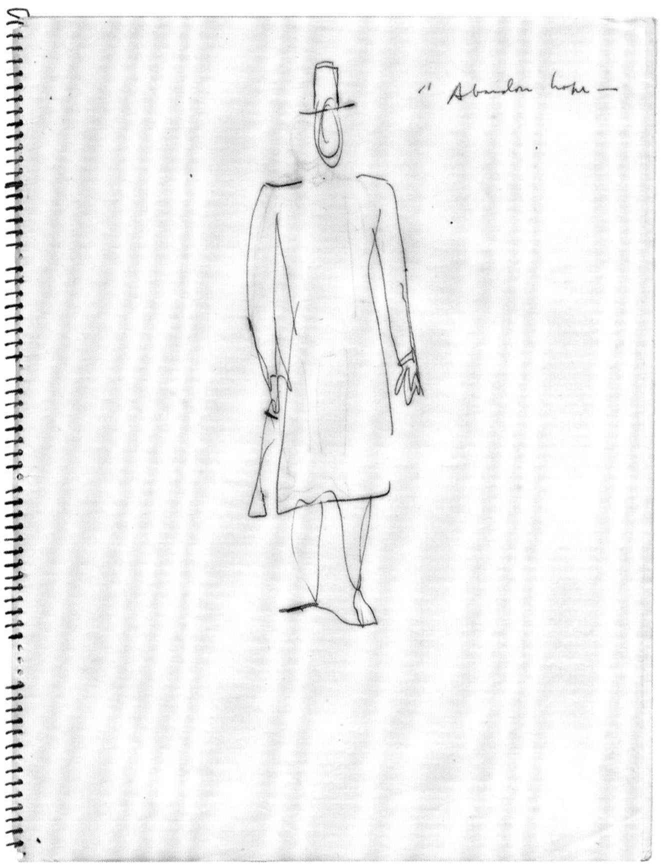

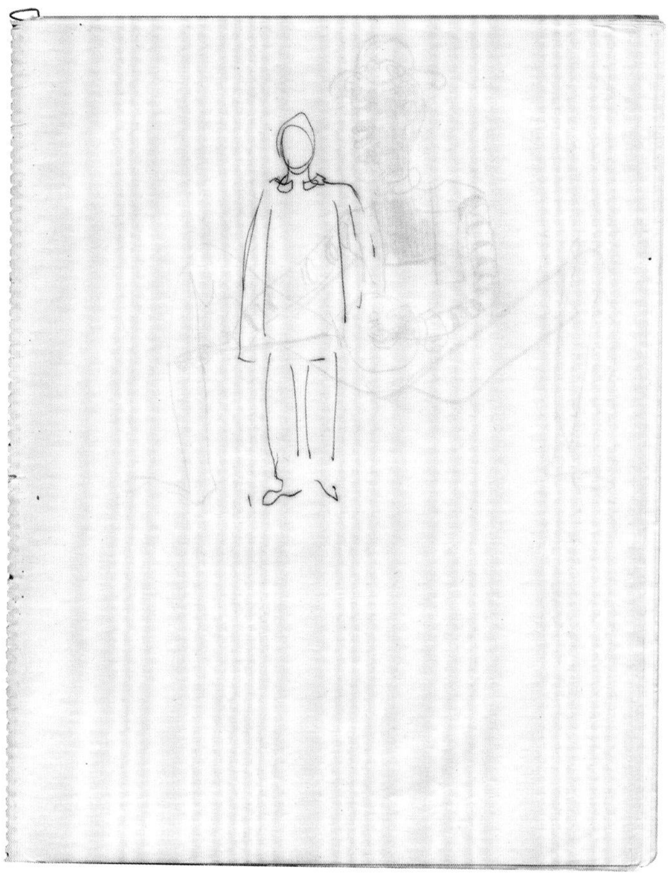

ABOVE: Staging and character notes; originals scanned for publication

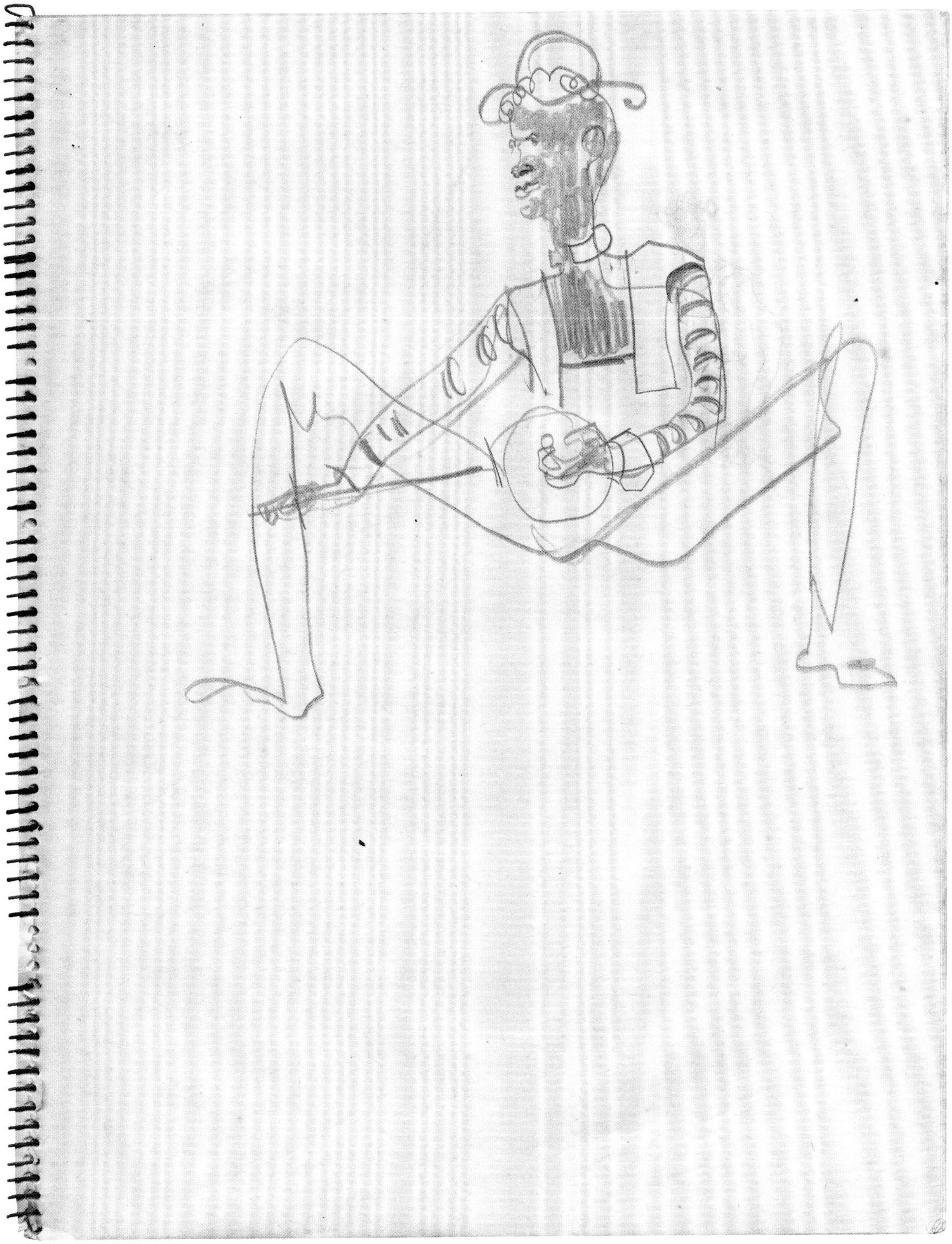

ABOVE: Staging and character notes; original scanned for publication

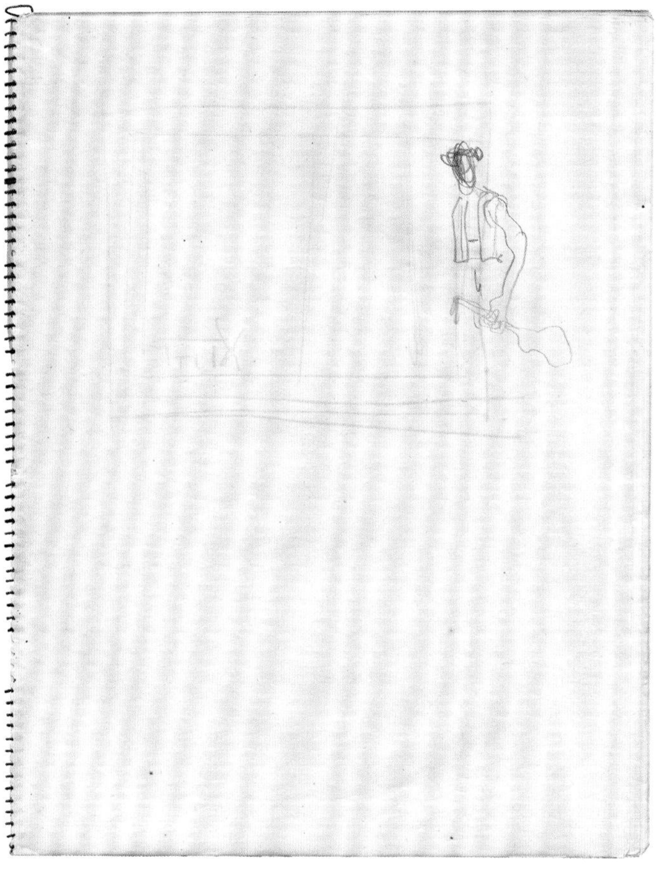

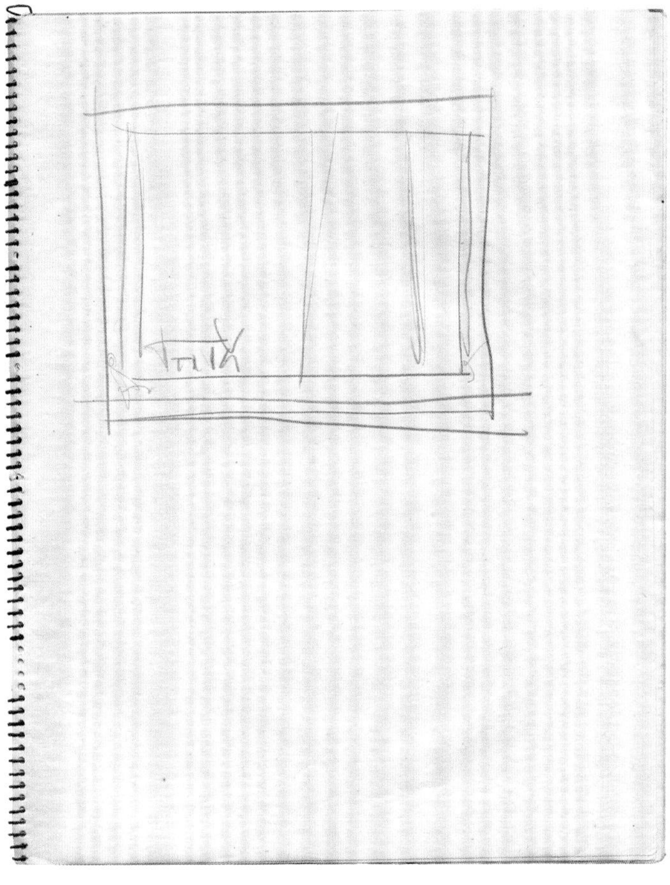

ABOVE: Staging and character notes; originals scanned for publication

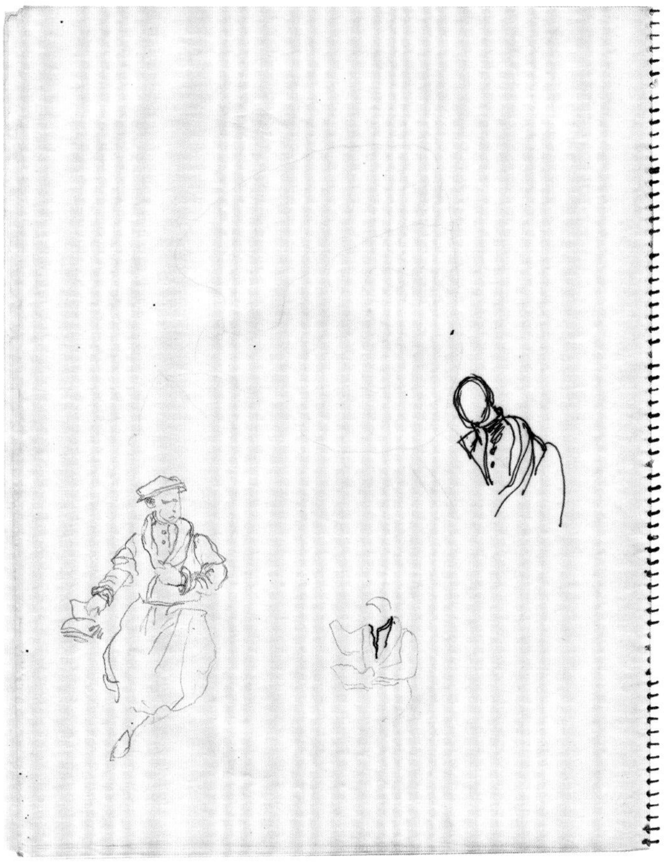

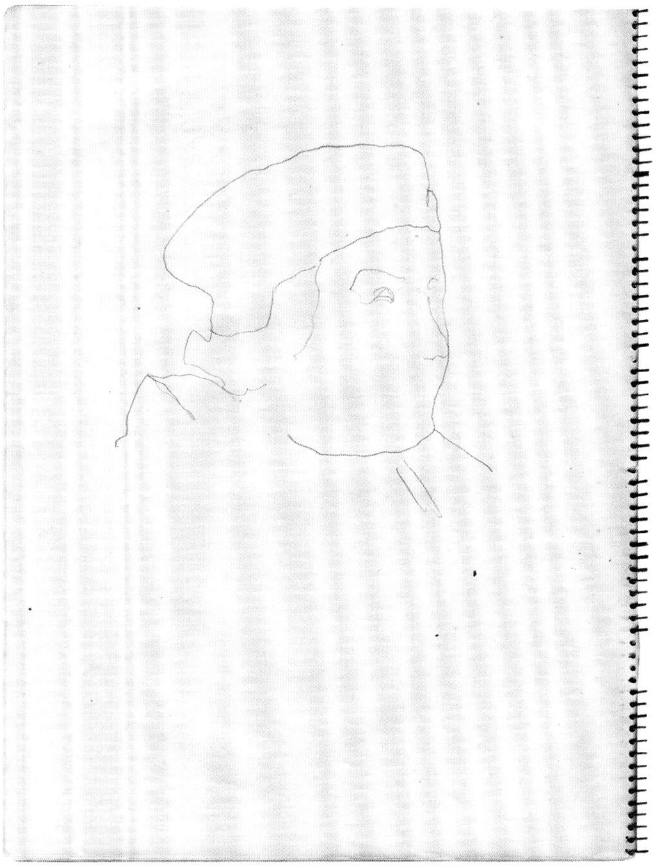

ABOVE: Staging and character notes; originals scanned for publication

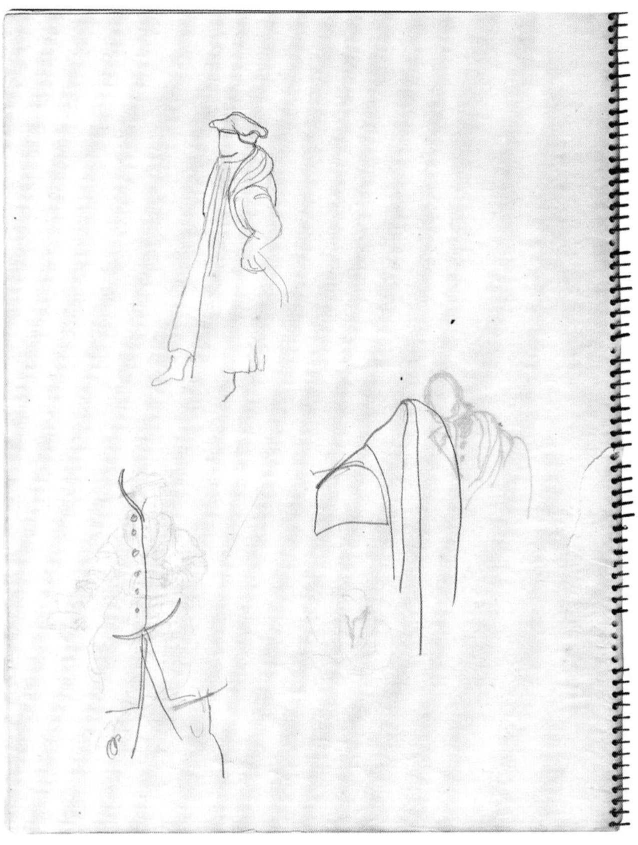
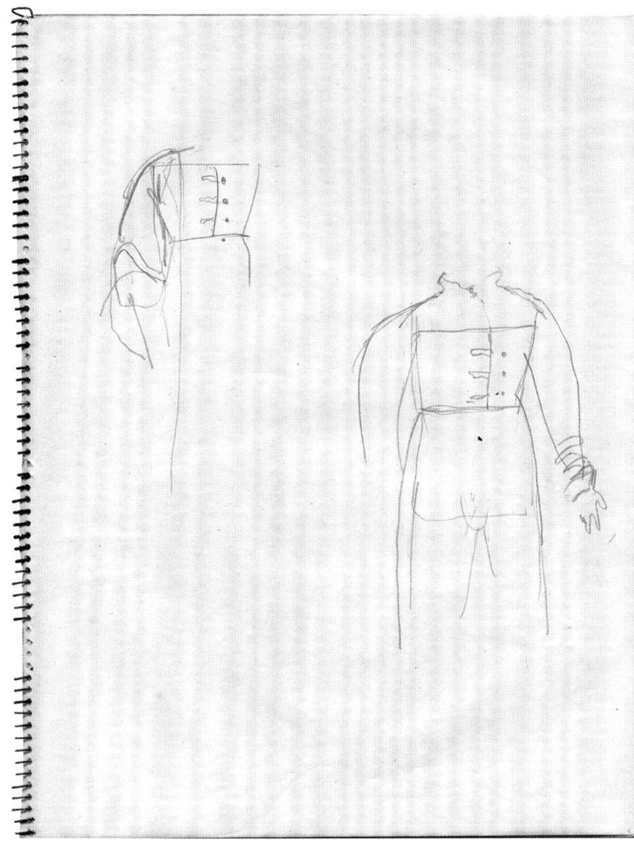

ABOVE: Staging and character notes; originals scanned for publication

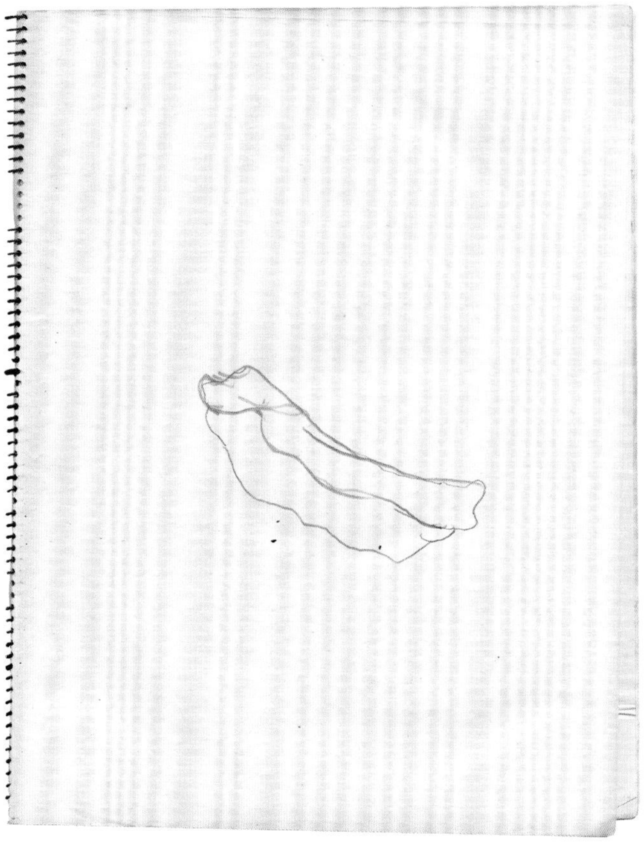

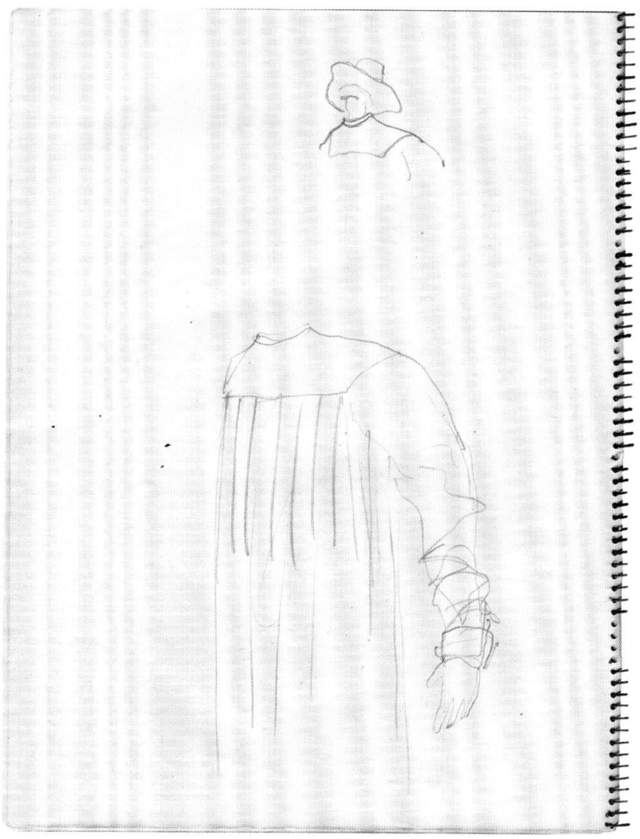

ABOVE: Staging and character notes; originals scanned for publication

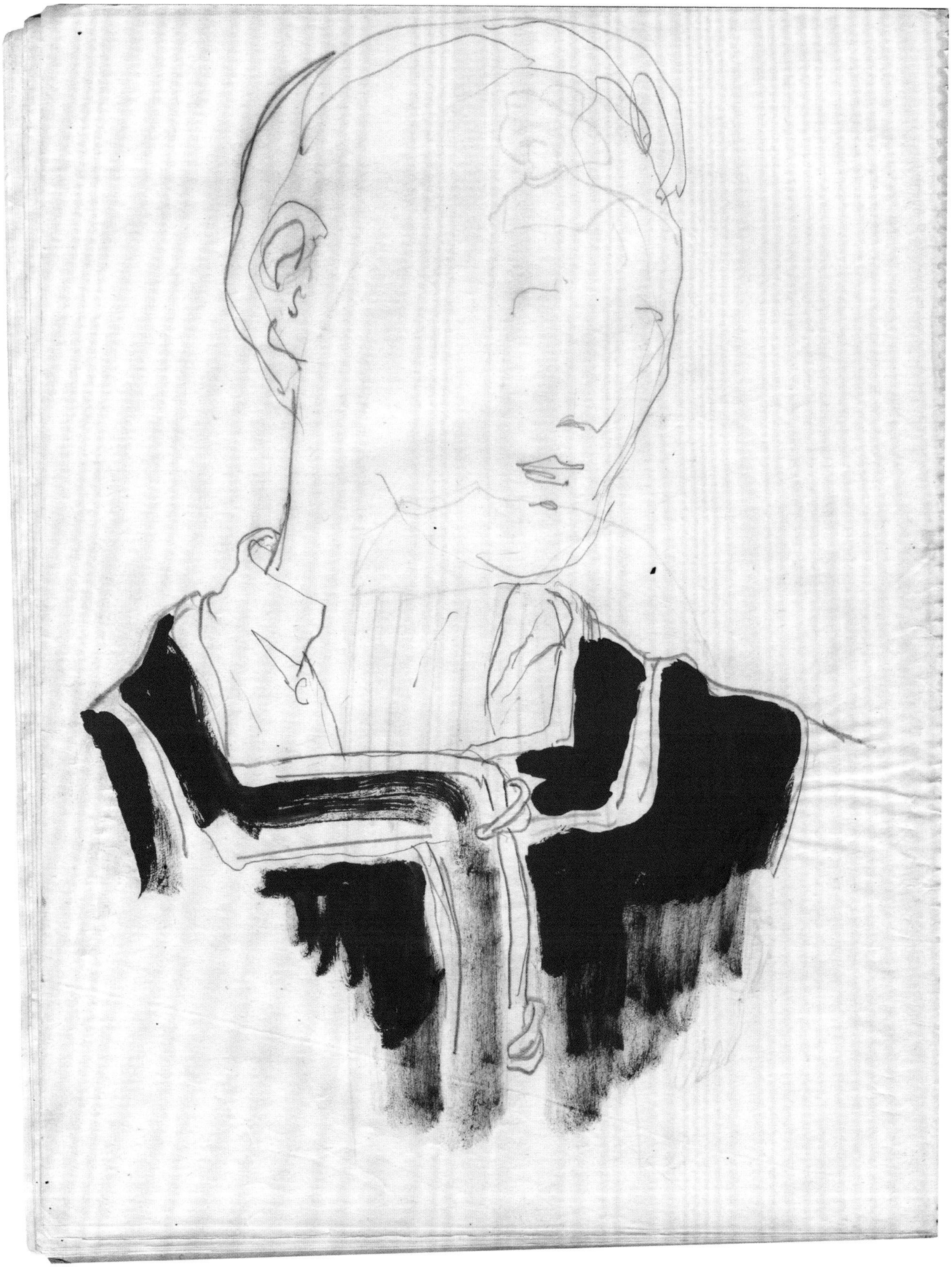

ABOVE: Staging and character notes; original scanned for publication

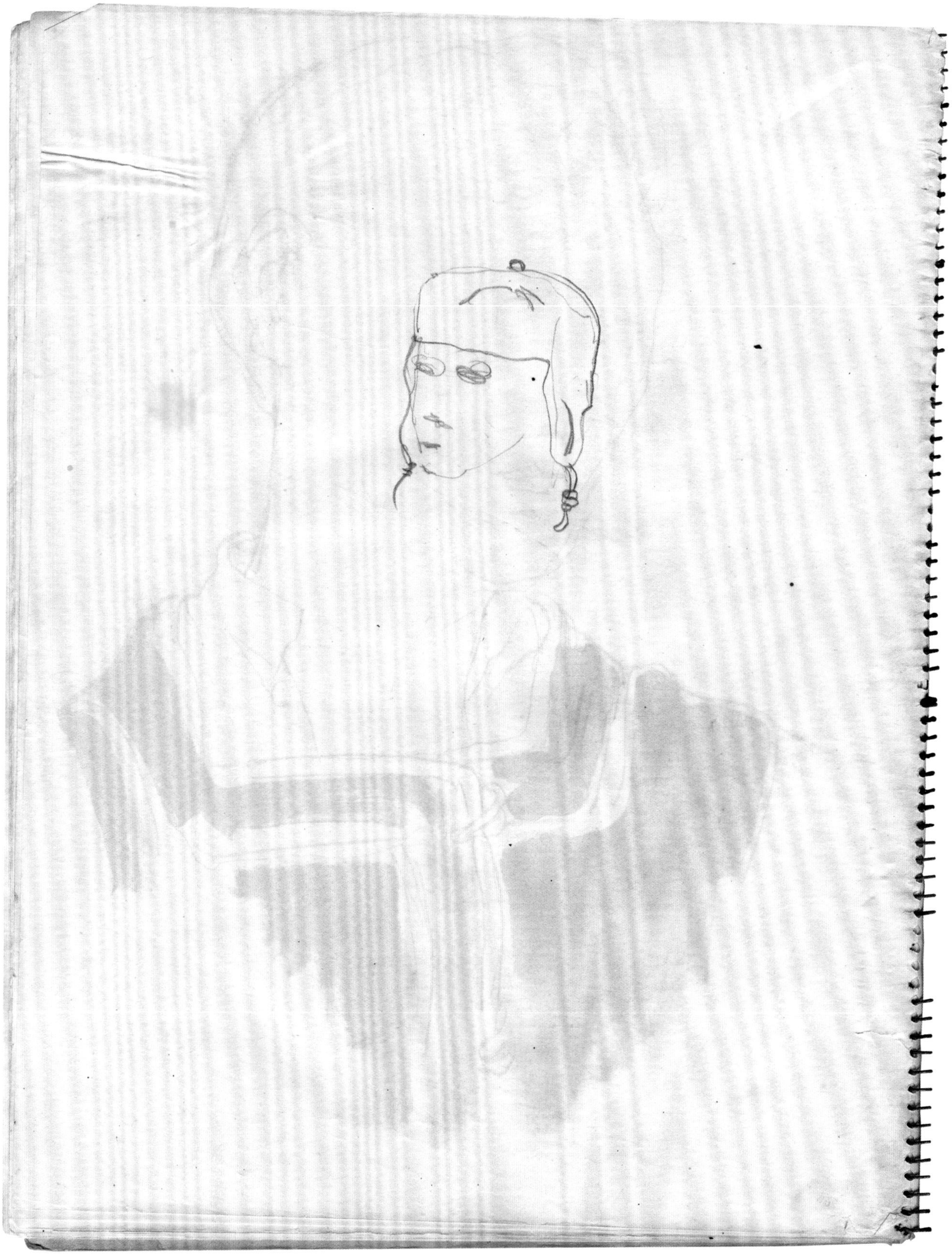

ABOVE: Staging and character notes; original scanned for publication

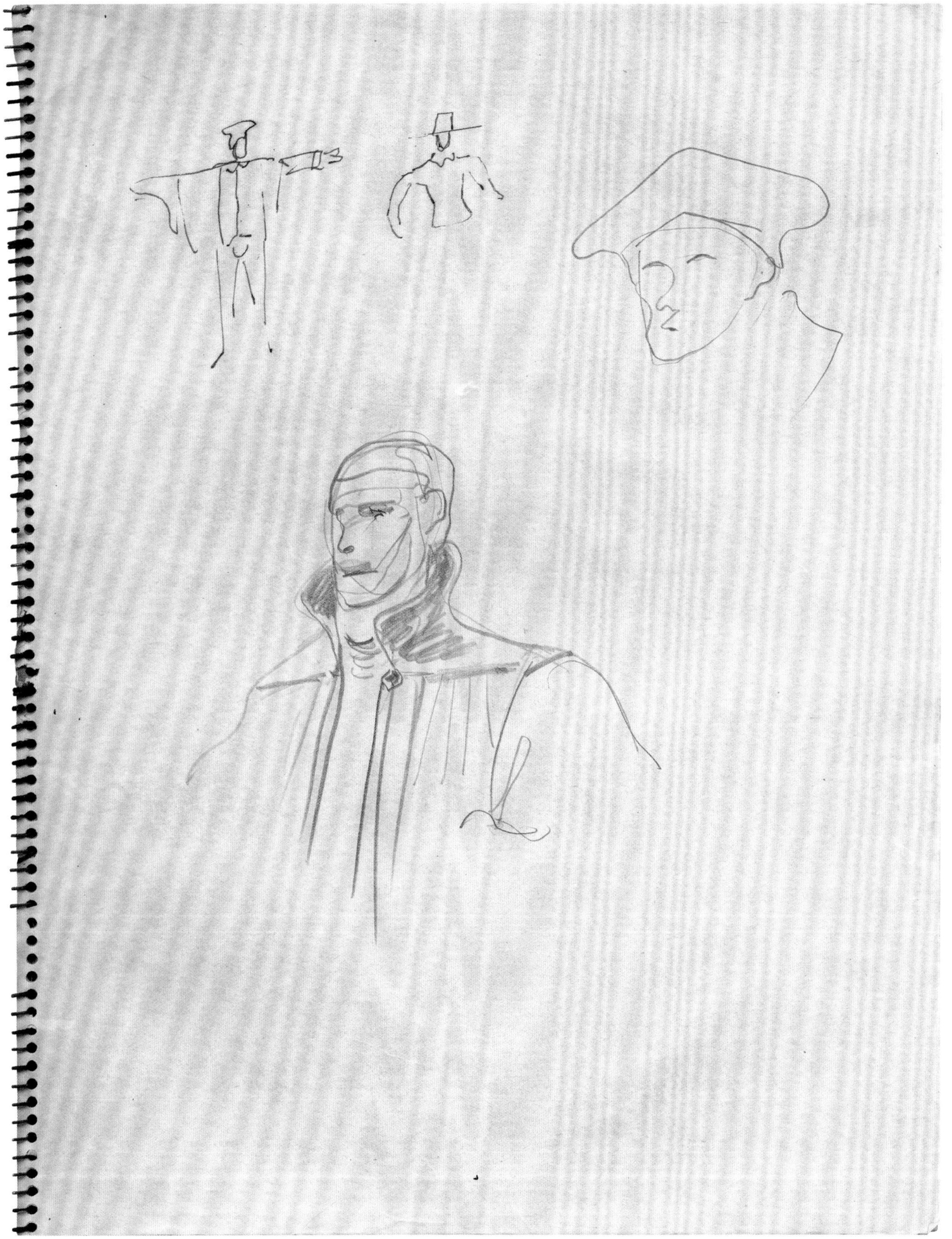

ABOVE: Staging and character notes; original scanned for publication

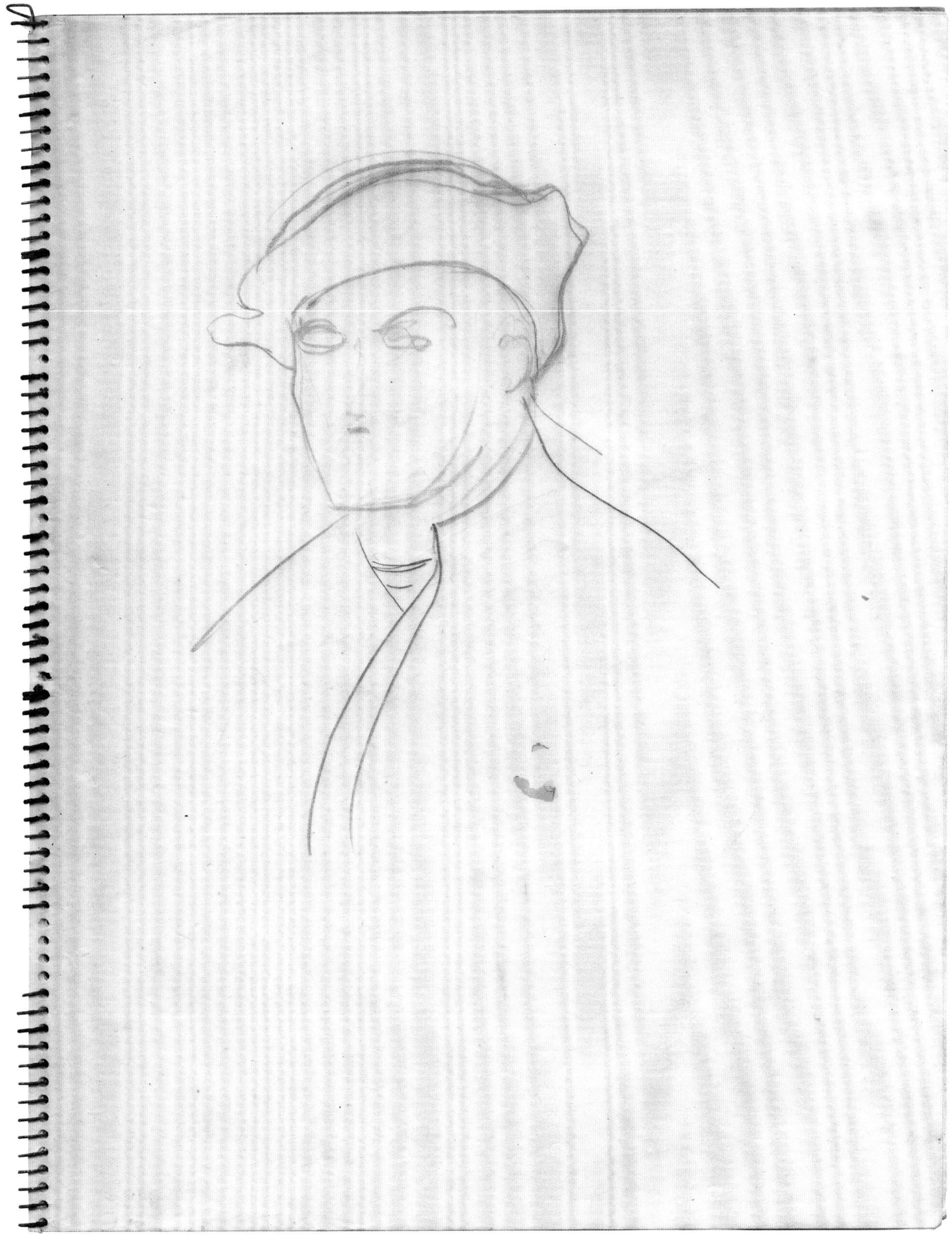

ABOVE: Staging and character notes; original scanned for publication

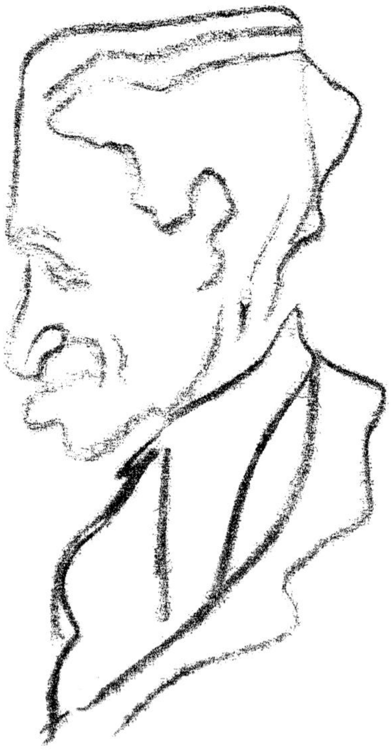

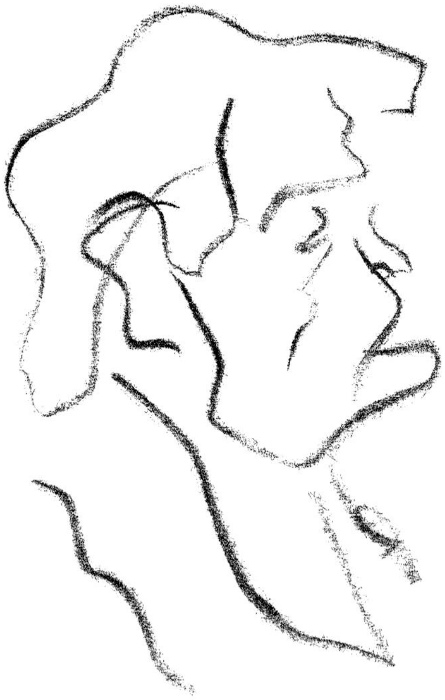

THE MERCURY THEATER ON THE AIR & THE CAMPBELL PLAYHOUSE

An entire book could – and perhaps should – be written about Welles's career in radio. In a few short years he came to dominate the medium, and might have continued to do so if the movies hadn't intervened. He acted in countless radio plays in the 1930s, somehow fitting them in around his formidable theater commitments, which alone would have exhausted a lesser mortal. His schedule was so hectic at one point that he needed an ambulance with lights flashing and siren blaring to ferry him from stage to studio through the Manhattan traffic.

He was no less prolific as a writer and director, presenting groundbreaking and masterful adaptations of literary classics with *The Mercury Theater On the Air* and, later, more commercial fare with *The Campbell Playhouse*. The list of productions Welles wrote, co-produced, directed and starred in between 1938 and 1940 is staggering. To cite *Julius Caesar, Heart of Darkness, The Bridge of San Luis Rey, Jane Eyre, Treasure Island, Les Misérables, Vanity Fair, Mutiny on the Bounty* and *The Murder of Roger Ackroyd* is to barely scratch the surface. He is as famous for his 1938 broadcast of *The War of the Worlds*, and the panic it induced in more credulous members of the American public, as he is for anything else, including *Citizen Kane*.

ABOVE: Sketches; scans supplied for publication

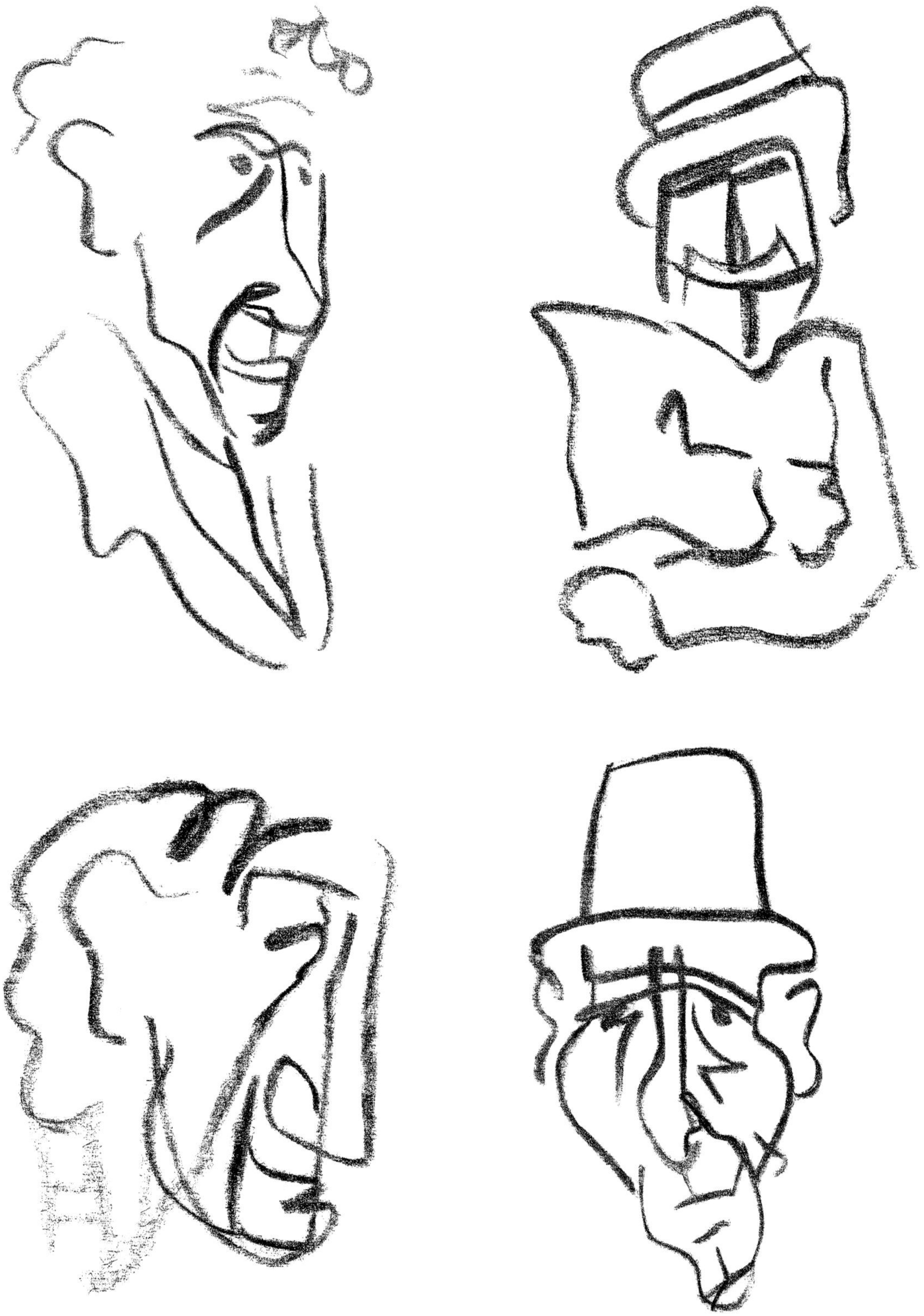

ABOVE: Sketches; scans supplied for publication

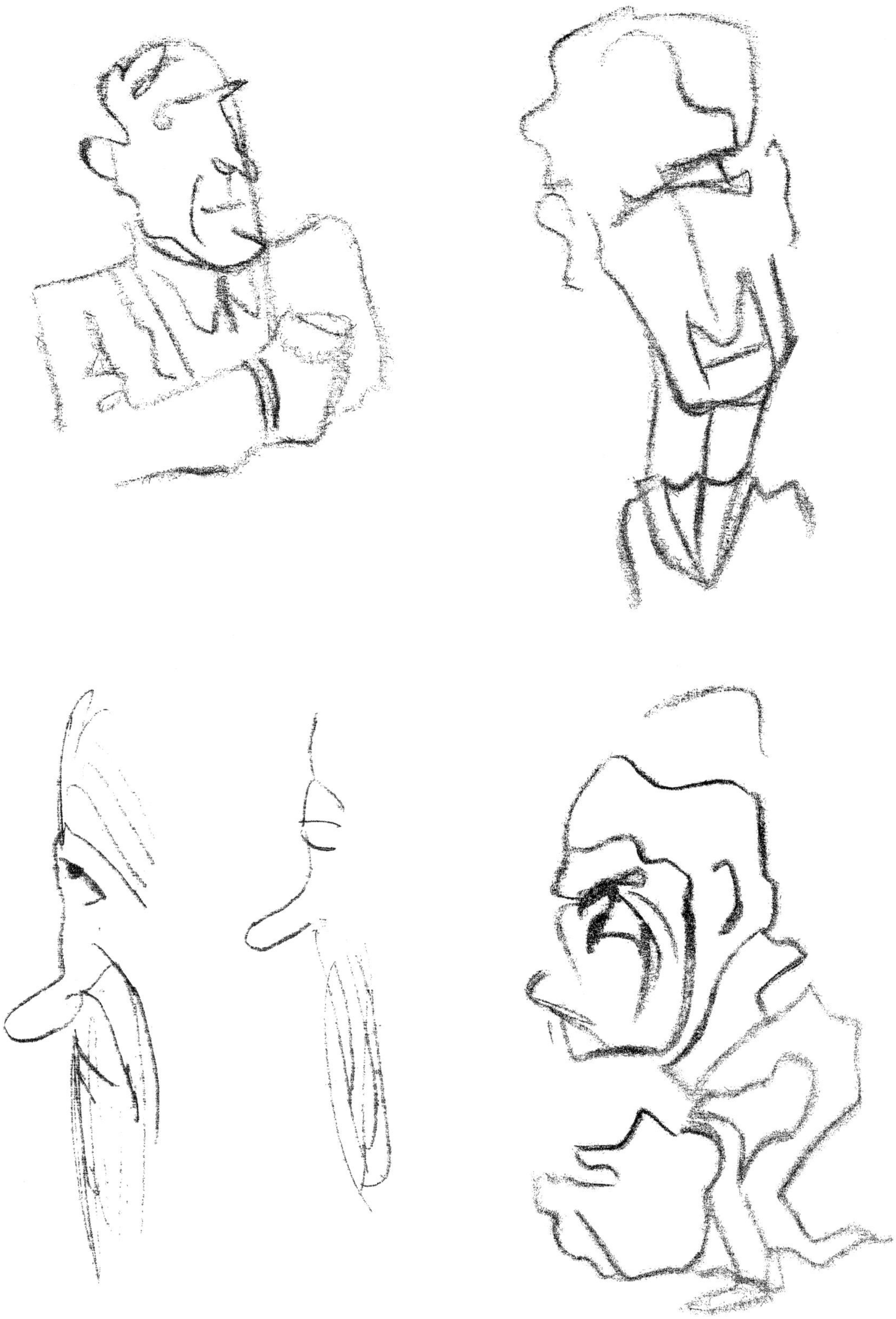

ABOVE: Sketches; scans supplied for publication

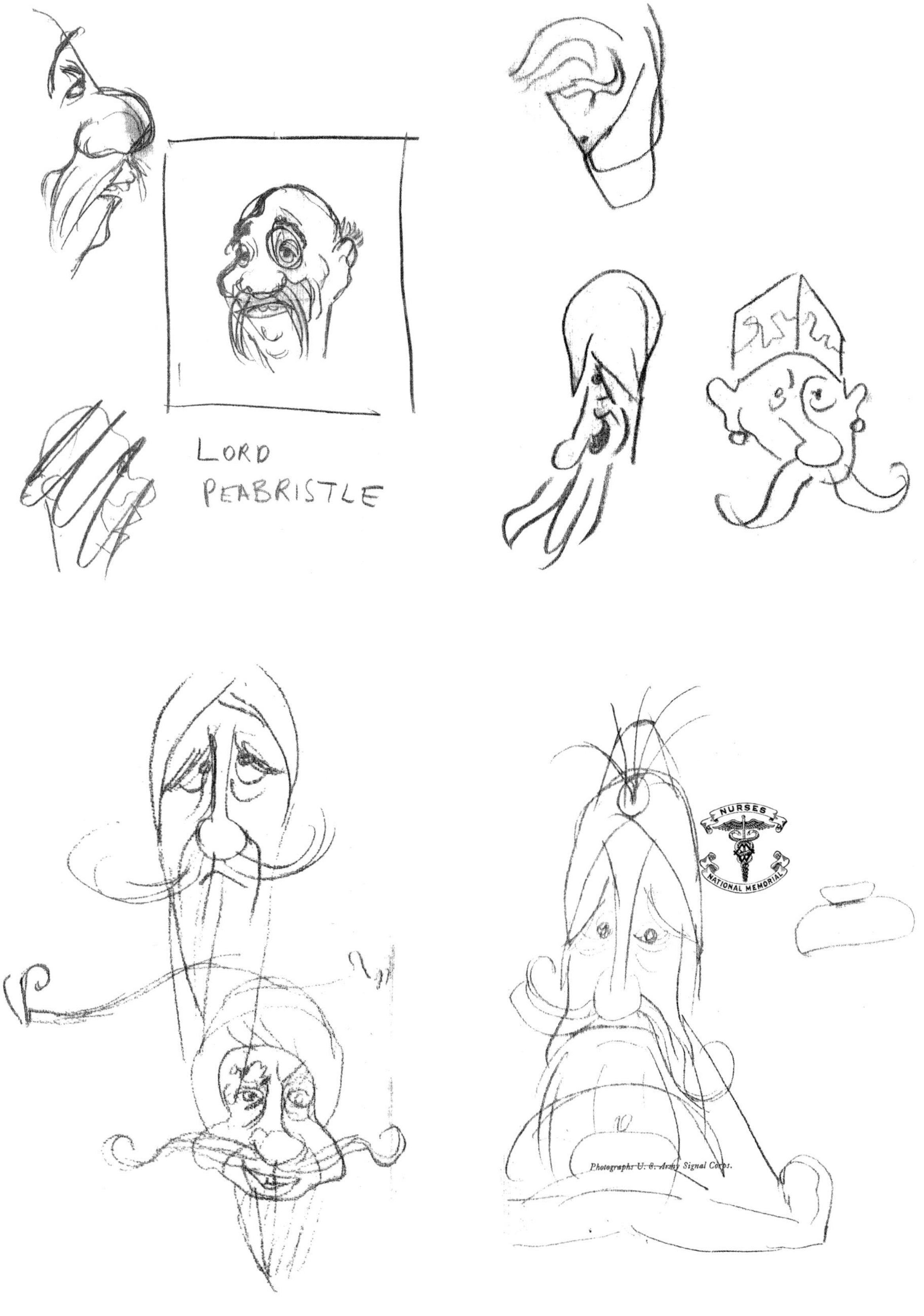

ABOVE: Sketches; scans supplied for publication

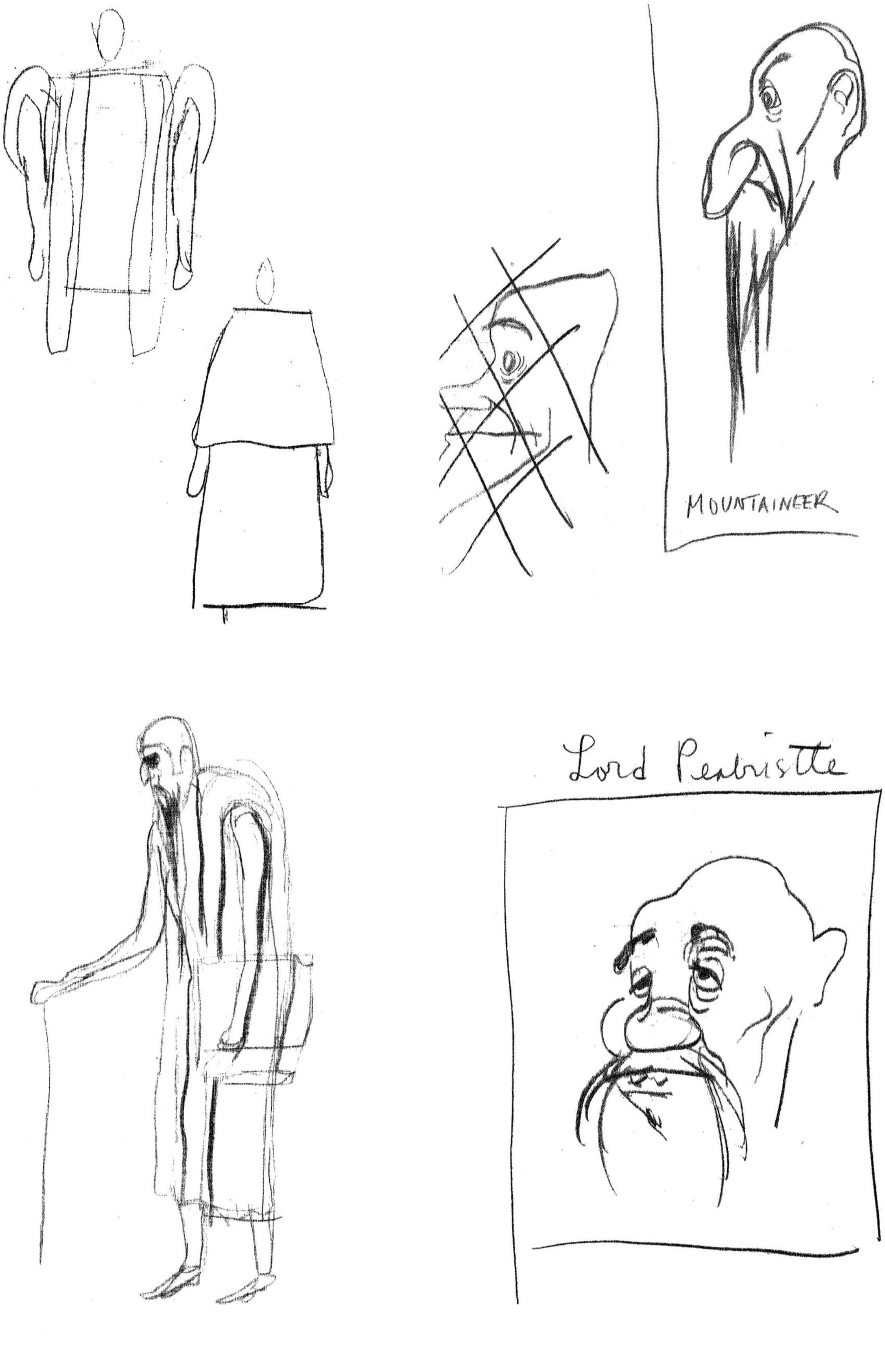

ABOVE: Sketches; scans supplied for publication

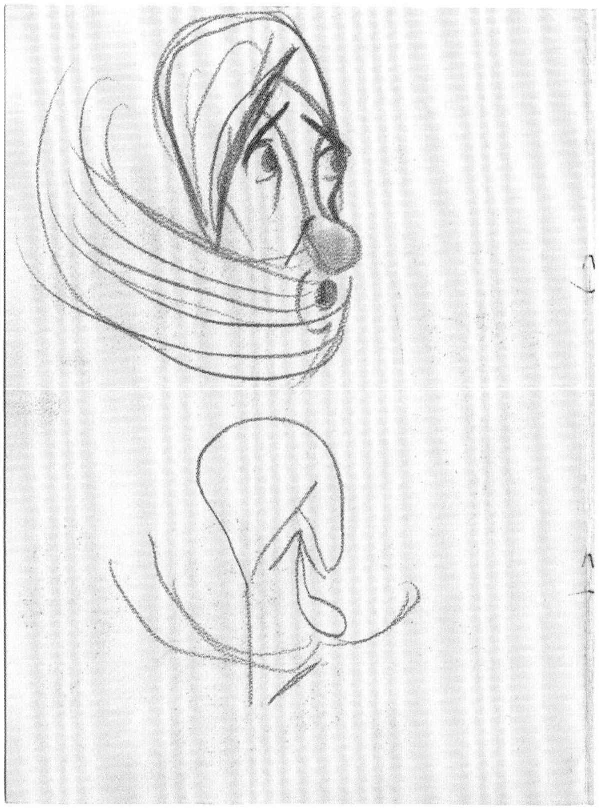

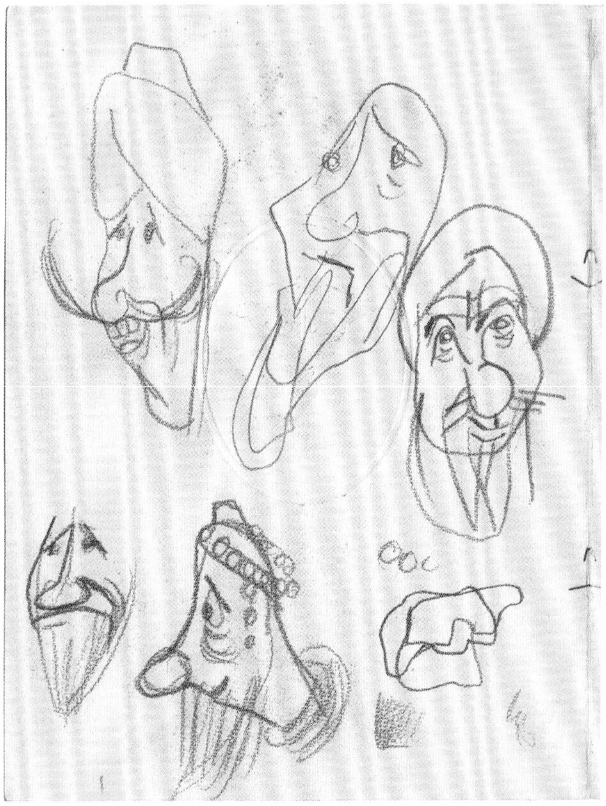

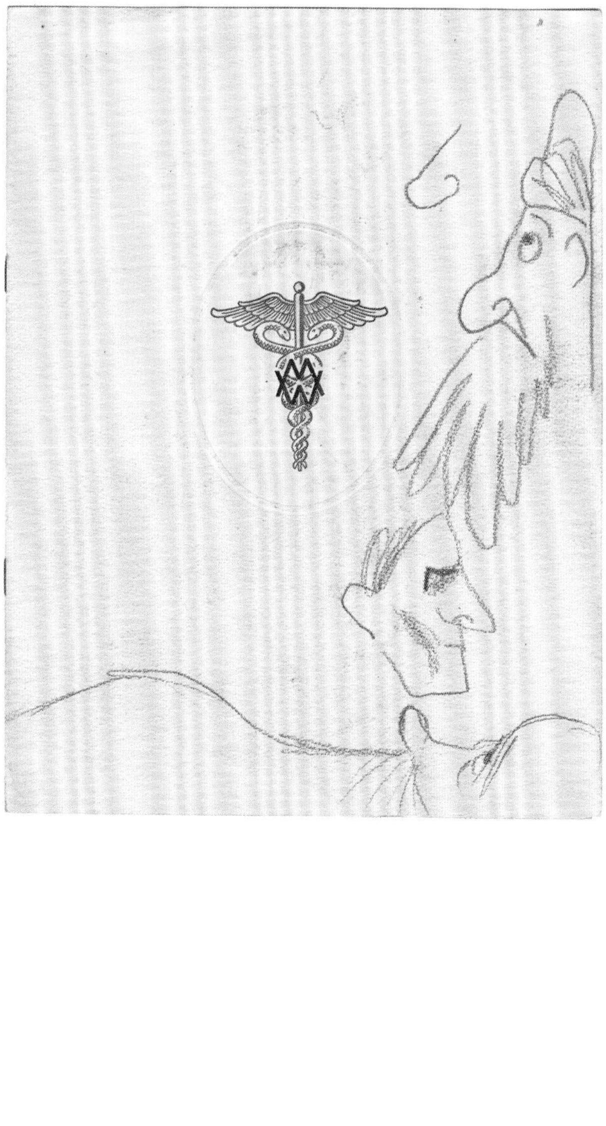

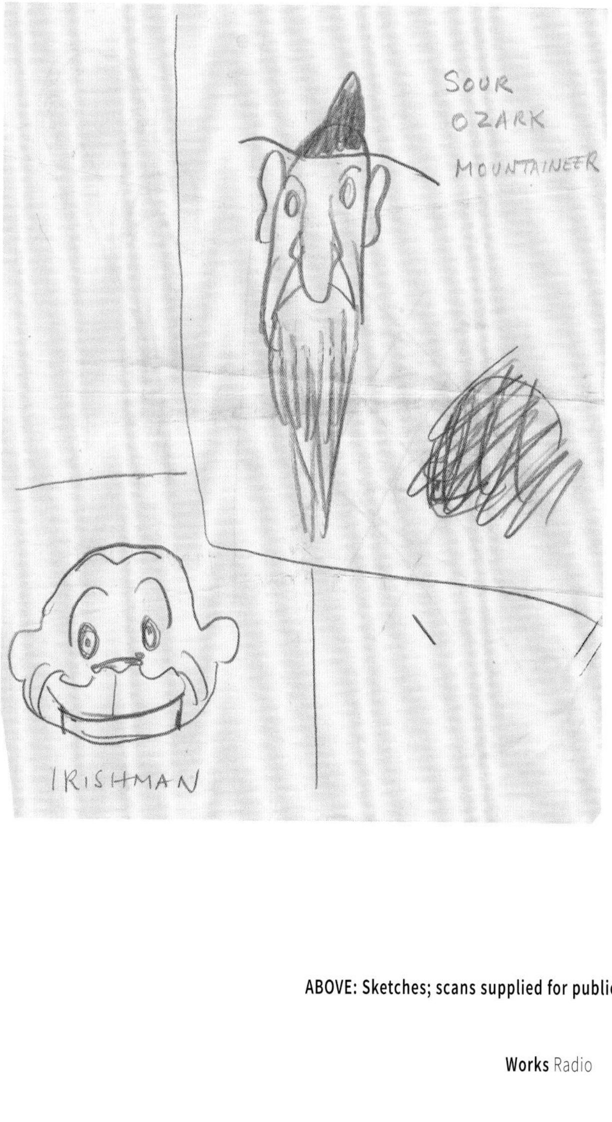

ABOVE: Sketches; scans supplied for publication

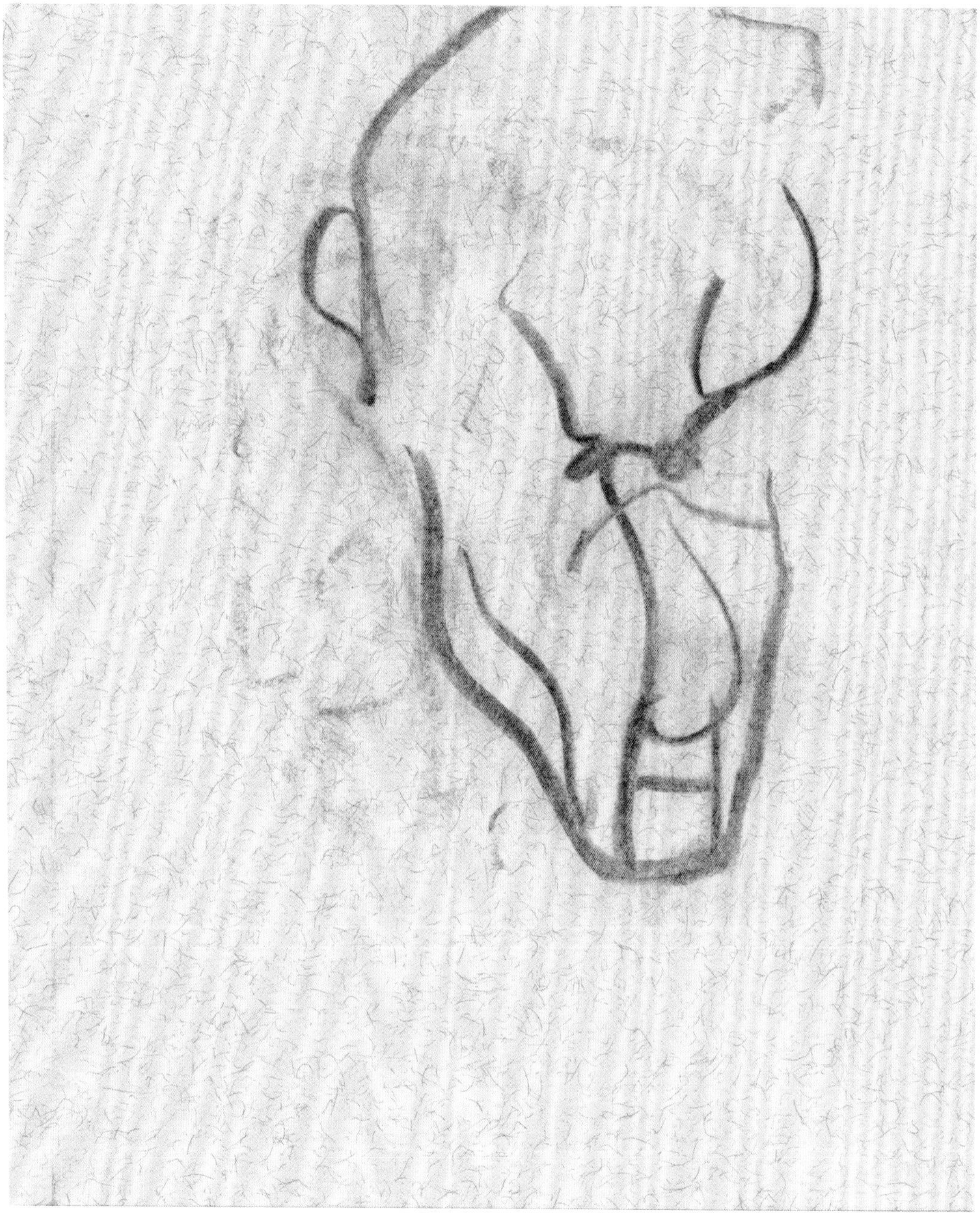

ABOVE: Sketches; scans supplied for publication

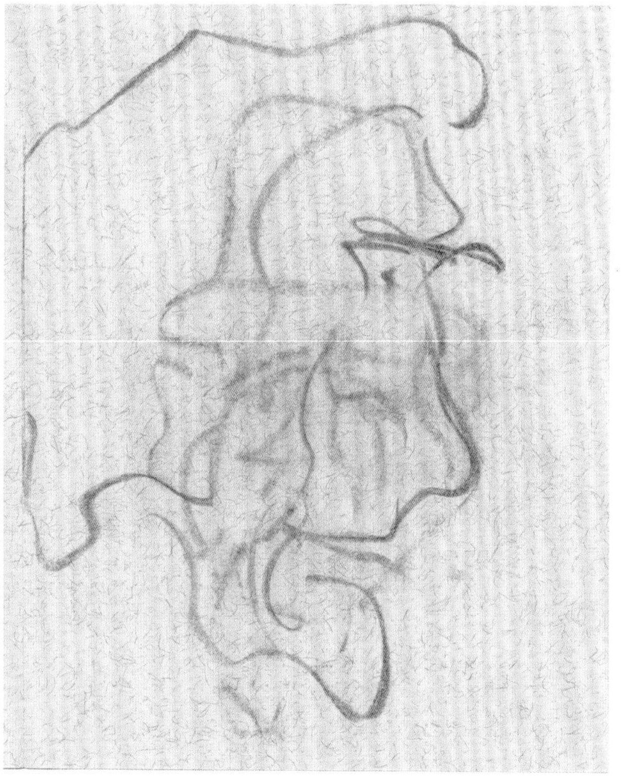

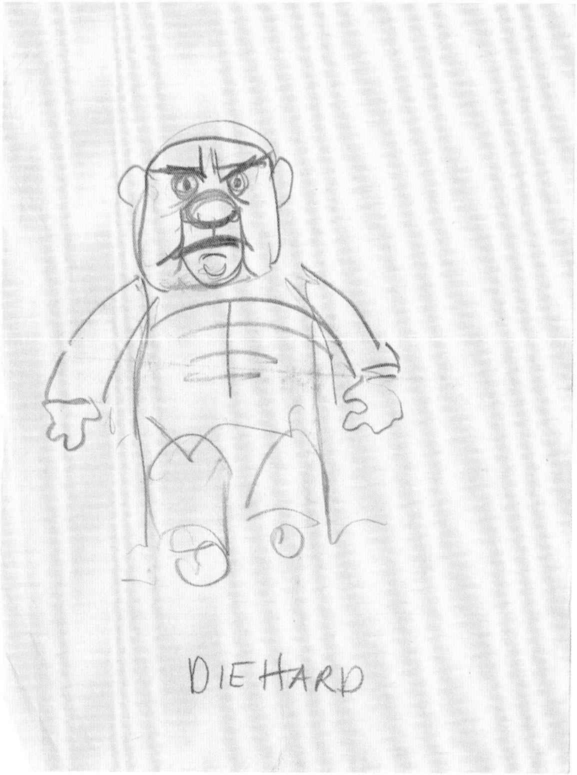

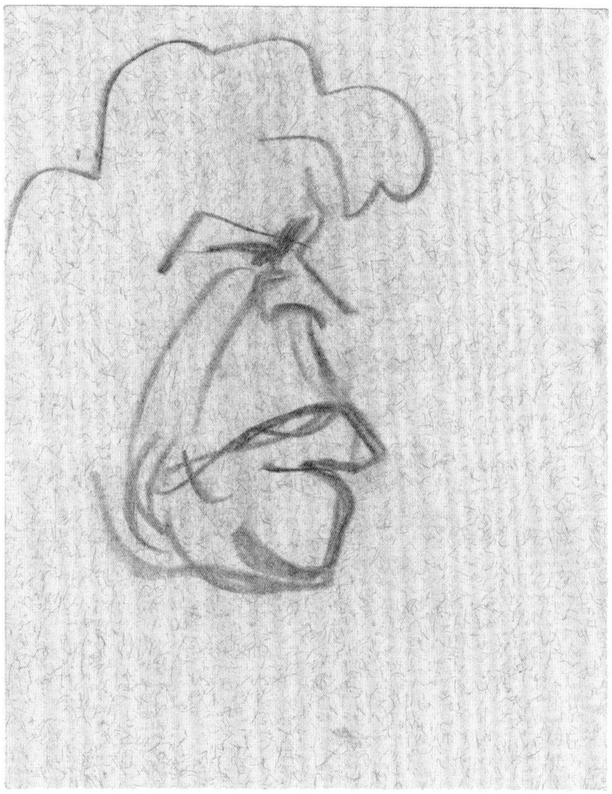

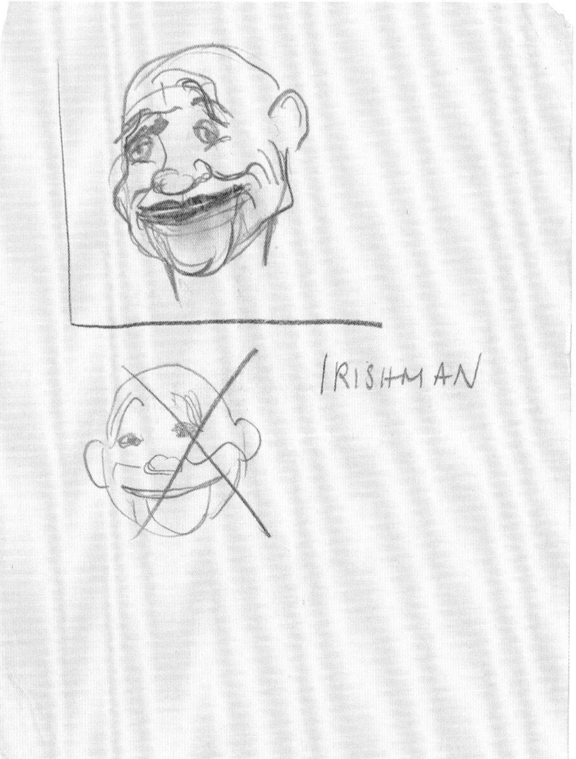

ABOVE: Sketches; scans supplied for publication

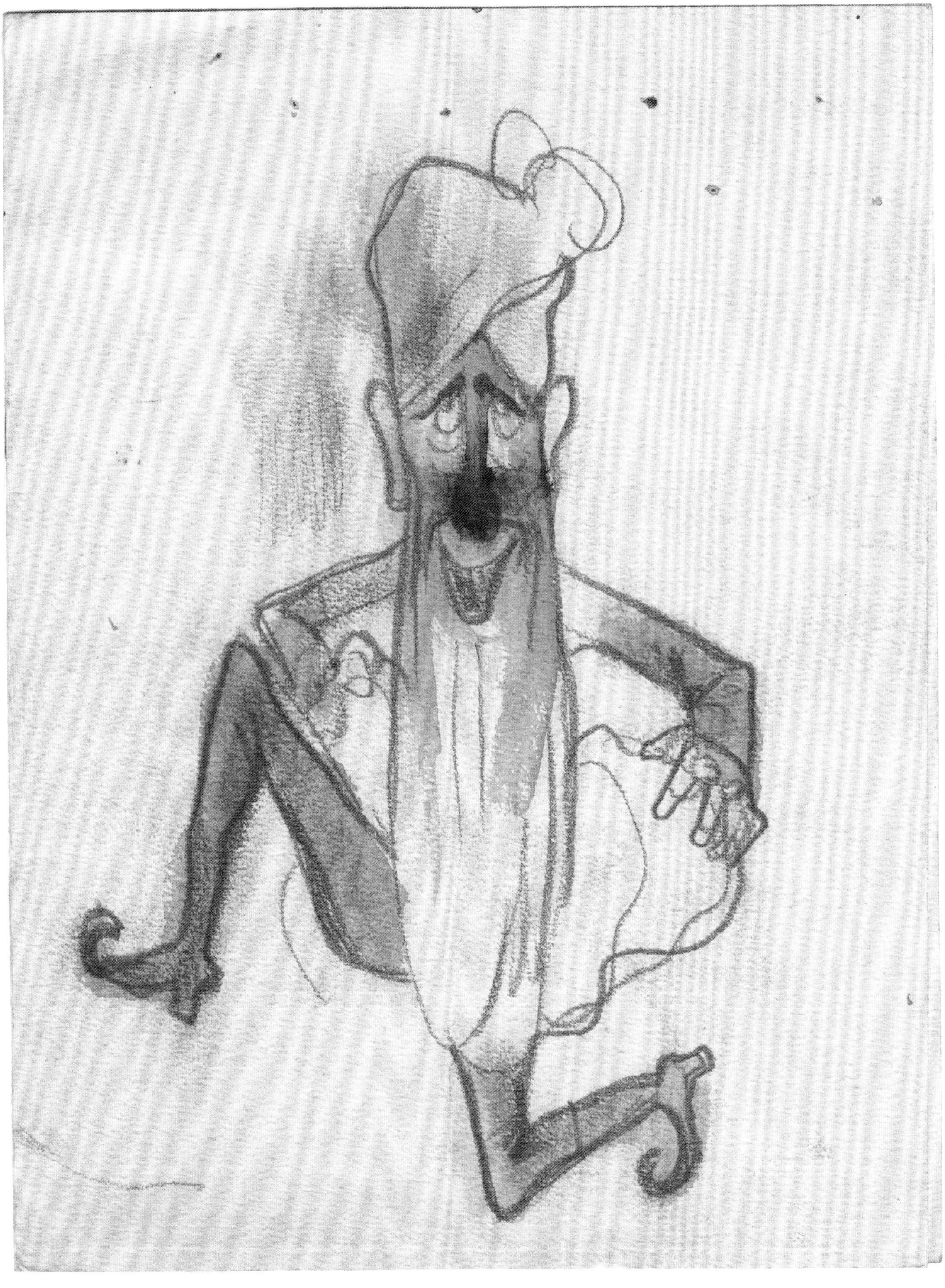

ABOVE: Watercolor sketch; scan supplied for publication

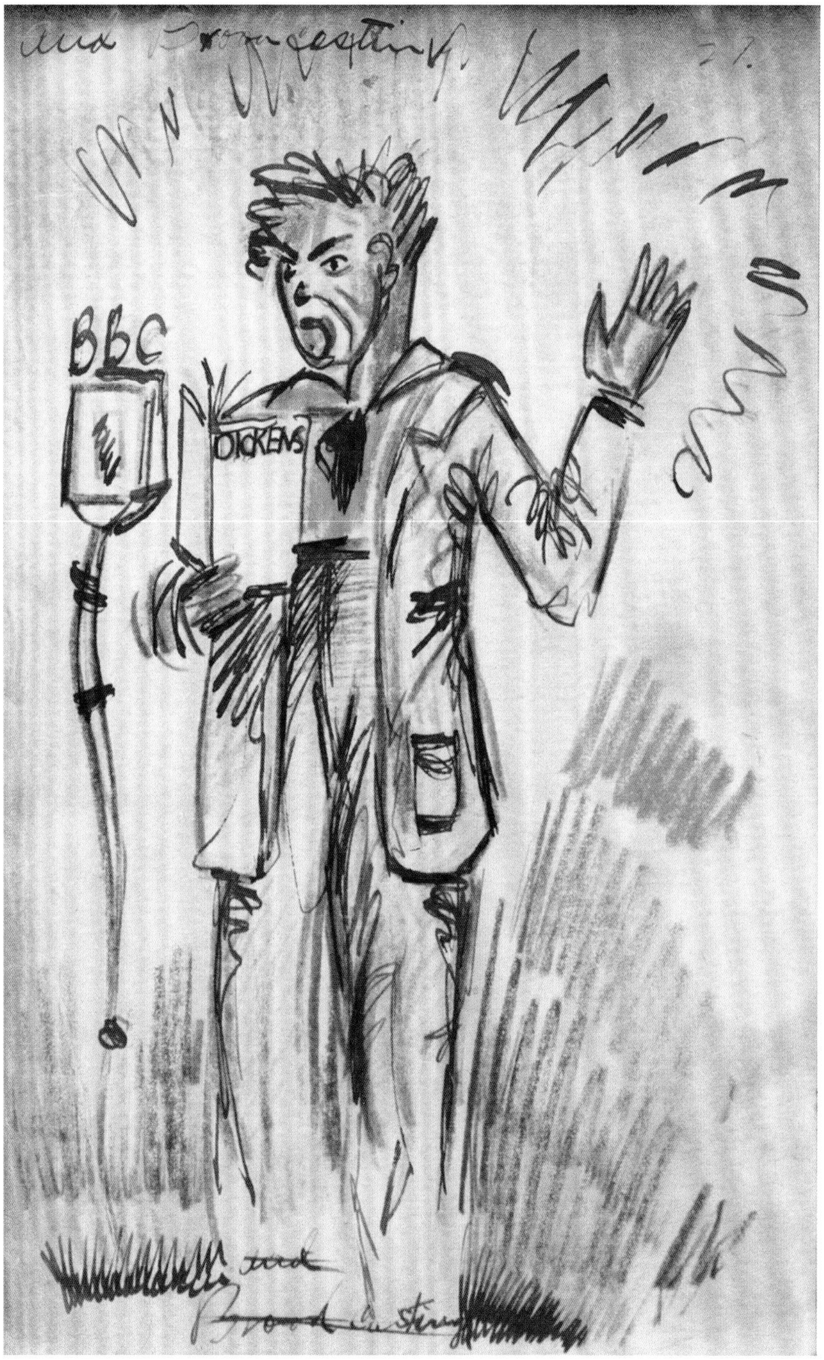

BBC

This marvelous sketch vividly captures the passion and energy Welles brought to his radio performances, although the BBC logo on the microphone tells us that his late '30s heyday was behind him.

In 1951, Welles was persuaded by British radio producer Harry Alan Towers to star in *The Adventures of Harry Lime*, an episodic prequel to *The Third Man* chronicling the exploits of Welles's character before his fateful reckoning in Vienna. The series was syndicated to the BBC and, thanks to its reimagining of the odious Lime as a likeable rogue, was a huge success.

Welles teamed with Towers again in 1952 for true-crime anthology *The Black Museum* and the following year for Towers' production of *The Adventures of Sherlock Holmes*, playing Moriarty in the final episode opposite John Gielgud as Holmes and Ralph Richardson as Watson. The series was broadcast on the BBC in 1954.

Welles did work directly for BBC radio on several occasions, on *Portrait of Robert Flaherty*, broadcast September 2, 1952, and *Song of Myself*, broadcast August 22, 1953, but the script he is clutching in the picture seems to be wishful thinking. Although he tackled *Oliver Twist, A Christmas Carol, The Pickwick Papers* and *A Tale of Two Cities* in the US, he never did Dickens at the Beeb.

ABOVE: And Broadcasting...; photo supplied for publication

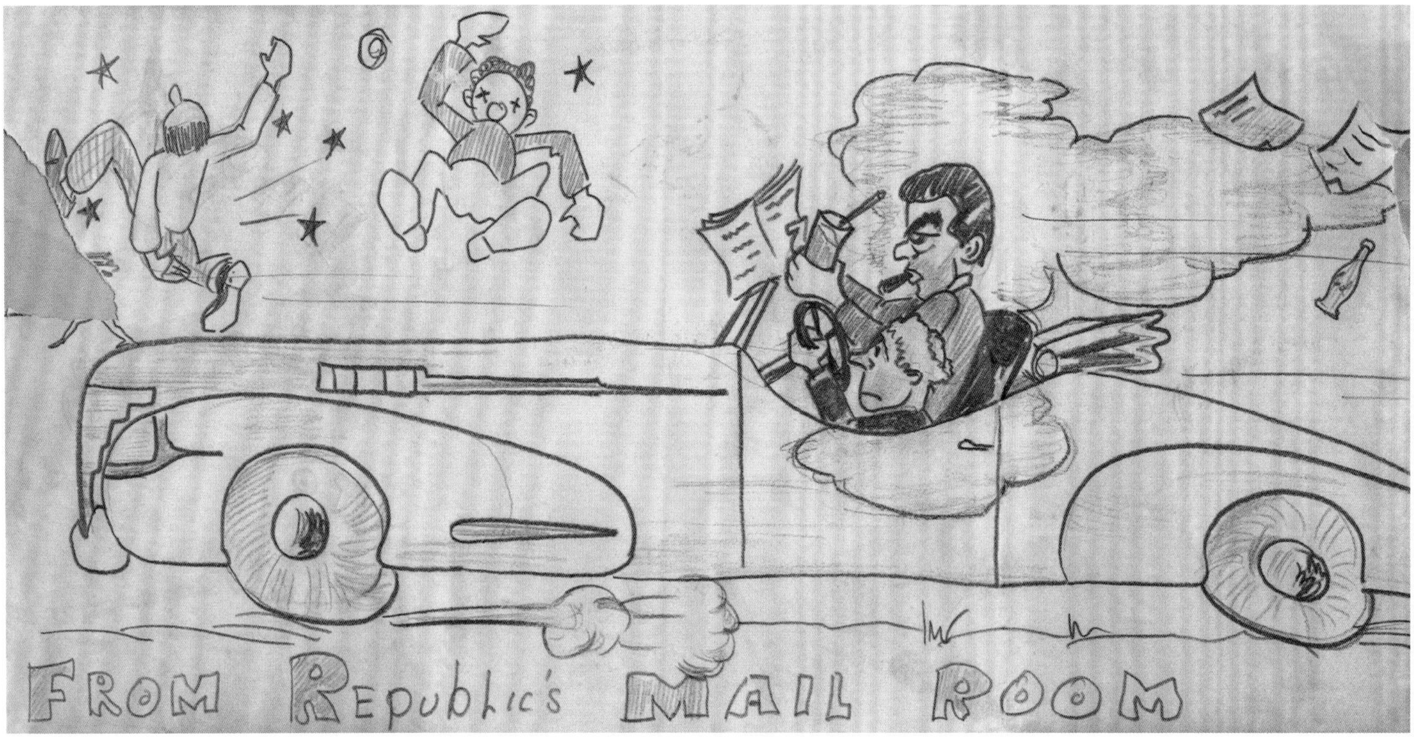

MACBETH

Welles told his biographer Barbara Leaming that his 1948 movie *Macbeth* was a bold charcoal sketch of the play. It's a fitting description, applicable to both the film's stark black-and-white photography and to his unflinching abstraction of the text. Welles was never afraid to take the pruning shears to Shakespeare – he positively reveled in it, in fact – and here he slashed the play's two-and-a-half-hour running time to a more screen-friendly 107 minutes.

It also finds echoes in the few pre-production sketches for *Macbeth* that survive, particularly the three leaden grey drawings for the castle set: hulking stone structures against lowering dark skies. It's obvious from these what look Welles was going for. His director of photography was John L. Russell, later Hitchcock's DOP on *Psycho* – not quite the recommendation it appears. Hitchcock used the crew from his TV show on *Psycho* to keep costs down. Russell worked fast and cheap; no Gregg Toland he. So, while he might get the credit, the visuals are unmistakably Welles.

The film was produced by Republic Pictures, an outfit better known for B-movie genre fare than the classics; other releases of 1948 included *Oklahoma Badlands, King of the Gamblers* and *Desperados of Dodge City*. The budget was set at $700,000 with a shooting schedule of twenty-three days, punishingly tight by anyone's standards.

A stage version of the production ran for four nights at the University Theater in Salt Lake City, Utah – rehearsals masquerading as public performance – before principal photography began on June 23, 1947 using sets left over from the low-budget westerns that were Republic's bread and butter. To save time and money, both in short supply, Welles had the entire cast pre-record their dialogue before shooting began.

Set design was credited to Republic's long-serving art director Fred Ritter, but, again, Welles's overarching influence is self-evident. The towers, ramparts

ABOVE: From Republic's Mail Room; scan supplied for publication

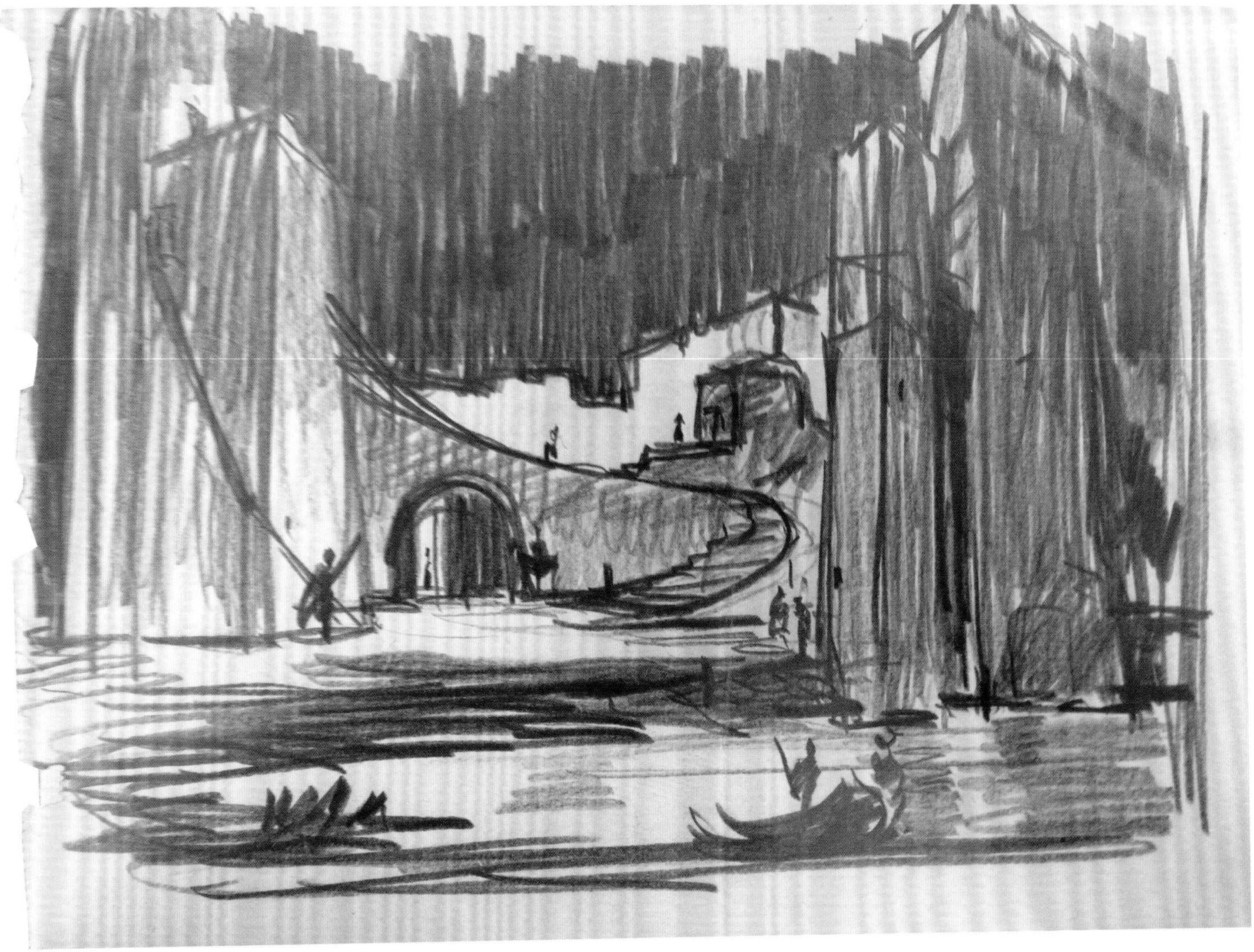

and sweeping staircases seen on screen are clearly taken from his sketches, which were based on sets for the Salt Lake City production. Minimal research reveals that they are, in effect, a massively scaled-up version of the stage set for Welles's 'Voodoo' *Macbeth* of the year before, with blasted heath standing in for verdant jungle. Elsewhere, the spidery branches of a dead tree, dashed off with customary economy by Welles, play a significant role in the film, looming menacingly over the scenes with the Weird Sisters.

The sketch titled 'HEATH' (captioned 'Soldiers behind Macbeth Misty Silhouettes in thick FOG'), might be short on detail, but it is hugely evocative nonetheless, the three witches spookily traced in outline only. It also hints strongly at the costumes Welles envisioned for Macbeth and his men: spiked helmets, chain mail and heavy furs that owe more to Genghis Khan than they do to medieval Scotland. Although, in the film, several characters sport the traditional kilt, a multi-purpose plaid cloak that bears little resemblance to the pleated skirts favored by Highland regiments and wedding guests today. Welles, with a nod to authenticity, believed it conveyed noble bearing. A publicity still of Welles in full battle dress – broadsword akimbo, spikes radiating from his headdress, his shoulders swathed in fur – shows the striking end result of these featureless yet expressive daubs.

Again, Welles received no official credit for costume design on *Macbeth*. But then, significantly, neither did anyone else. The costumes themselves were assembled from pieces rented from Western Costumes, a Hollywood institution since the silent era – and they are marvelous, despite their off-the-shelf origins. Welles did not agree. Years later he expressed his dissatisfaction with his own outfit to filmmaker Peter Bogdanovich. It made him look, he claimed, like the Statue of Liberty.

ABOVE: Set design; scan supplied for publication

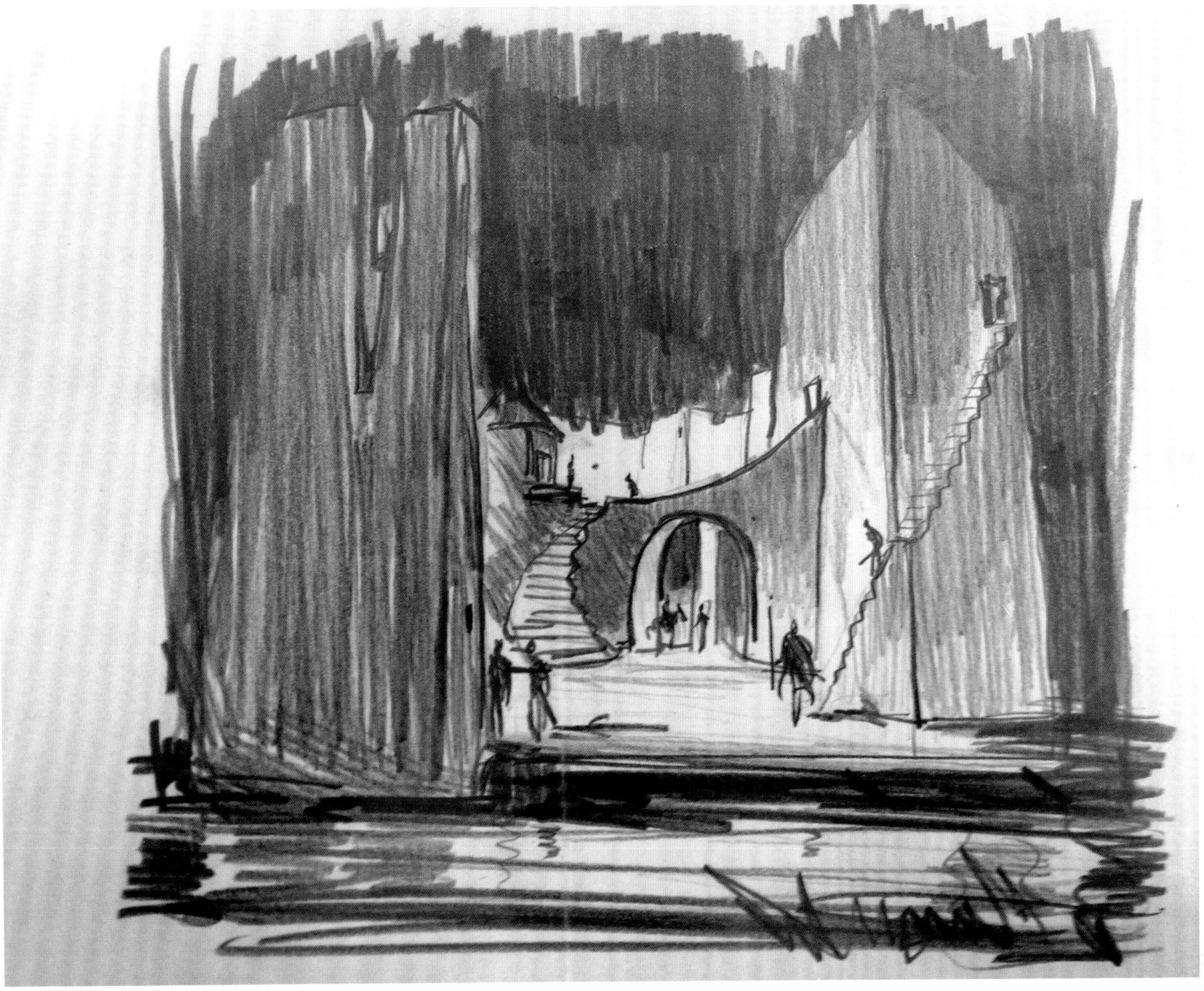

ABOVE: Set design; scan supplied for publication

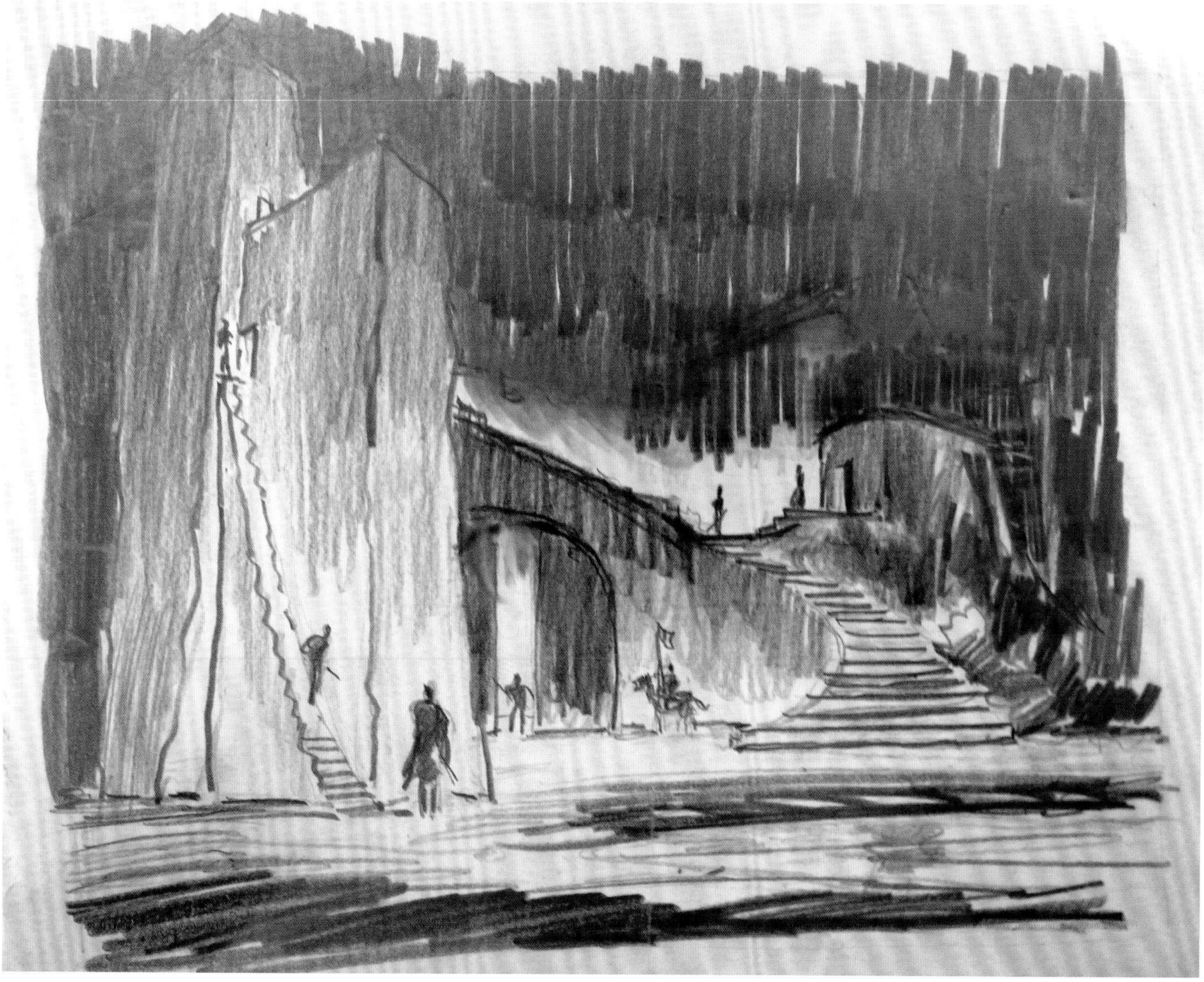

ABOVE: Set design; scan supplied for publication

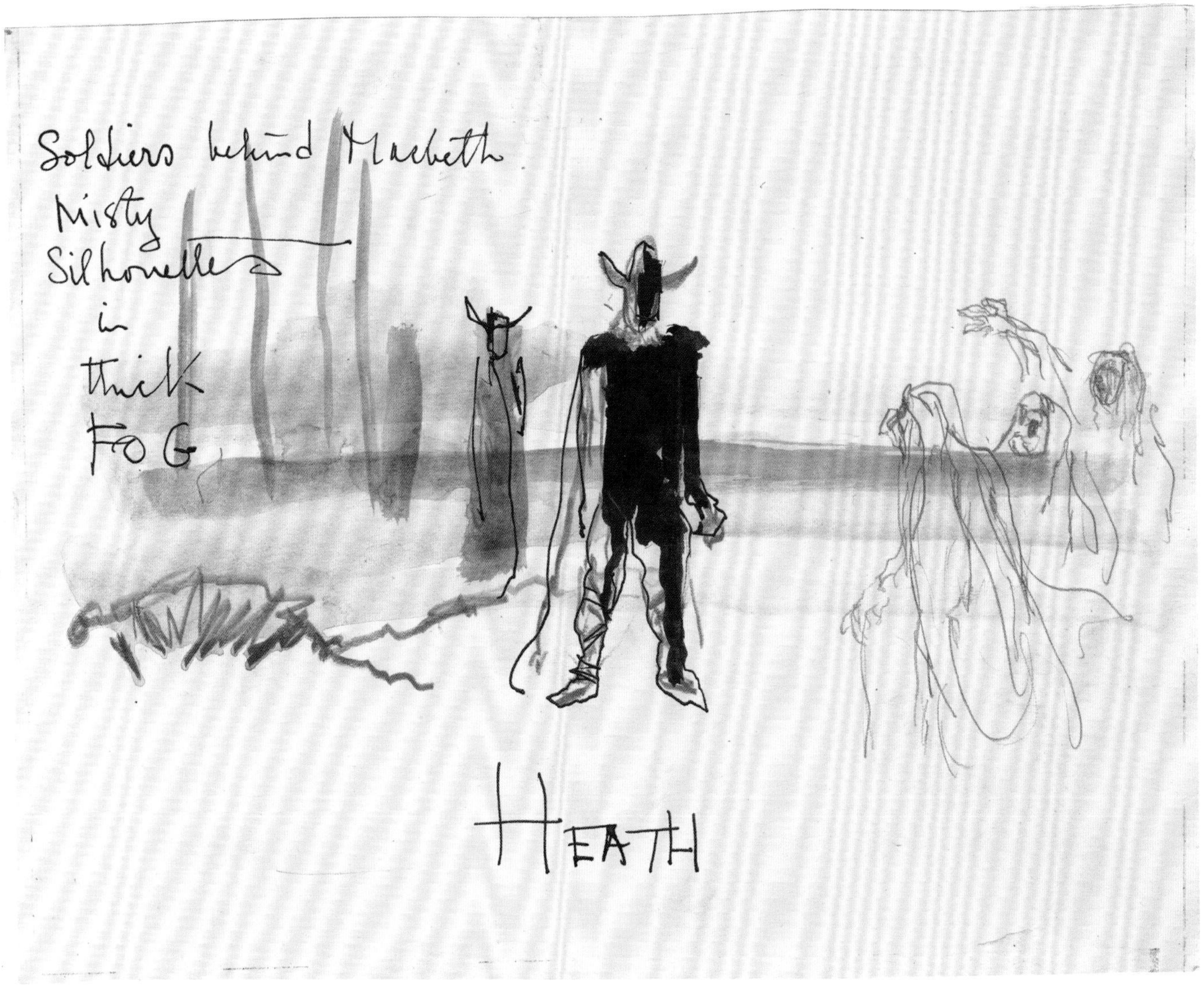

ABOVE: Staging sketch; scan supplied for publication

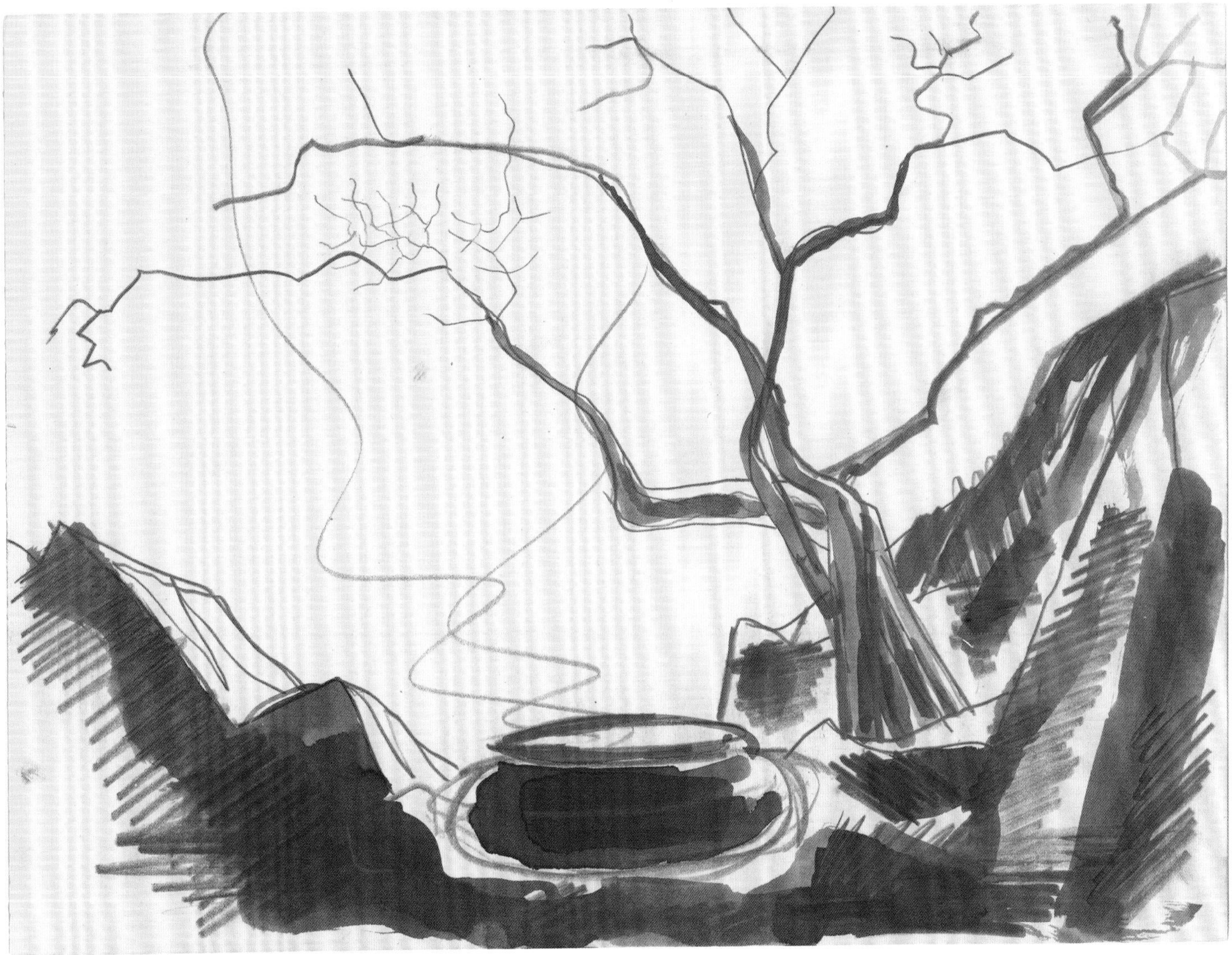

ABOVE: Staging sketch; scan supplied for publication

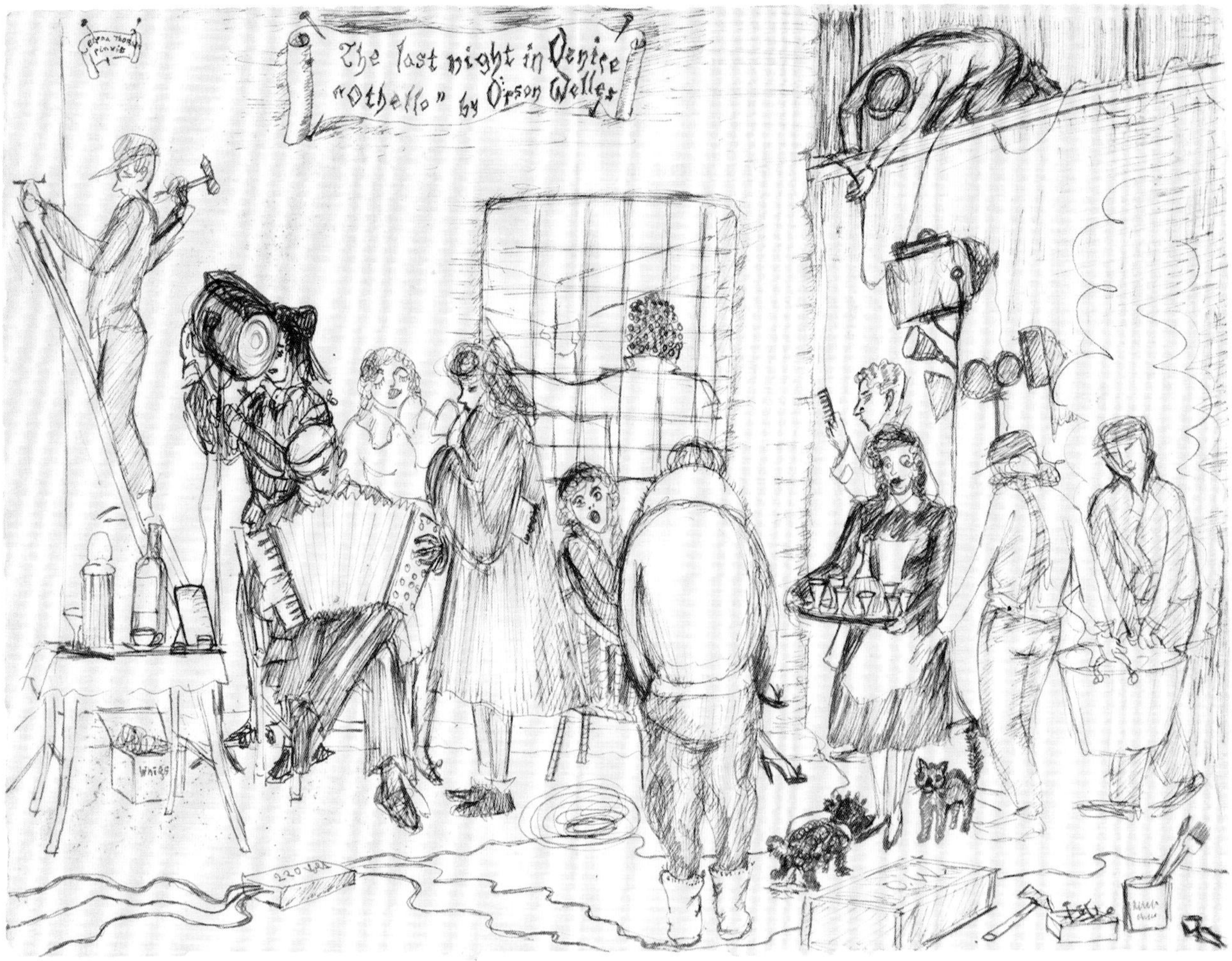

OTHELLO

In 1948, Welles found himself in what was becoming a familiar situation. He had taken the lead role in Gregory Ratoff's movie *Black Magic* for the paycheck and now found himself in Europe weighing up his options, one of which was an adaptation of *Cyrano de Bergerac* for producer Alexander Korda. When that went south, he turned his attention to a screen version of *Othello*.

Early signs were promising. Welles wrote the script with customary irreverence for the source text, and funding was on the table from Italian mogul Montatori Scalera. All systems were go, until, with wearying inevitability, Scalera went bust and the financing evaporated. This left Welles, his cast and crew stranded in the Moroccan city of Mogador with no money and no costumes.

Undeterred, Welles ploughed on, opting to shoot the scene of Rodrigo's murder in a Turkish bath (in reality a converted fish market) meaning only towels were required. This kind of ingenuity would come to serve him well, now that studio resources were a thing of the past.

Thereafter, filming progressed in fits and starts over the next three years, with Welles pumping his own money into the project whenever he was able.

Othello was shot mostly in Morocco, but a list of other locations, including Venice, Rome, Tuscany, Viterbo and Perugia, gives an idea of how erratic proceedings were. Welles summed it up in a later interview: 'Iago steps from the portico of a church in Torcello, an island in the Venetian lagoon, into a Portuguese cistern off the coast of Africa. Rodrigo kicks Cassio in Massaga and gets punched back in Ortega, a thousand miles away.' Getting the cast together was a constant nightmare. Legend has it that the role of Desdemona had to be re-cast four times to accommodate the schedule (or lack thereof). Whenever the company did convene, however, a festive atmosphere prevailed – as this sketch of the Venice wrap party attests. Ever the bon vivant, Welles made sure that whatever else might be lacking (costumes, for instance), his cast never wanted for sumptuous food and fine wines.

In 1974 Welles began work on a highly personal making-of documentary called *Filming Othello*, which also, somewhat fittingly, took a full three years to complete. Among the outtakes and interviews it contains a sequence where Welles glides through the canals of Venice in a gondola, pointing out locations where various scenes had been shot. It's pleasing to imagine that one of them was where this happy, chaotic celebration took place.

ABOVE: The Last Night in Venice; photo supplied for publication

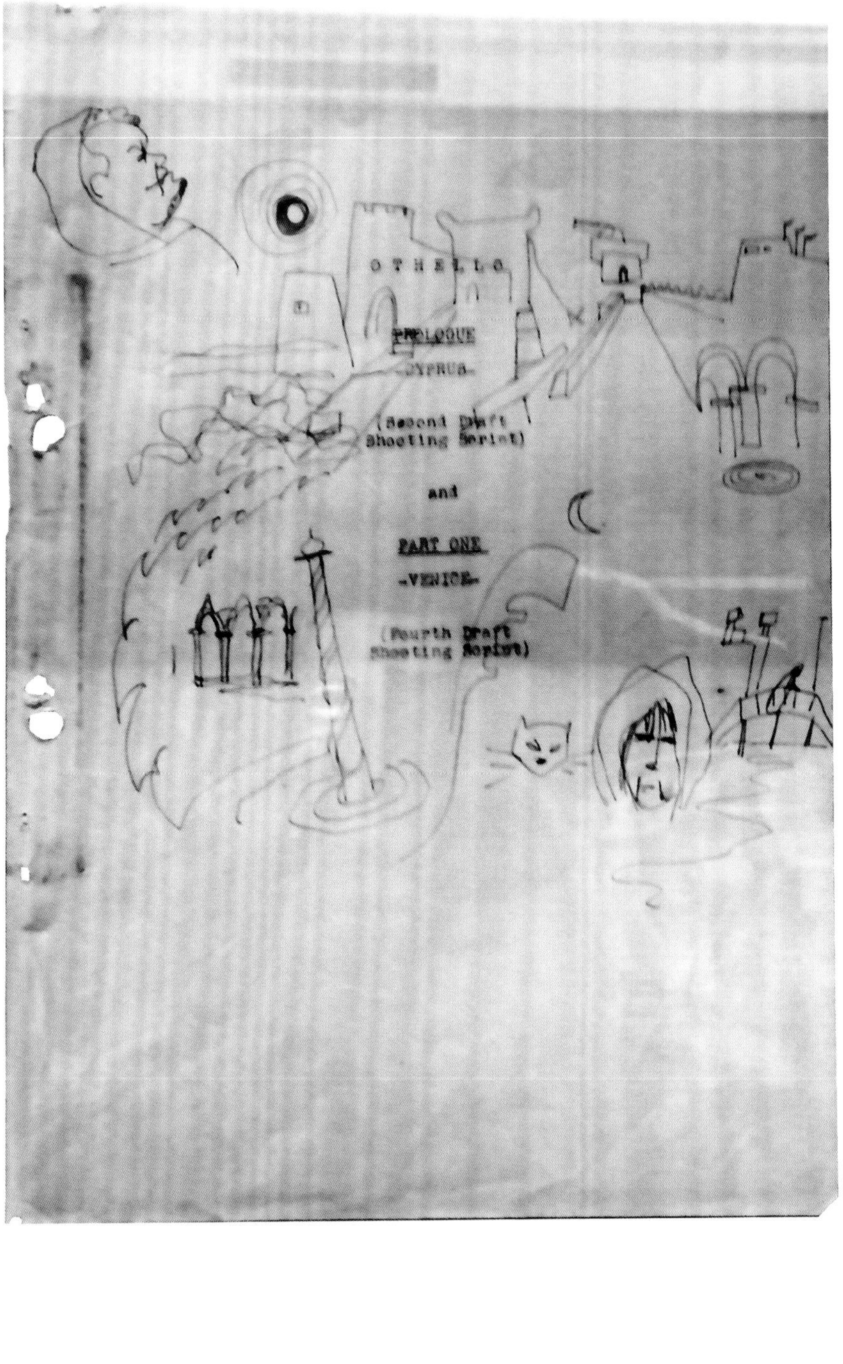

ABOVE: Sketches on title page of script; photo supplied for publication

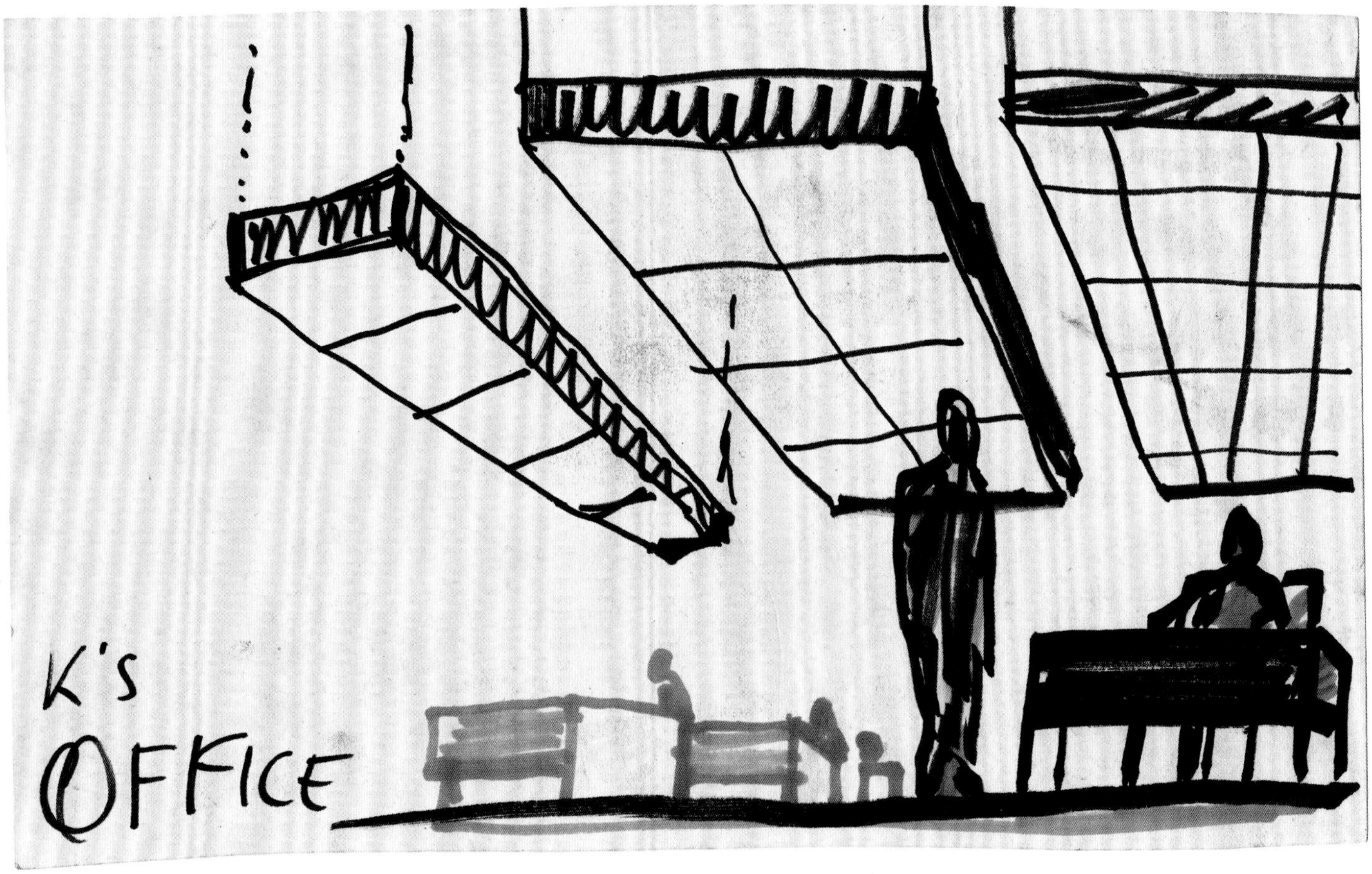

THE TRIAL

In 1960, producer siblings Alexander and Michael Salkind offered to finance a film for Welles and gave him a list of projects to choose from. He settled on an adaptation of Franz Kafka's novel *The Trial*. The Salkinds then set about the arduous task of raising funds.

Principal photography began in Yugoslavia in 1962 and continued until, inevitably, the money ran out. The Salkinds voted to suspend operations. Welles had other ideas. He moved the entire production to Paris and carried on filming in the abandoned shell of the Gare d'Orsay.

If this was a case of any port – or railway station – in a storm, it was a serendipitous one. The cavernous interiors of the old building, with its vaulted ceilings and massive windows, suited the tone of the film perfectly, dwarfing the actors and evoking the oppressive, totalitarian state of Kafka's imagining.

The film was released in December 1962 to mixed notices. Many critics were unhappy with Welles's casting of Anthony Perkins as Joseph K, the ill-fated everyman, trapped in an endless bureaucratic nightmare after he is accused of an unnamed crime. Most of them, to Welles's annoyance, felt he was insufficiently mousey. 'It's very clearly stated in the book,' he thundered, 'that K is a young executive on his way up.' It was, he said, Perkins' pugnacious approach to the character that landed him the role.

Although it still has the power to polarize opinion, like much of Welles's later work, *The Trail* has received serious critical re-appraisal and is now widely considered a minor masterpiece.

ABOVE: Set design; original scanned for publication

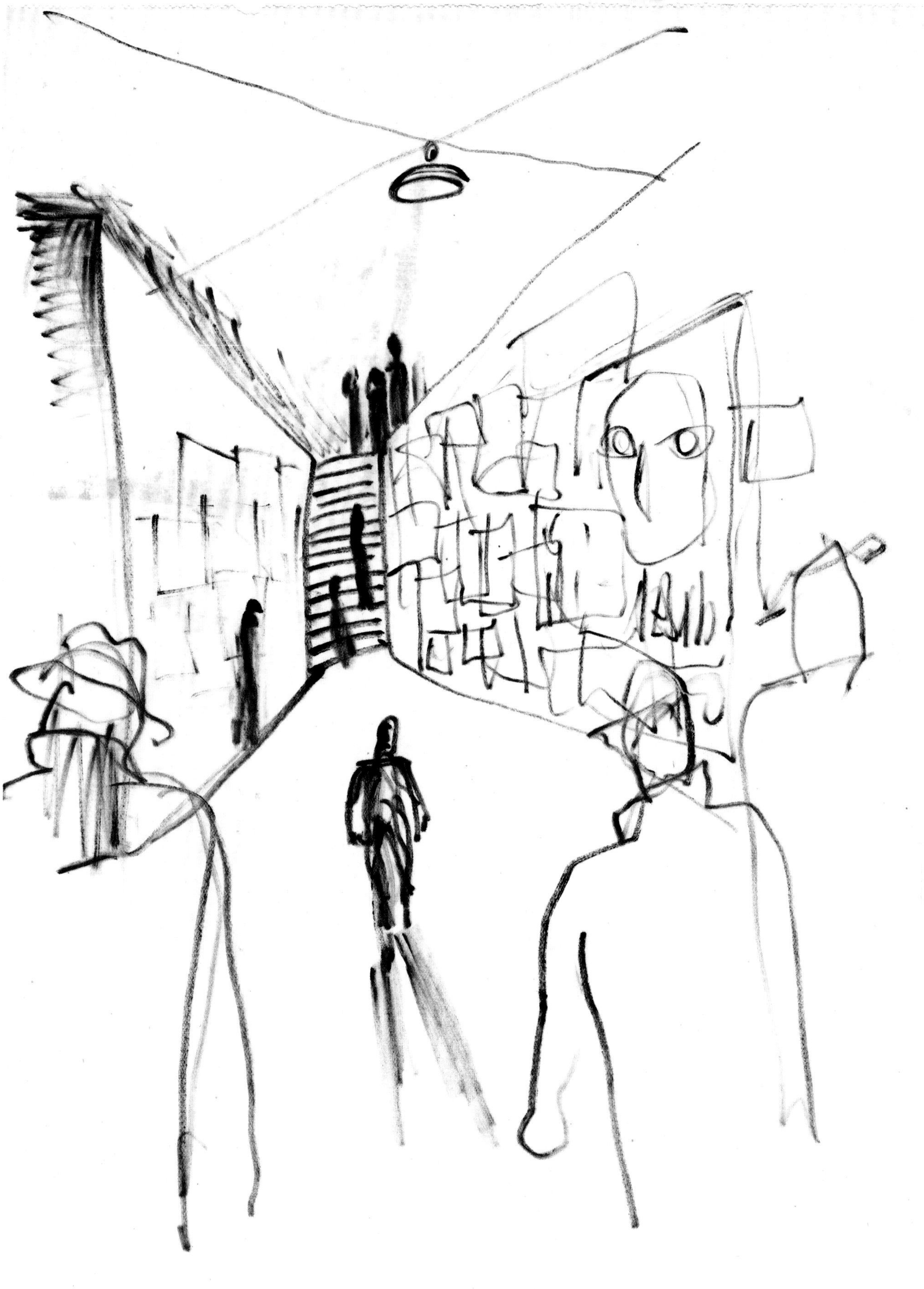

ABOVE: Set design; original scanned for publication

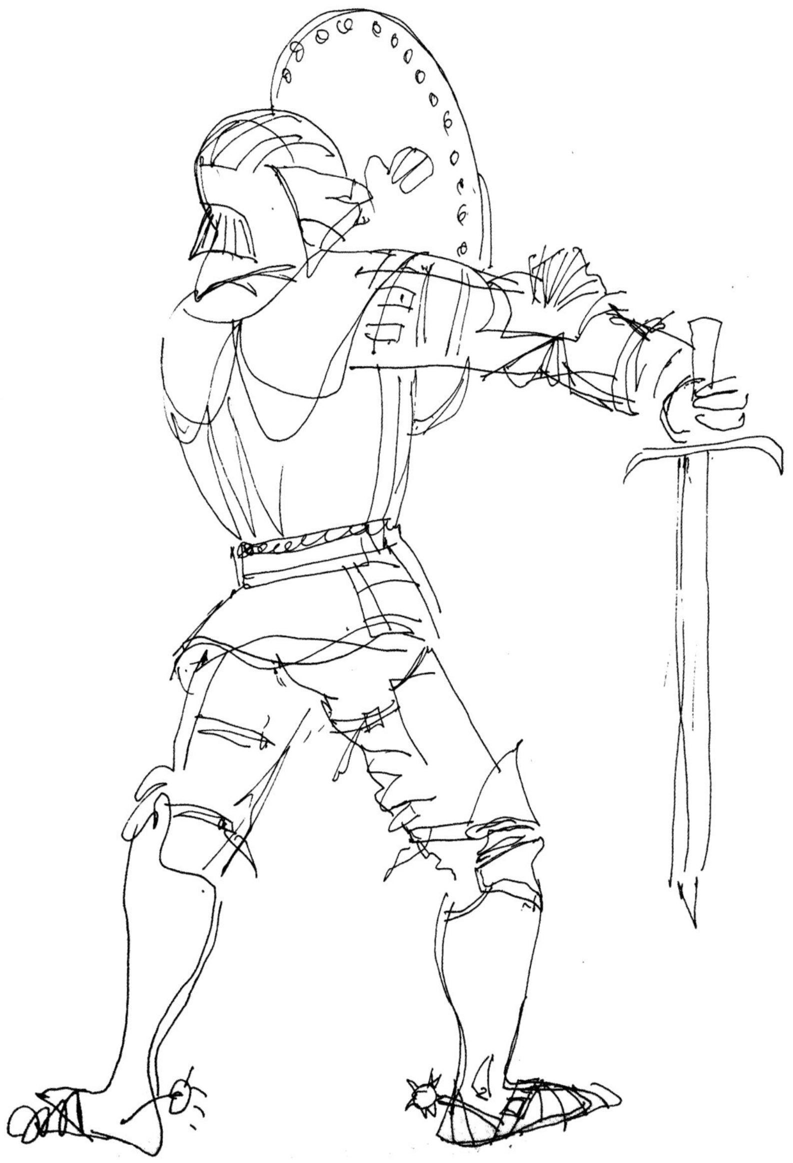

CHIMES AT MIDNIGHT

If Welles's costume designs for *Chimes at Midnight* are not as generously detailed as those for *Faustus*, they are marvelous nevertheless. Mostly pen-and-ink sketches of minor characters and knights in armor, they are acutely expressive. One, captioned 'a recruit for the ragged army' is of a peasant boy whose pinched little face gazes out from the page in comic consternation; it's as if he's been caught by the flash of a modern camera.

The knights, several of them on horseback, in the thick of battle, are particularly thrilling. Brandishing lances and clubs, their features hidden behind metal visors, they appear more menacing than noble – which was precisely the intention. Despite the film's cakes-and-ale whimsy, Welles is careful to remind us how brutal and bloody the age of chivalry was, and he does so most forcefully in the brilliantly shot and edited Battle of Shrewsbury sequence. It's here that romantic notions of Arthurian gallantry perish in the mud and the chaos and the carnage.

A Valentine of sorts to the myth of Merrie England, *Chimes at Midnight* was a monumental amalgamation of no less than five Shakespeare plays (*Henry IV Parts 1* and *2*, *Henry V*, *Richard II* and *The Merry Wives of Windsor*) that Welles had staged in its theatrical guise of *Five Kings* on Broadway in 1939 and at Dublin's Gate Theatre in 1960. Neither production was a success. It was shot between September 1964 and April 1965 on an array of locations in Spain, many of them chosen on the spur of the moment. The budget was a paltry $800,000, and Welles had to resort to unprecedented levels of skullduggery to get that.

In 1964, on the hunt for financing, he had flushed out Spanish film producer Emiliano Piedra, who was keen to work with him but unwilling to sink his money into a Shakespearean mash-up that had already failed in the theater. Instead, he proposed a version of *Treasure Island*, with Welles as Long John Silver. Welles agreed – on the proviso that he could make *Chimes at Midnight* at the same time. His argument was that most of the sets would be interchangeable, never mind that *Treasure Island* was set in the mid-eighteenth century and *Chimes* in 1403. That was, ultimately, by-the-by, since Welles had no intention of making *Treasure*

ABOVE: Costume design; scan supplied for publication

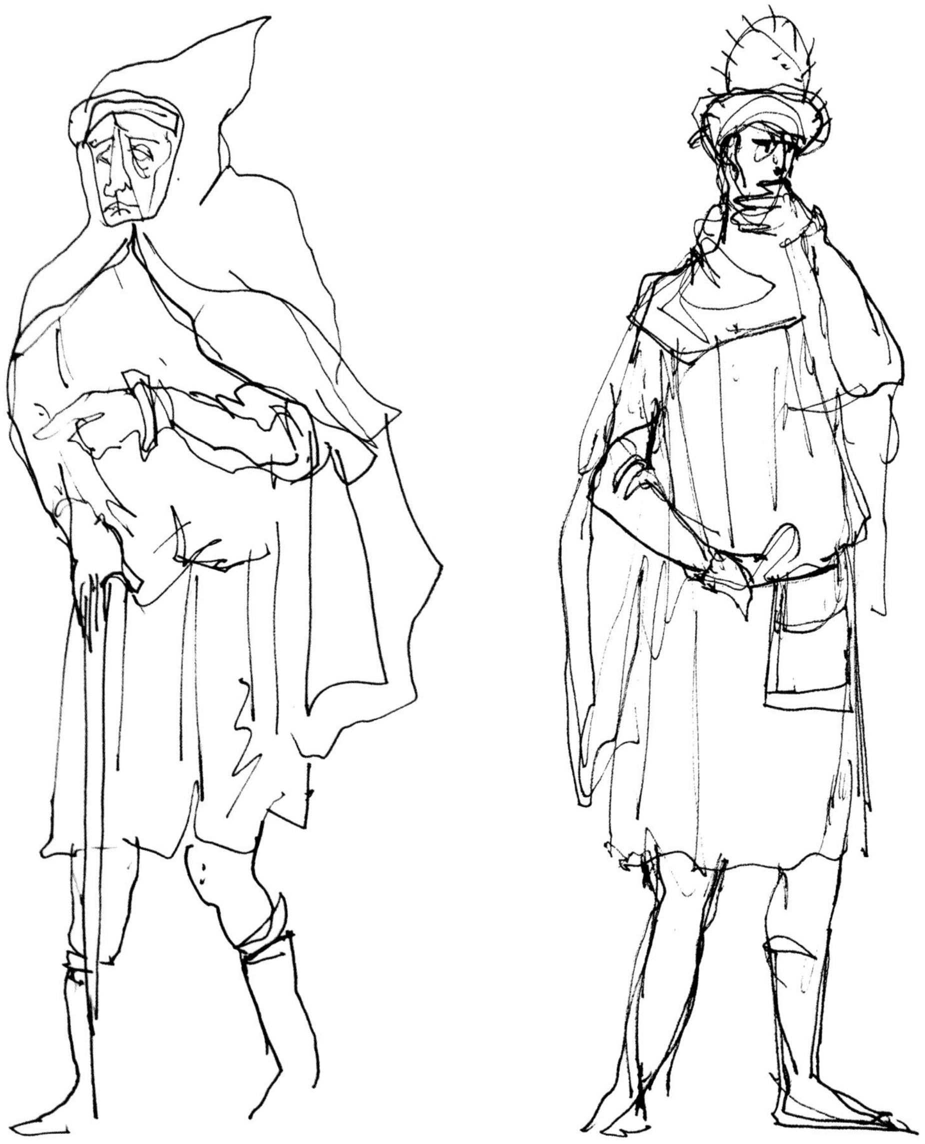

Island in the first place. Naturally, he kept that under his hat. When John Gielgud arrived to play King Henry IV, Piedra fully believed he was there to play Squire Trelawney as well. Whether Gielgud believed the same is highly doubtful.

That Welles got away with the ruse is a miracle, but get away with it he did. And, by all accounts, *Chimes* was a highly convivial shoot for all its long hours and poverty-stricken privations. The tireless ringmaster as ever, Welles (cast as Falstaff – who else?) made sure the company was well taken care of, even though facilities were scarce.

'We were in Avila and it was absolutely *freezing*,' recalls Beatrice Welles, who played Falstaff's page. 'There was no heat, nowhere to change, no nothing. But everyone, even Sir John, was happy to be there. I remember shooting a scene in the Blue Boar Tavern and I was sitting next to Margaret Rutherford [cast as Mistress Quickly]. She was so wonderful, she used to help me with my lines, and she was just *shaking* with cold. My father asked Keith [Pyott, veteran British character actor] to ask her if she wanted a little brandy. She said, "Oh no. I'm not cold. Orson is my sunshine." Isn't that a wonderful thing to say. And she meant it.'

The second-hand costumes, a threadbare challenge to Welles's magnificent designs, were a particular source of amusement. Gielgud complained drolly about his smelly tights: 'Shall I catch something from them?' he asked. 'I've never had Spanish Fly, I don't want Spanish Crabs.' Keith Baxter, playing Prince Hal, scrounged his outfit from a pile of Samuel Bronston Company cast-offs. He appears on screen resplendent in a pair of knitted chain mail leggings and a leather jerkin worn by Jayne Mansfield in *The Sheriff of Fractured Jaw*.

It mattered not at all. *Chimes at Midnight*, despite its shoestring budget, is a triumph, a rollicking, bittersweet evocation of medieval life and an ultimately tragic meditation on the theme of fathers and sons, a subject uncomfortably close to Welles's heart.

'If I wanted to get into Heaven on the basis of one movie,' Welles said in 1982, 'that's the one I would offer up.'

ABOVE: Costume designs; scans supplied for publication

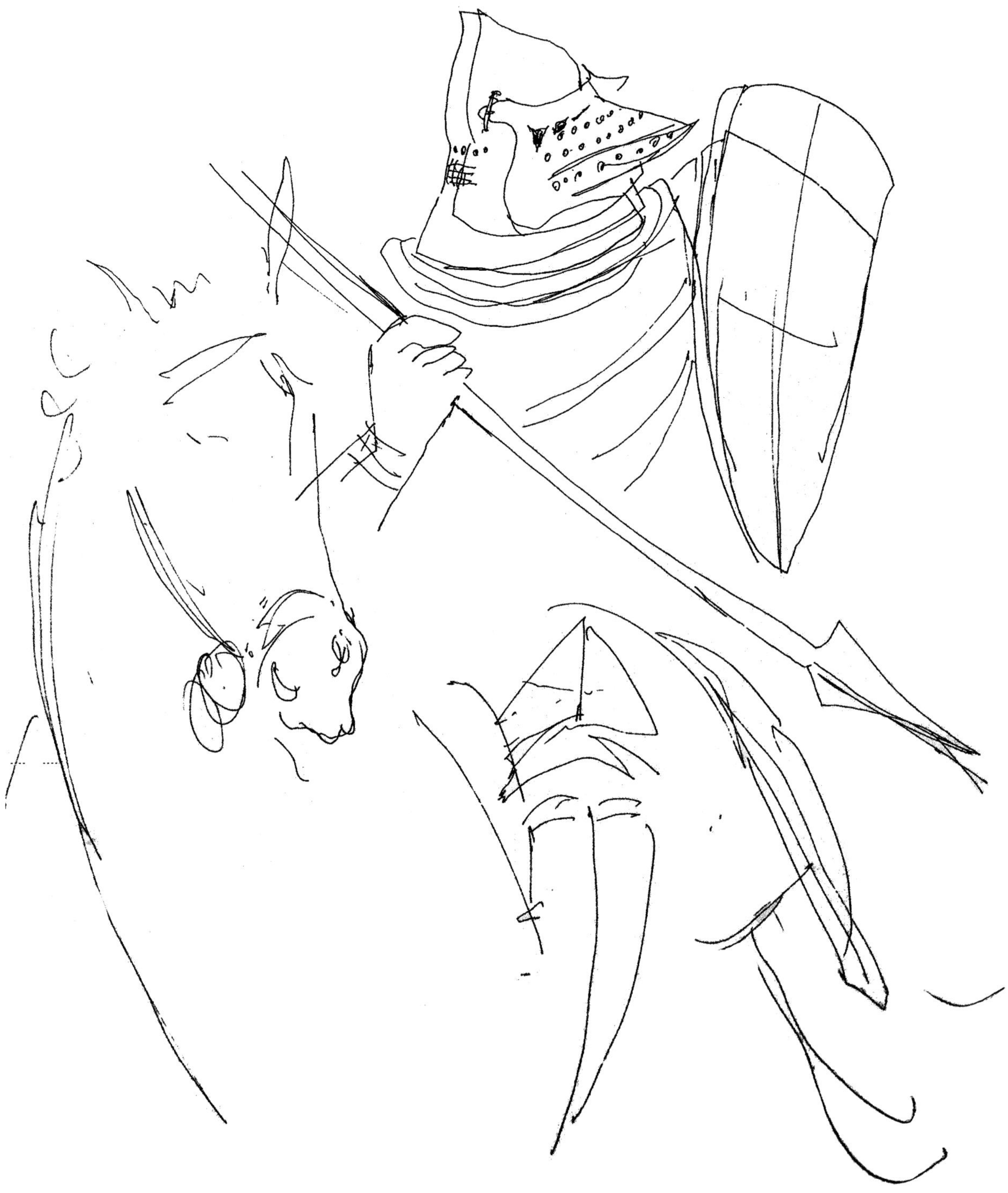

ABOVE: Costume design; scan supplied for publication

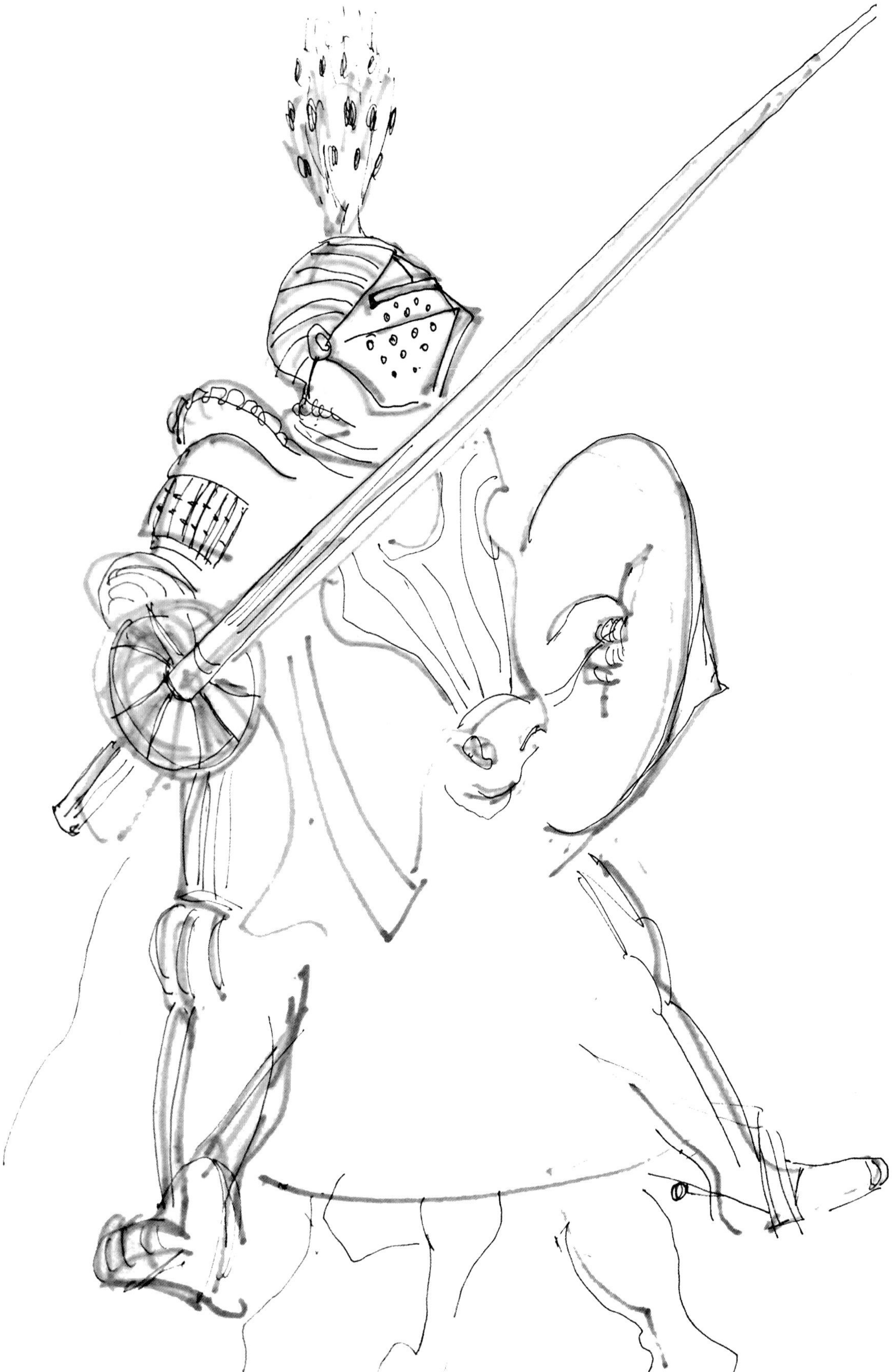

ABOVE: Costume design; scan supplied for publication

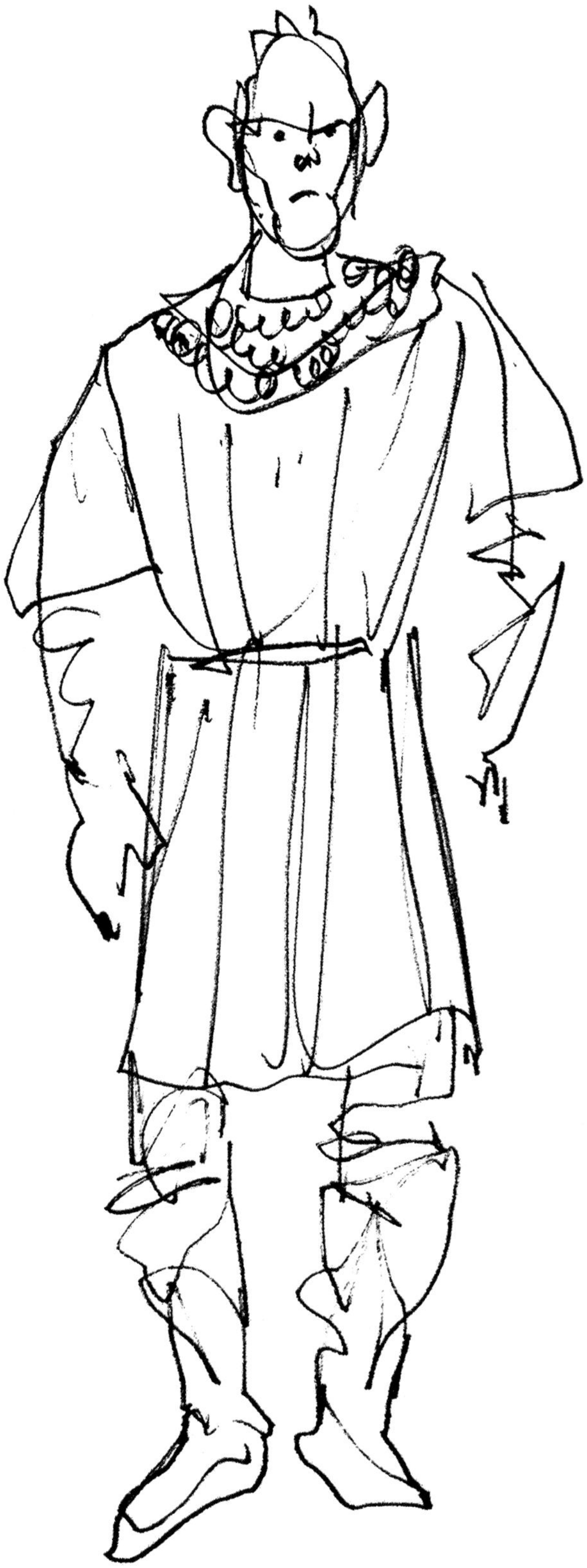

ABOVE: Costume design; scan supplied for publication

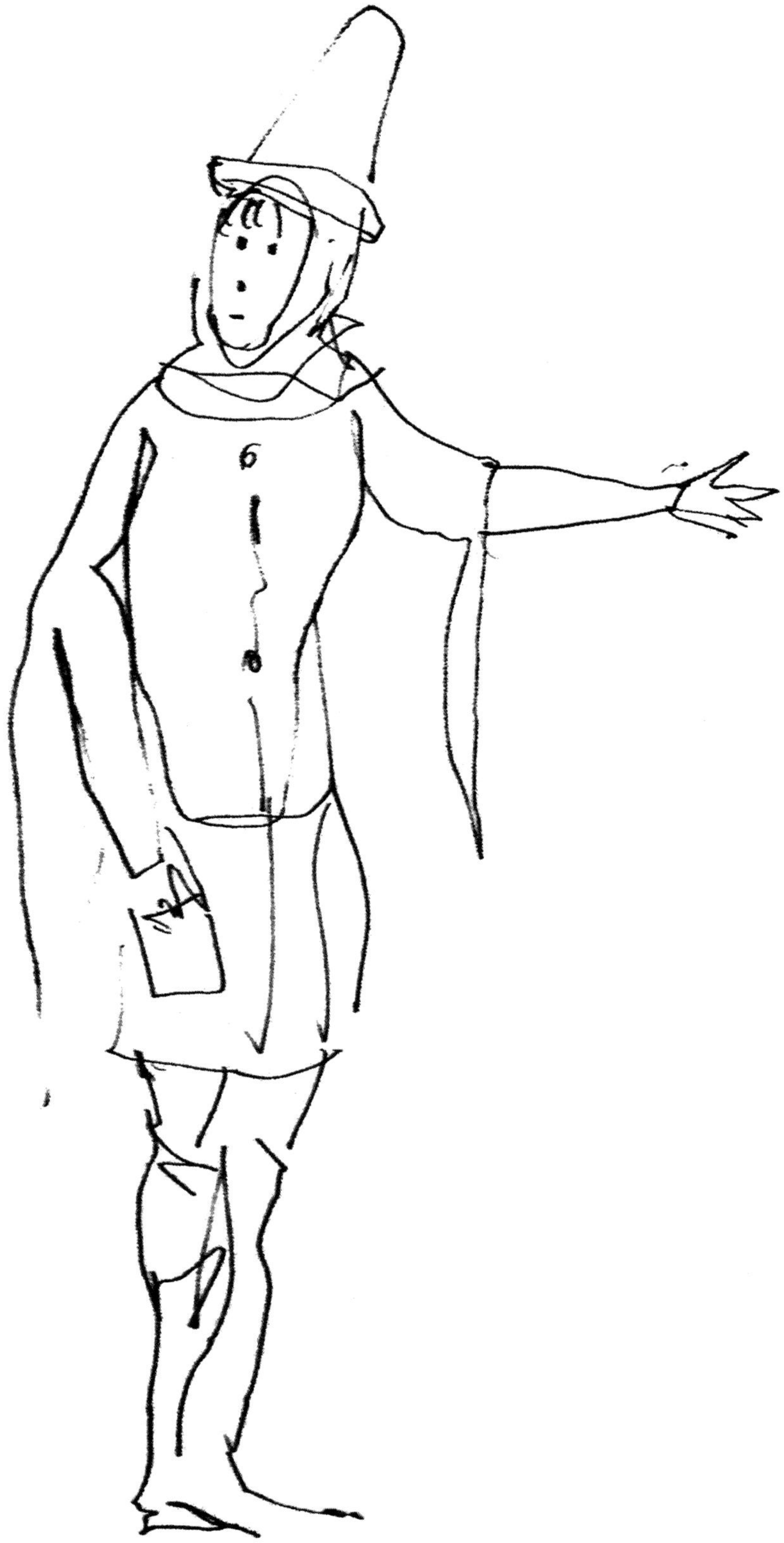

ABOVE: Costume design; scan supplied for publication

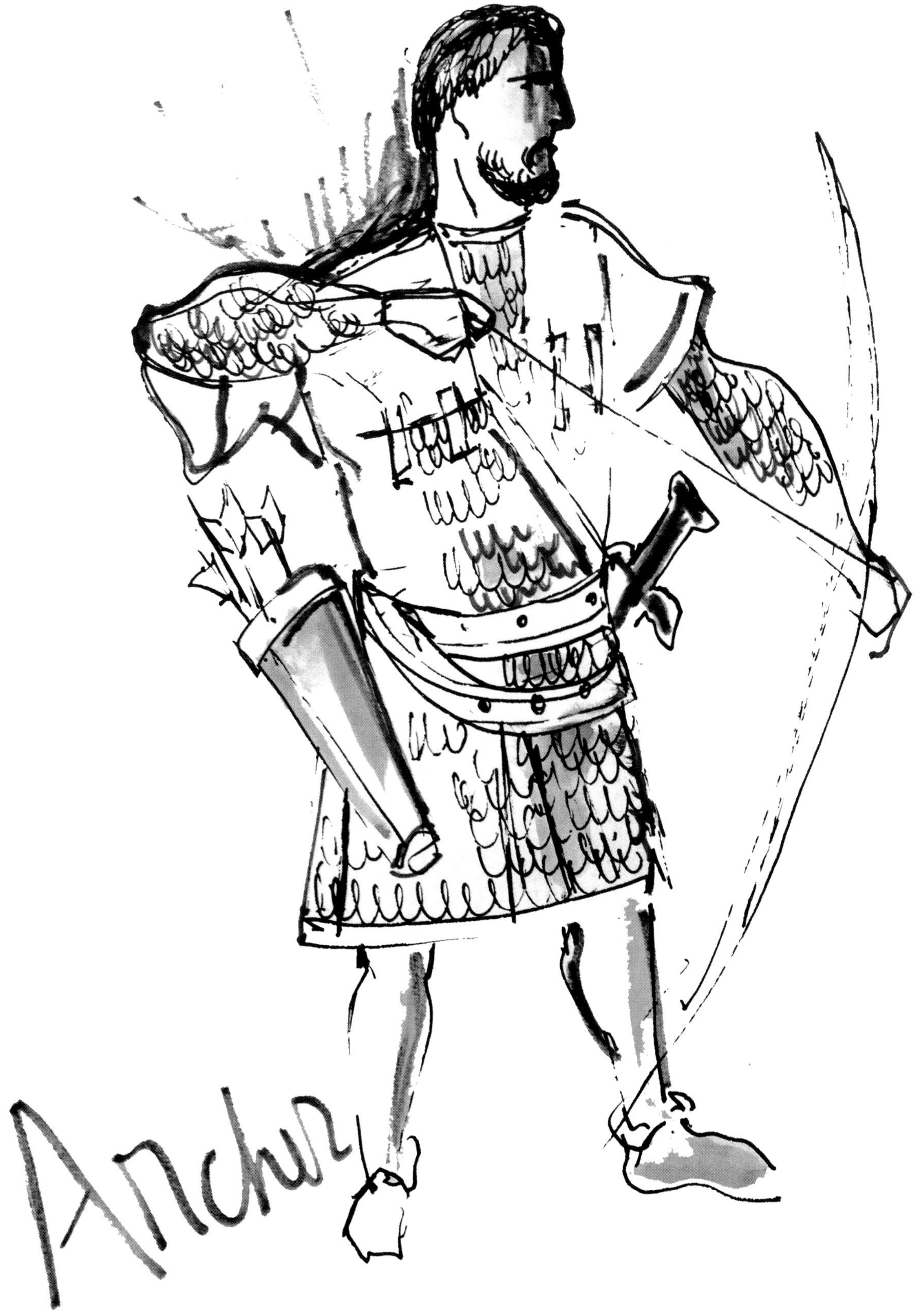

ABOVE: Costume design; scan supplied for publication

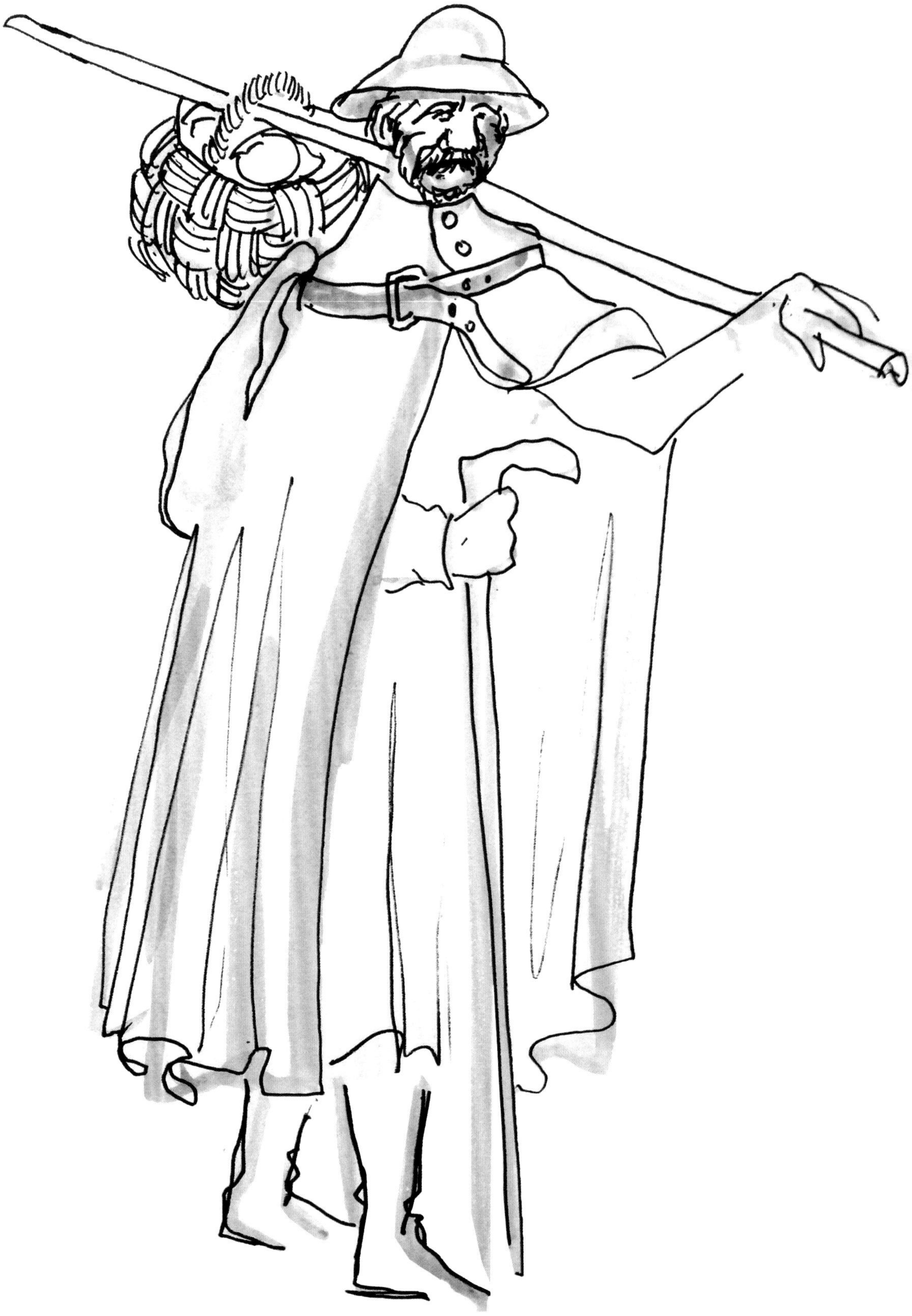

ABOVE: Costume design; scan supplied for publication

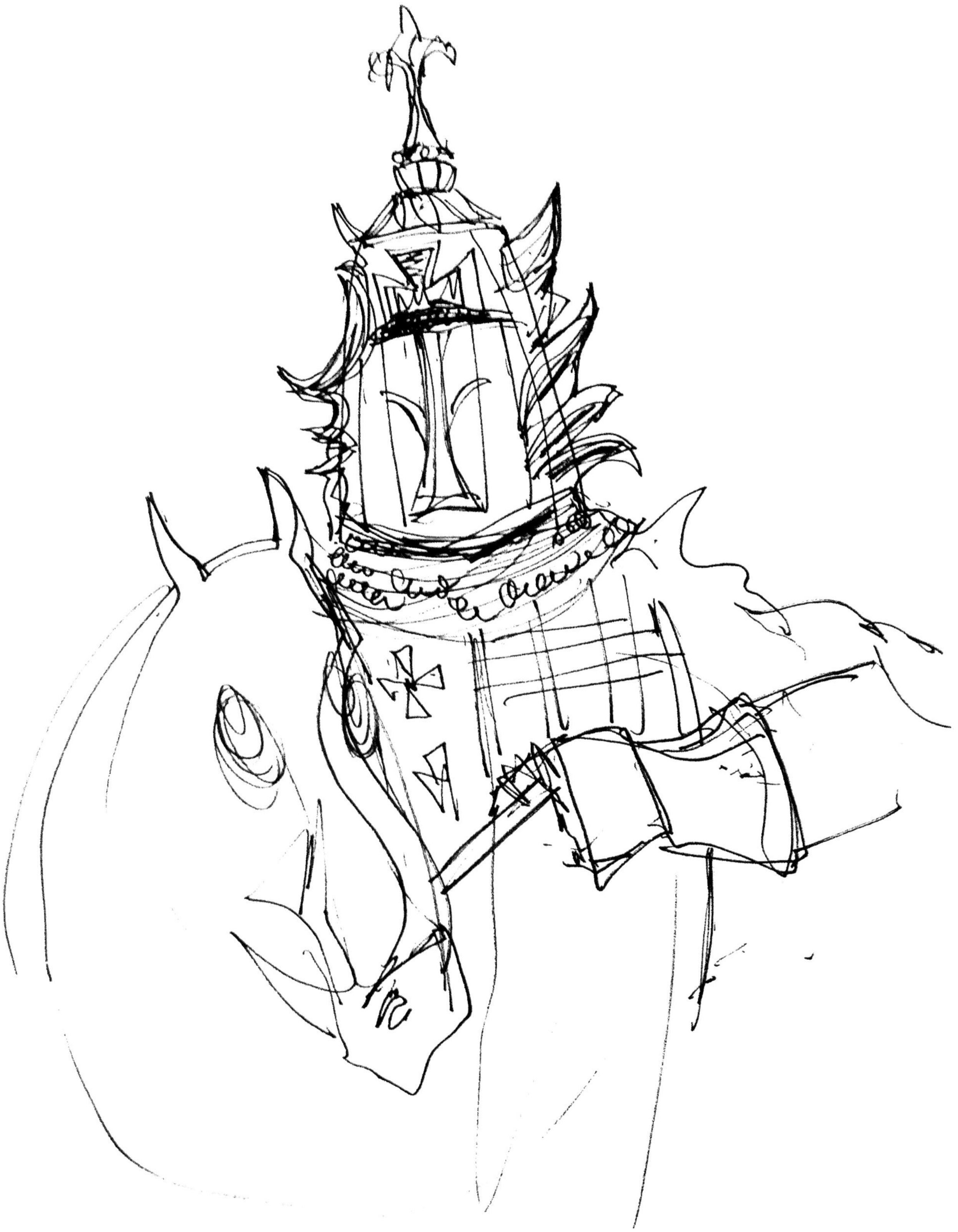

ABOVE: Costume design; scan supplied for publication

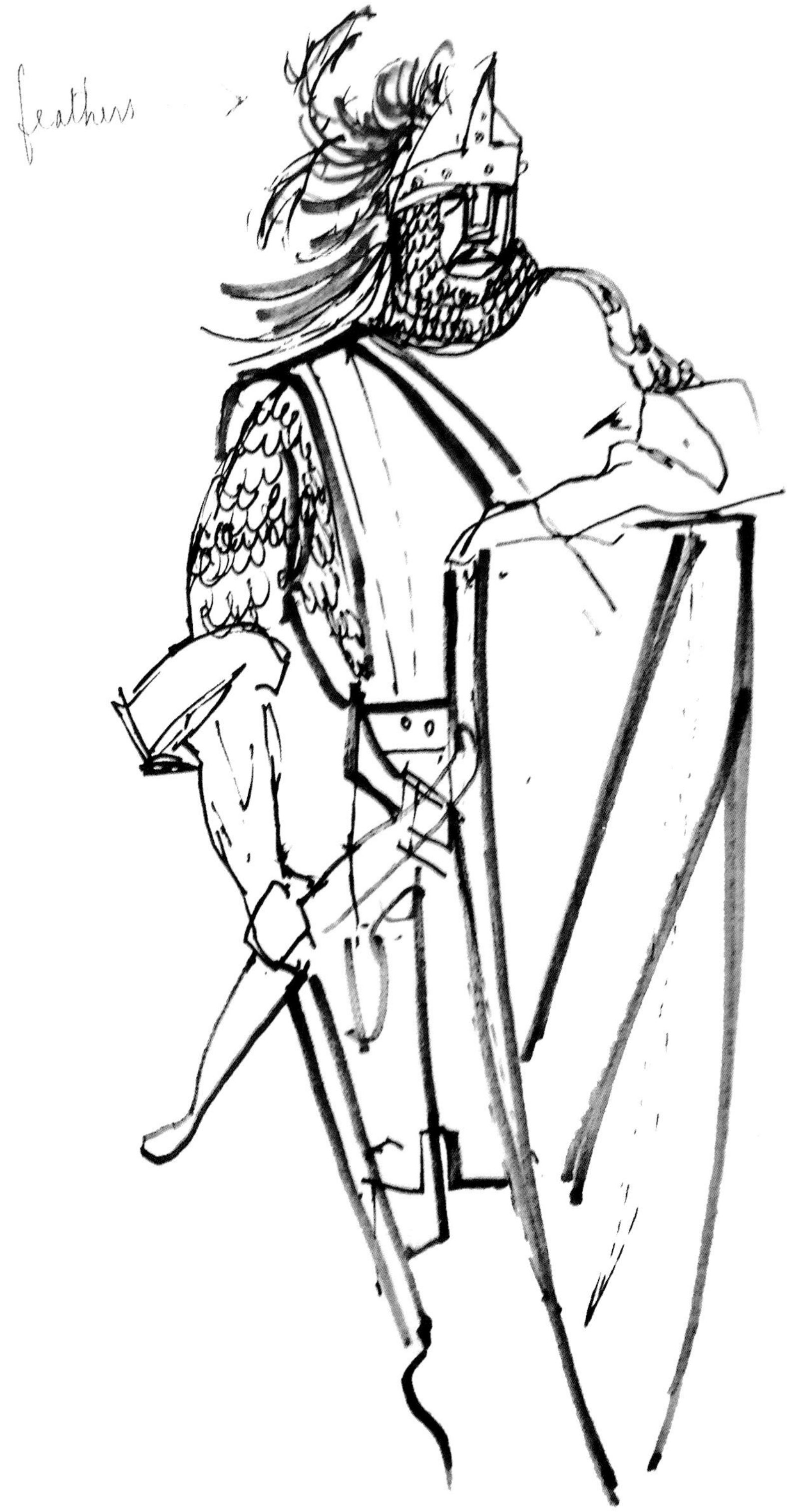

ABOVE: Costume design; scan supplied for publication

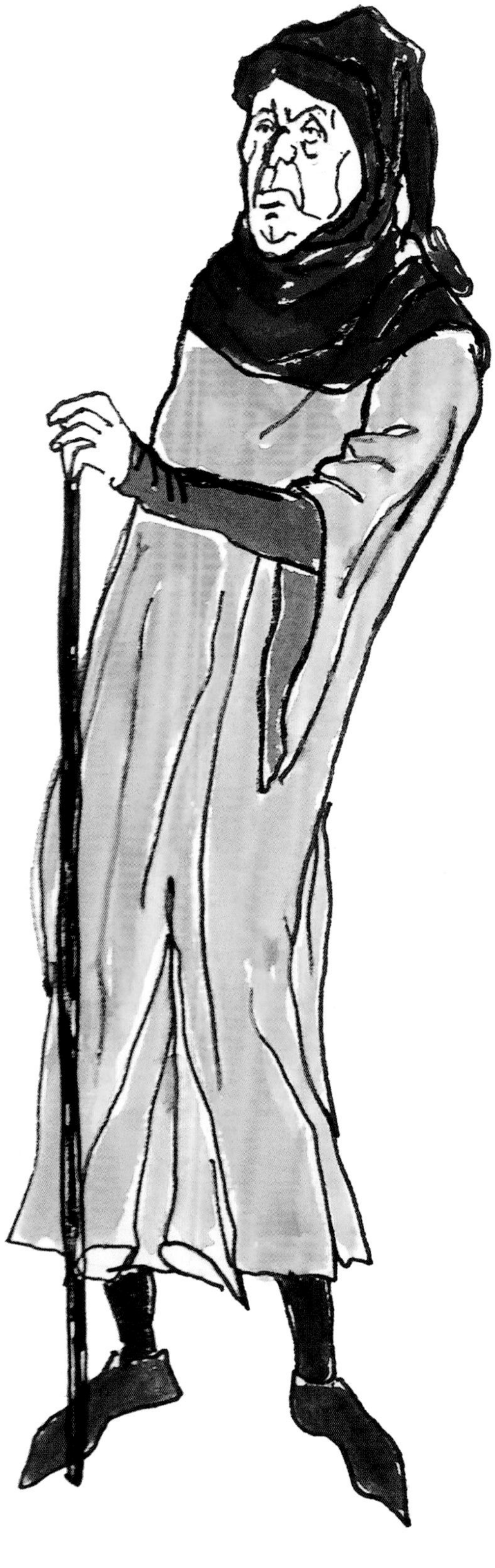

ABOVE: Costume design; scan supplied for publication

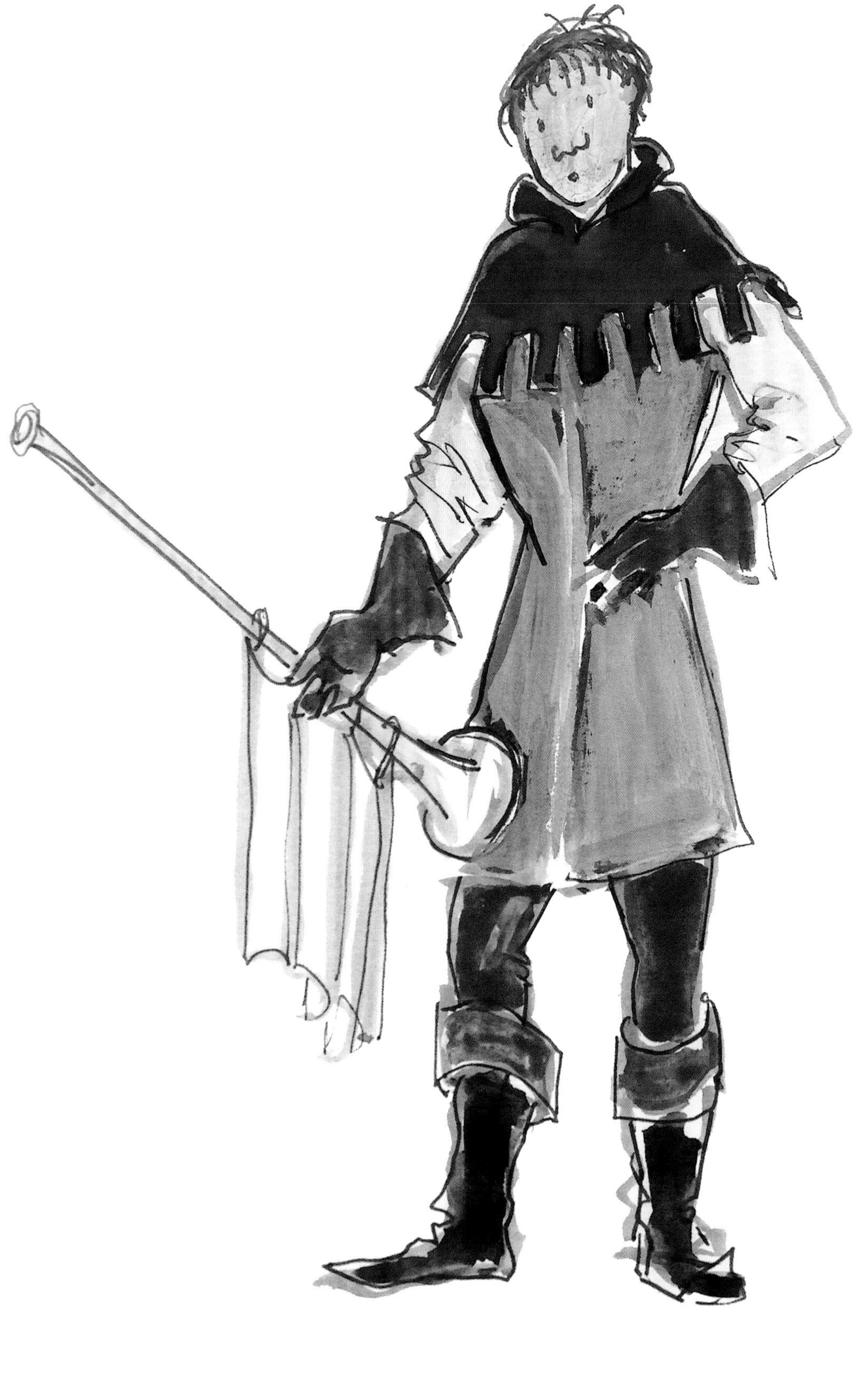

ABOVE: Costume design; scan supplied for publication

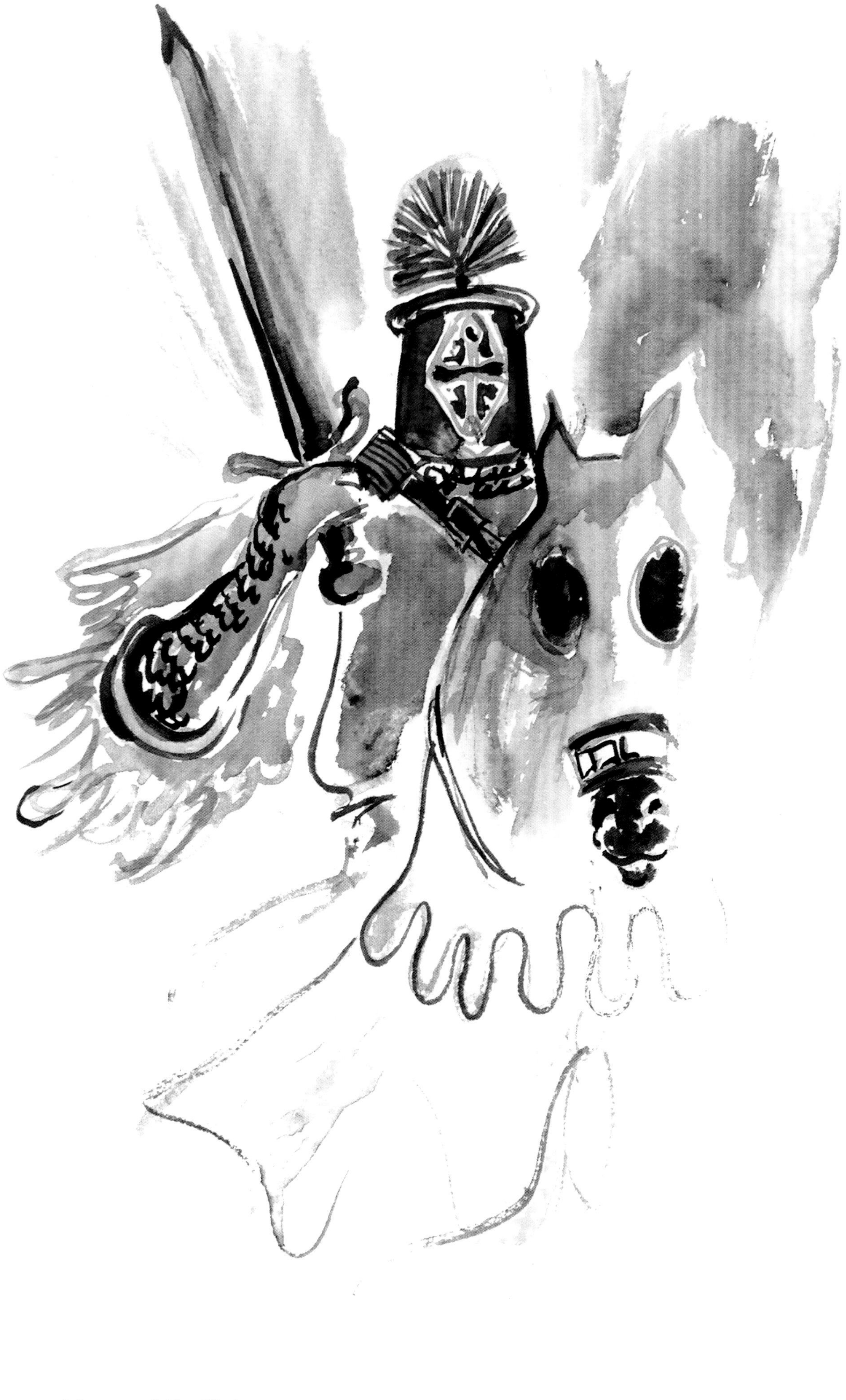

ABOVE: Costume design; scan supplied for publication

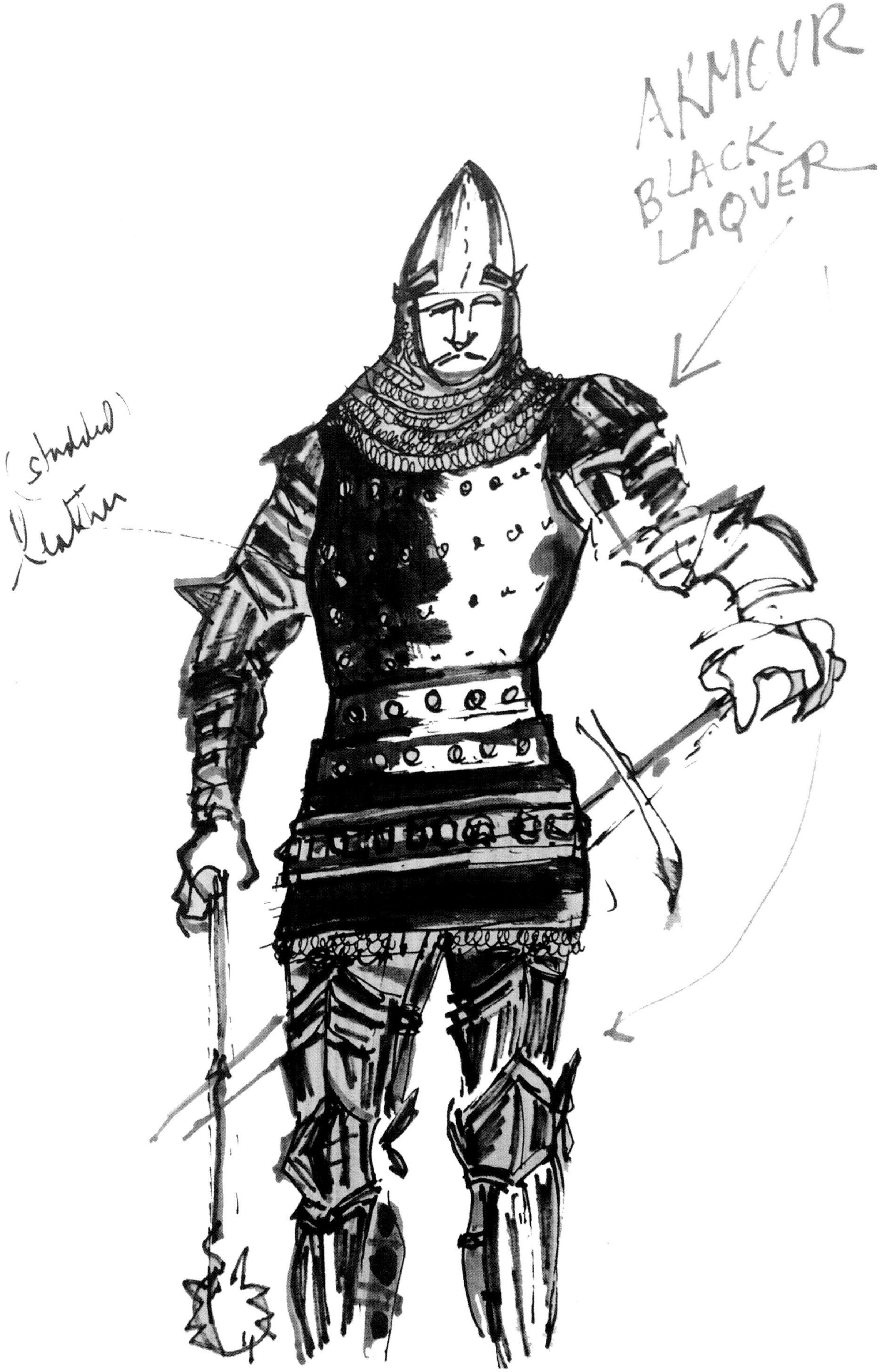

ABOVE: Costume design; scan supplied for publication

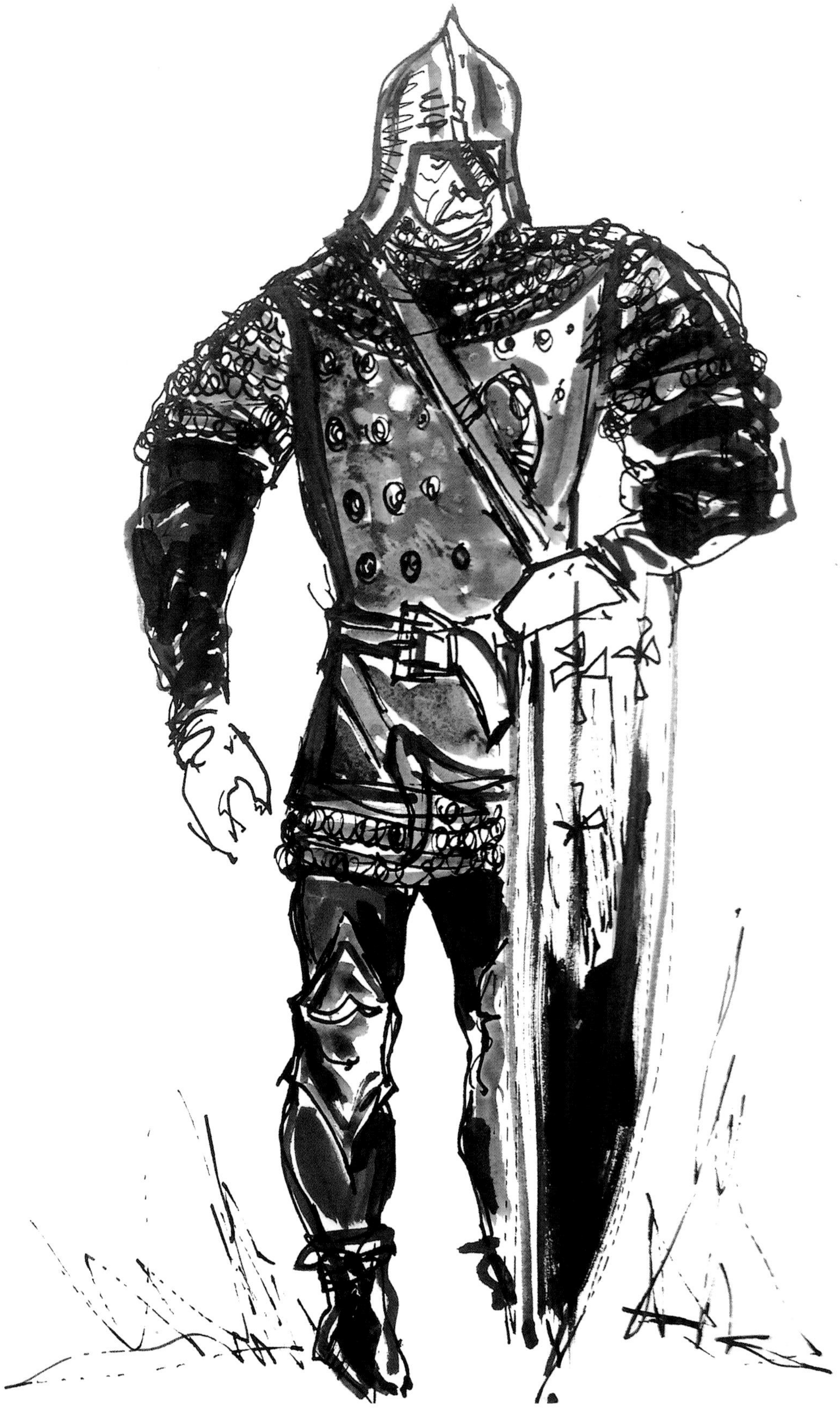

ABOVE: Costume design; scan supplied for publication

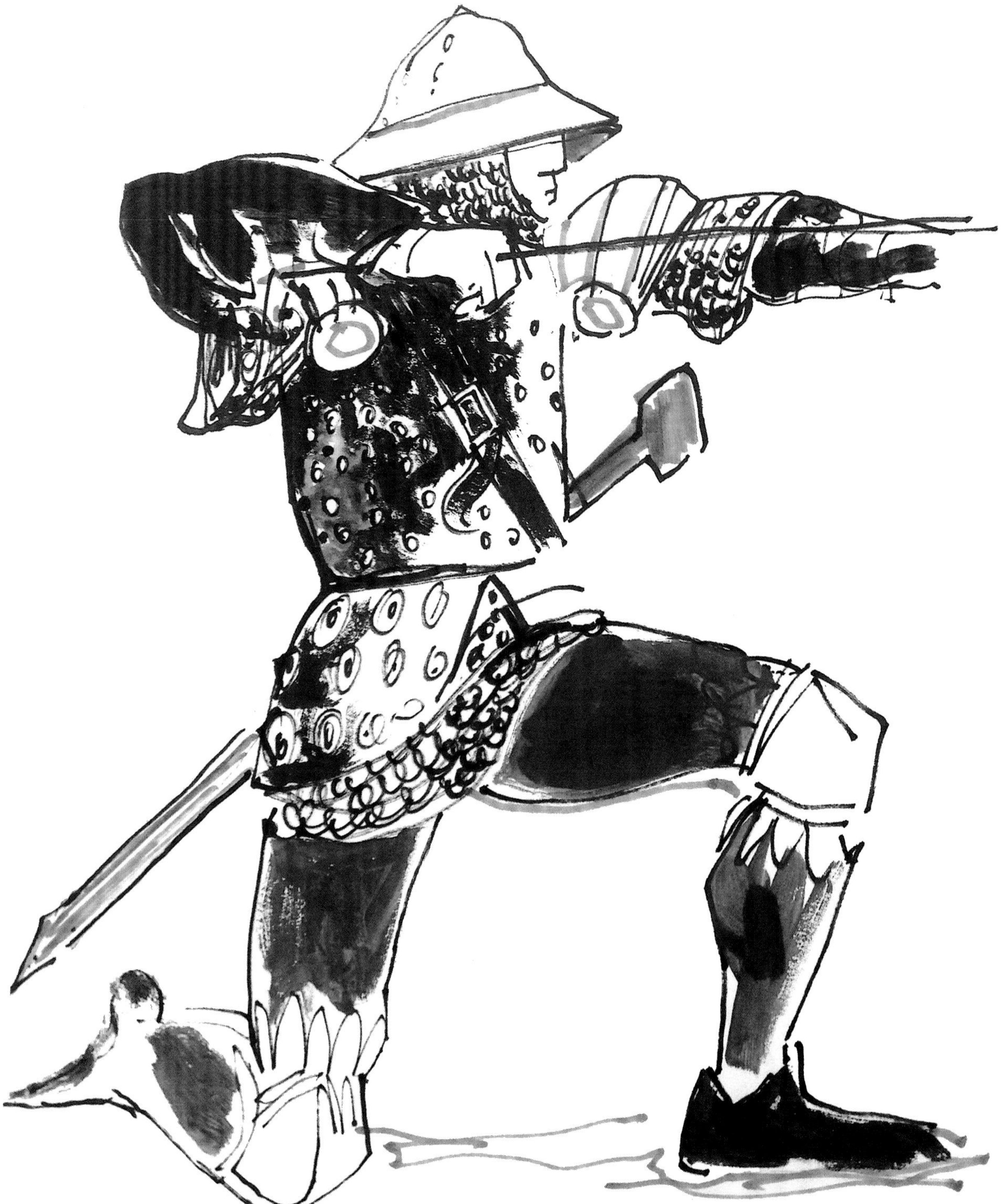

ABOVE: Costume design; scan supplied for publication

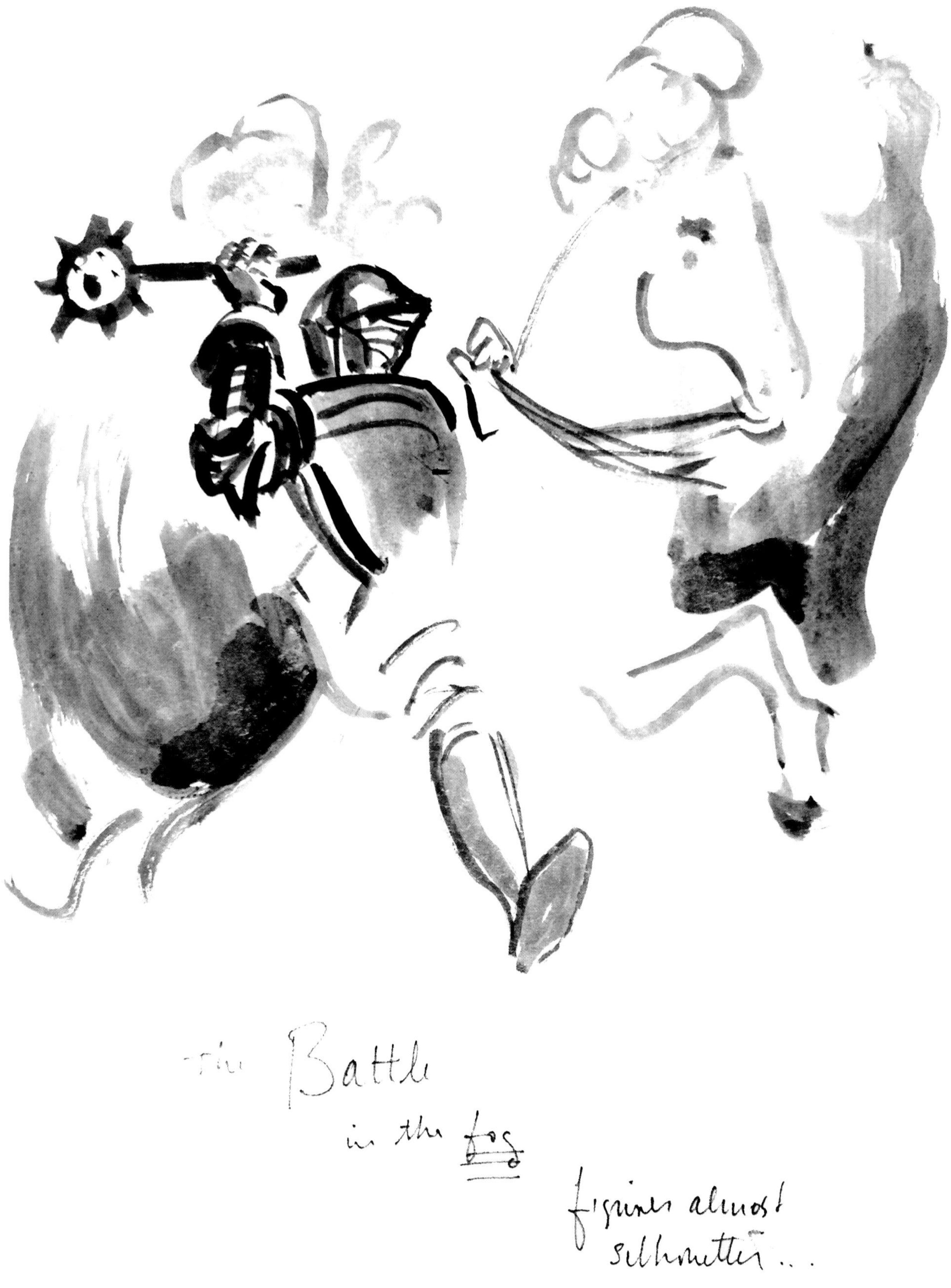

ABOVE: Costume design; scan supplied for publication

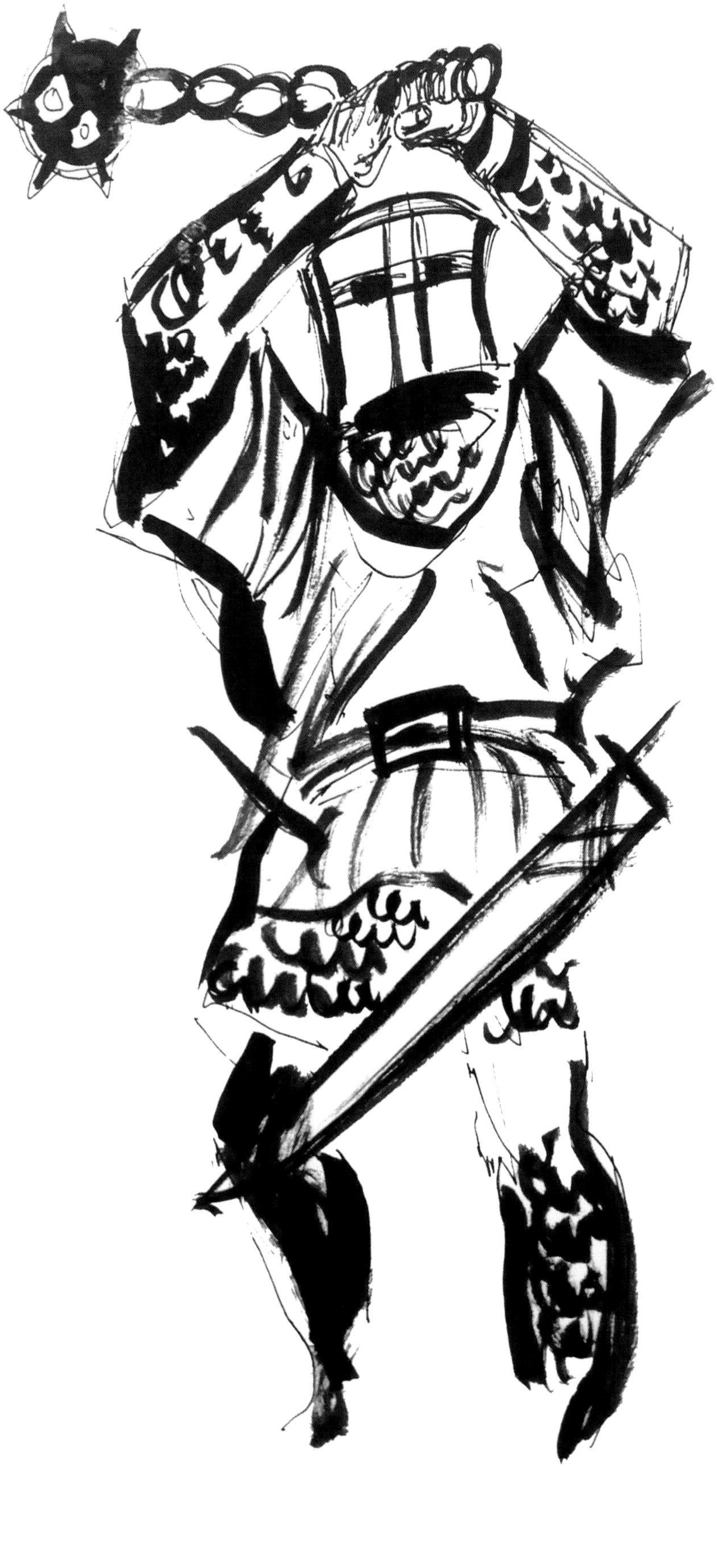

ABOVE: Costume design; scan supplied for publication

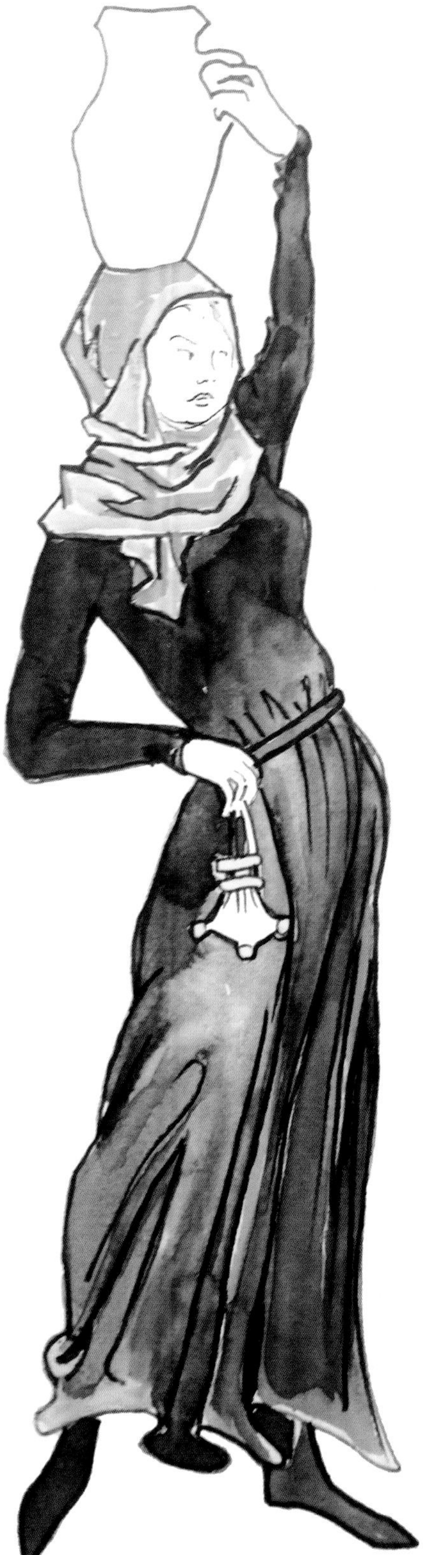

ABOVE: Costume design; scan supplied for publication

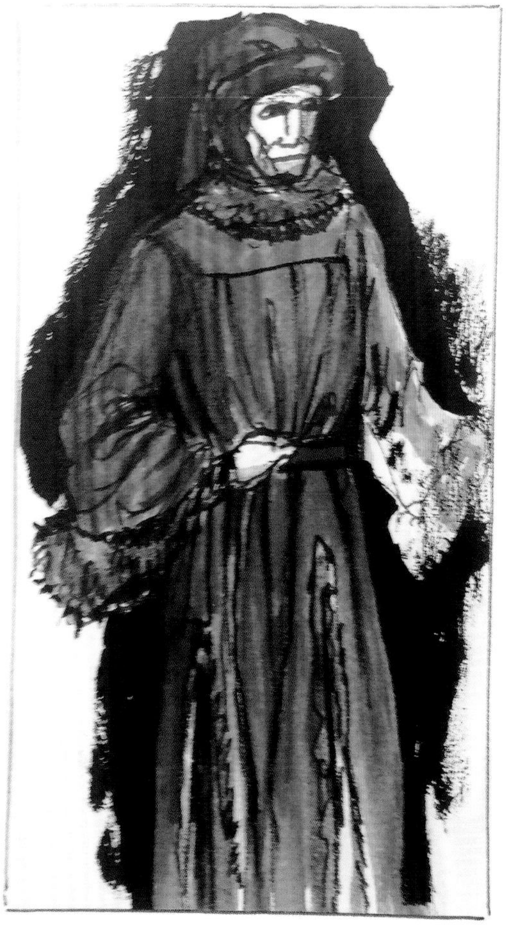

ABOVE: Costume design; scan supplied for publication

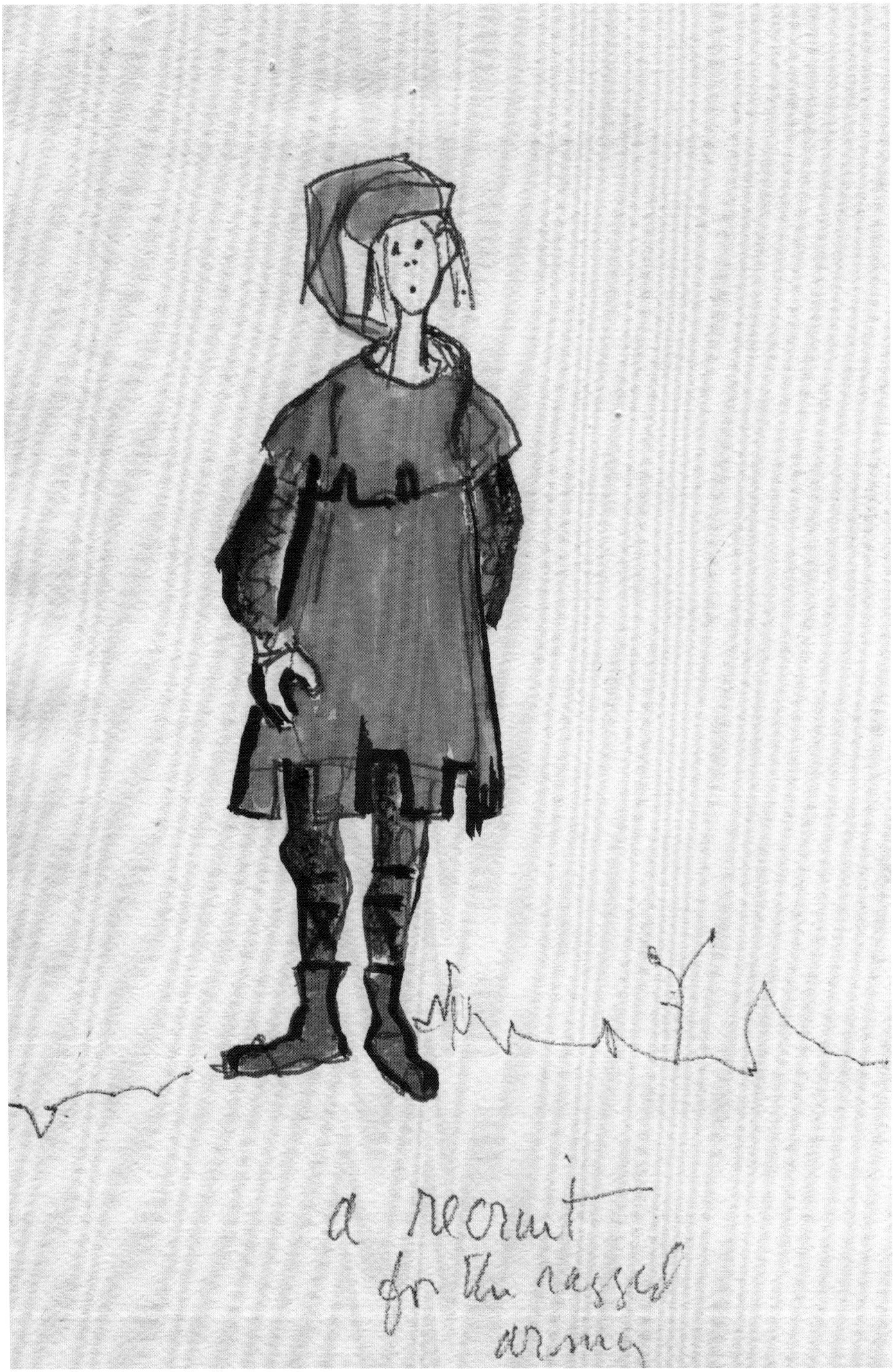

ABOVE: Costume design; scan supplied for publication

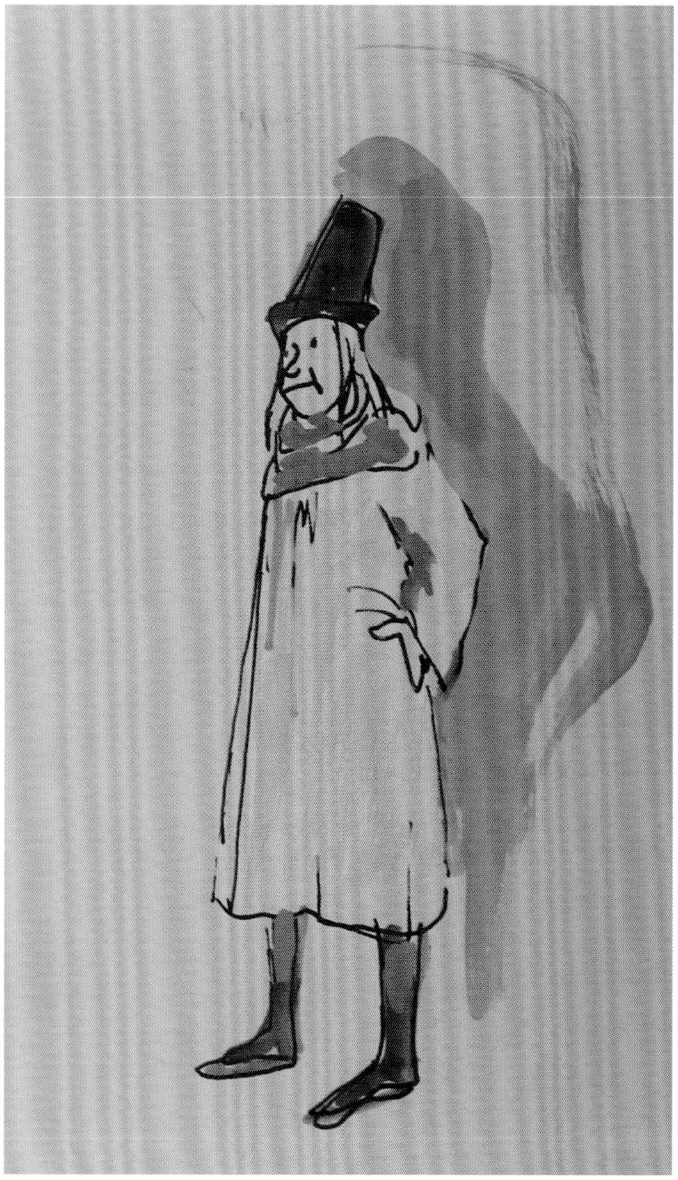

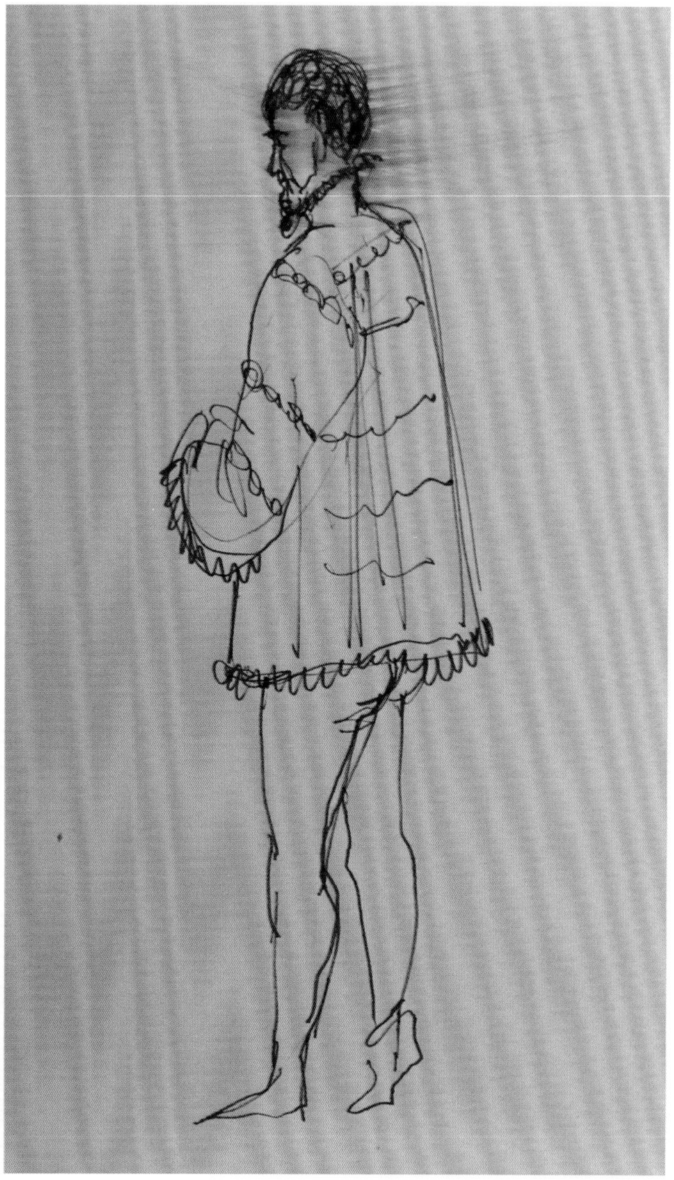

ABOVE: Costume designs; photos supplied for publication

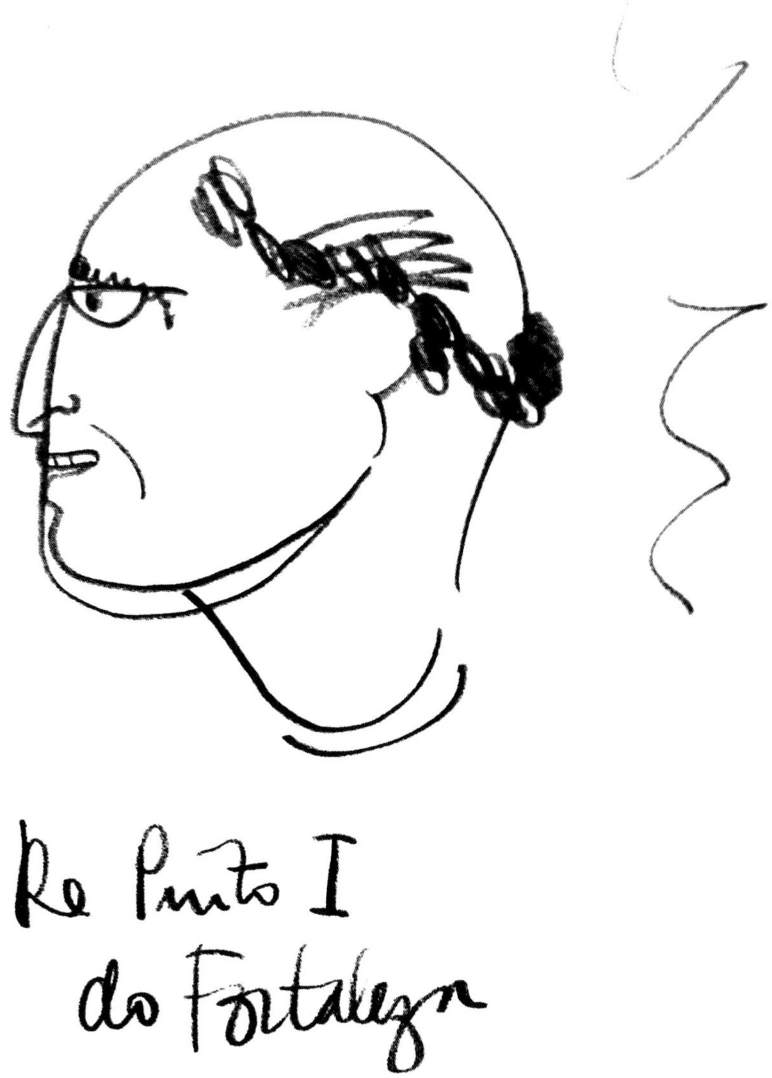

IT'S ALL TRUE

Welles's third film for RKO was a monumentally ambitious mix of documentary and docudrama shot in South America and spanning the history of samba, the true-life tale of a fighting bull saved from the corrida by a young boy's love, and the heroic struggle of Brazilian fishermen against exploitation. Just the sort of thing, in short, to endear him to the studio execs.

The film was co-produced by the Office of the Coordinator of Inter-American Affairs, meaning Welles was not just an employee of RKO, but a goodwill ambassador for the US government to boot. Even so, the film was never finished, which is not, in hindsight, a great shock. What is shocking is how brutally it was abandoned and the effects its termination had on Welles's life and career. Following a major shake-up at RKO he lost control of *The Magnificent Ambersons*, which was edited in his absence, *It's All True* was suspended, Mercury Productions was expelled from the lot and his contract was cancelled. Welles was, effectively, banished from Hollywood.

ABOVE: Sketch for Richard Wilson; photo supplied for publication

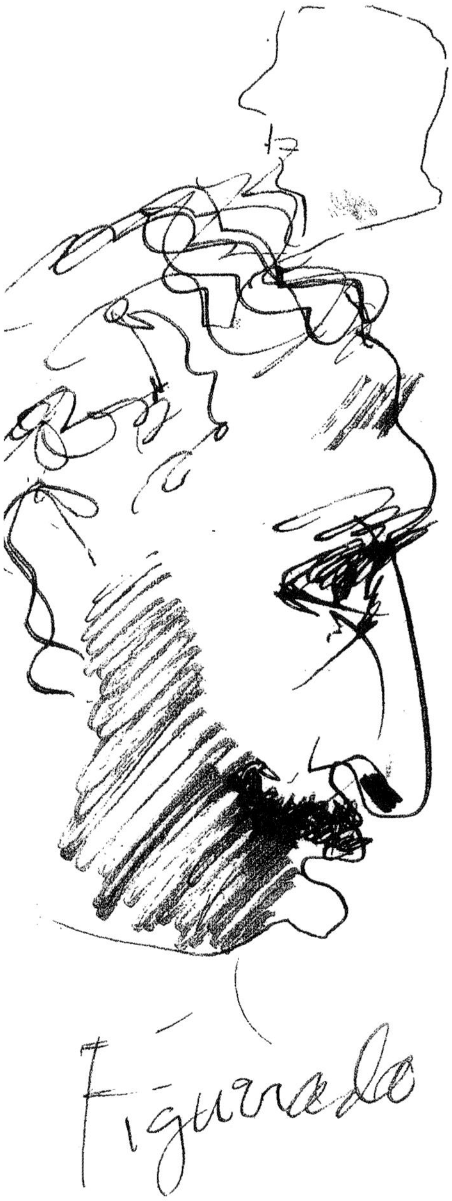

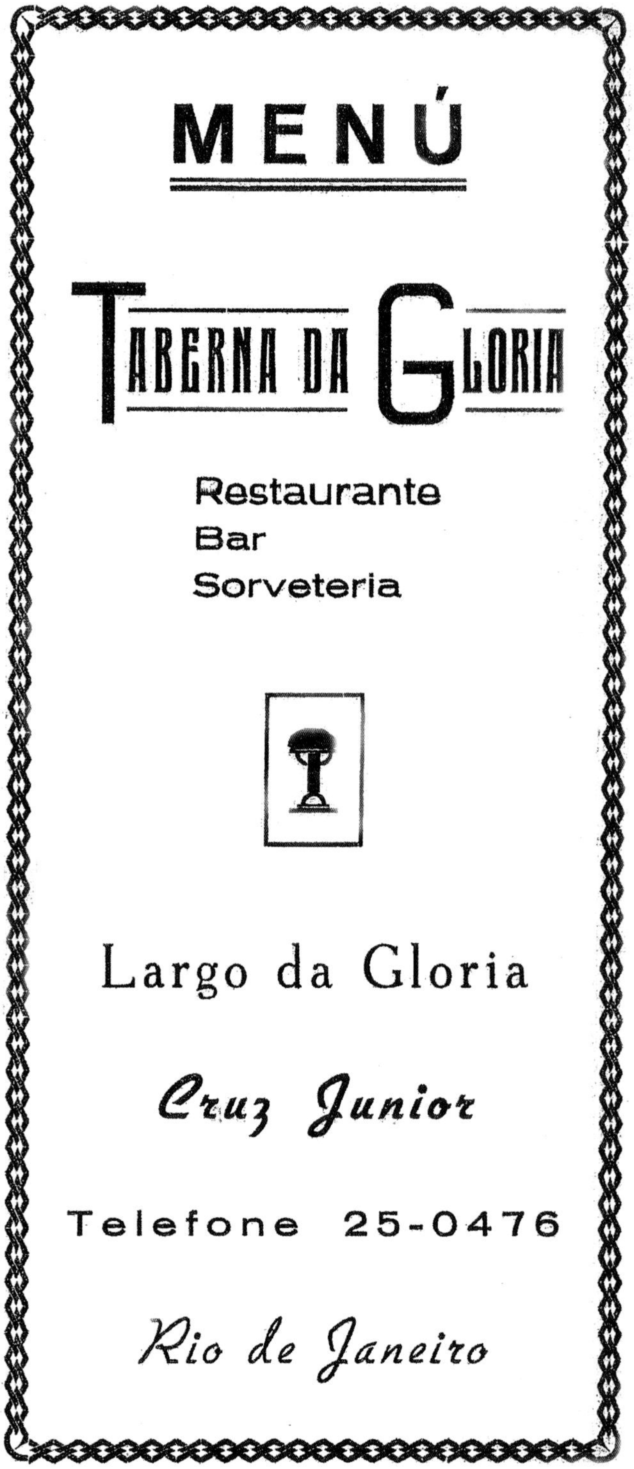

ABOVE: Sketch on restaurant menu; scan supplied for publication

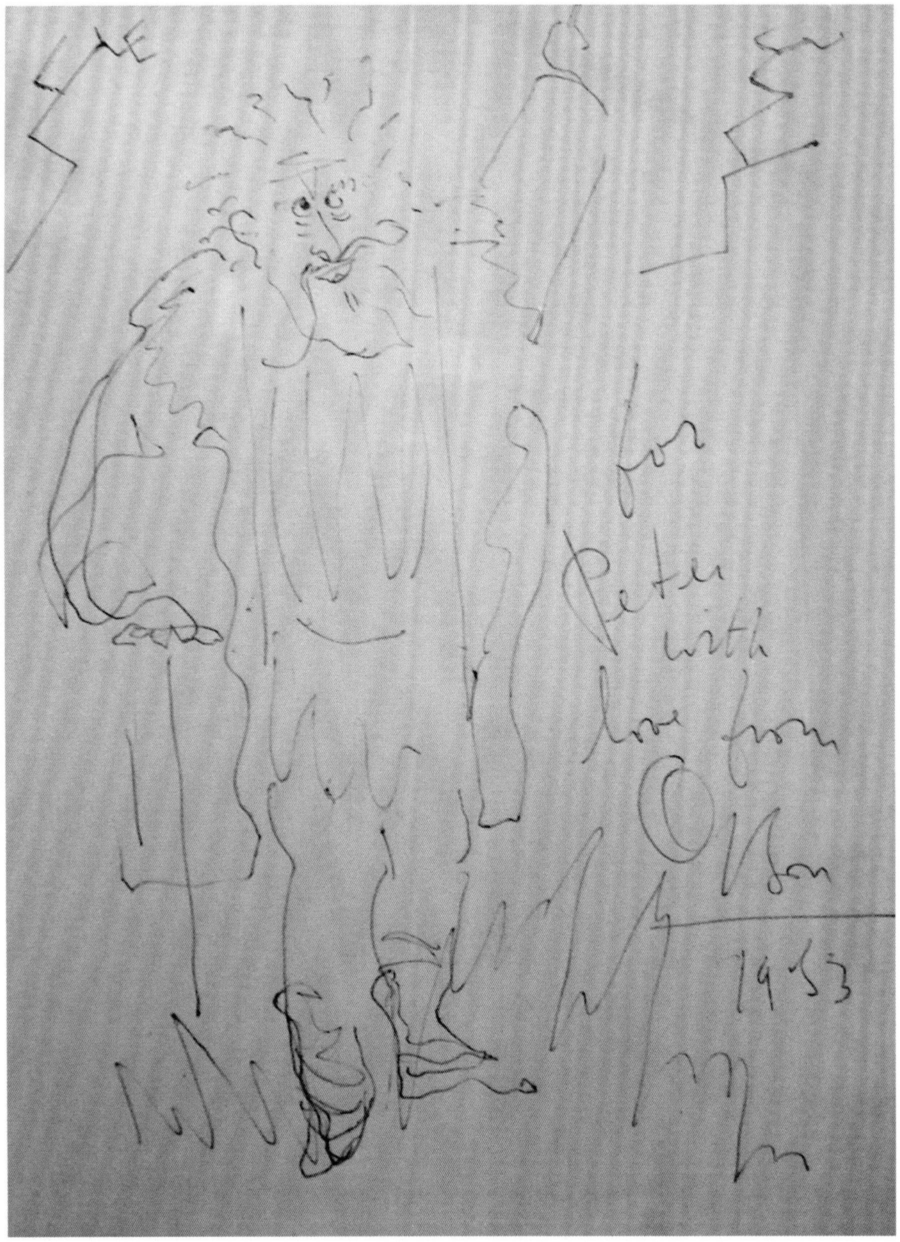

KING LEAR

What might be another Falstaff is, in fact, Welles's depiction of himself as King Lear, a gift to Peter Brook, in whose adaptation of the play he starred in 1953. At thirty-eight, Welles was patently too young for the role – or would have been, were it not for a longstanding history of playing much older characters, the octogenarian Charles Foster Kane among them.

Taking his cue from Welles, Brook cut *Lear* to the bone, dispensing with the characters Edgar and Edmund entirely and expanding the role of Oswald to compensate. 'Poor Tom', played by Welles's Gate Theatre guru Micheál MacLiammóir, was promoted to an actual character (in the text he is Edgar in disguise). Cordelia was played by Brook's wife, Natasha Parry.

Directed by Andrew McCullough, the production was broadcast live in the US on the prestigious CBS arts program *Omnibus*, hosted by legendary British broadcaster Alistair Cooke.

Welles, whose performance was deemed 'enormously impressive' by the *New York Herald Tribune*, had to return from exile abroad to take part. He was accompanied throughout his stay by IRS agents and, on his departure, saw his entire fee, minus expenses, seized to pay his tax bill. He returned to England immediately after the broadcast, no doubt in a rage to do Lear proud.

ABOVE: Sketch for Peter Brook; photo supplied for publication

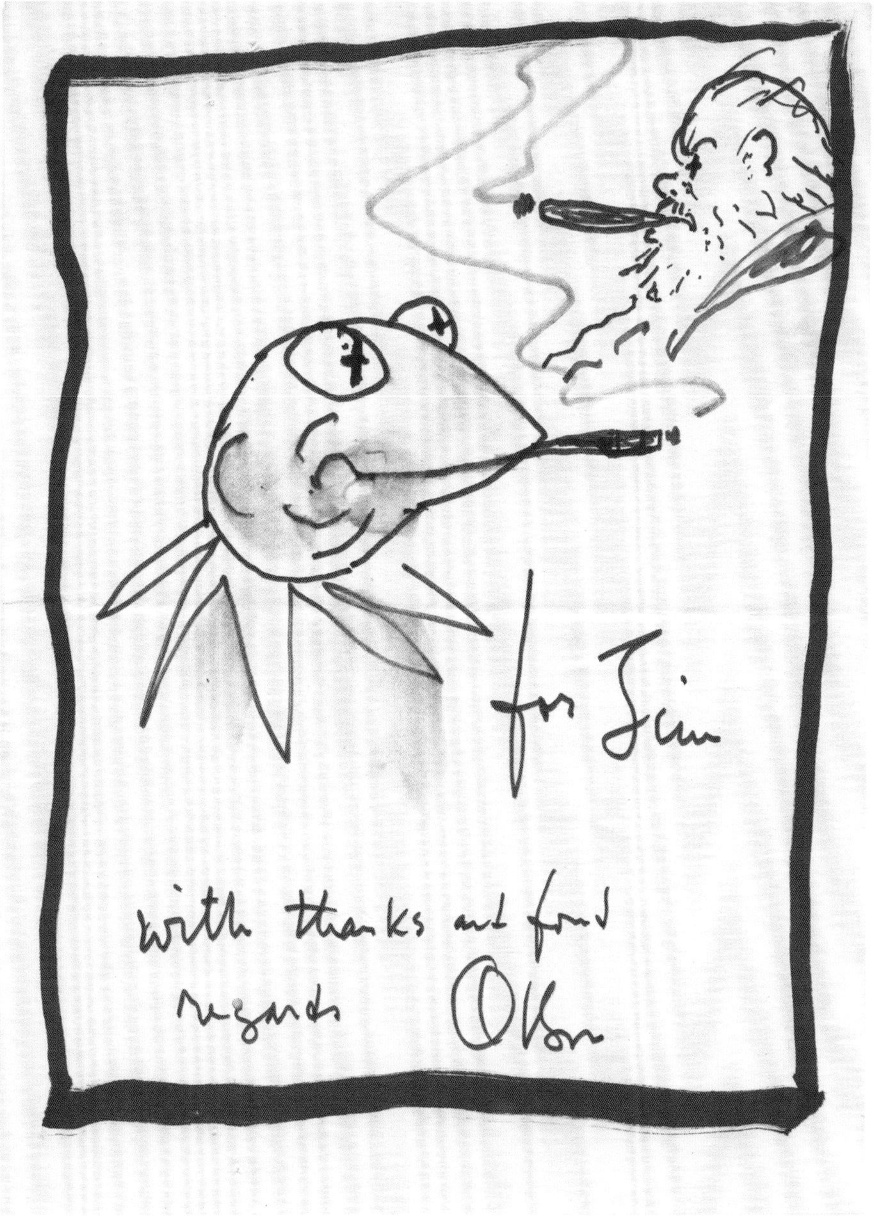

THE ORSON WELLES SHOW

In the late 1970s, Welles attempted to launch a career as a TV talk show host. The pilot for *The Orson Welles Show* was shot on a shoestring budget between September 1978 and February 1979. It was never picked up and has never aired anywhere in its entirety. Which is a shame, since, on paper at least, and judging by the few clips that have since surfaced, it looks like a lot of fun.

The guests were Angie Dickinson and Burt Reynolds, who handled an audience Q&A session with his trademark rascally charm, despite the decidedly mundane nature of the questions. Surprisingly, given their lack of imagination, these had been pre-scripted by Welles to make the footage easier to edit (Welles could only afford one camera; traditionally, talk shows use two).

The stand-out of the show were taped segments featuring Welles and an assortment of Muppets, including Kermit, Fozzie Bear, Animal and Gonzo the Great. Muppet maestros Jim Henson, Frank Oz and Jim Goetz were also interviewed by Welles, who had a cameo in 1979's *The Muppet Movie* as show-biz impresario Lew Lord. He had one line: 'Miss Tracy, prepare the standard 'Rich and Famous' contract for Kermit the Frog and Company.'

This charming little sketch was Welles's thank you note to Henson. Kermit, with jauntily angled cigar, is the star, fittingly taking center stage while the host stays in the background. It's a simple but personal token of affection and gratitude, capturing Welles on fine self-deprecating form.

ABOVE: Sketch for Jim Henson; scan supplied for publication

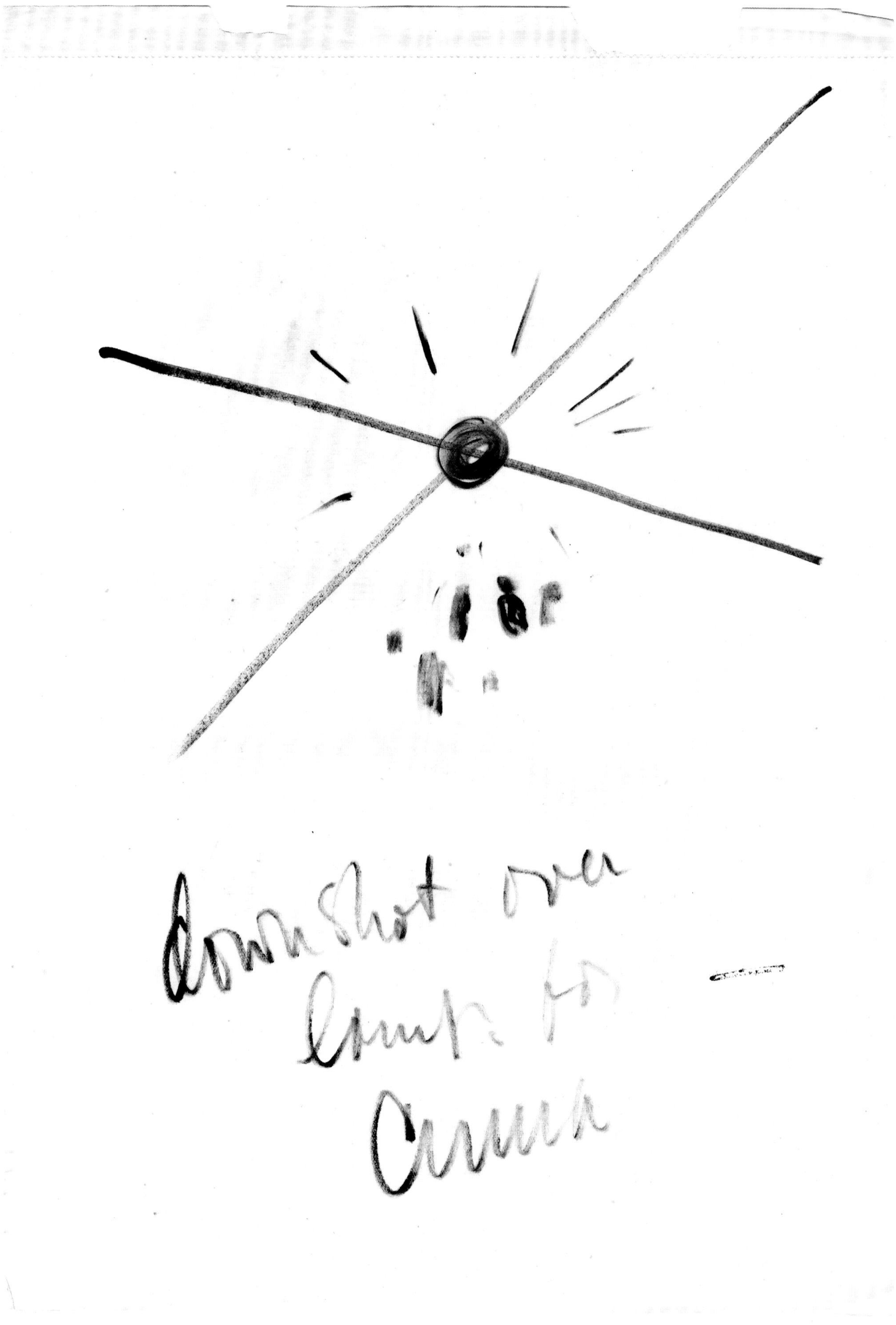

ABOVE: Unidentified storyboard (possibly for unfilmed *Caesar* project, unused); original scanned for publication

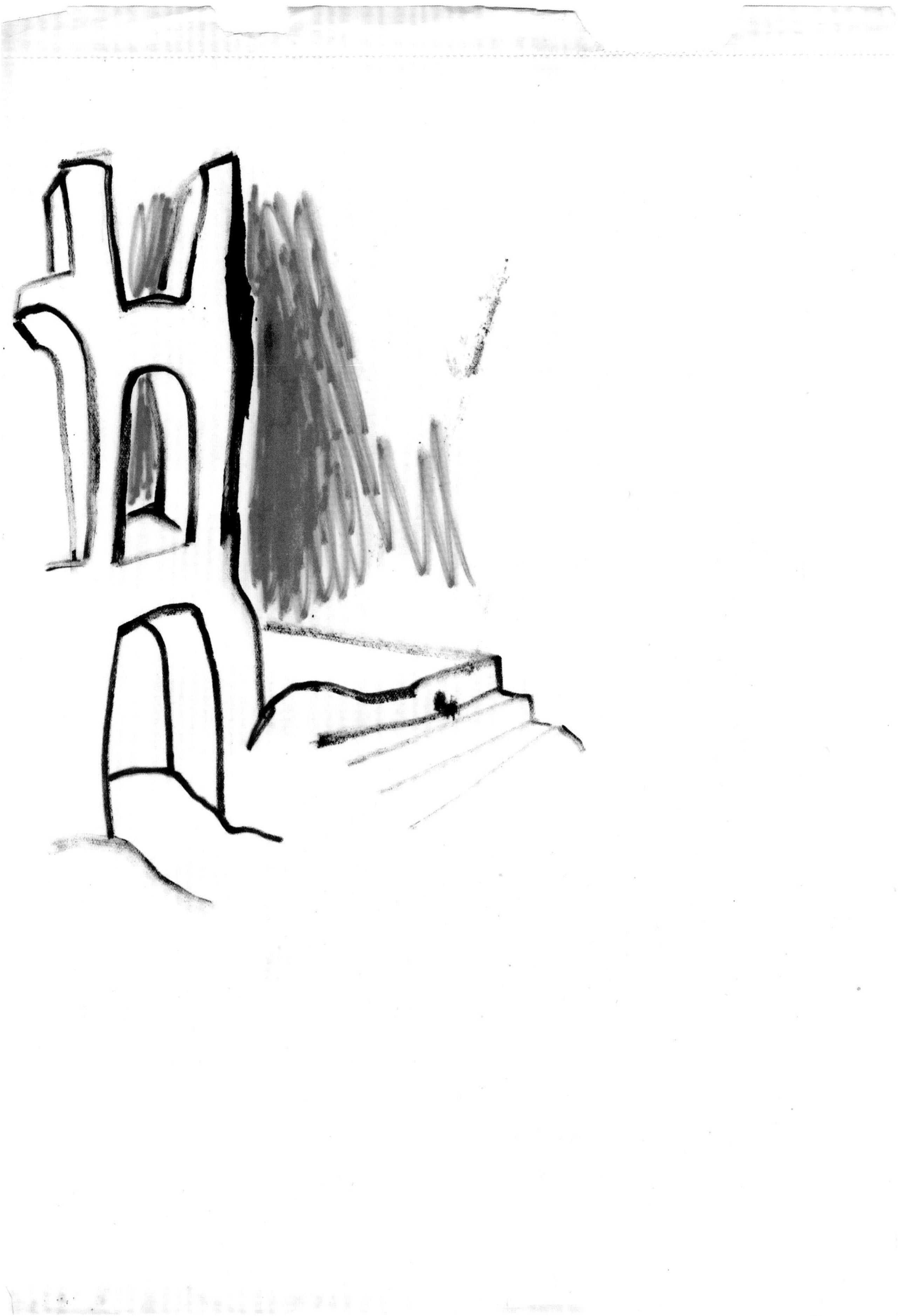

ABOVE: Unidentified storyboard (possibly for unfilmed *Caesar* project, unused); original scanned for publication

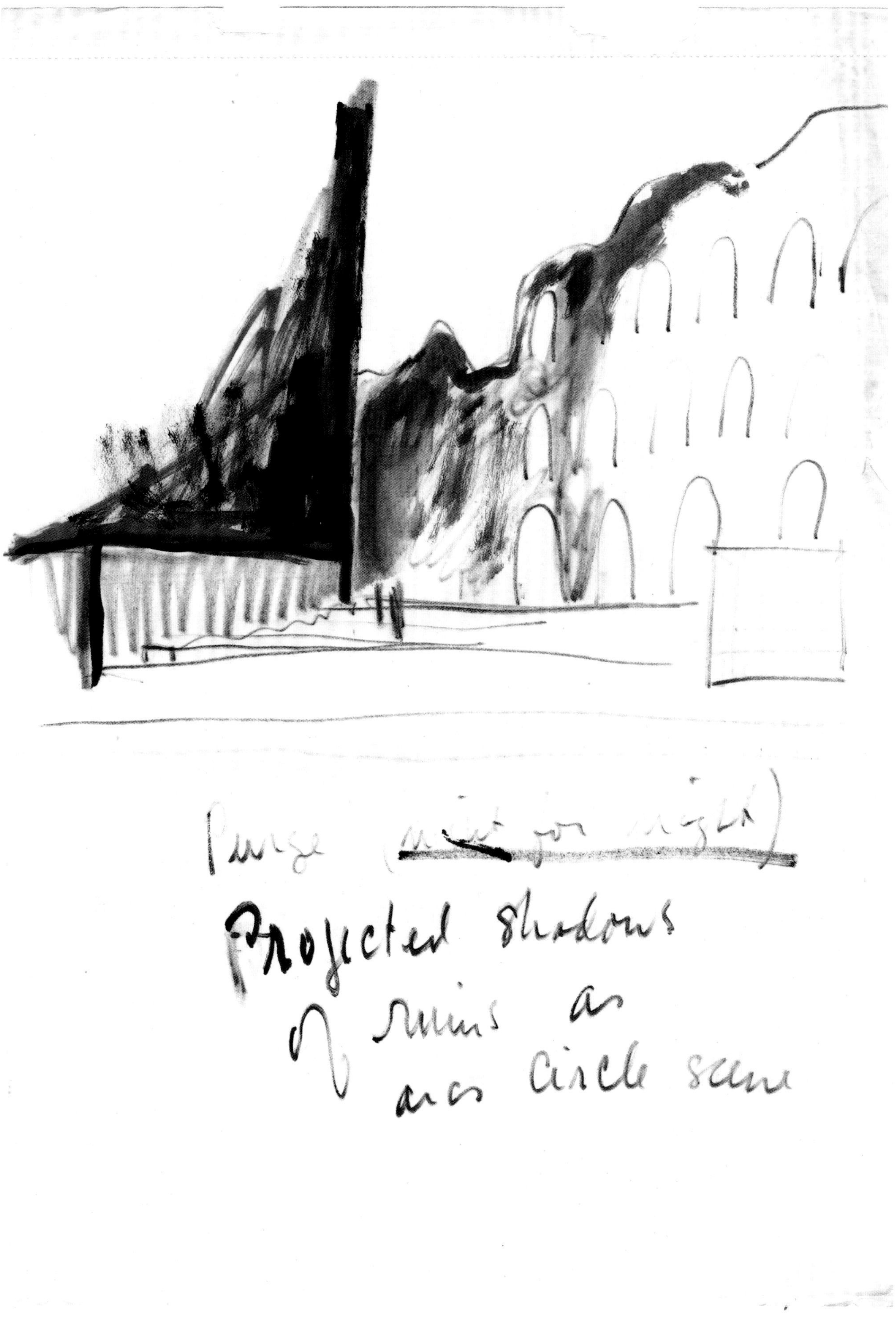

ABOVE: Unidentified storyboard (possibly for unfilmed *Caesar* project, unused); original scanned for publication

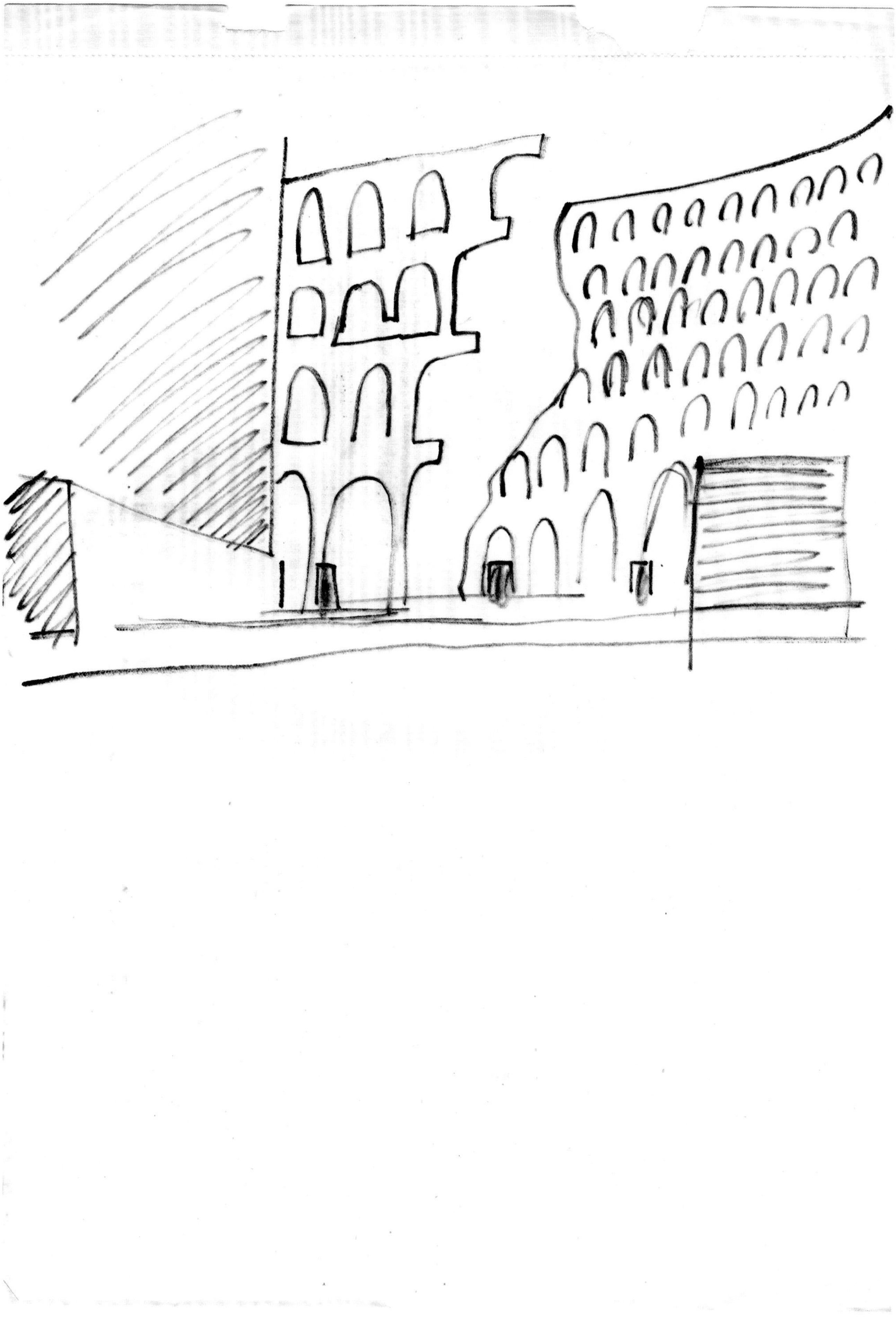

ABOVE: Unidentified storyboard (possibly for unfilmed *Caesar* project, unused); original scanned for publication

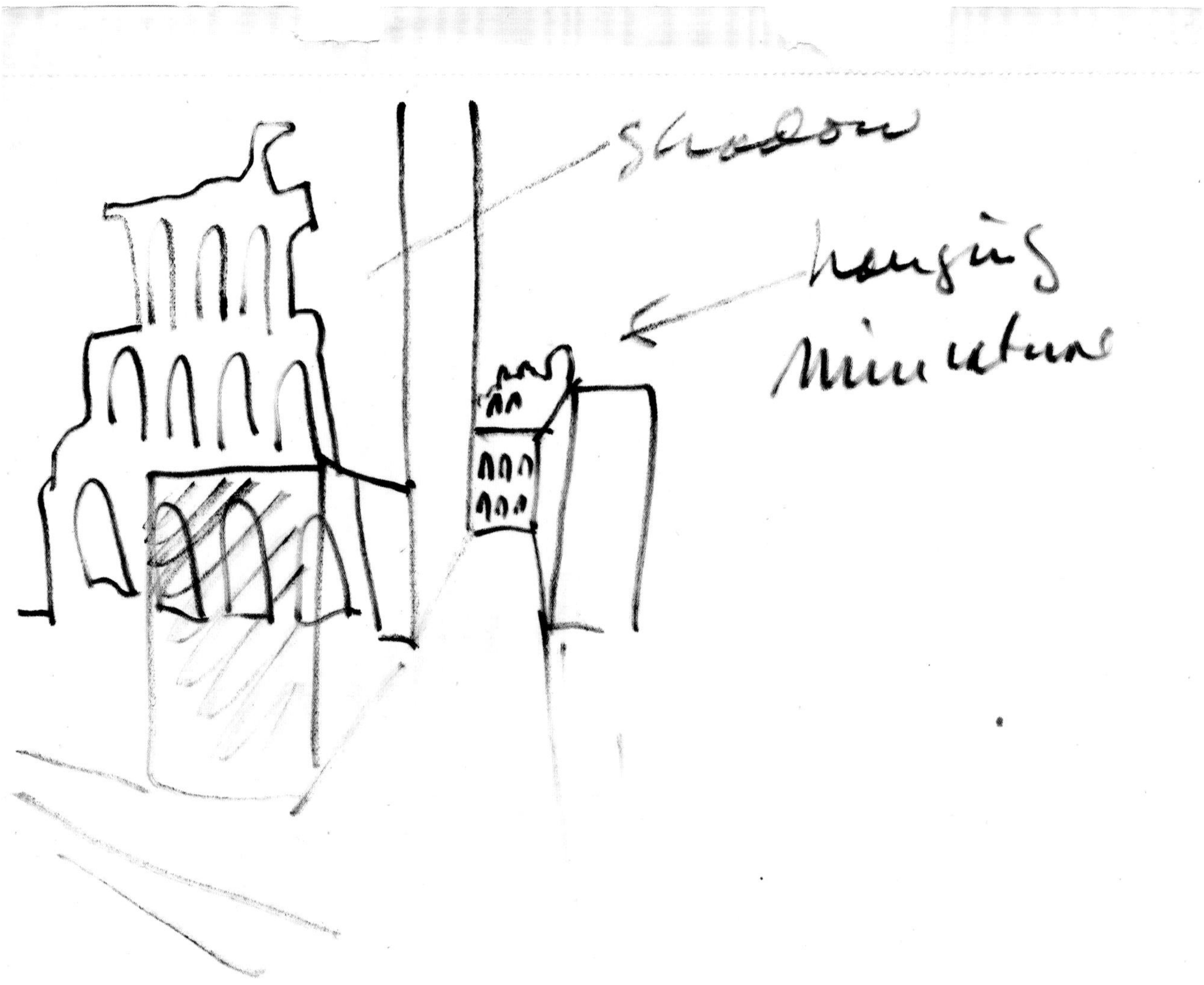

ABOVE: Unidentified storyboard (possibly for unfilmed *Caesar* project, unused); original scanned for publication

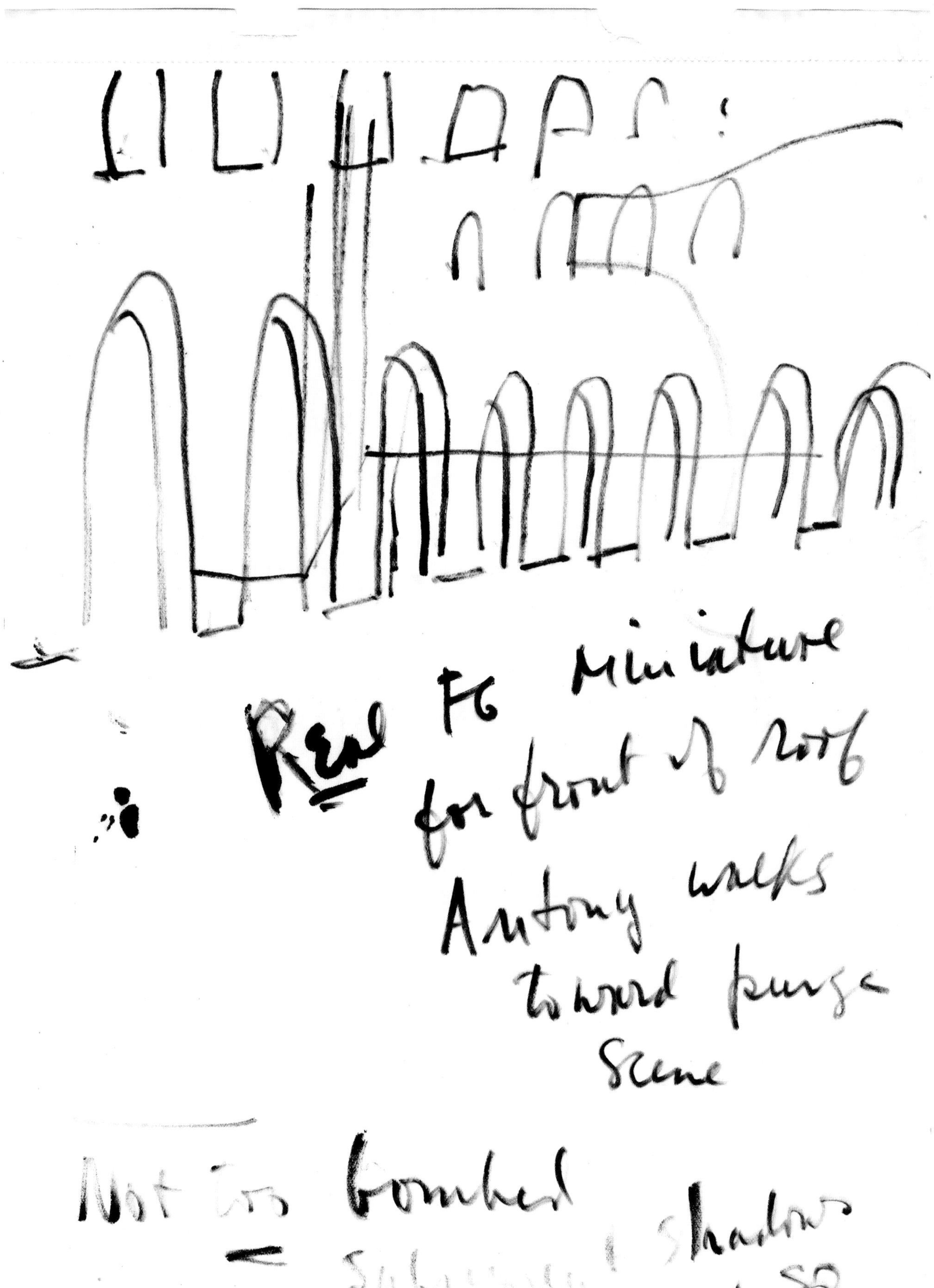

ABOVE: Unidentified storyboard (possibly for unfilmed *Caesar* project, unused); original scanned for publication

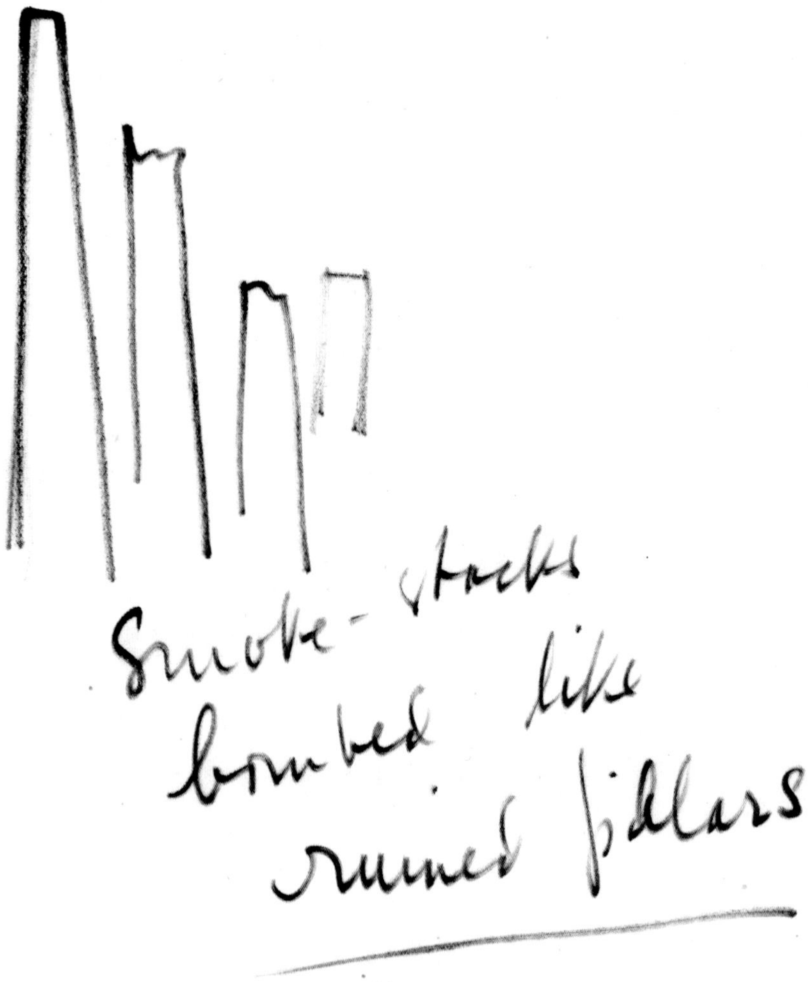

ABOVE: Unidentified storyboard (possibly for unfilmed *Caesar* project, unused); original scanned for publication

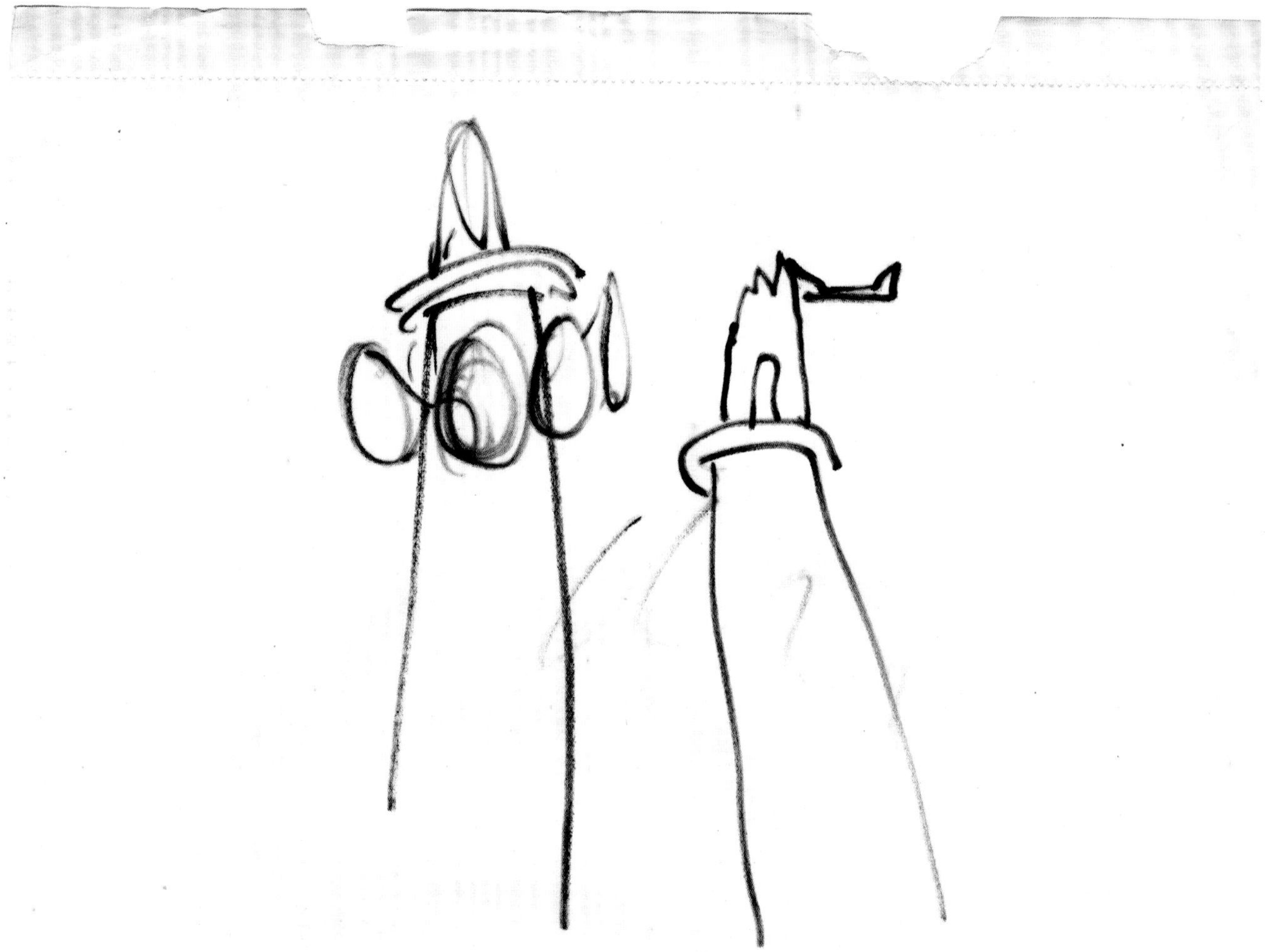

ABOVE: Unidentified storyboard (possibly for unfilmed *Caesar* project, unused); original scanned for publication

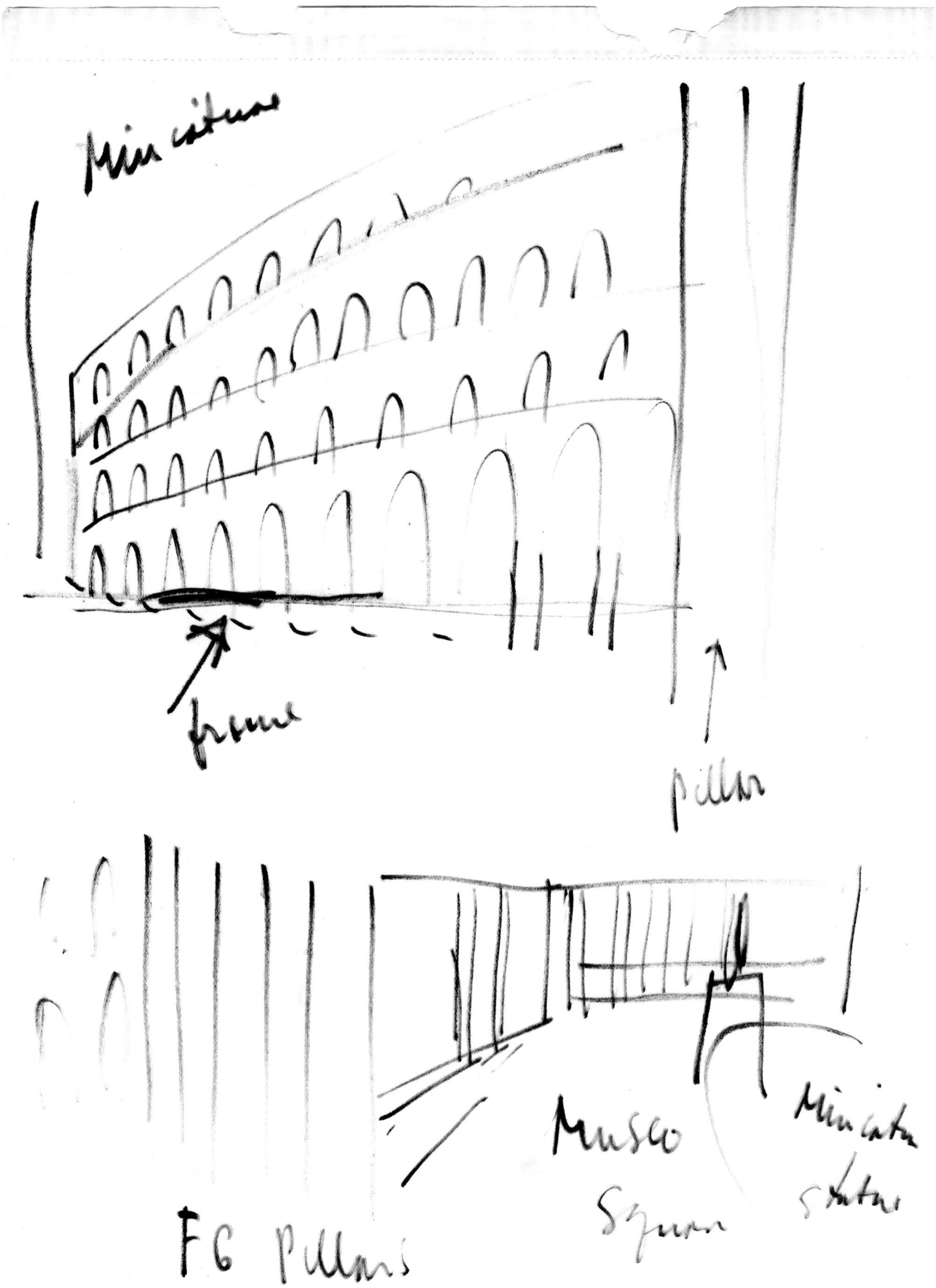

ABOVE: Unidentified storyboard (possibly for unfilmed *Caesar* project, unused); original scanned for publication

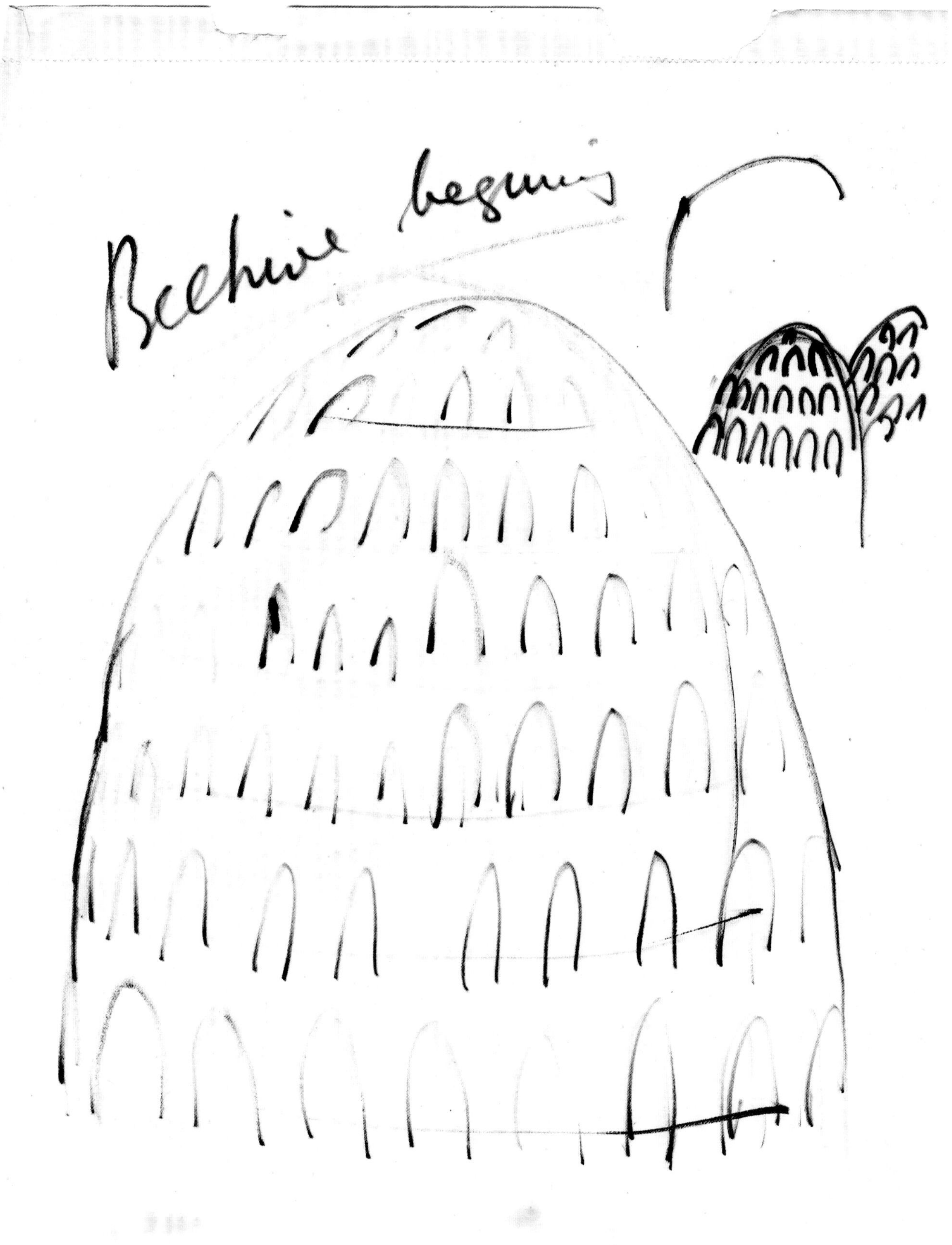

ABOVE: Unidentified storyboard (possibly for unfilmed *Caesar* project, unused); original scanned for publication

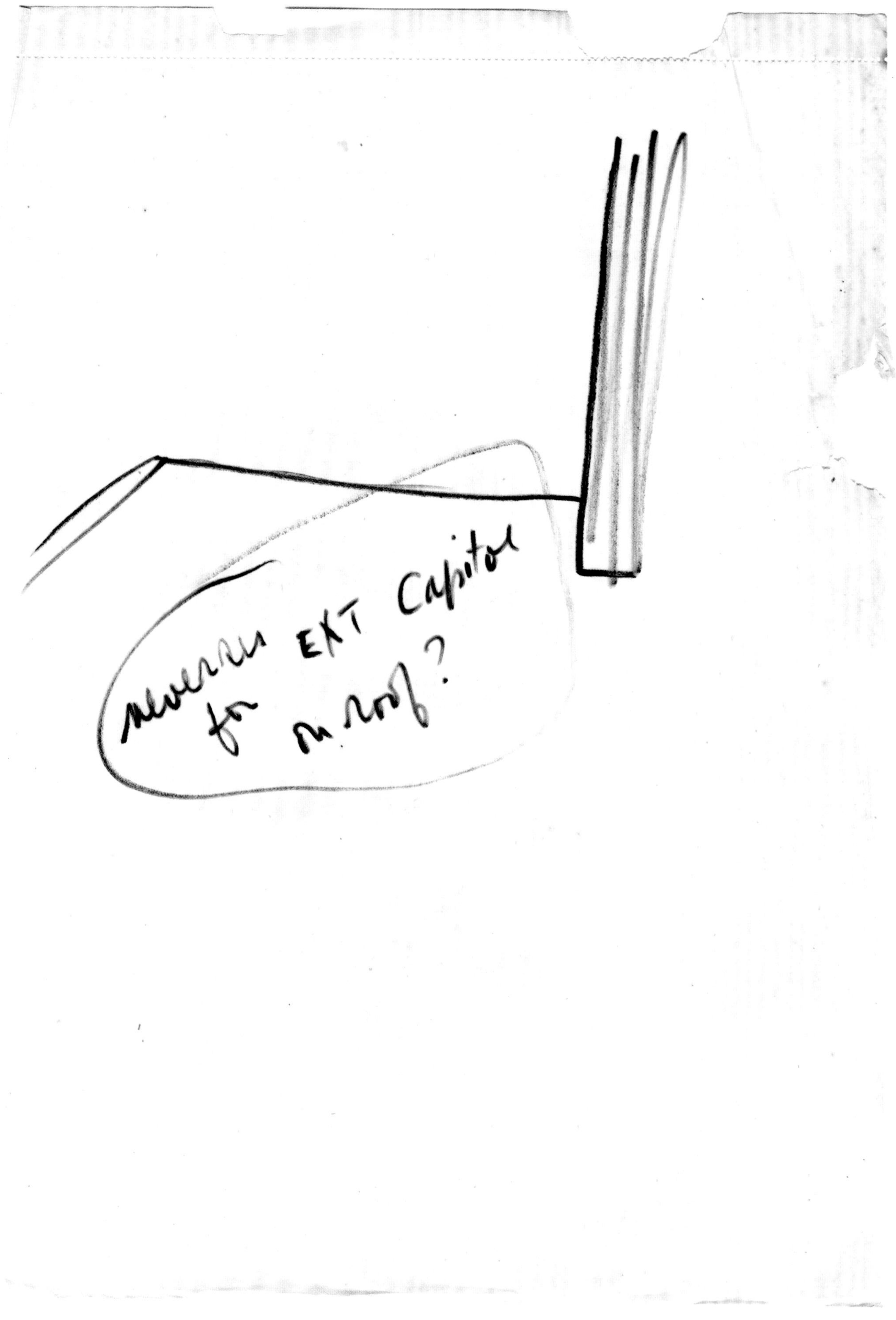

ABOVE: Unidentified storyboard (possibly for unfilmed *Caesar* project, unused); original scanned for publication

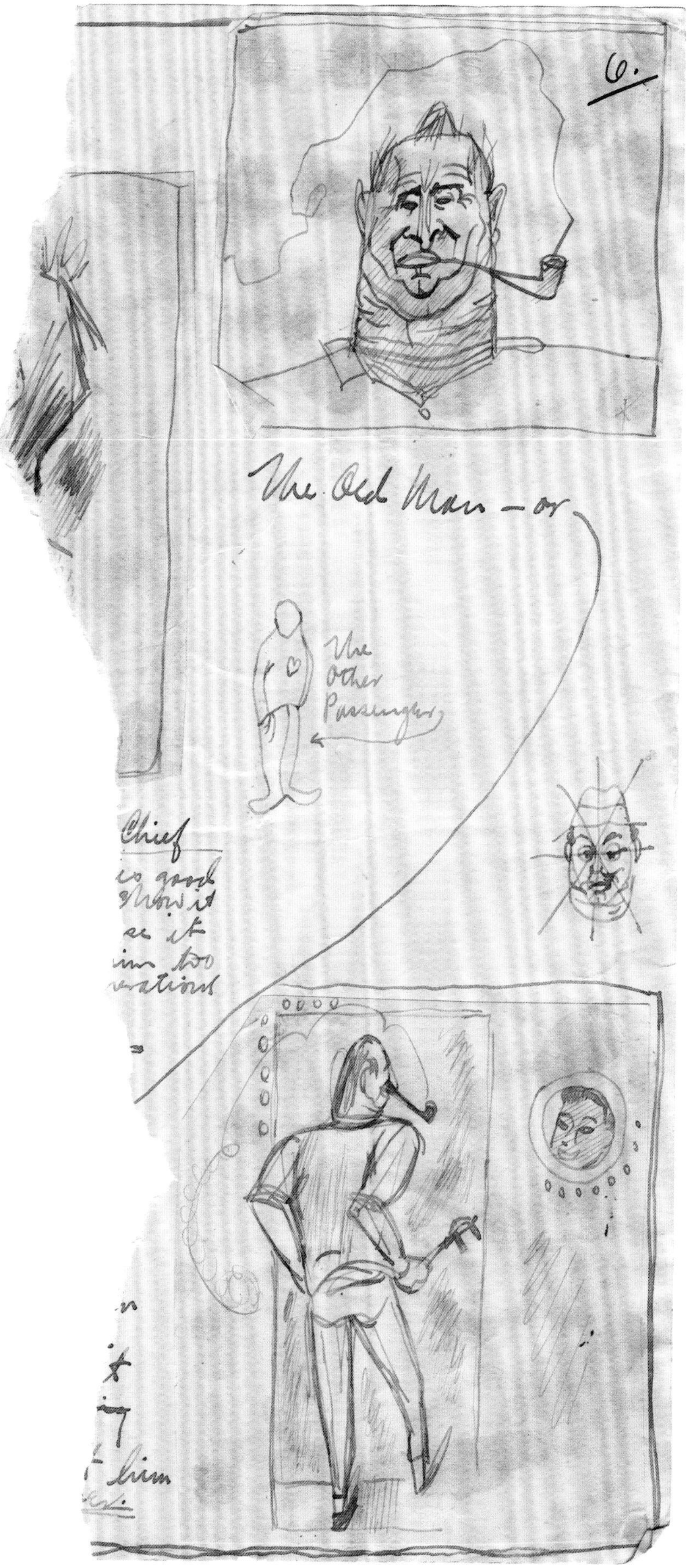

ABOVE: Unidentified scene notes; original scanned for publication

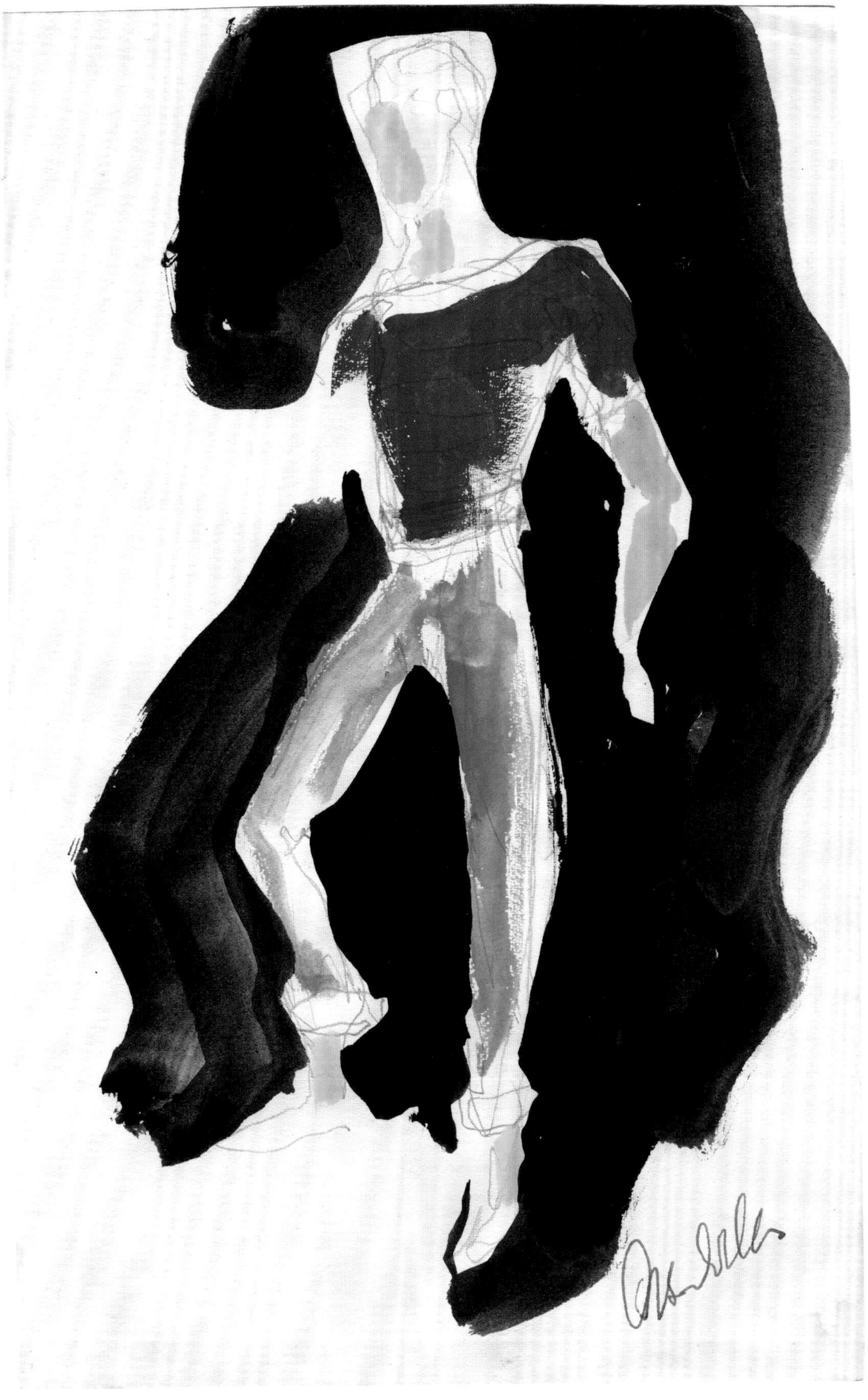

ABOVE: Unidentified costume design; original scanned for publication

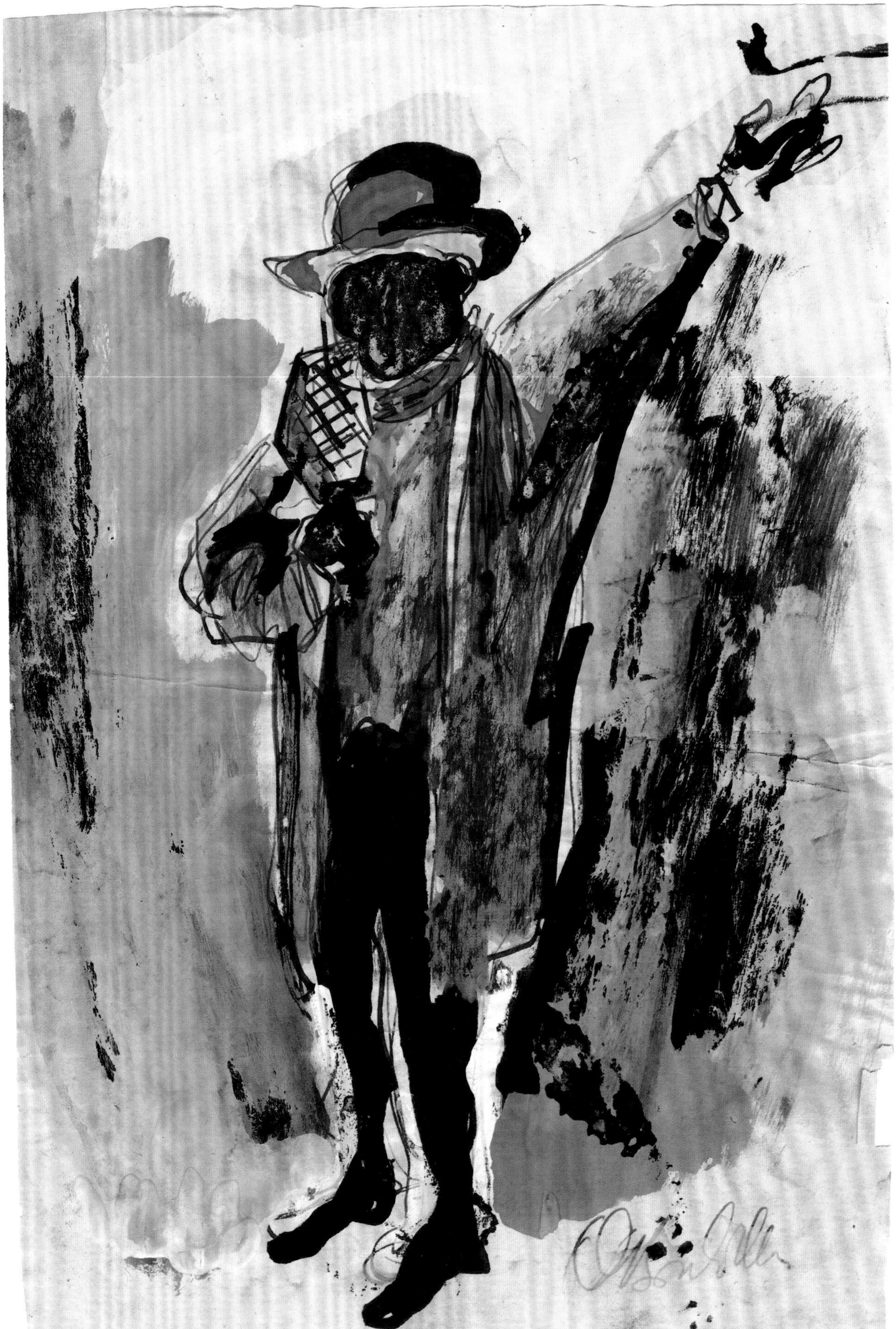

ABOVE: Unidentified costume design; original scanned for publication

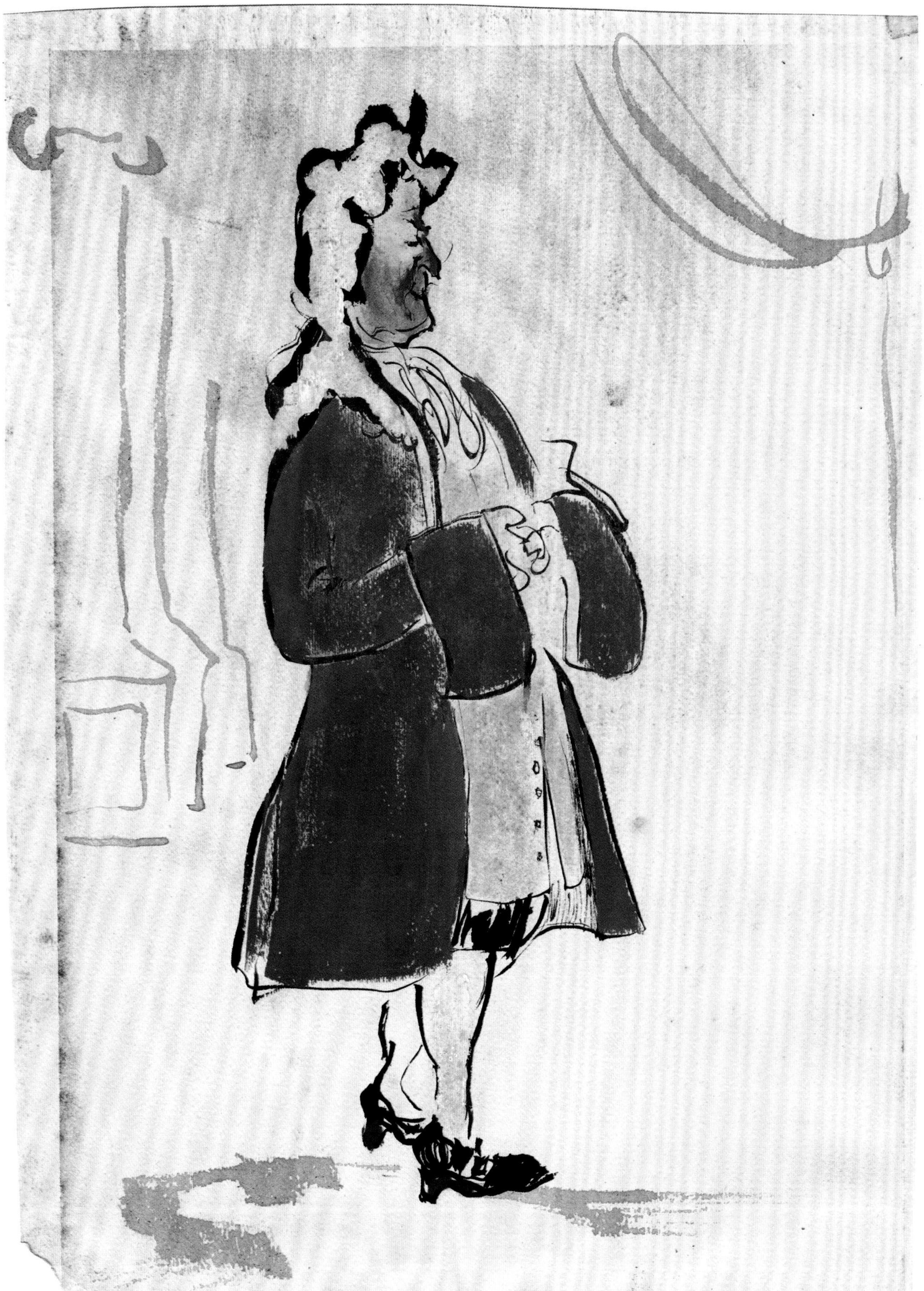

ABOVE: Unidentified costume design; original scanned for publication

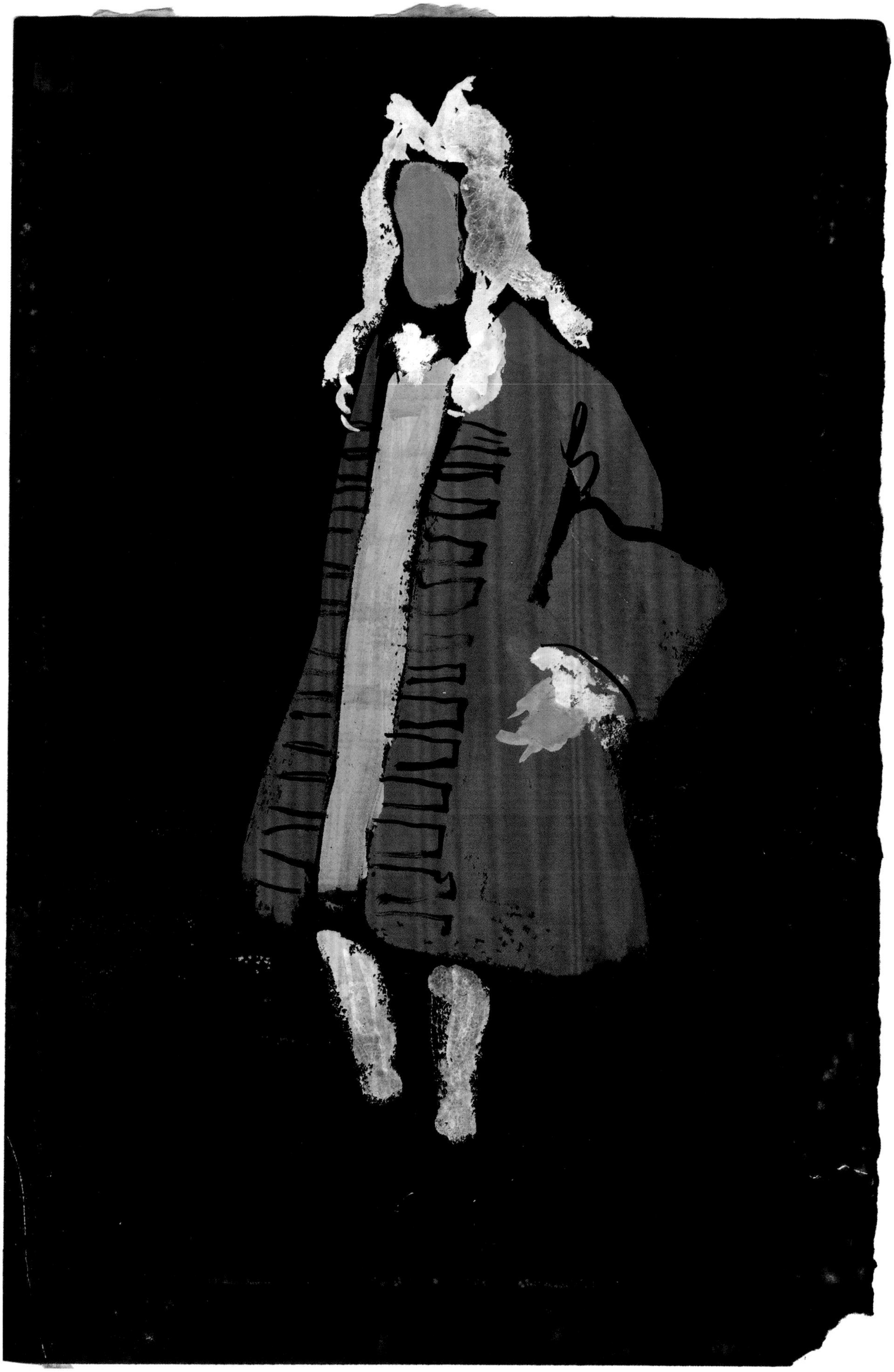

ABOVE: Unidentified costume design; original scanned for publication

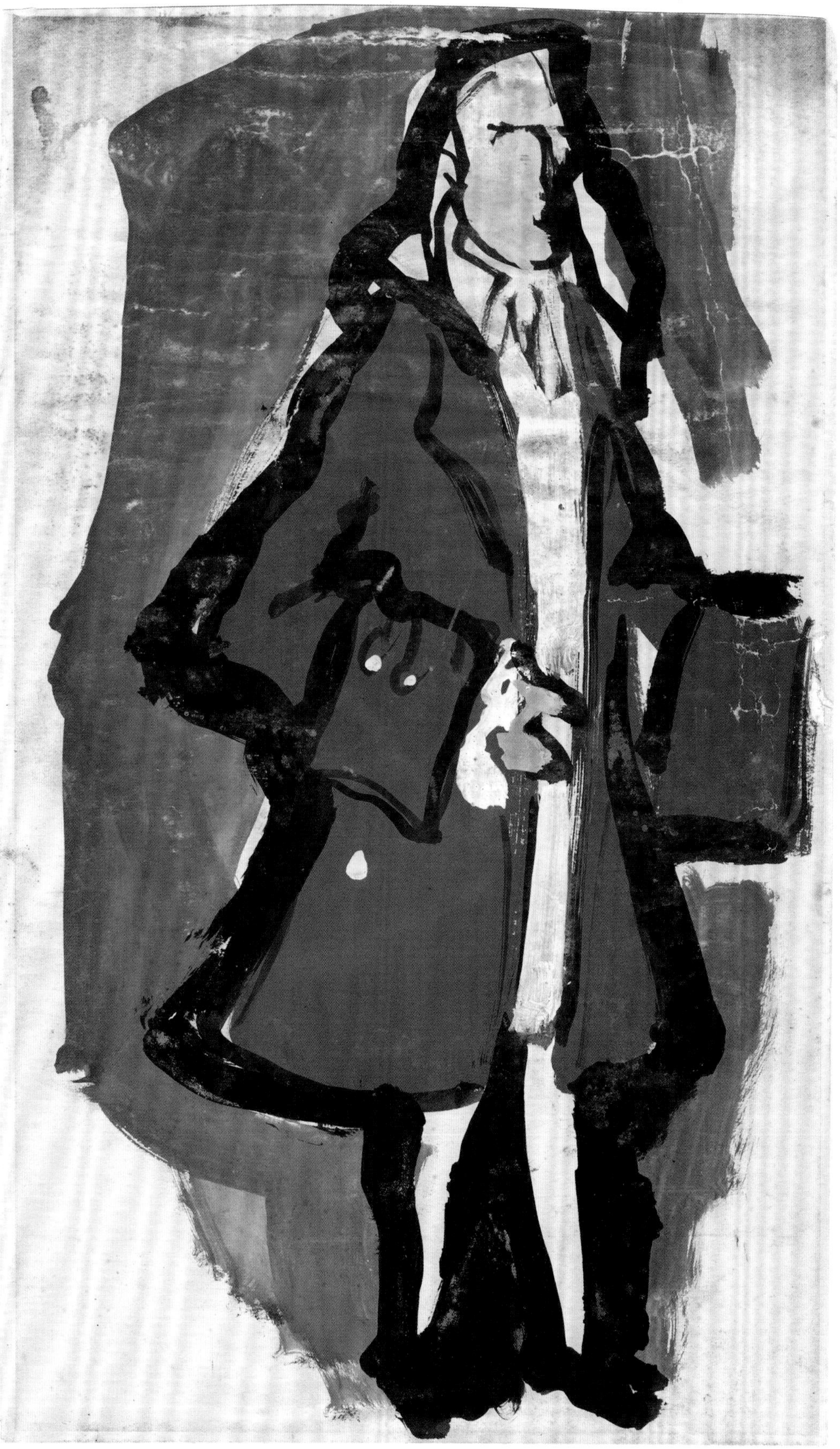

ABOVE: Unidentified costume design; original scanned for publication

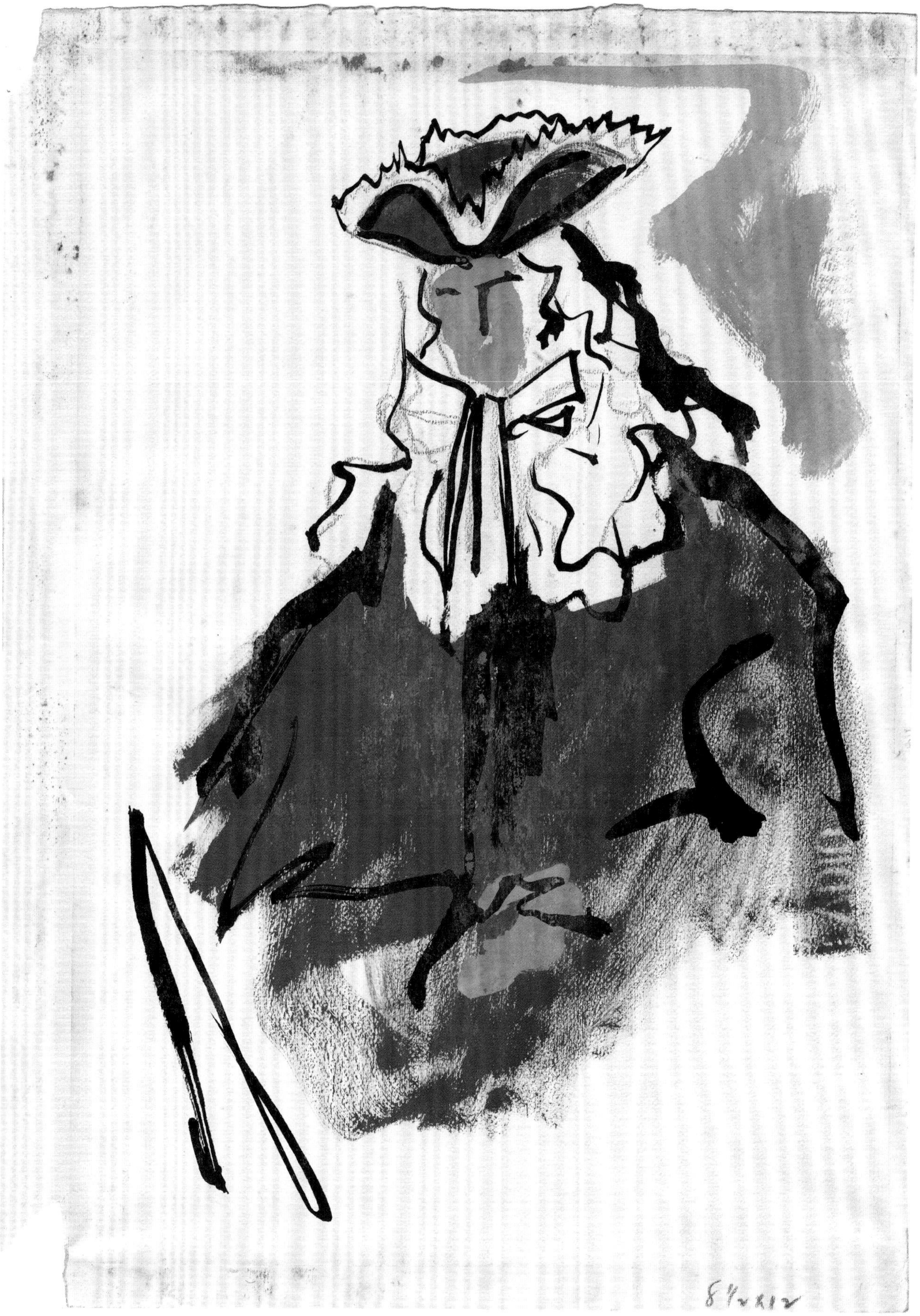

ABOVE: Unidentified costume design; original scanned for publication

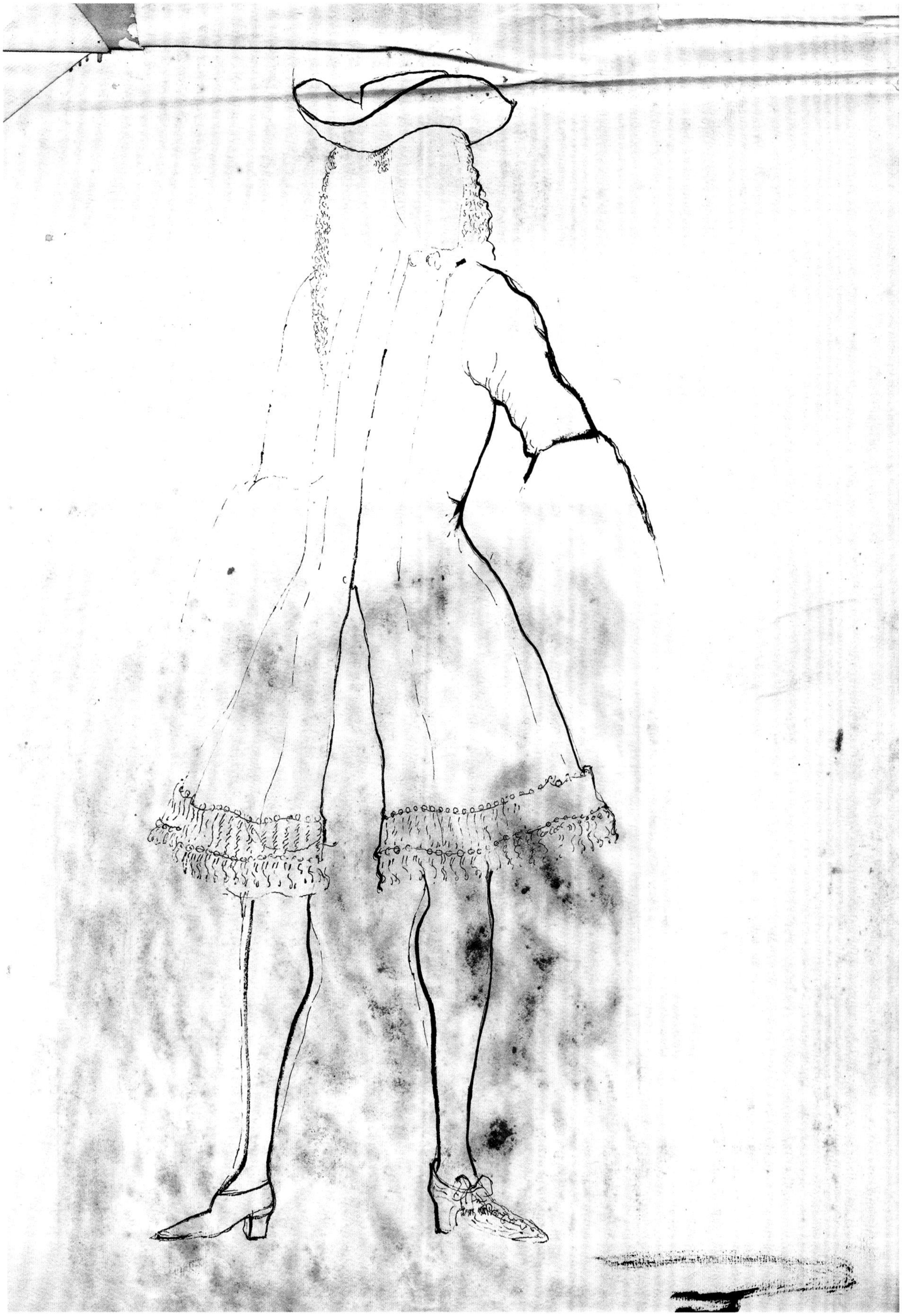

ABOVE: Unidentified costume design; original scanned for publication

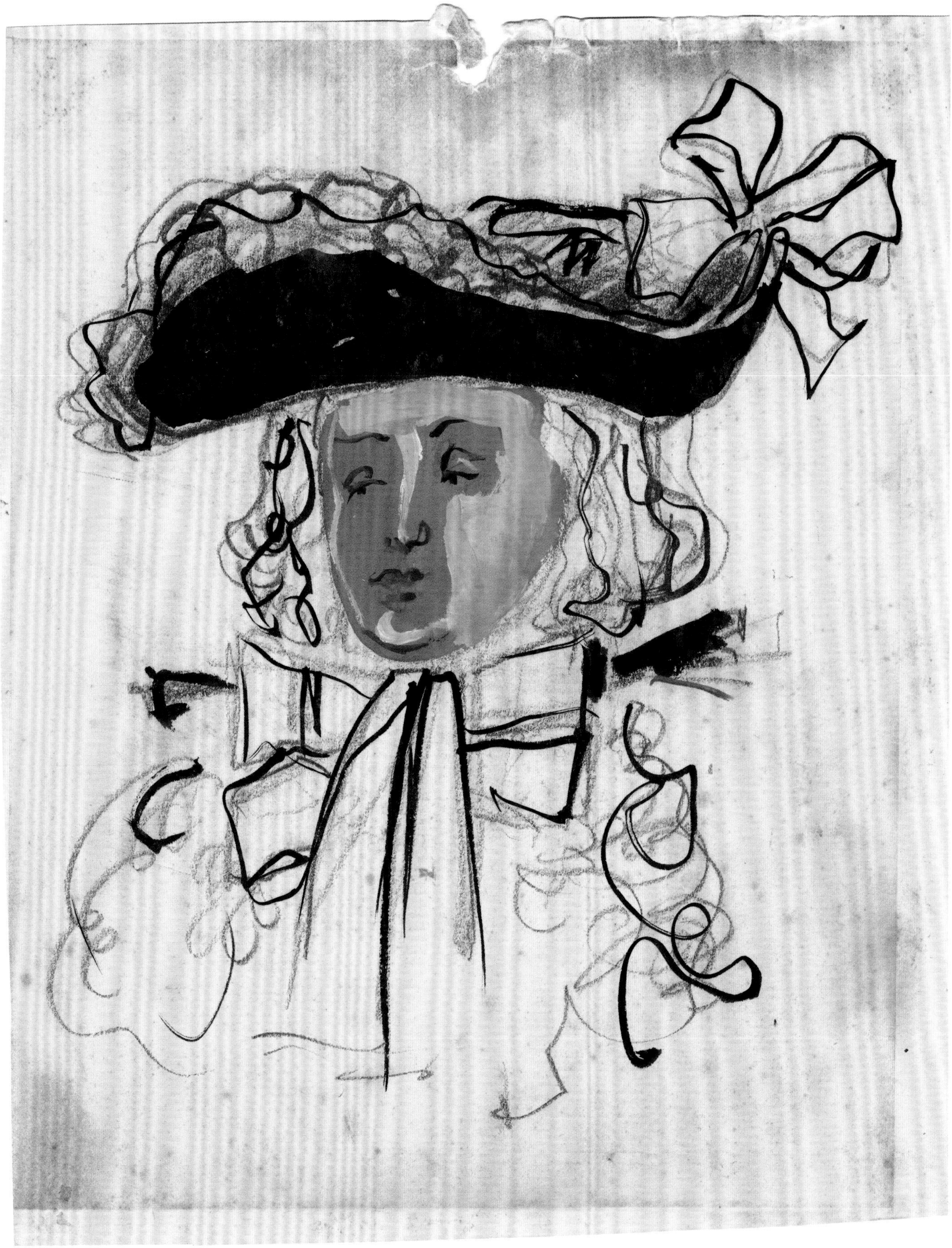

ABOVE: Unidentified costume design; original scanned for publication

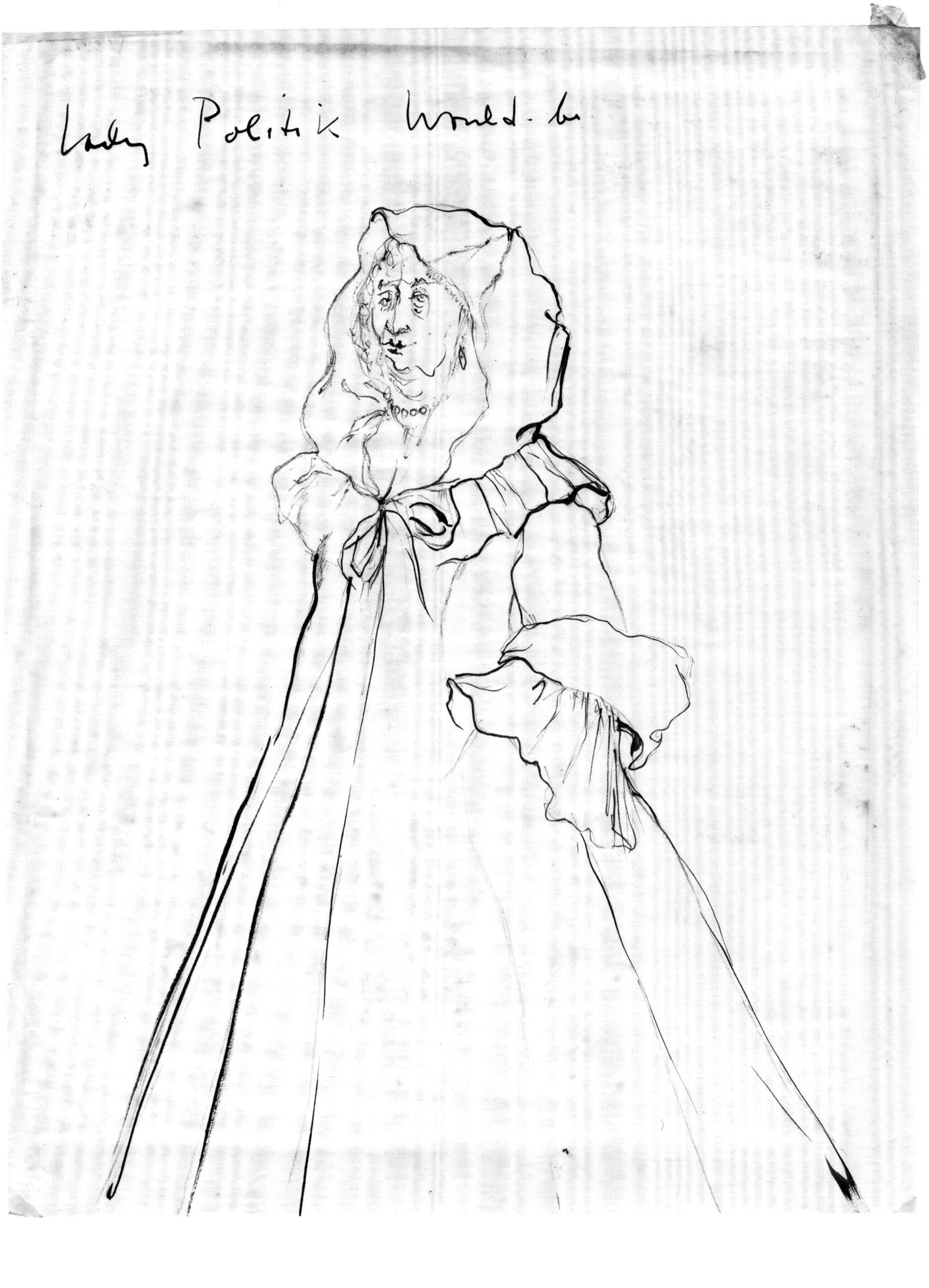

ABOVE: Unidentified costume design 'Lady Politik'; original scanned for publication

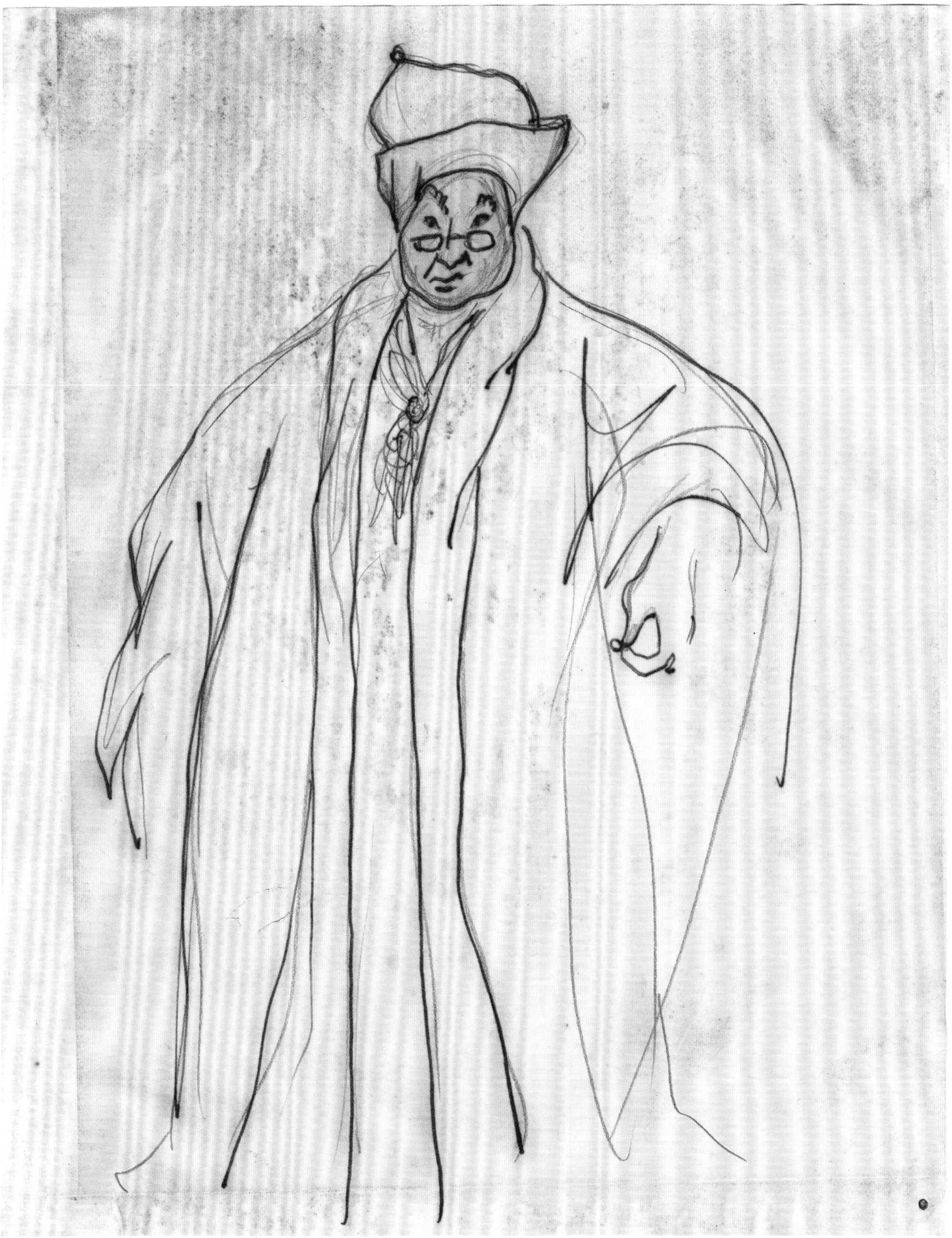

ABOVE: Unidentified costume design; original scanned for publication

ABOVE: Unidentified costume design; original scanned for publication

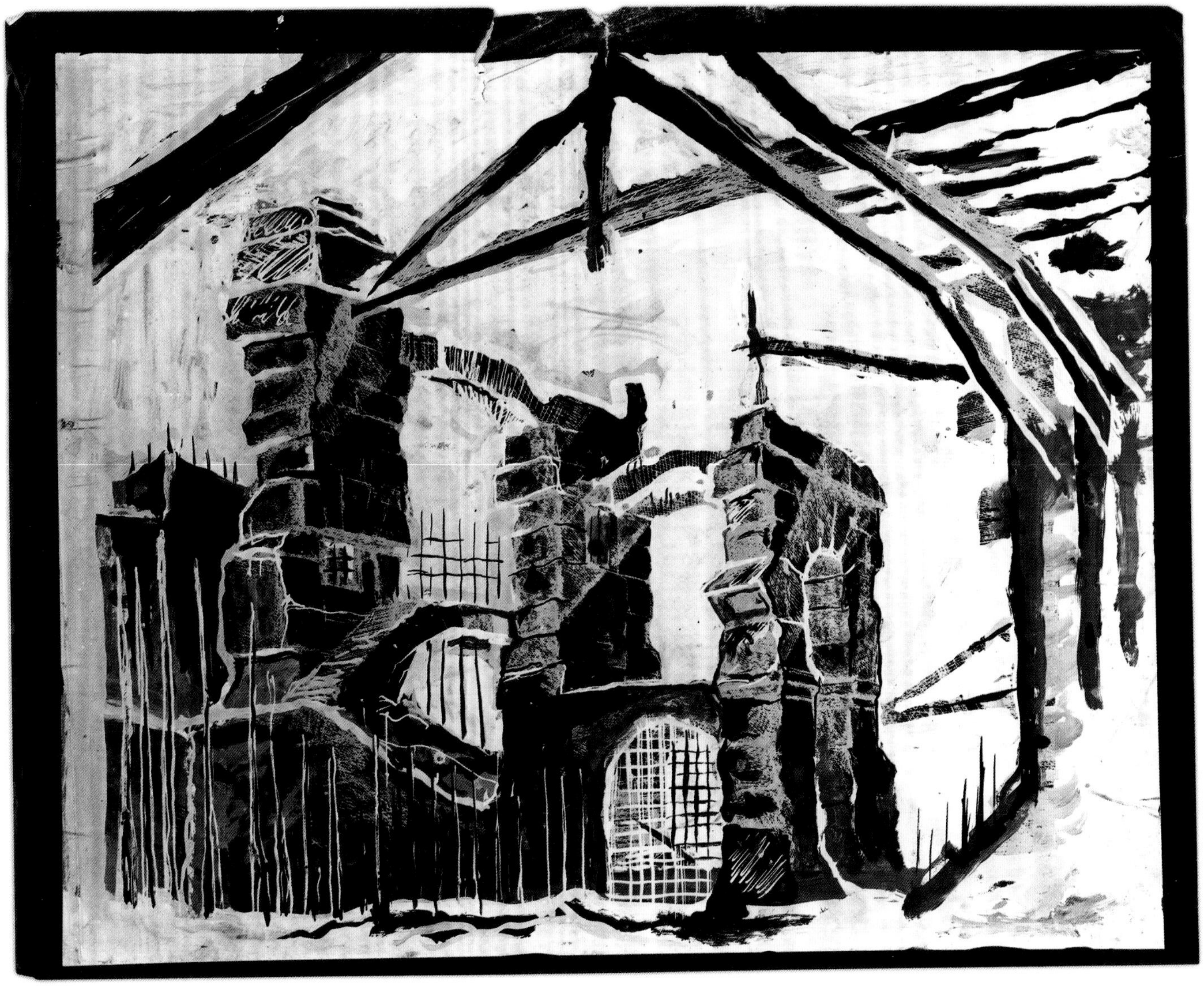

ABOVE: Unidentified set design; original scanned for publication

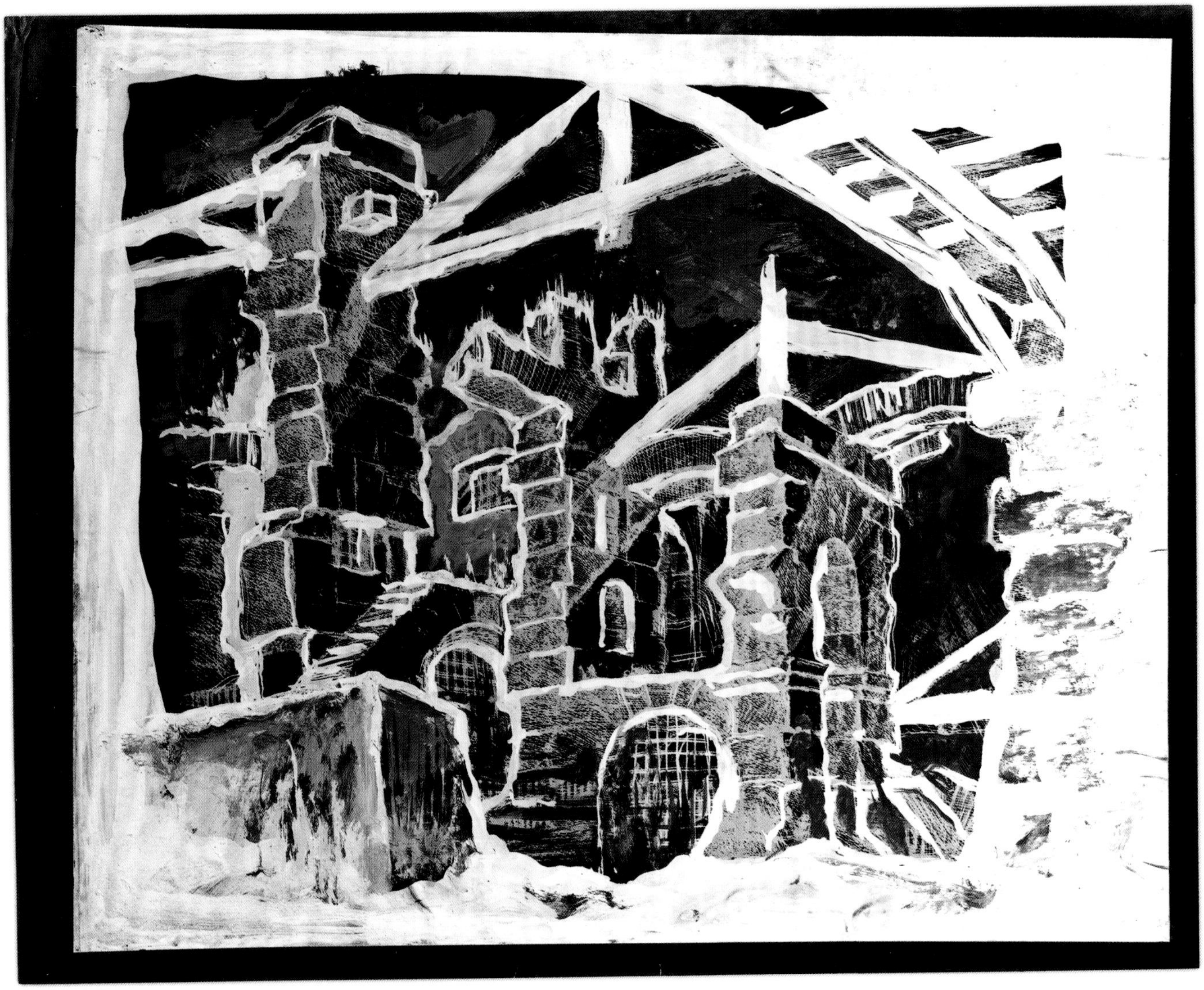

ABOVE: Unidentified set design; original scanned for publication

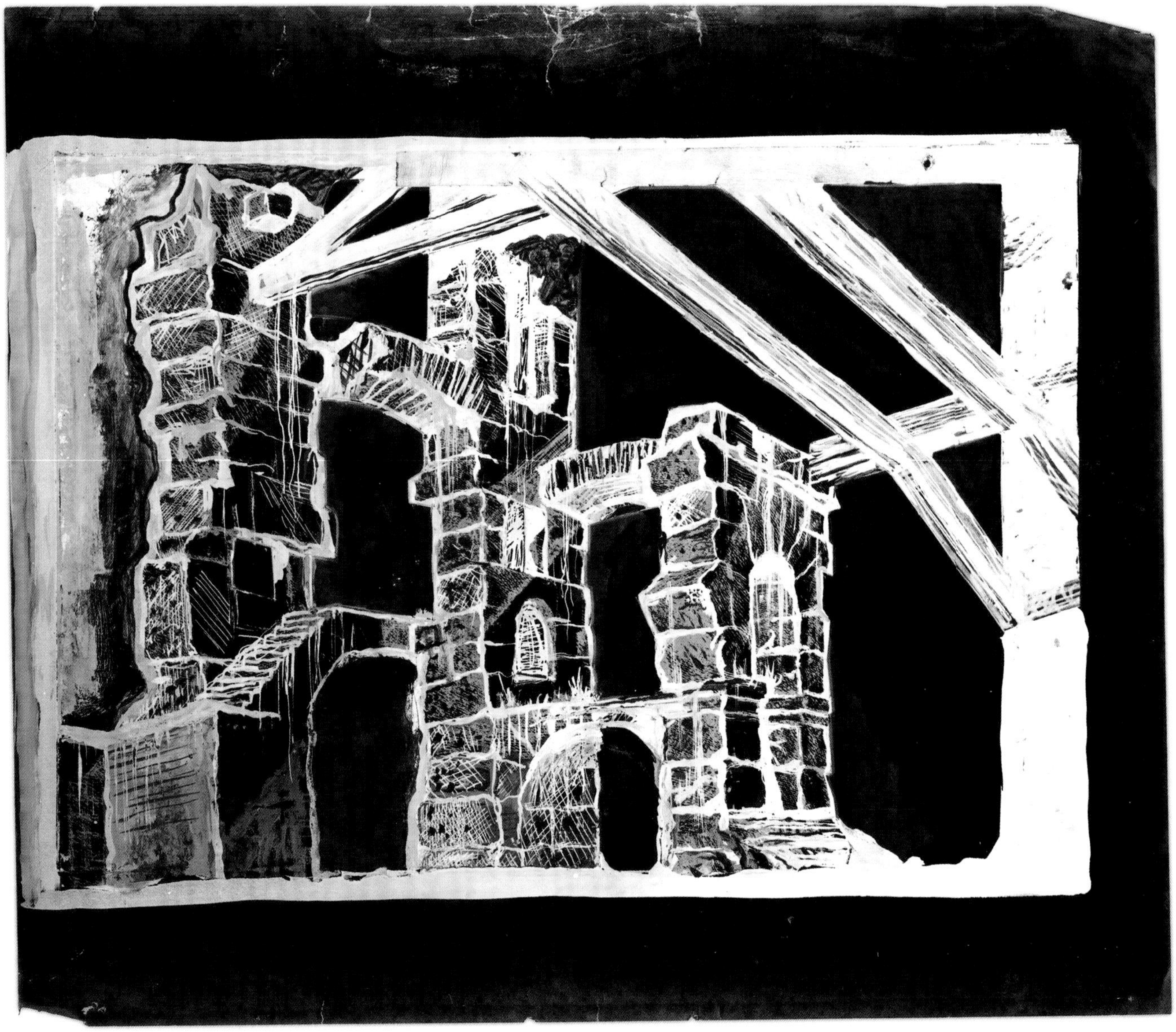

ABOVE: Unidentified set design; original scanned for publication

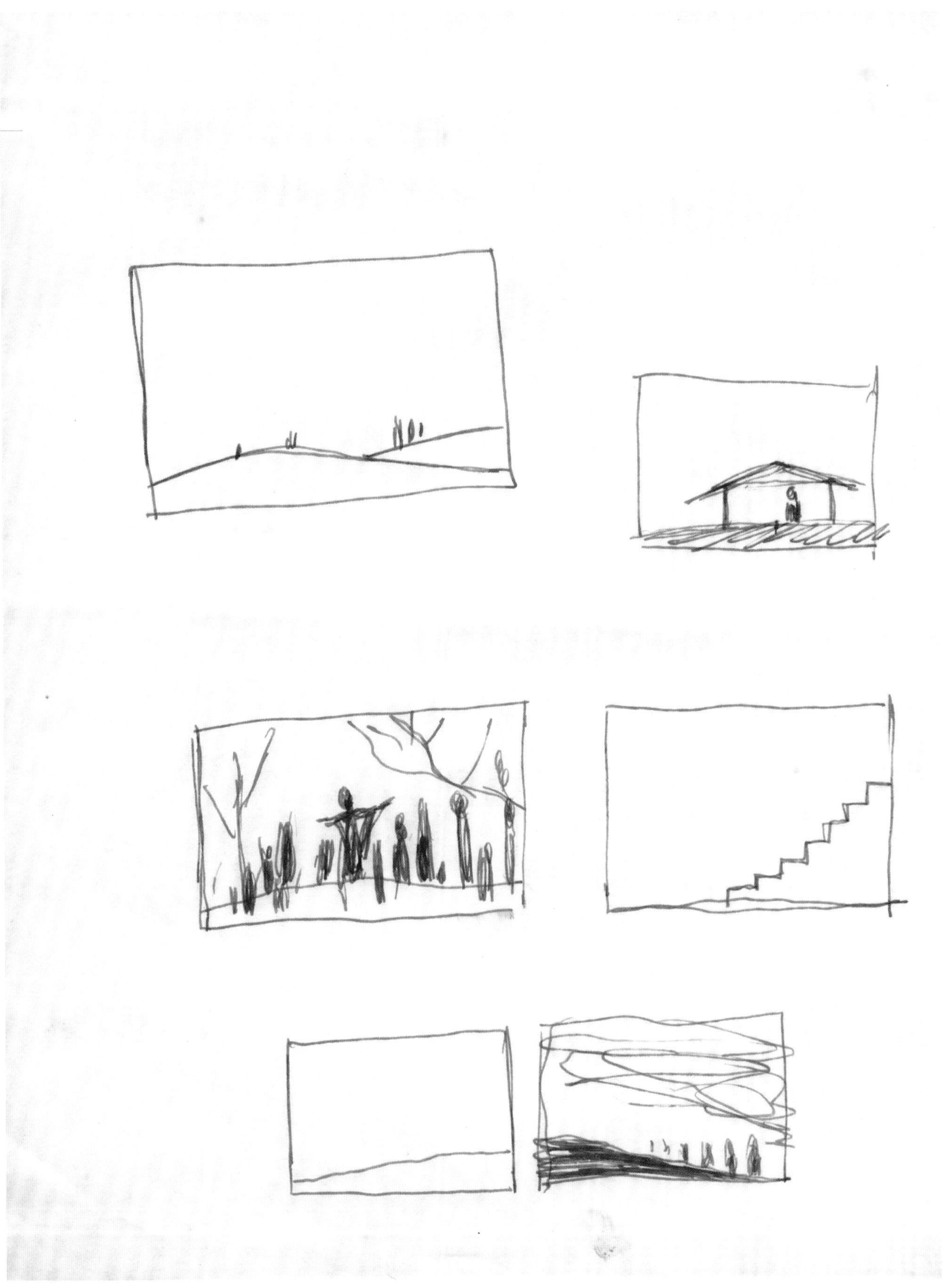

ABOVE: Unidentified storyboards; scan supplied for publication

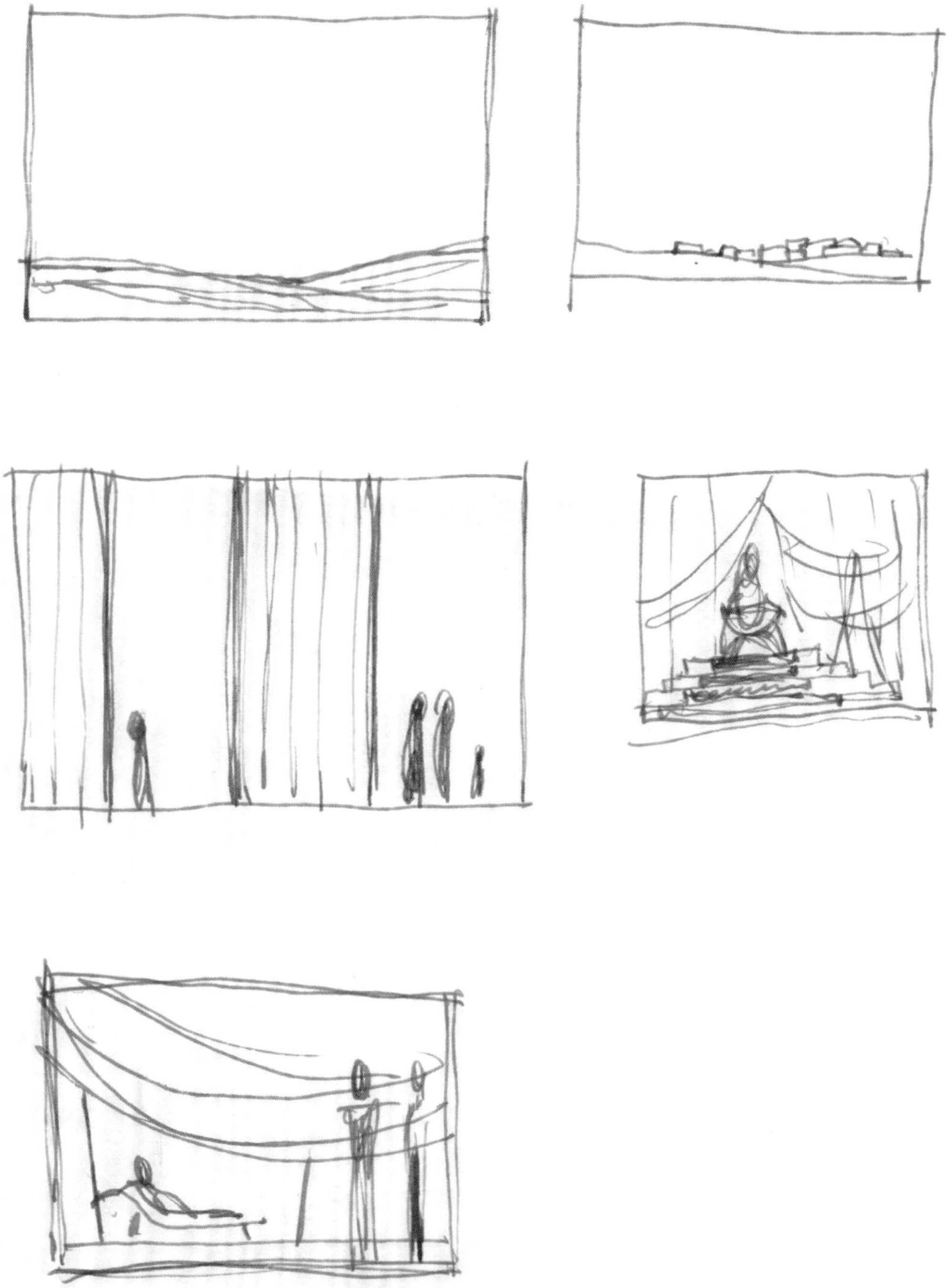

ABOVE: Unidentified storyboards; scan supplied for publication

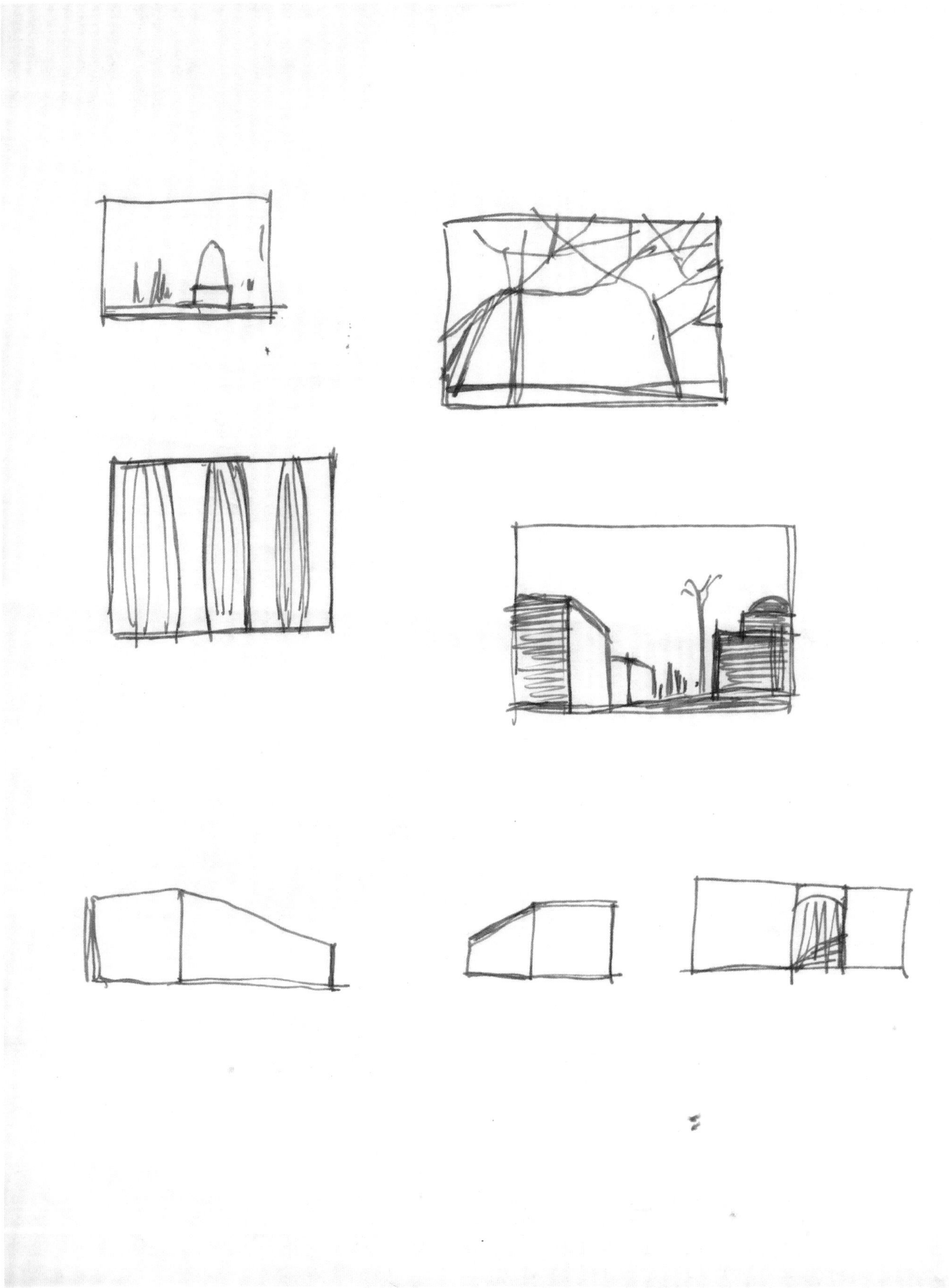

ABOVE: Unidentified storyboards; scan supplied for publication

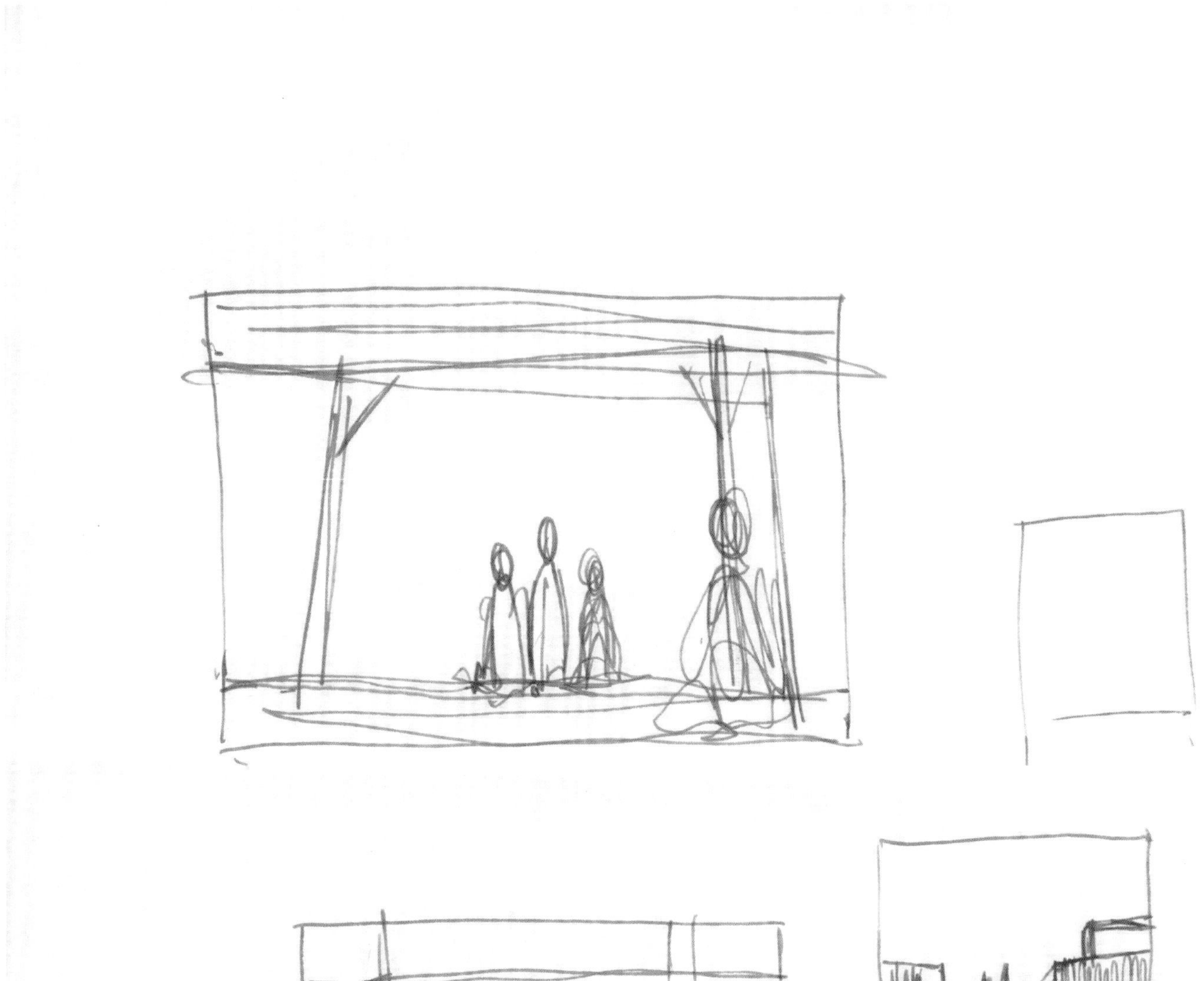

ABOVE: Unidentified storyboards; scan supplied for publication

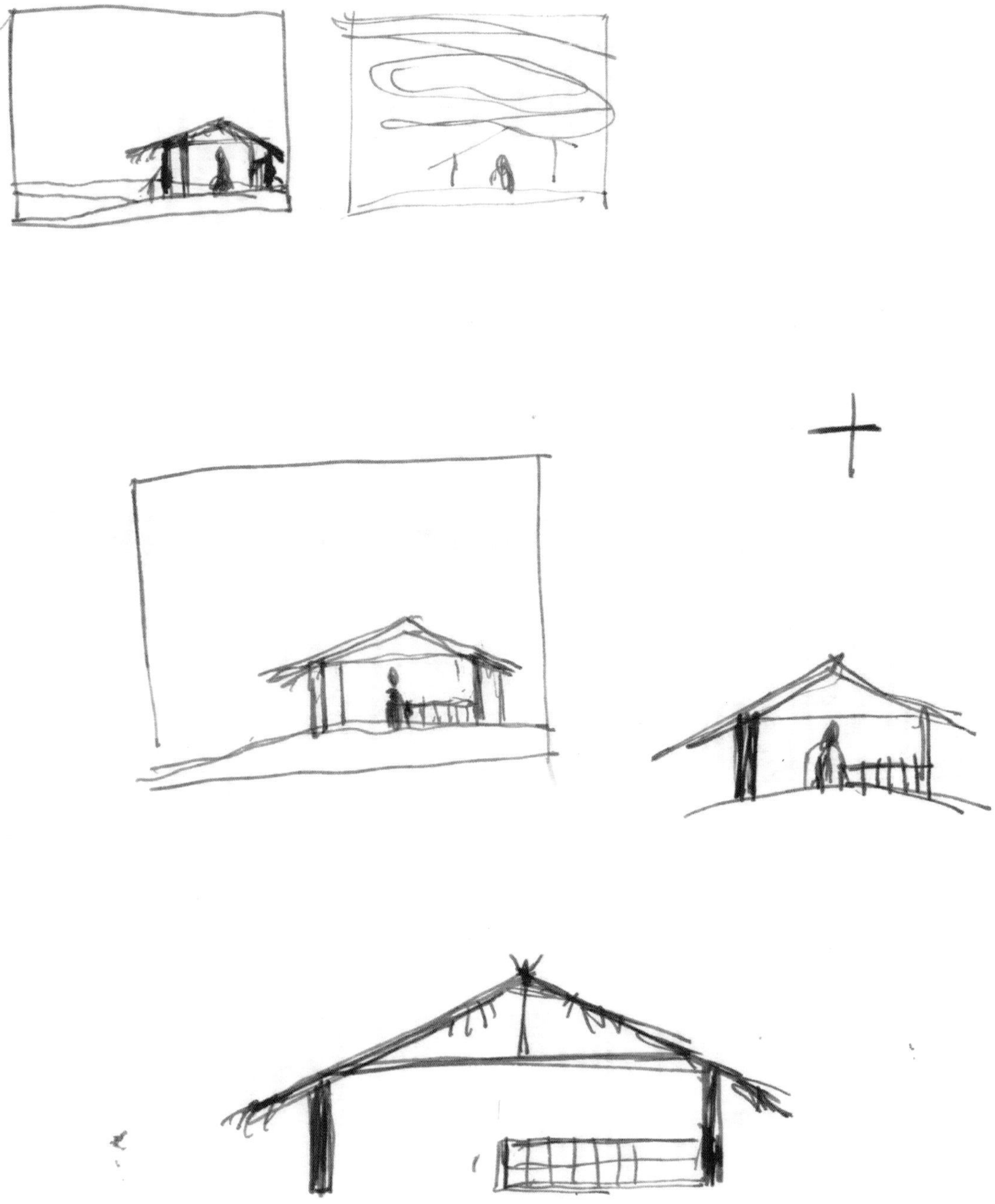

ABOVE: Unidentified storyboards; scan supplied for publication

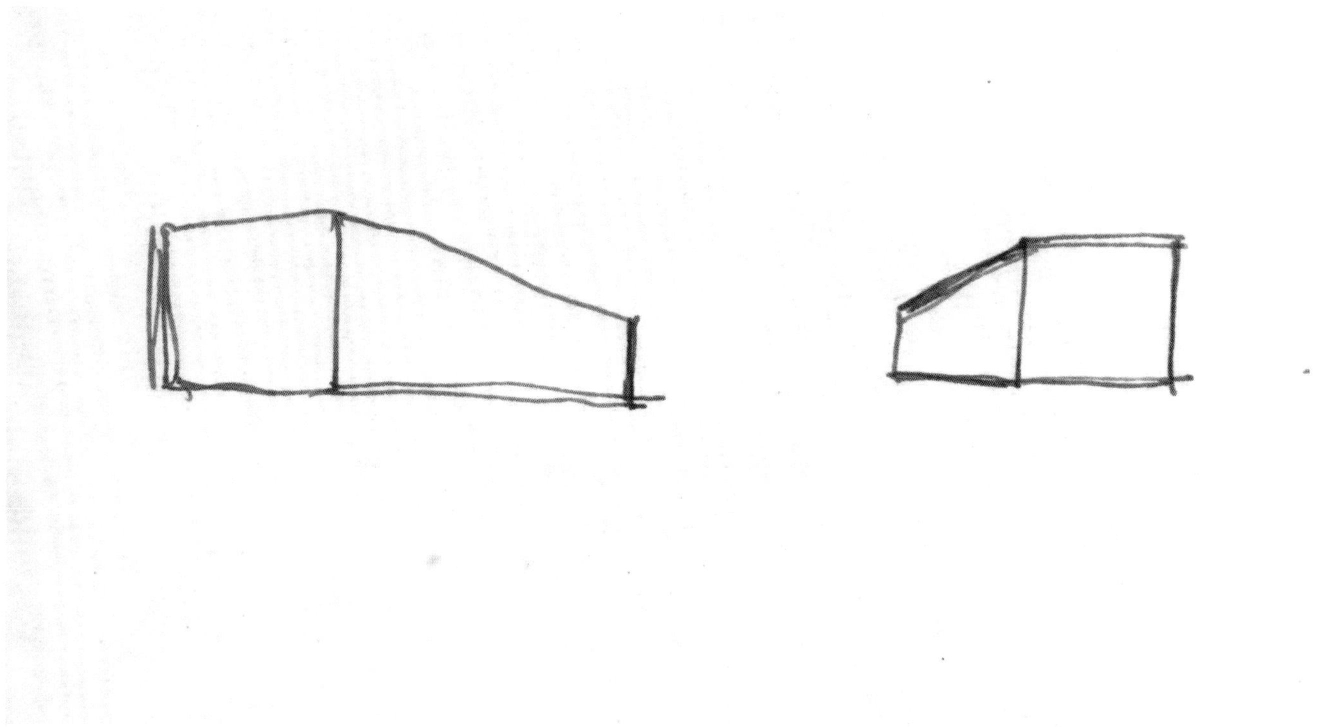

ABOVE: Unidentified sketch; scan supplied for publication

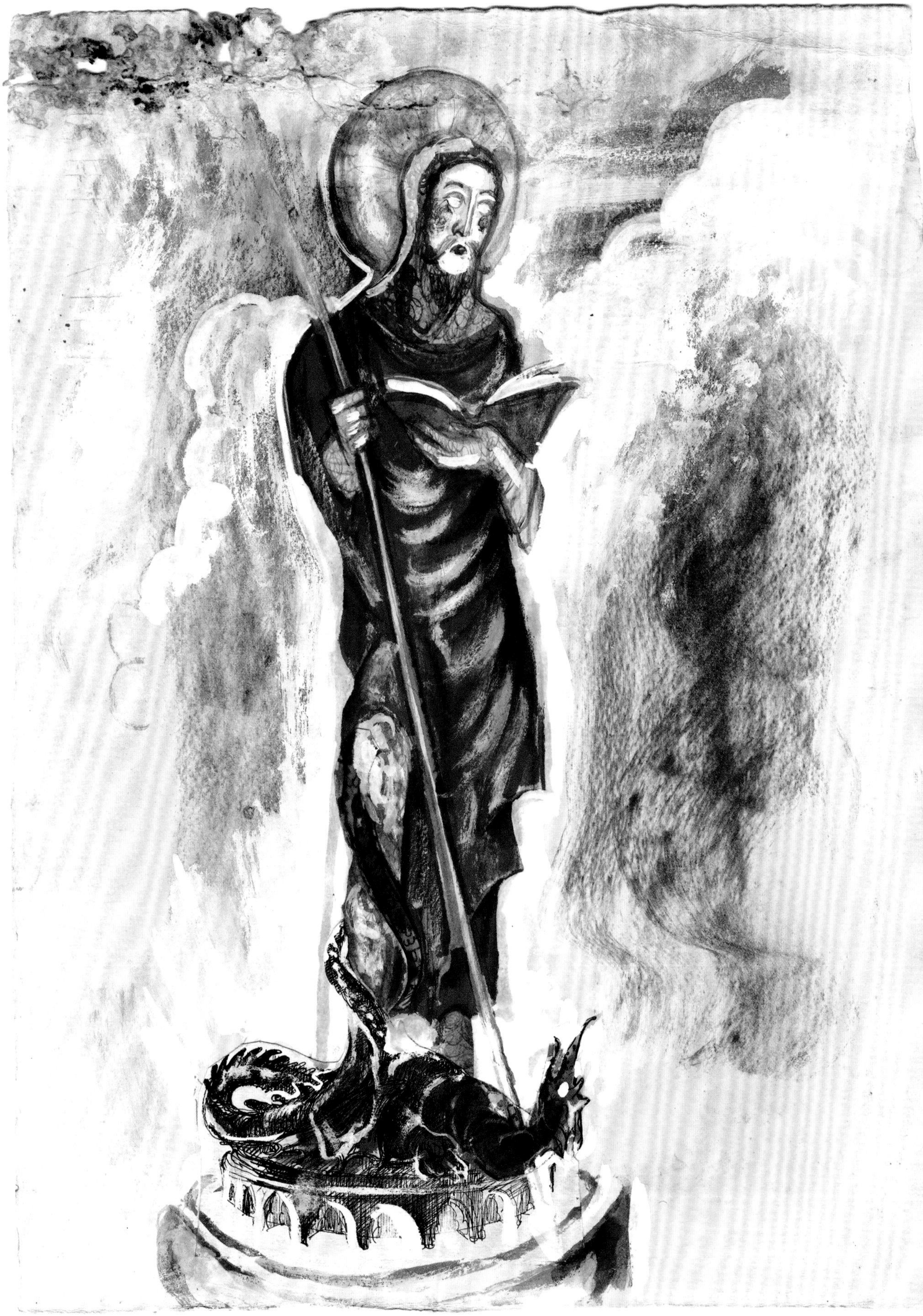

ABOVE: Unidentified St. George slaying the dragon statue watercolor sketch; original scanned for publication

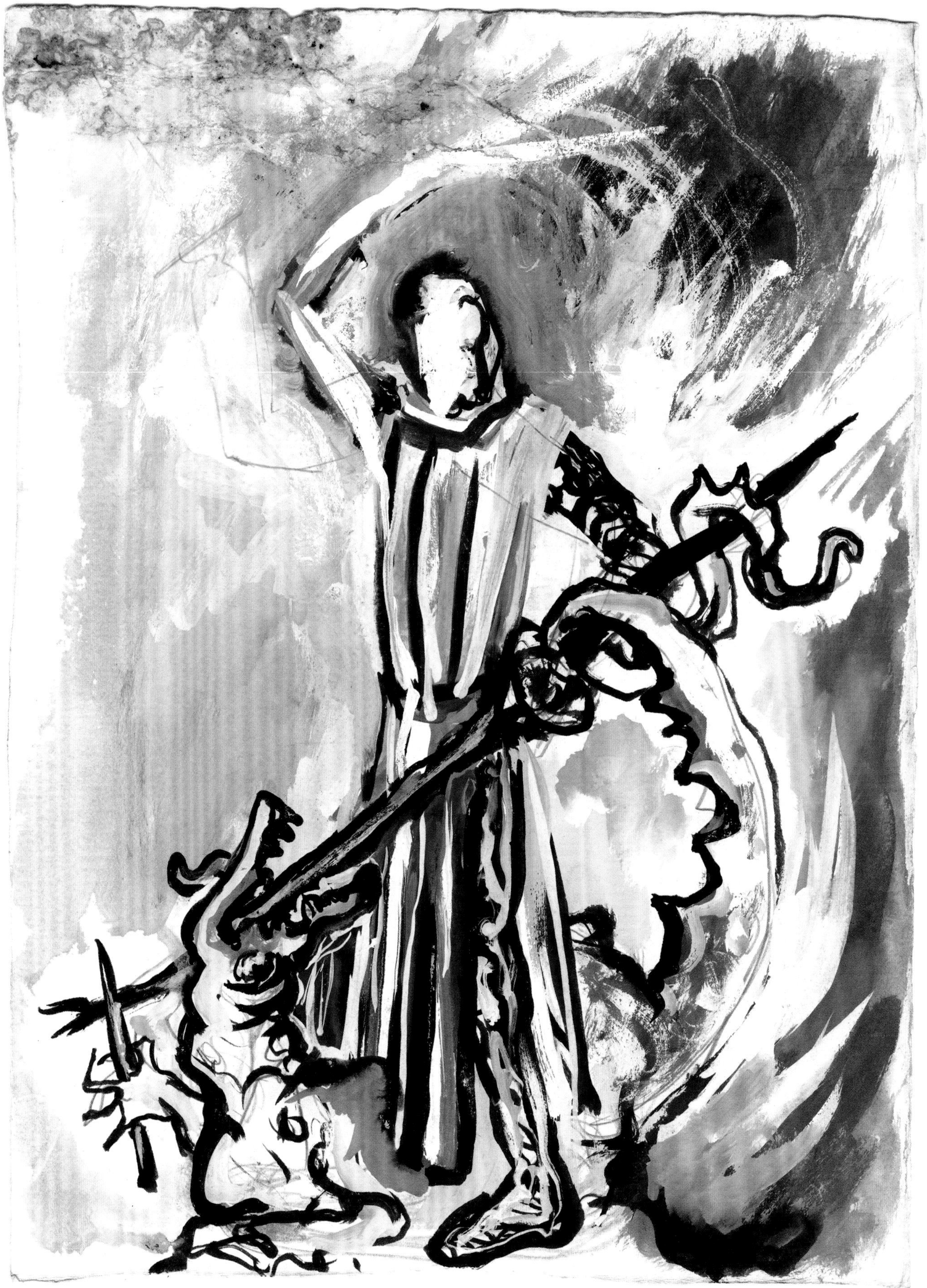

ABOVE: Unidentified St. George slaying the dragon statue watercolor sketch; original scanned for publication

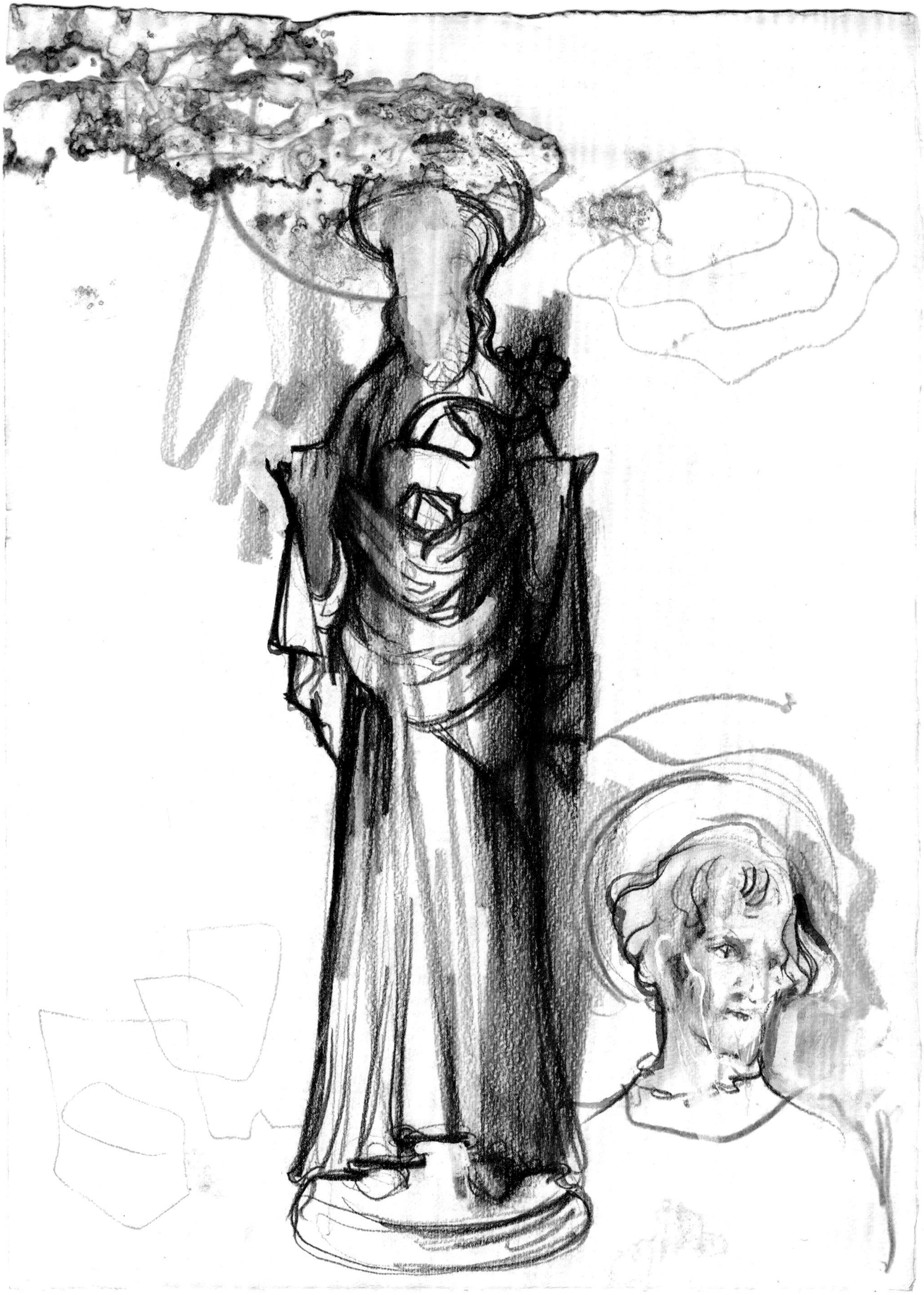

ABOVE: Unidentified St. Francis statue watercolor sketch; original scanned for publication

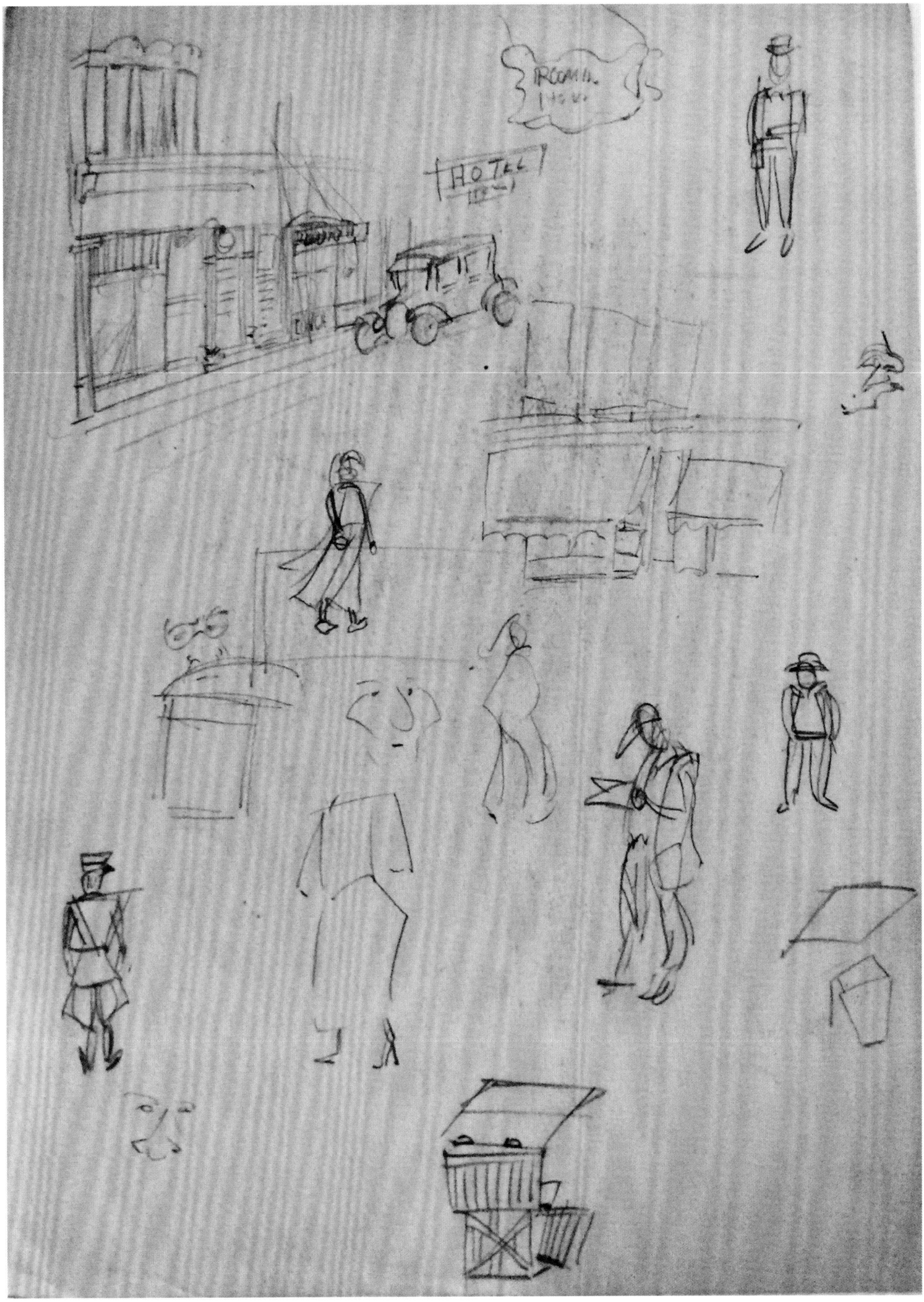

ABOVE: Unidentified sketch; scan supplied for publication

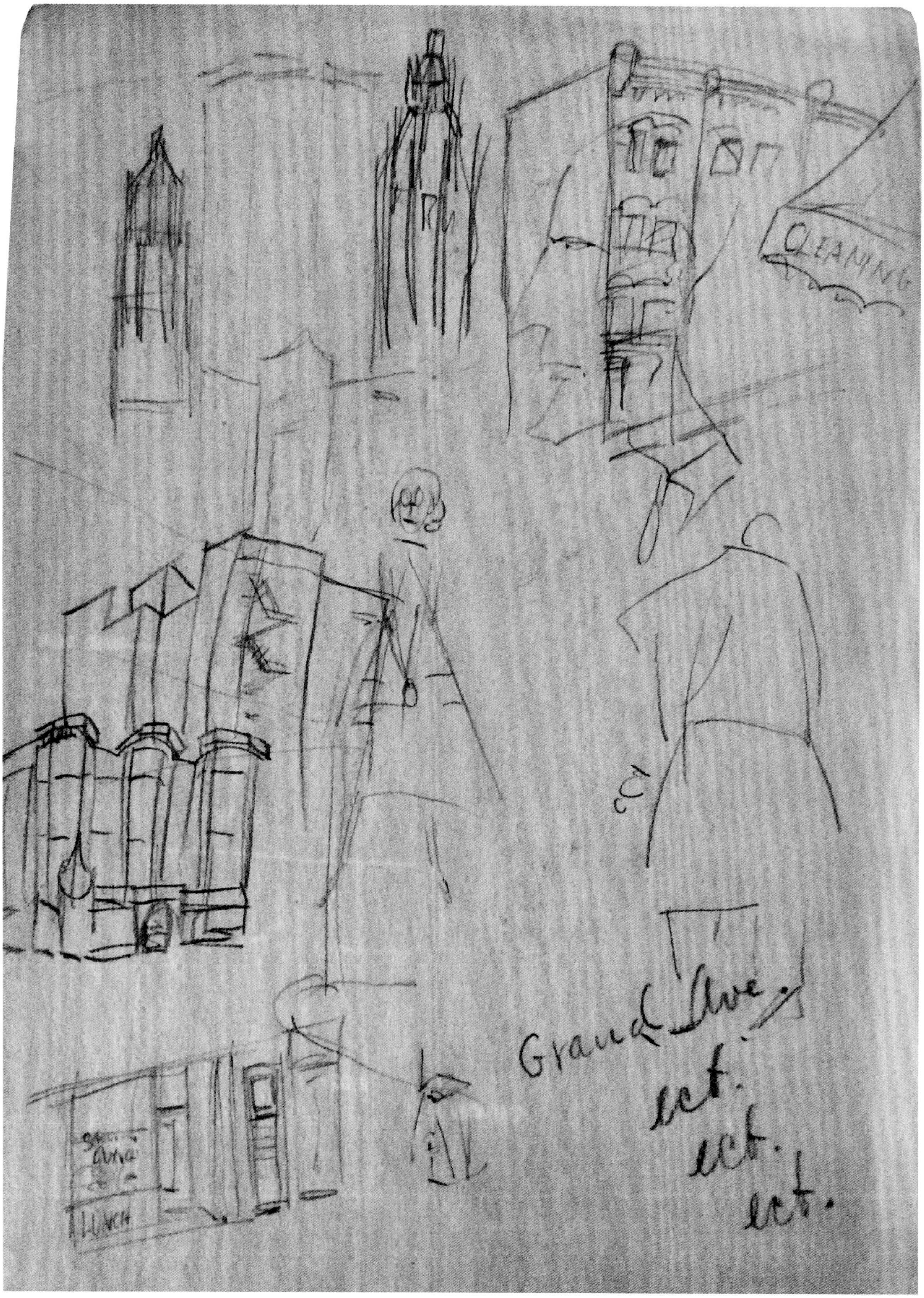

ABOVE: Unidentified sketch; scan supplied for publication

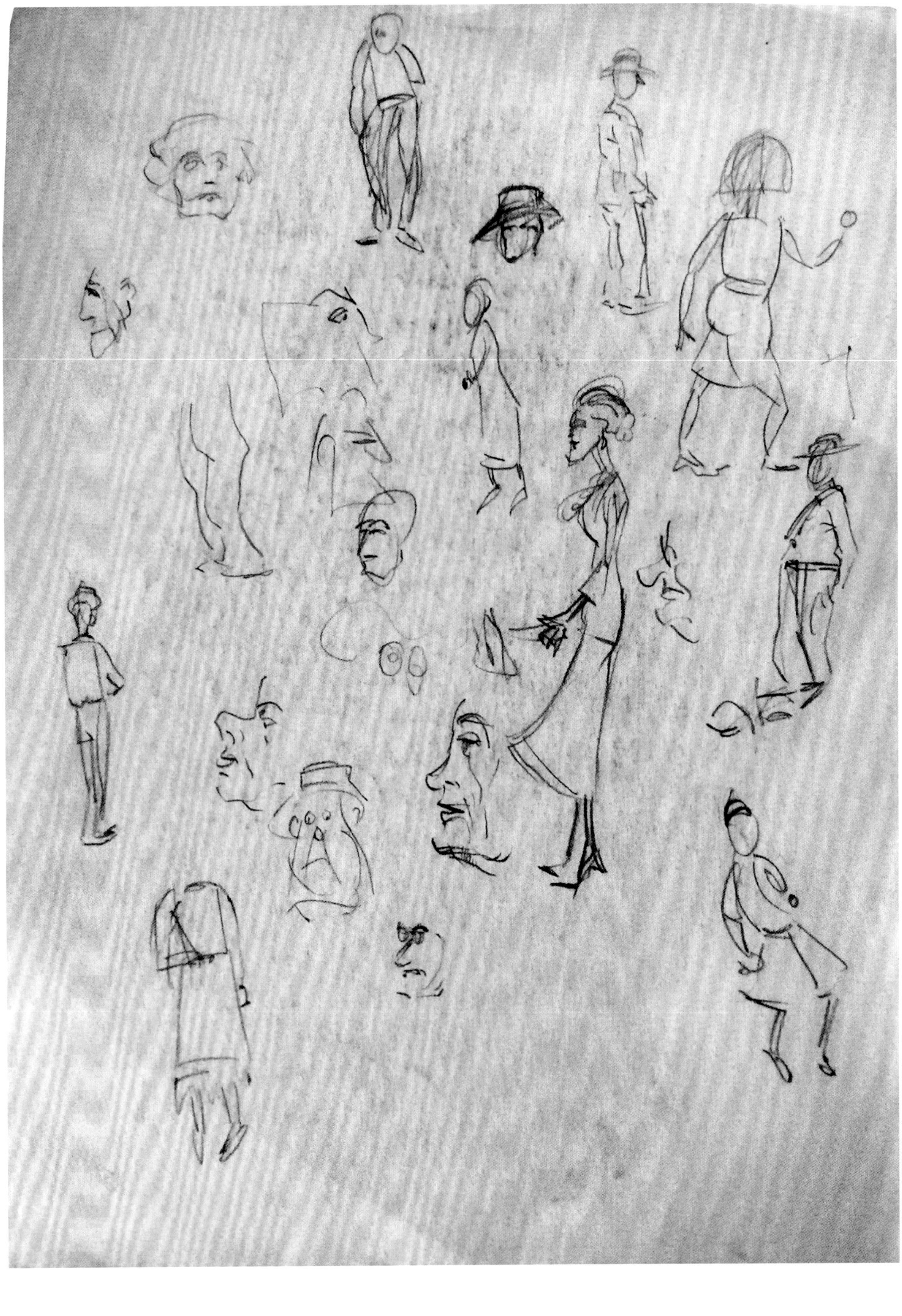

ABOVE: Unidentified sketch; scan supplied for publication

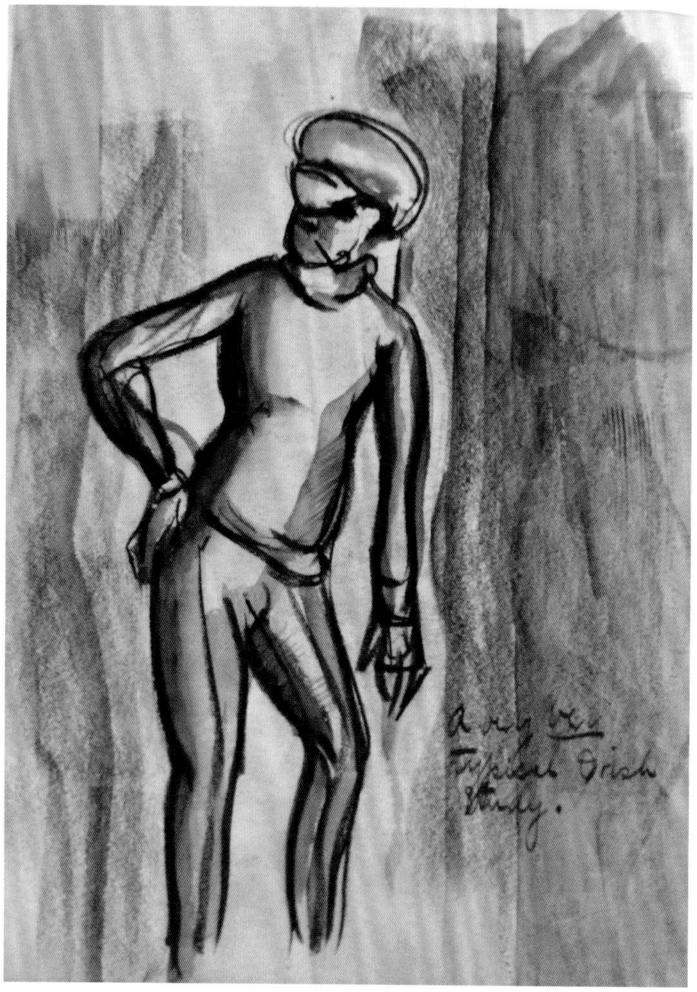

IRELAND

Welles's globe-trotting lifestyle began early. Before he was in his teens, his alcoholic father decided that the small fortune he'd made as an inventor would be best spent funding his carousing, which he did on a global scale, usually with his young son in tow. Before he enrolled in high school, Welles had visited China, Japan, Jamaica, Cuba and an assortment of European capitals, Budapest being a particular favorite. In later life, he traveled extensively, partly to satisfy his own wanderlust and partly in the unceasing pursuit of financing for his film projects.

In late summer of 1931, at the tender age of sixteen – if he can be said to have had a tender age – Welles was packed off on a painting tour of Ireland. It was hoped by his legal guardian, Dr. Maurice Bernstein, a slightly shady character who had assumed the role on Welles's father's death in December 1930, that the trip would distract him from a worrying obsession with the theater and point him in the direction of a traditional education. It was a plan that backfired in spectacular fashion.

Welles landed in Galway and from there set out on a journey of discovery aboard a cart pulled by a donkey he named Sidheog (pronounced Sheeog). He was instantly besotted with the country, indulging in the hospitality of its people and enthralled by its unspoiled landscapes and ancient mythology. Making up his own itinerary, he ventured as far as the Aran Islands – not coincidentally the source of inspiration for and adopted home of Irish playwright J.M. Synge.

The journal Welles kept is liberally peppered with sketches, but he destroyed the paintings he did there. His true passion, despite his protestations to the contrary, was always the theater. With that in mind, he traded Sidheog and the cart in for a bicycle named Ulysses and plotted a course for Dublin. Almost on arrival he engineered a meeting with the co-founders of the Gate Theatre, Hilton Edwards and Micheál MacLiammóir. Claiming he was two years older than he actually was and a veteran of the American stage – a story that neither Edwards nor MacLiammóir believed a word of – he somehow persuaded them to give him an audition. And the rest, as they say…

ABOVE: Sketch; scan supplied for publication

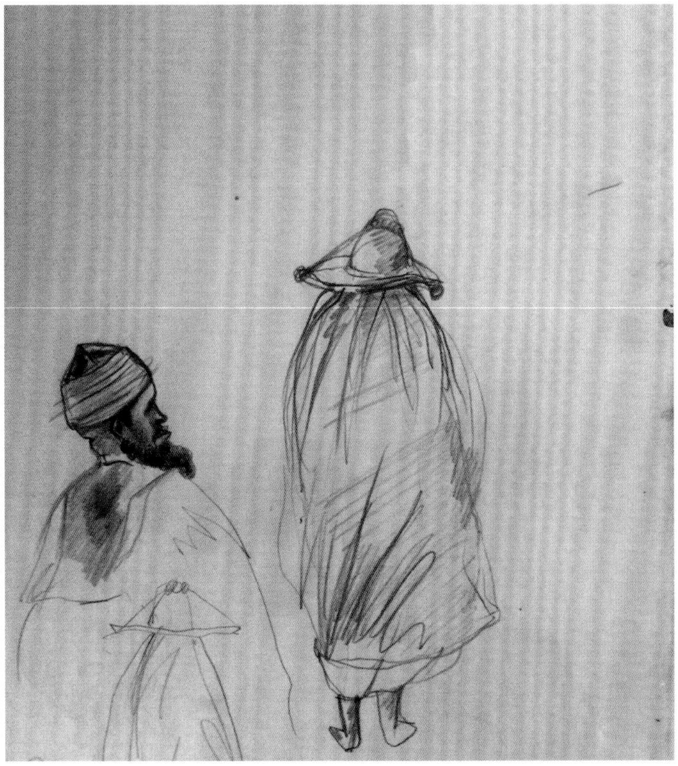

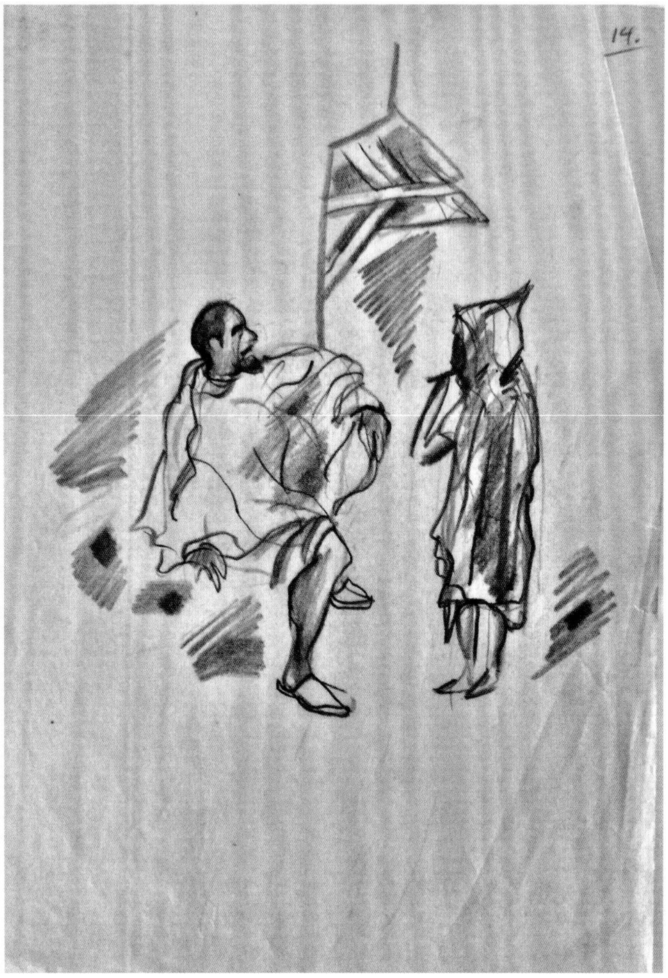

MOROCCO

In 1933, to remedy the sense of ennui that had afflicted him since graduating from the Todd School, Welles booked a second-class passage on board the American Export Lines freighter *Exermont* and headed for Morocco. Laden down with volumes of Elizabethan drama, his plan was to write and draw the illustrations for the *Everybody's Shakespeare* book while exploring the country, an extremely intrepid undertaking in those days.

According to Welles, he landed in Tangier, where he met and befriended an elderly Dutchman, a curator of the Rijksmuseum. It was through this rather mysterious Dutchman that he came to enjoy the lavish hospitality of Thami El-Glaoui, the legendary Pasha of Marrakech. This, claimed Welles, included feasting, dancing, daily picnics and, at night, the attentions of the Thami's concubines. That he found time to do any sketching at all is a miracle.

Another less colorful version of events is that Welles actually landed in Casablanca, where he stayed for a while in a house owned by the Coca-Cola Company, of which Thami El-Glaoui was vice-president. From there, he traveled to Tangier and then on to Seville.

ABOVE: Sketches; scans supplied for publication

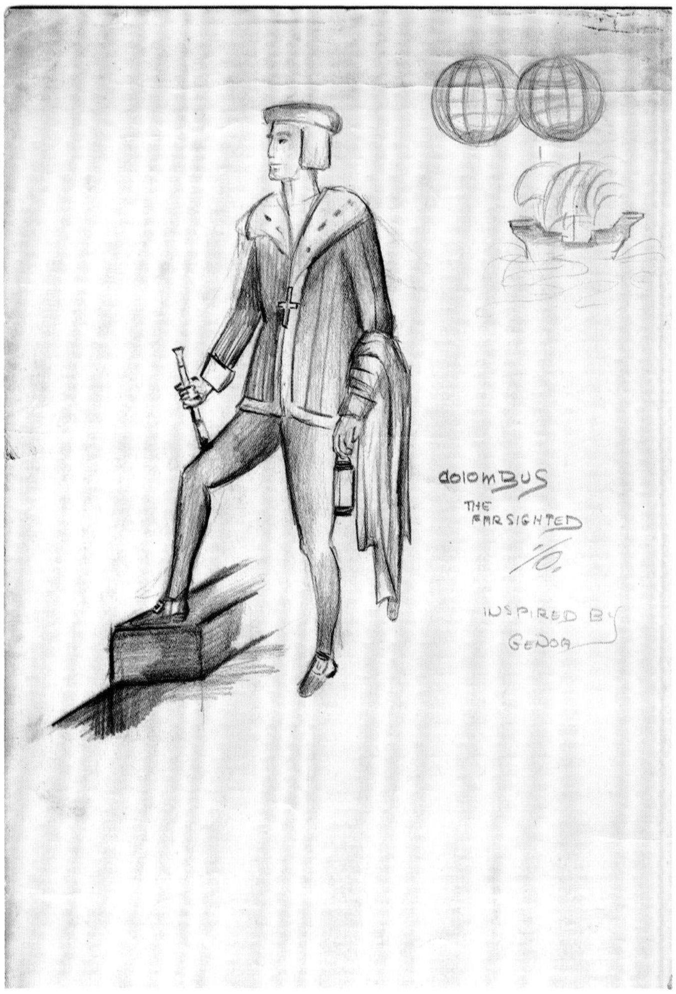

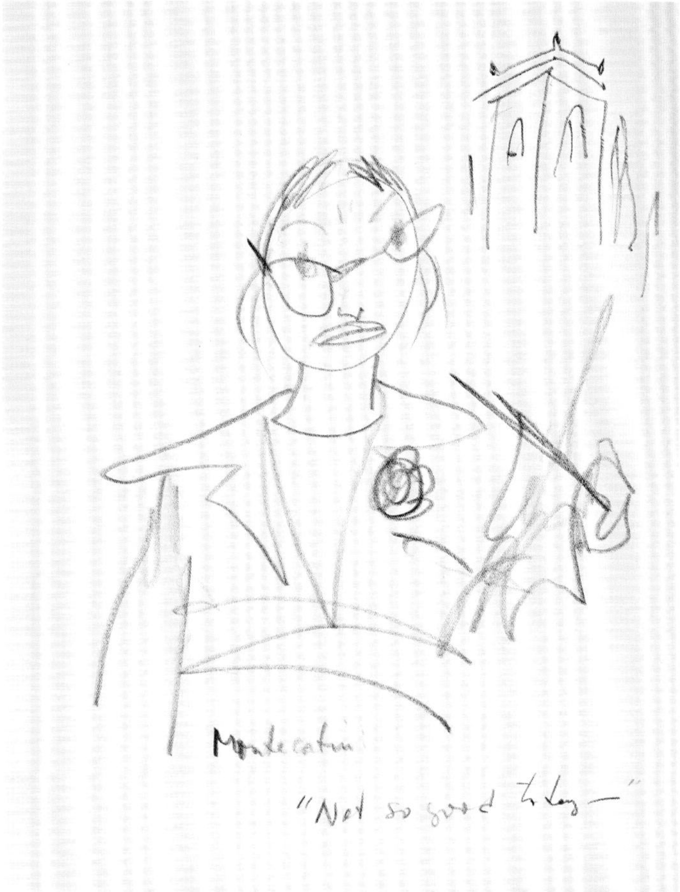

ABOVE: Genoa pencil drawing; original scanned for publication

ABOVE: Montecatini sketch of Paola; photo supplied for publication

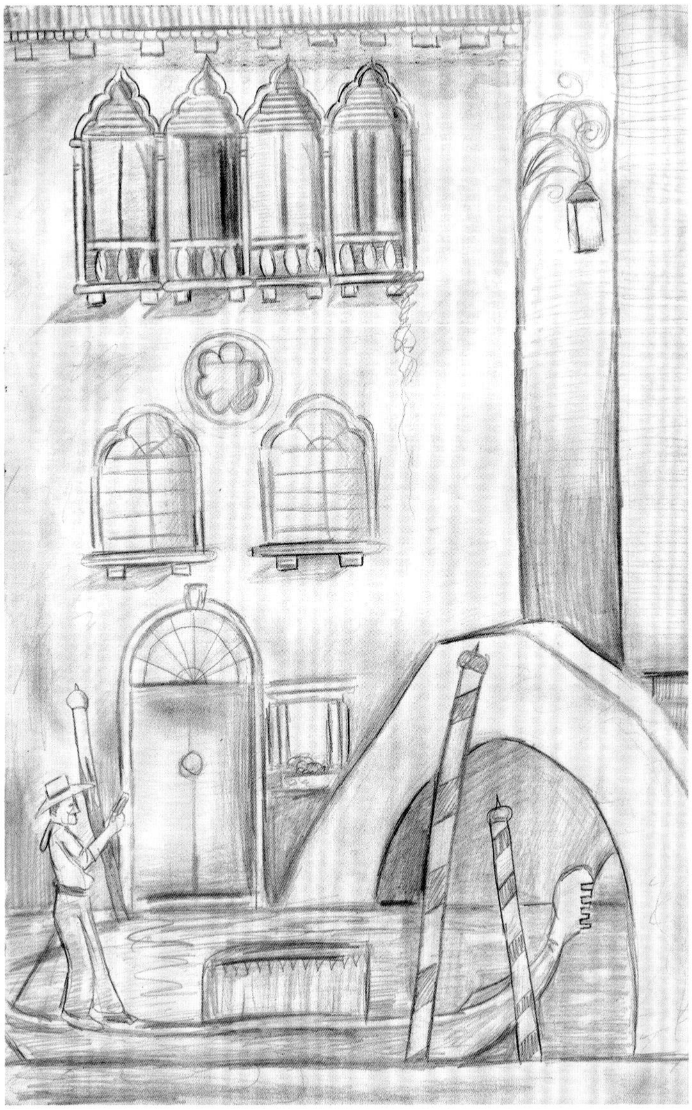

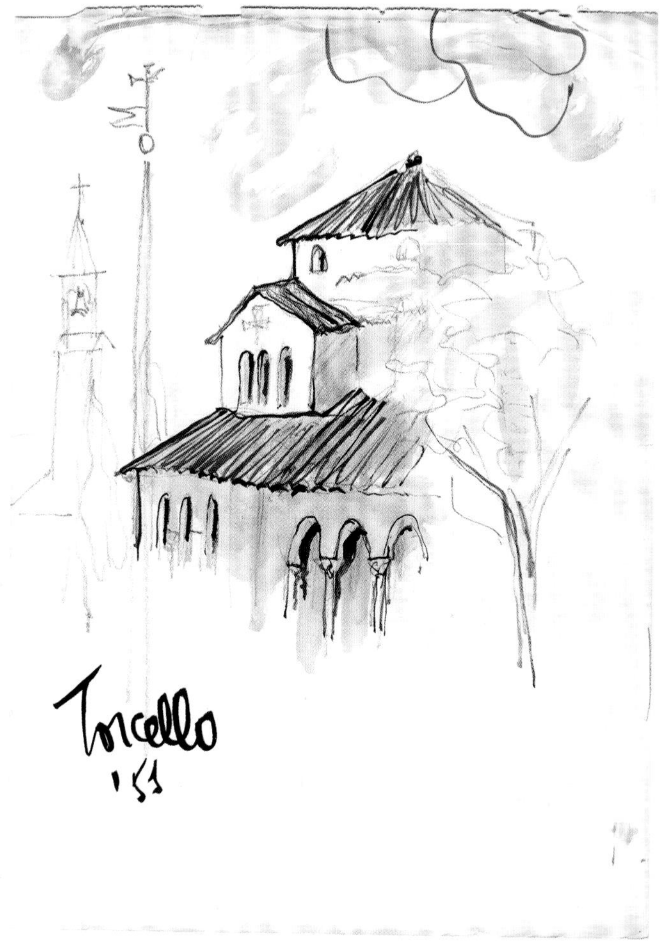

VENICE, ITALY

Although Welles spent a good deal of time in Venice, it was not, according to his daughter Beatrice, among his favorite places. 'He thought it was beautiful architecturally,' she says, 'and he filmed a lot of *Othello* there. But it was never a case of, "Ooh, let's all go to Venice!" When he was there it was always because there was something going on: the film festival or a meeting with someone or a film he was shooting. I went with him often, and it's not my favorite place in the world either. It's very beautiful, but I find it depressing and eerie, and a bit smelly.'

ABOVE: Venice pencil drawing and Torcello, Venice watercolor sketch; originals scanned for publication

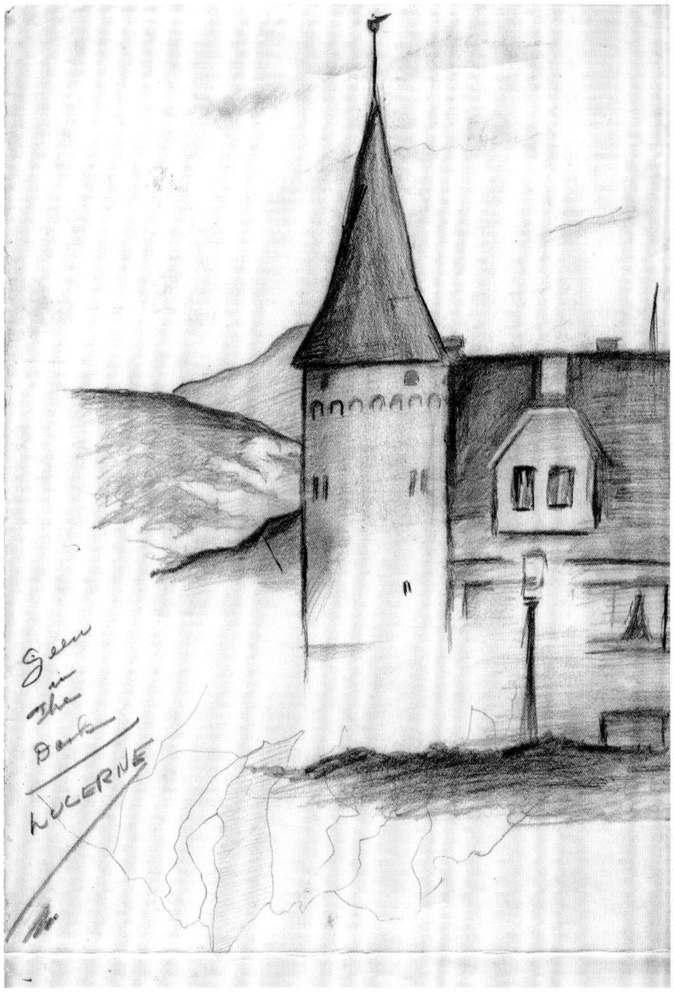

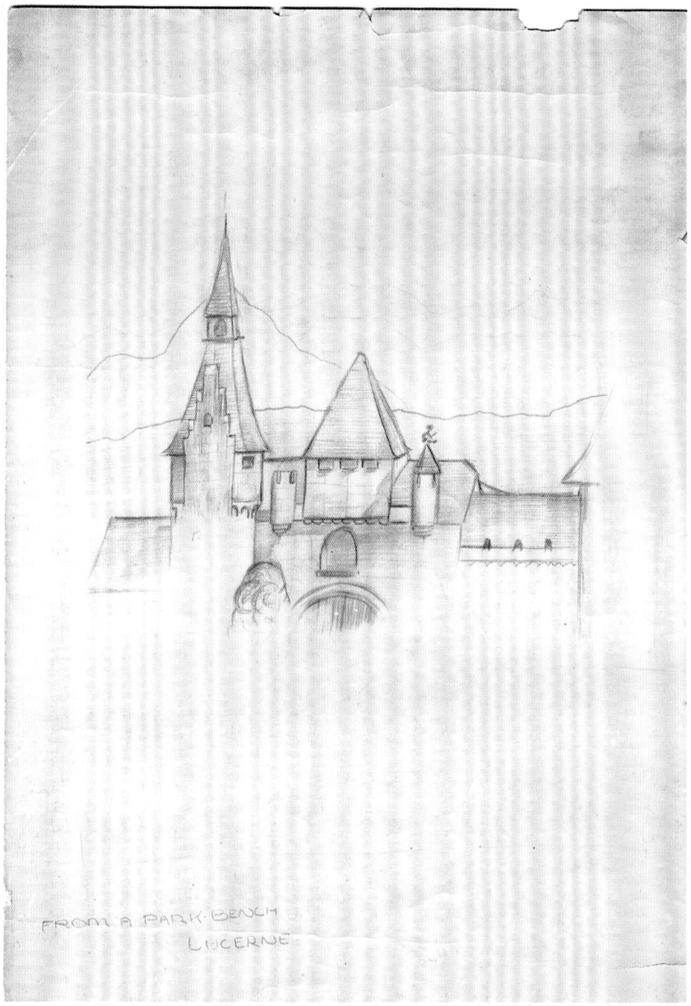

SWITZERLAND

Although the sketches are of Lucerne, Welles's regular haunt in Switzerland – certainly in the late 1950s and early 1960s – was actually the ski resort of Klosters. 'We went there for years,' recalls his daughter Beatrice, 'because a lot of his friends would be there, people like Deborah Kerr and Peter Viertel [author and screenwriter, and Kerr's second husband]. We rented a house one year, but mostly stayed at the Hotel Walserhof, where Prince Charles stays.'

ABOVE: Lucerne pencil drawings; originals scanned for publication

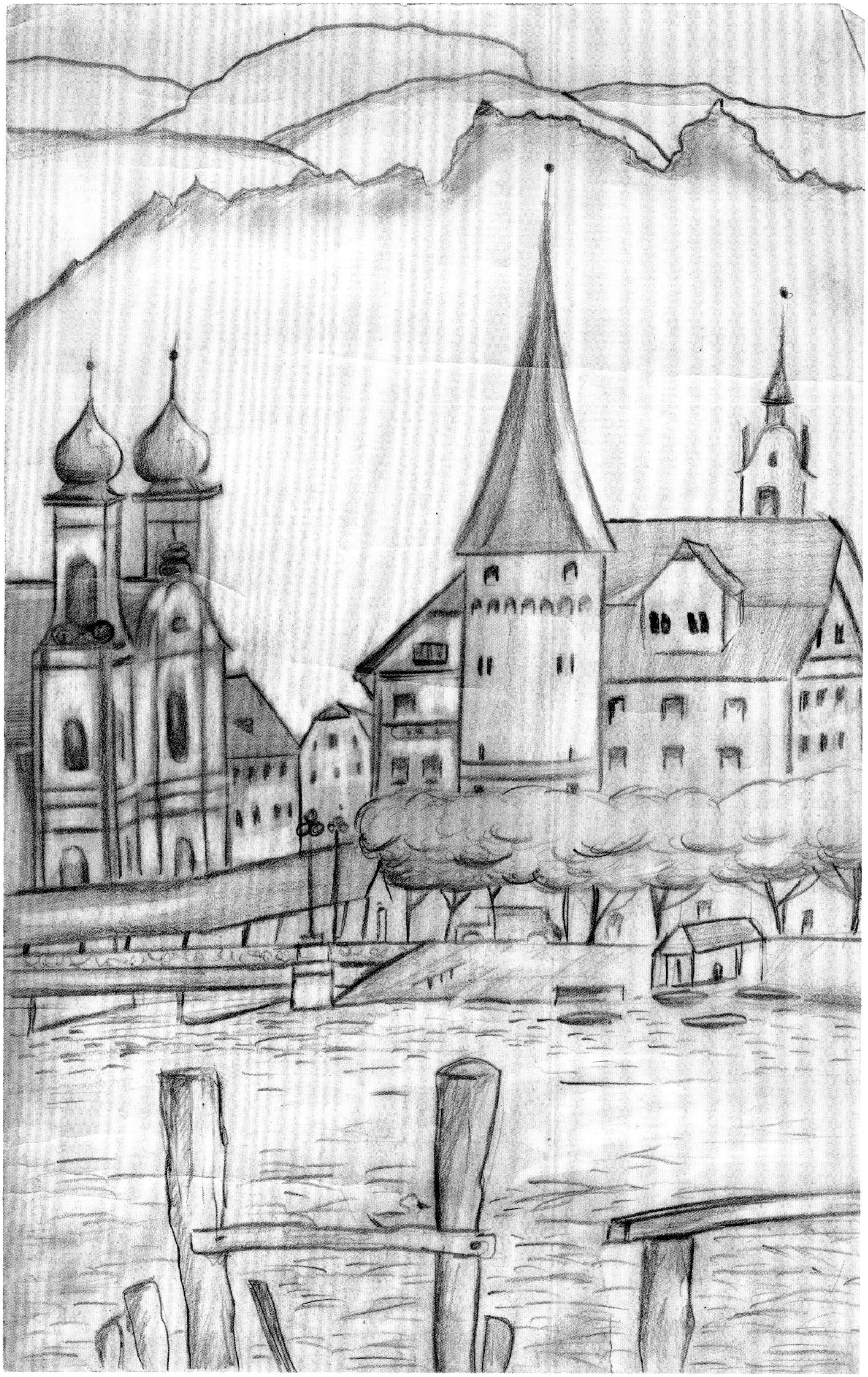

ABOVE: Lucerne pencil drawing; original scanned for publication

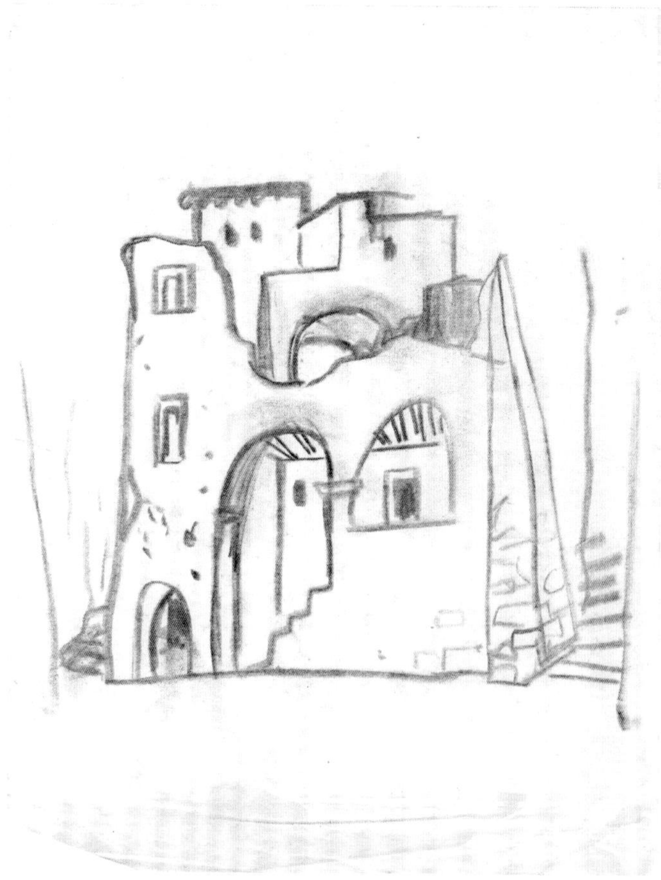

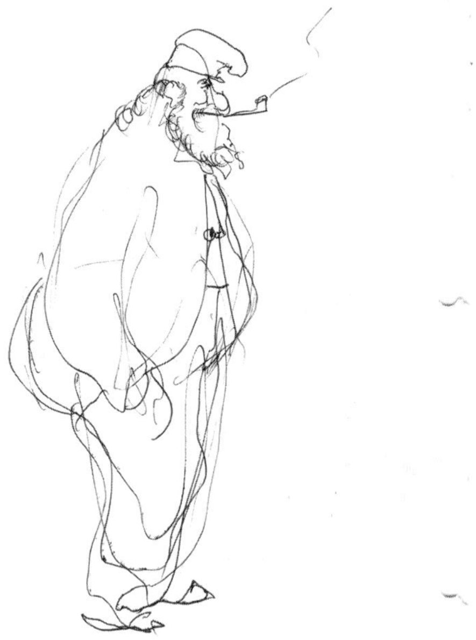

ABOVE: Sketches; originals scanned for publication

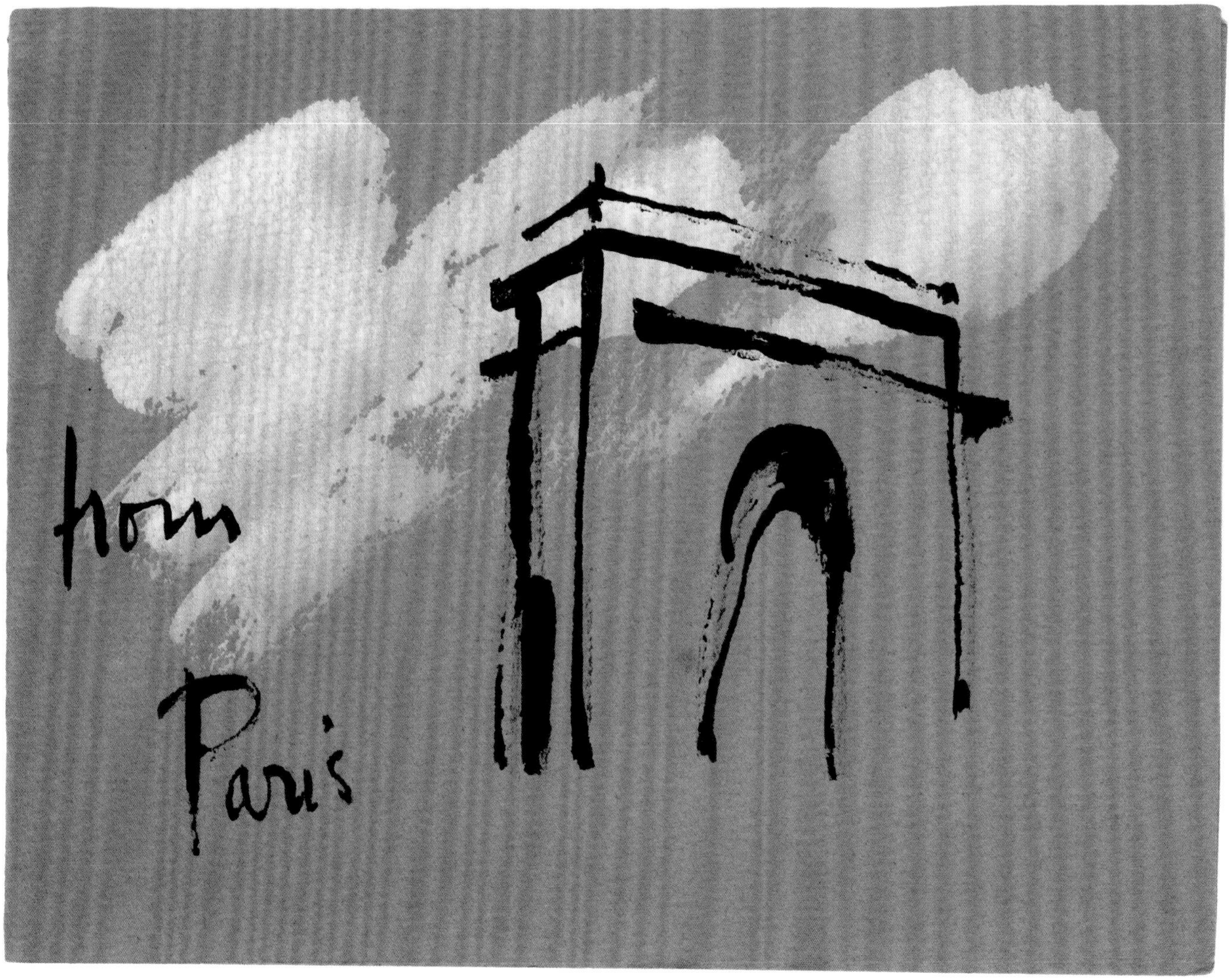

PARIS, FRANCE

Welles visited Paris for the first time in 1931, shortly after his adventures in Ireland and a brief stay in London. According to one biographer, he spent his time there 'Drinking, dining and attending parties.' He returned many times throughout his life, never settling, but enjoying the best of its deluxe hotels. He filmed an episode of his TV series *Around the World with Orson Welles* there in 1955, in which he was seen visiting Jean Cocteau and the singer Juliette Gréco.

The longest period Welles spent in Paris was in 1962 when he was filming his adaptation of Franz Kafka's *The Trial*, a location shoot that put the vast, empty interiors of the derelict Gare d'Orsay to spectacularly dramatic use.

ABOVE: Paris postcard; original scanned for publication

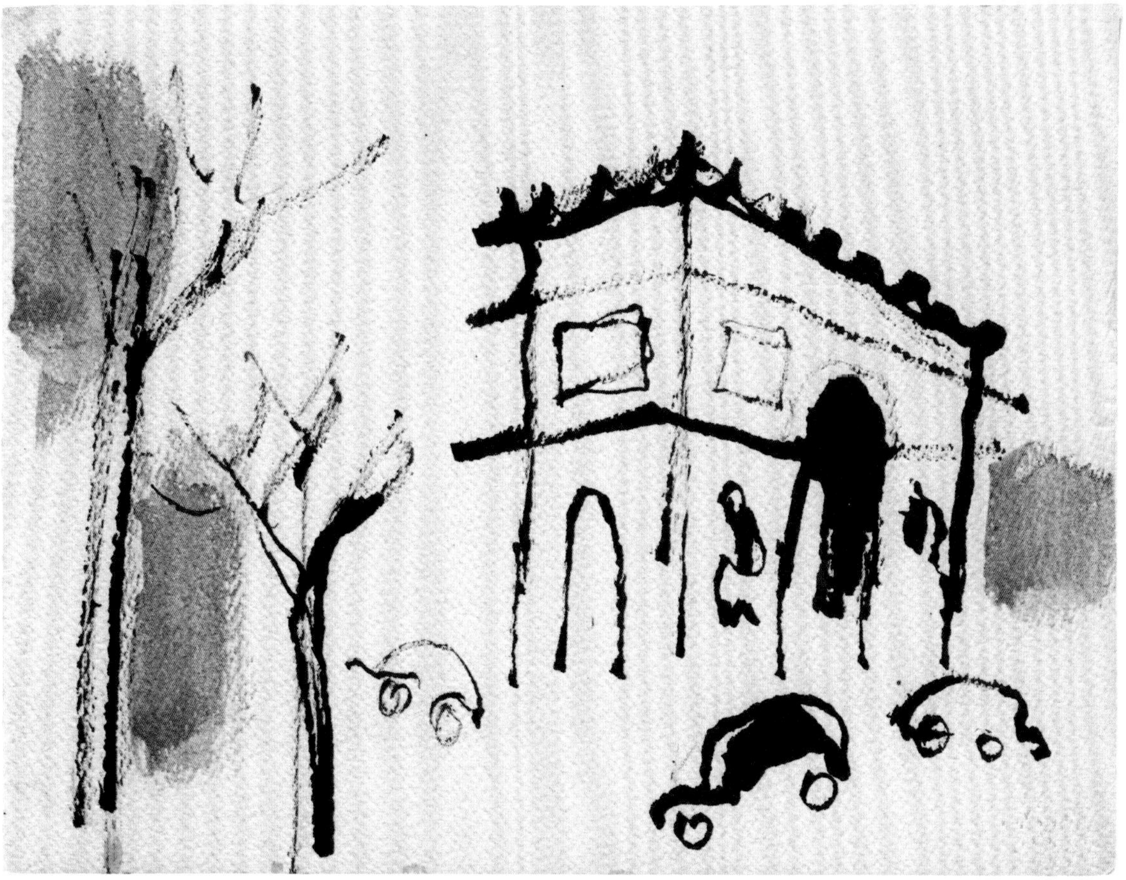

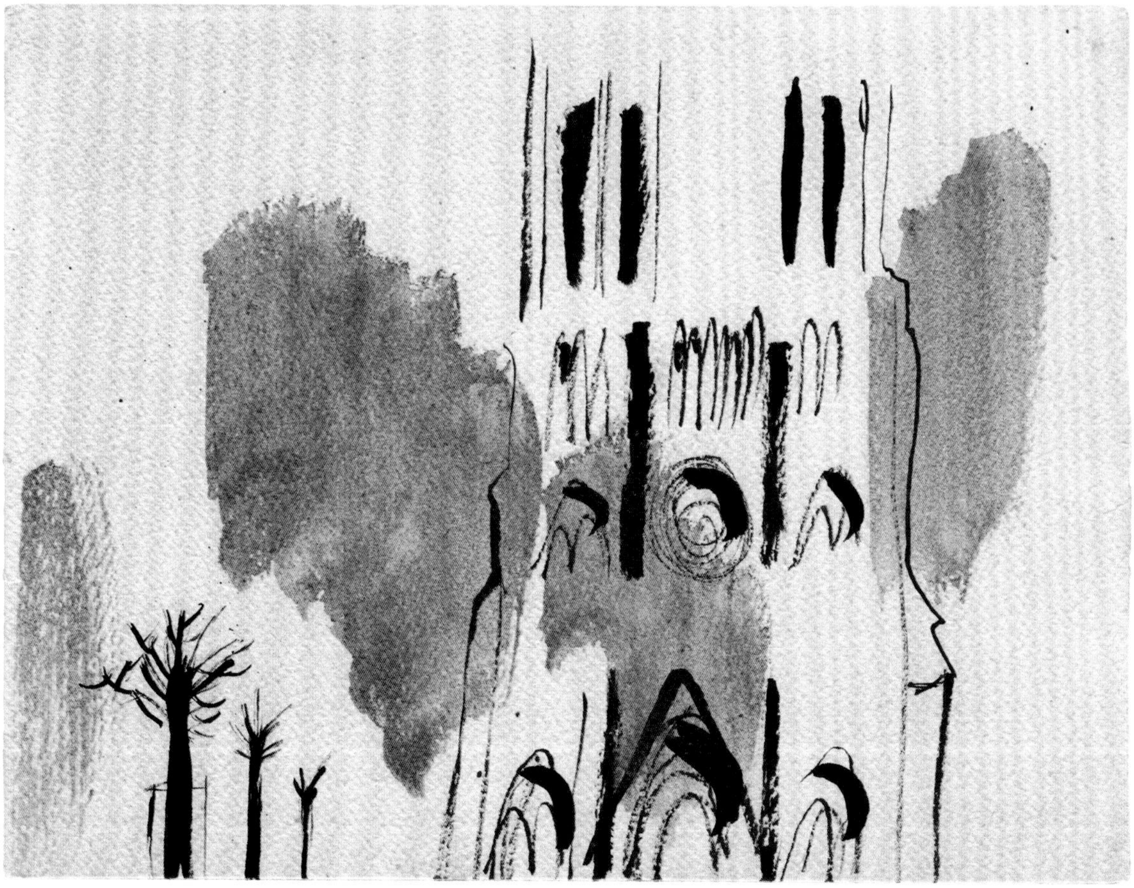

ABOVE: Paris postcards; originals scanned for publication

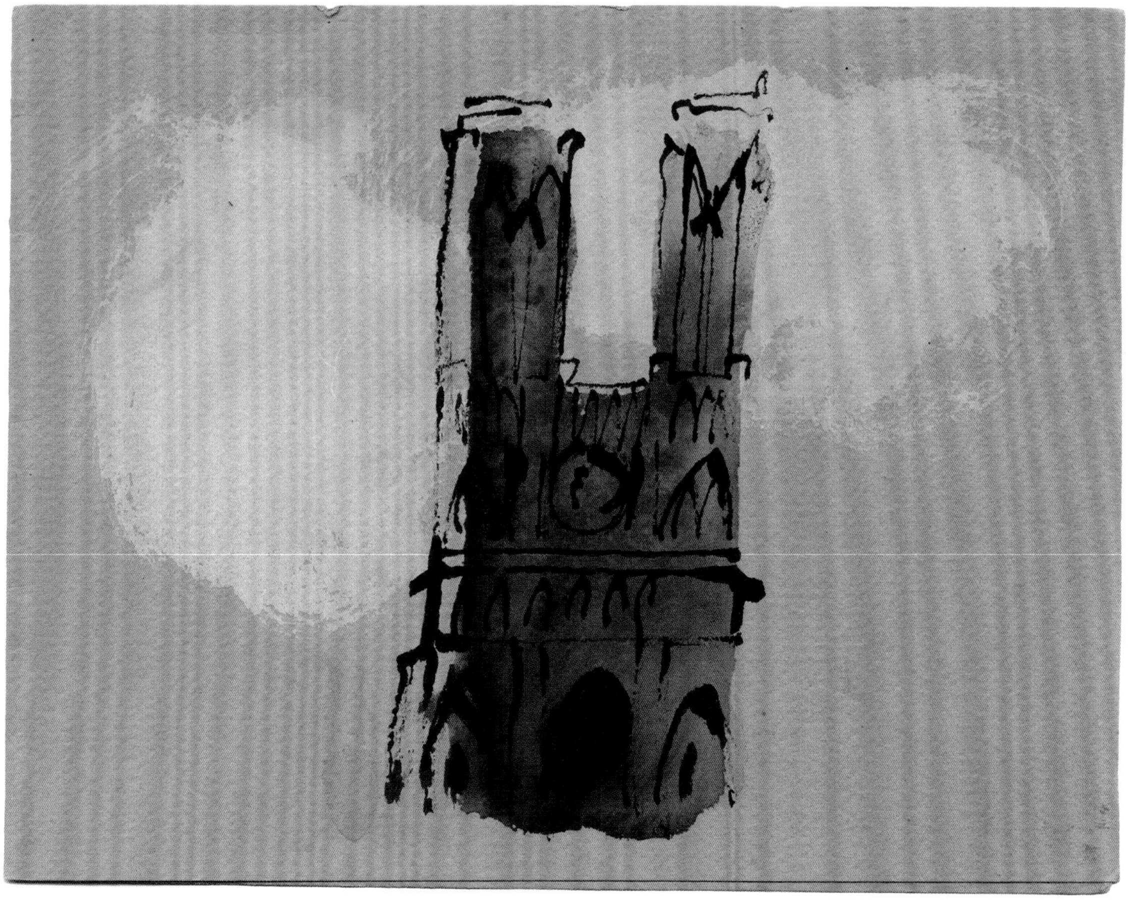

ABOVE: Paris postcards; originals scanned for publication

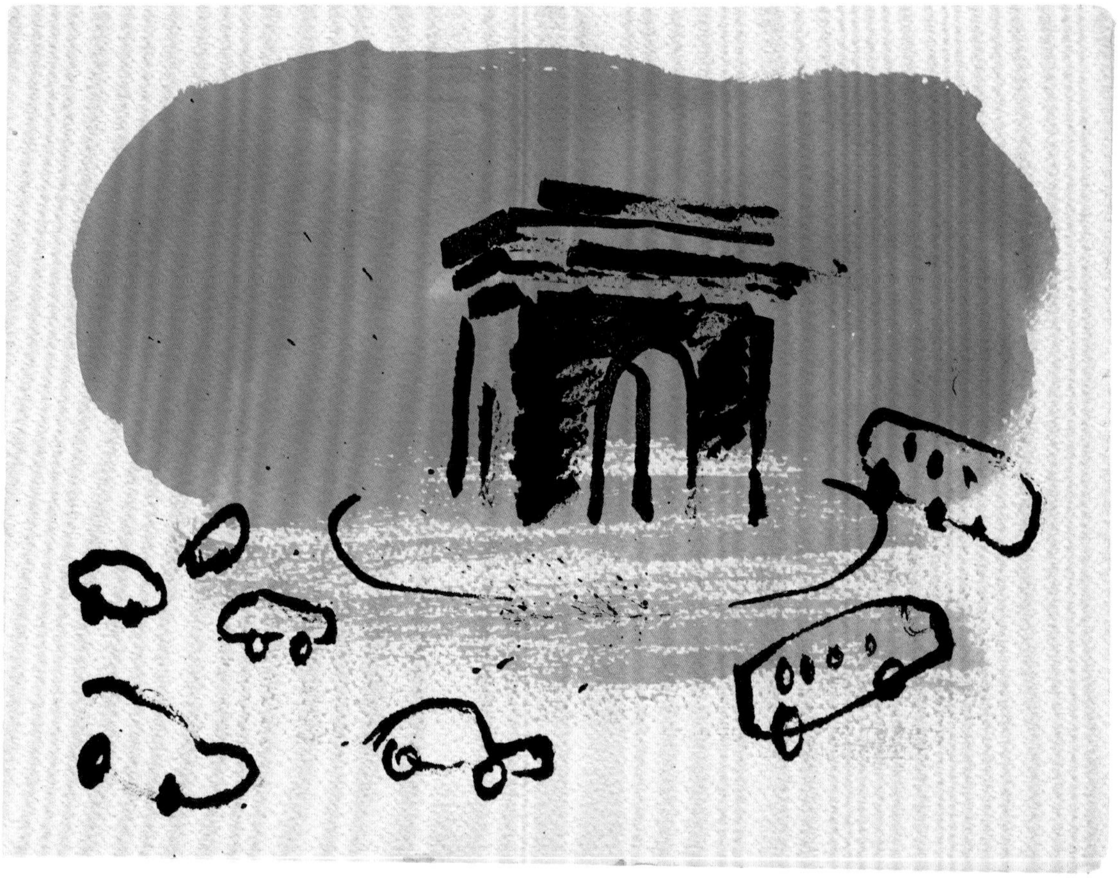

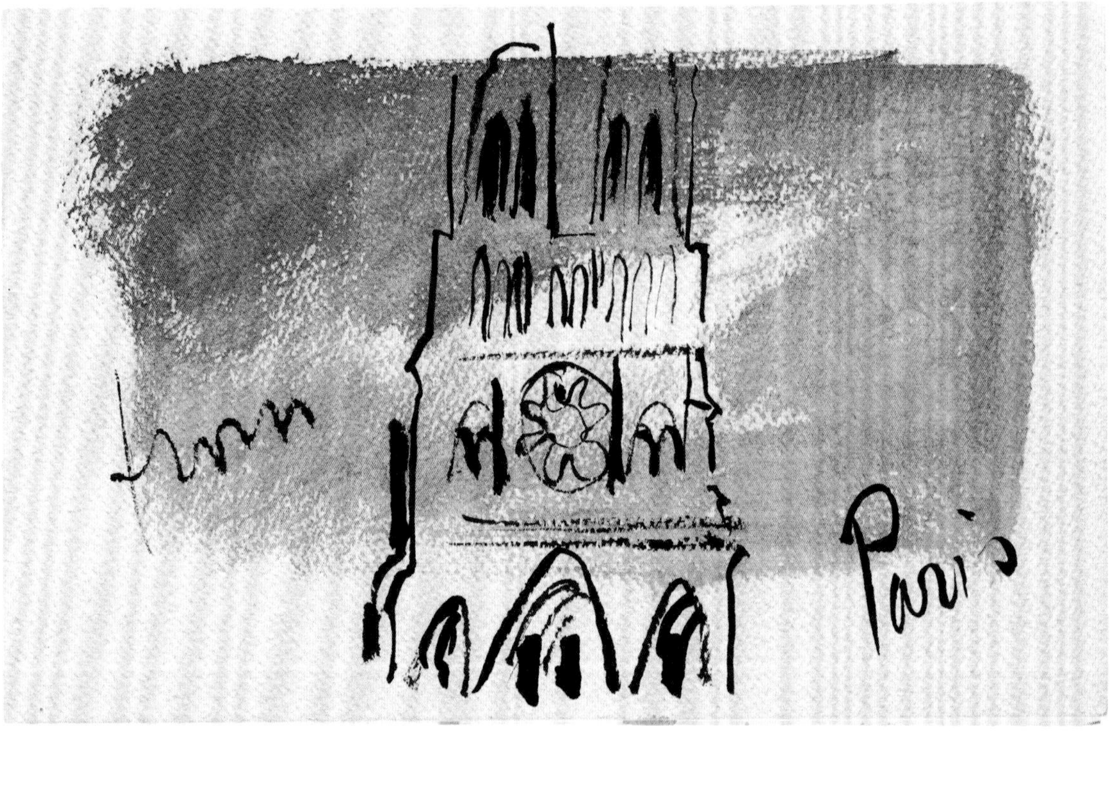

ABOVE: Paris postcards; originals scanned for publication

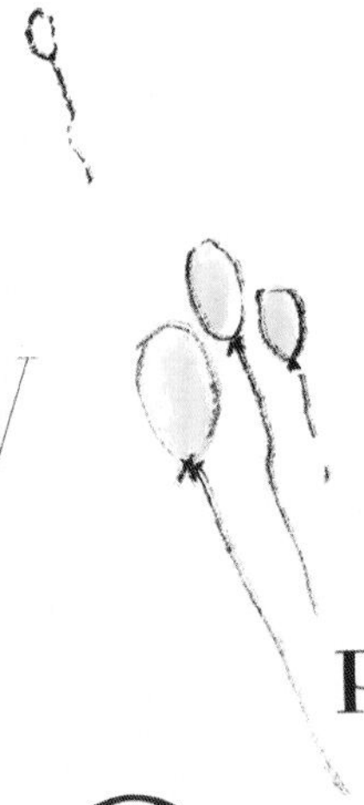

VOGUE
PAR
ORSON WELLES

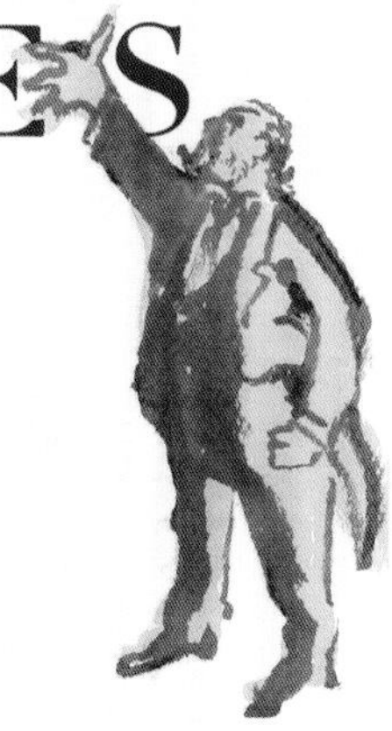

As the darling of the *Cahiers du Cinéma* crowd, Welles's stock was always buoyant in France even while it nosedived elsewhere. In 1982, he was asked to guest edit the Christmas edition of *Vogue Paris*. The invitation came with the assurance that he could say whatever he liked. Welles took them at their word.

The cover photograph depicts him as a stage magician in mid-levitation. Inside, the copy makes much of the notion that magicians were the founding fathers of cinema. The issue is respectfully dedicated to the greatest of them all, the 'incomparable Georges Méliès.'

In short order, however, with Welles appearing to be in conversation with himself, the subject of magicians and the 'animated photographs' they inspired is jettisoned in favor of American politics and its increasing overlap with show business. 'The last time I saw our current leader,' writes Welles, referring to then-President Ronald Reagan, 'he was playing stooge to a monkey in a Universal picture called *Bedtime for Bonzo*.' Things get really interesting when he muses on the relative powerlessness of the president. 'If I was to be leader,' he says, 'I'd want to be made King of the World. Nothing Constitutional. I would only accept total, global tyranny.' This is accompanied by the absolutely marvelous caricature of King Orson, crown askew and a face like thunder (overleaf). What has sparked his glowering fury, it turns out, is Christmas – or, more accurately, the commercialization of it. He describes Santa Claus as 'A tirelessly jolly Coca-Cola salesman,' lamenting that children no longer believe in him. 'Christmas should belong to them, and them alone,' he decrees. His solution is to ban Christmas outright 'under penalty of the most serious punishment to all citizens over the age of nine.' Another illustration shows him angrily planting a spurred boot up the backside of a 'Coca-Cola Santa'.

Elsewhere, a still-glowering King Orson towers over a Christmas tree pointing an admonitory finger. There are echoes here of both Welles's illustrations for the *Everybody's Shakespeare* books and the personally drawn Christmas cards he made for friends and family.

ABOVE: Watercolor illustration; *Vogue Paris* No 632 scanned for publication

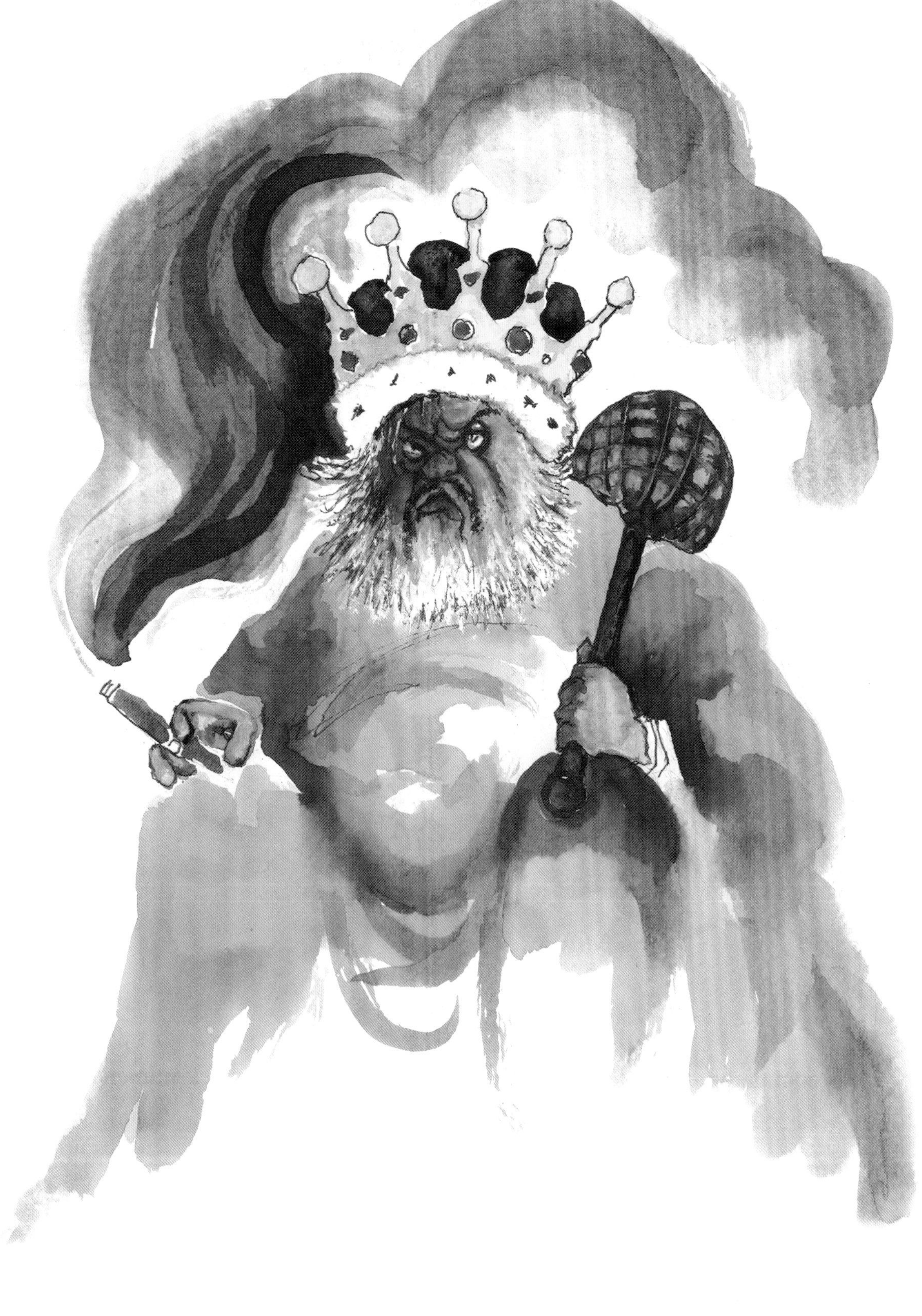

ABOVE: Watercolor illustration; *Vogue Paris* No 632 scanned for publication

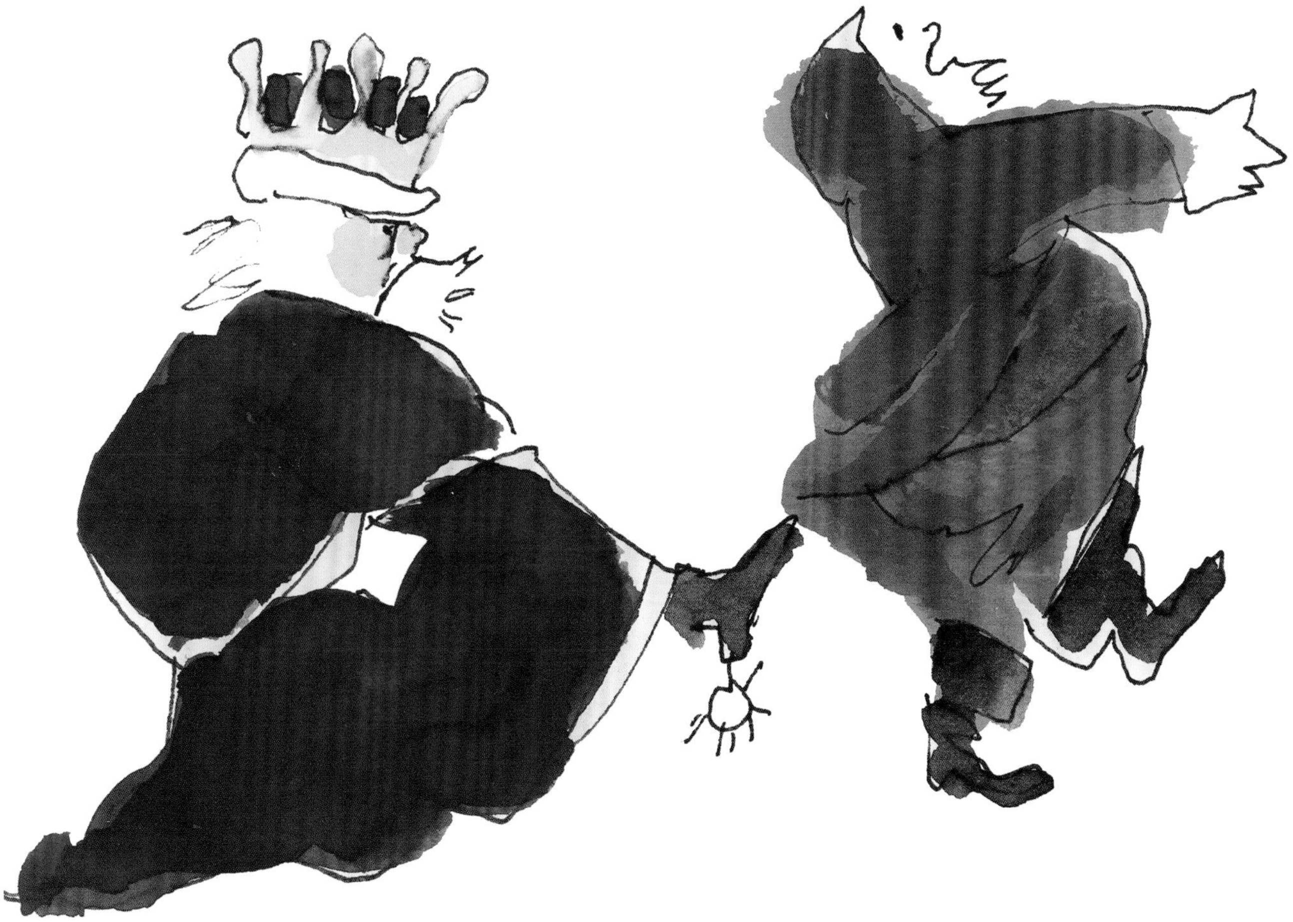

ABOVE: Watercolor illustration; *Vogue Paris* No 632 scanned for publication

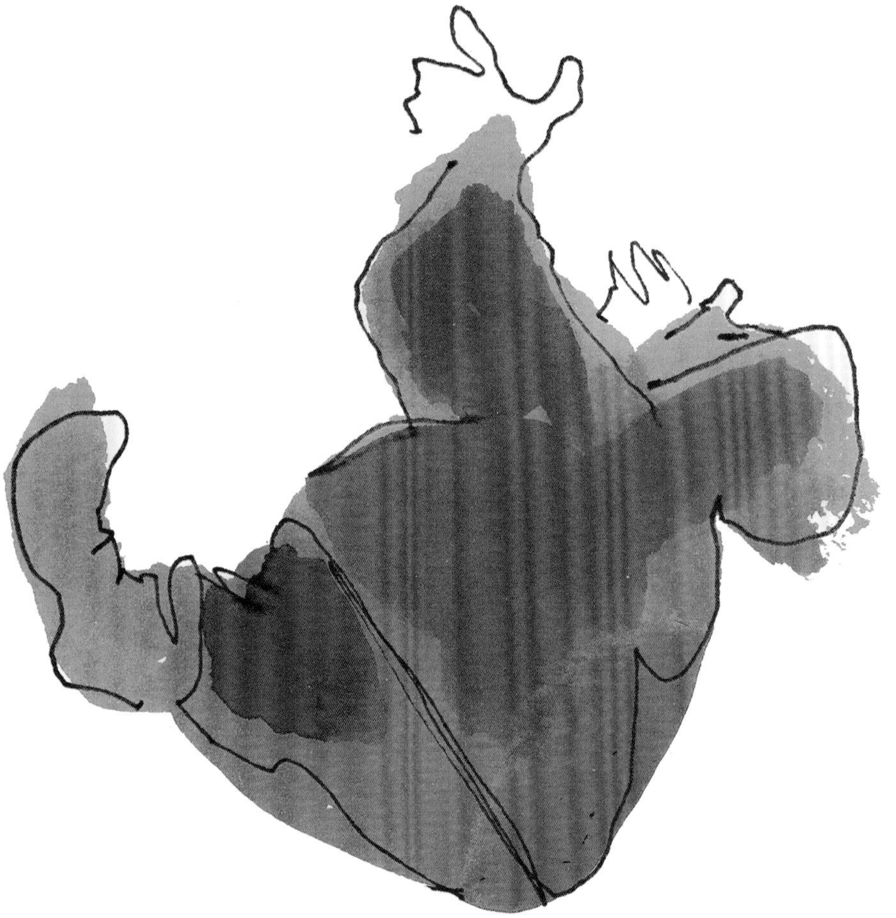

ABOVE: Watercolor illustration; *Vogue Paris* No 632 scanned for publication

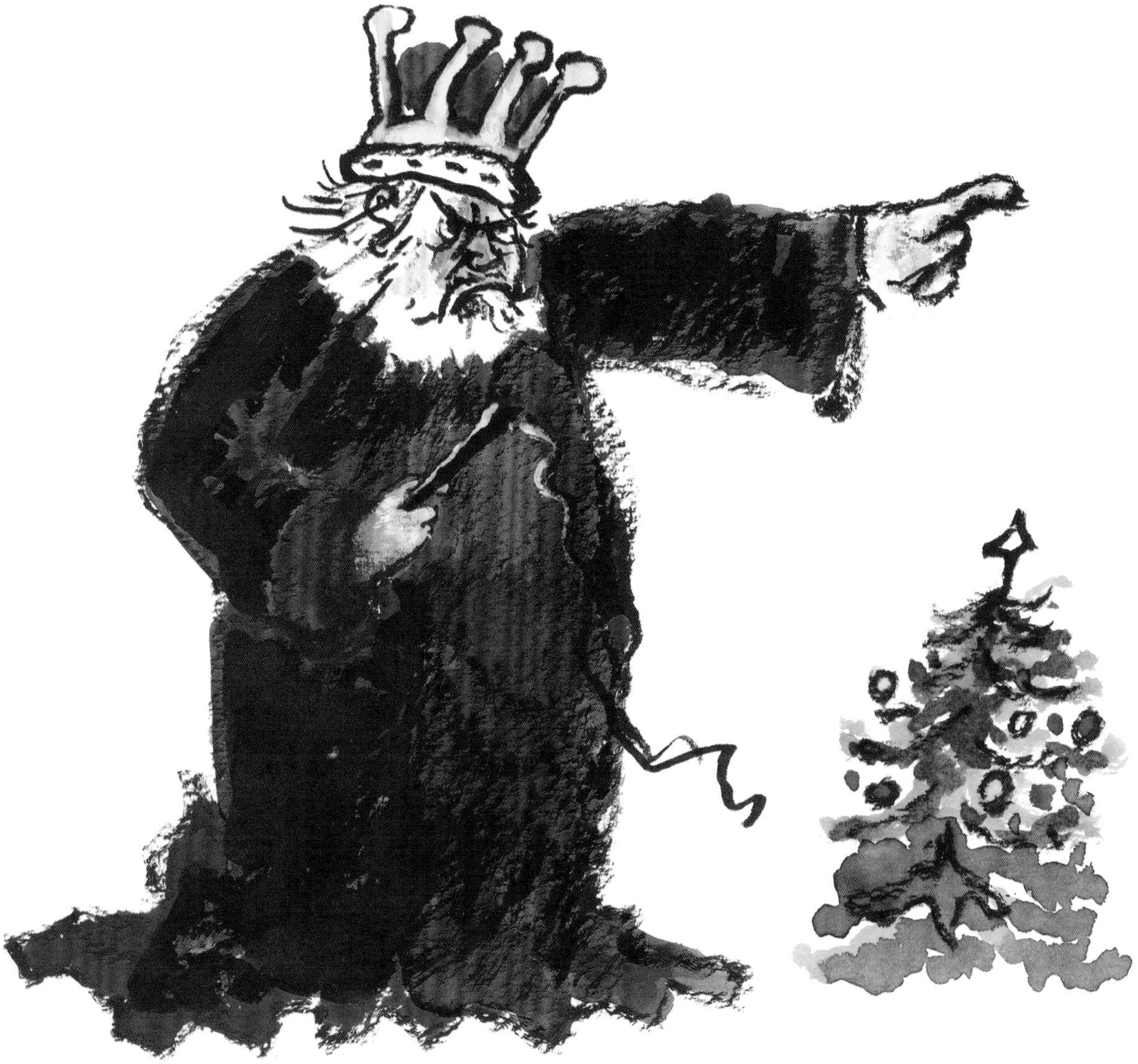

ABOVE: Watercolor illustration; *Vogue Paris* No 632 scanned for publication

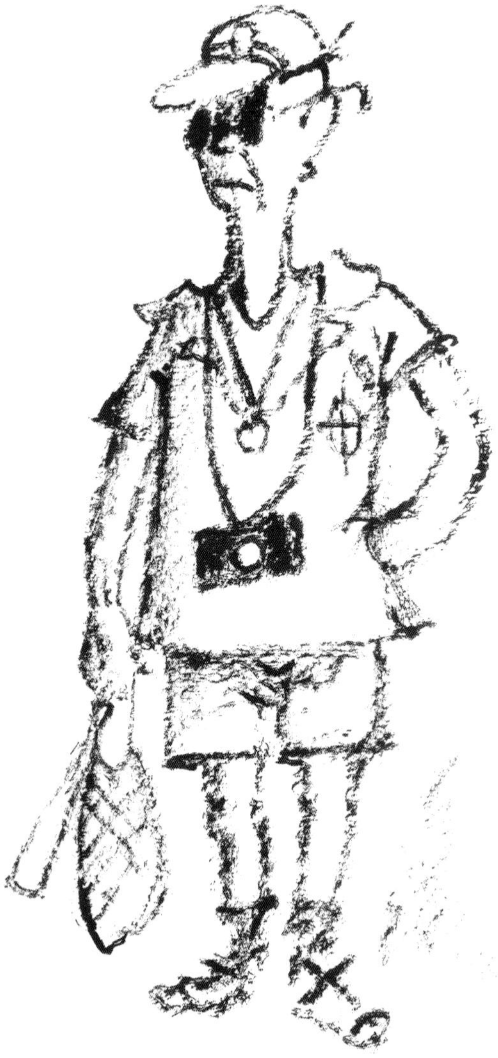

Later, he launches into a tirade against tourists and the tourist industry, comparing its 'economic considerations' to the pseudo-science of phrenology. 'By nature,' he rants, 'the average tourist is a species of delinquent. He's left courtesy at home to die of hunger with his cat.' There is, of course, a representative of the species for us to examine, complete with baseball cap, ugly shorts, socks-and-sandals-combo and the ubiquitous camera slung round his neck. King Orson's solution to this scourge is to outlaw summer holidays.

Further on, with conjuring tricks and animated photographs now completely forgotten, he advocates social engineering on a grand scale: 'Where once the Arab oil sheiks paraded themselves, we'll see the population of the slums. The poor and elderly, those whose only address is a park bench, or who share a cardboard box with rats, we'll receive them in the finest hotels with a bow, with flowers and champagne on demand. Everything will be free. It's my party!' And how will the King of the World pay for all this? 'Tax!'

Throughout the piece, the illustrations are a delight, and it's terrific fun to see Welles sending up his megalomaniacal image with such glee. But for all the comedy bluster, his comments have a core of seriousness. Welles really did love Christmas and hated to see it tarnished, and his concern over the worlds of entertainment and politics blurring into one is remarkably prescient.

ABOVE: Pencil illustration; *Vogue Paris* No 632 scanned for publication

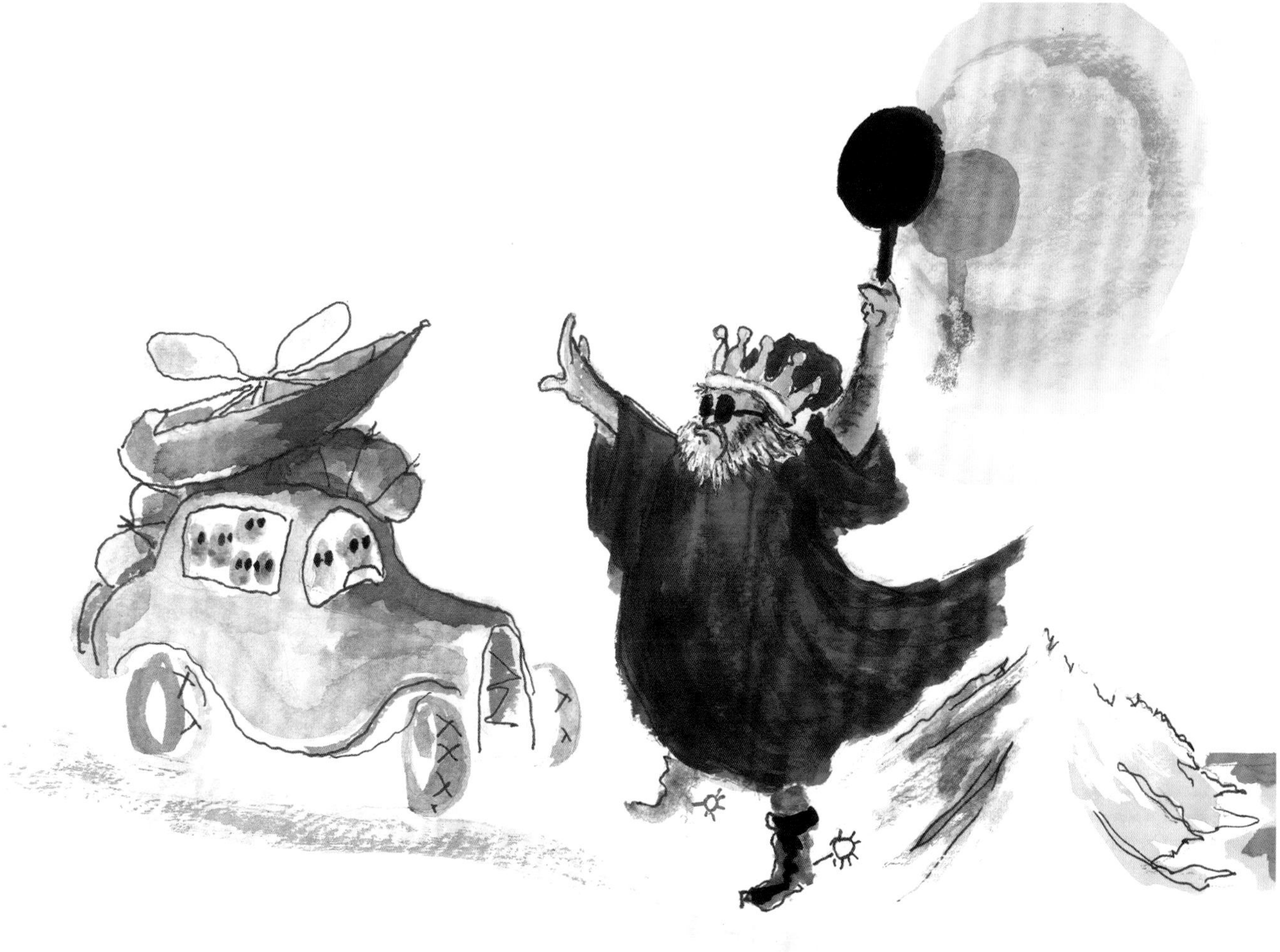

ABOVE: Watercolor illustration; *Vogue Paris* No 632 scanned for publication

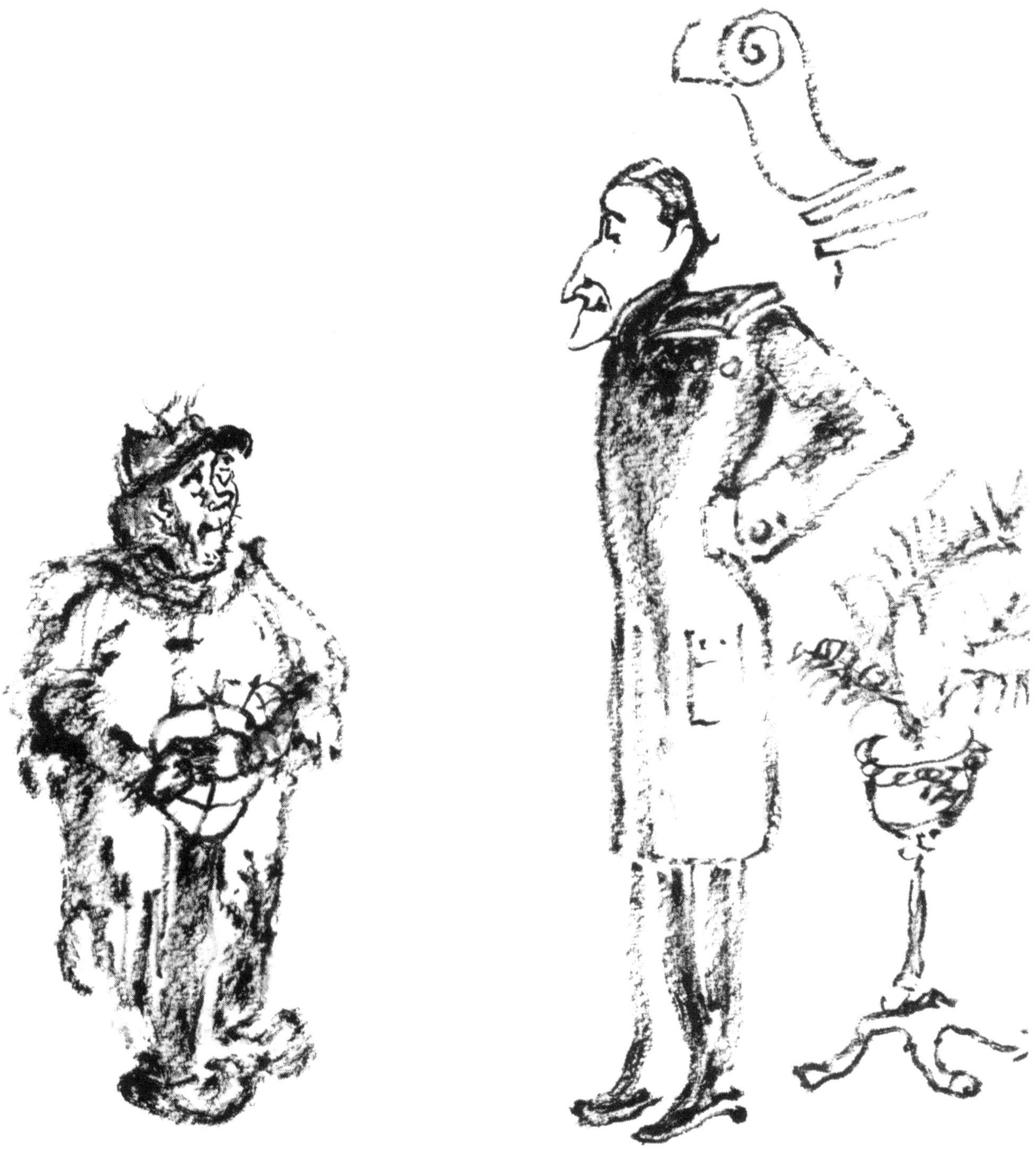

ABOVE: Pencil illustration; *Vogue Paris* No 632 scanned for publication

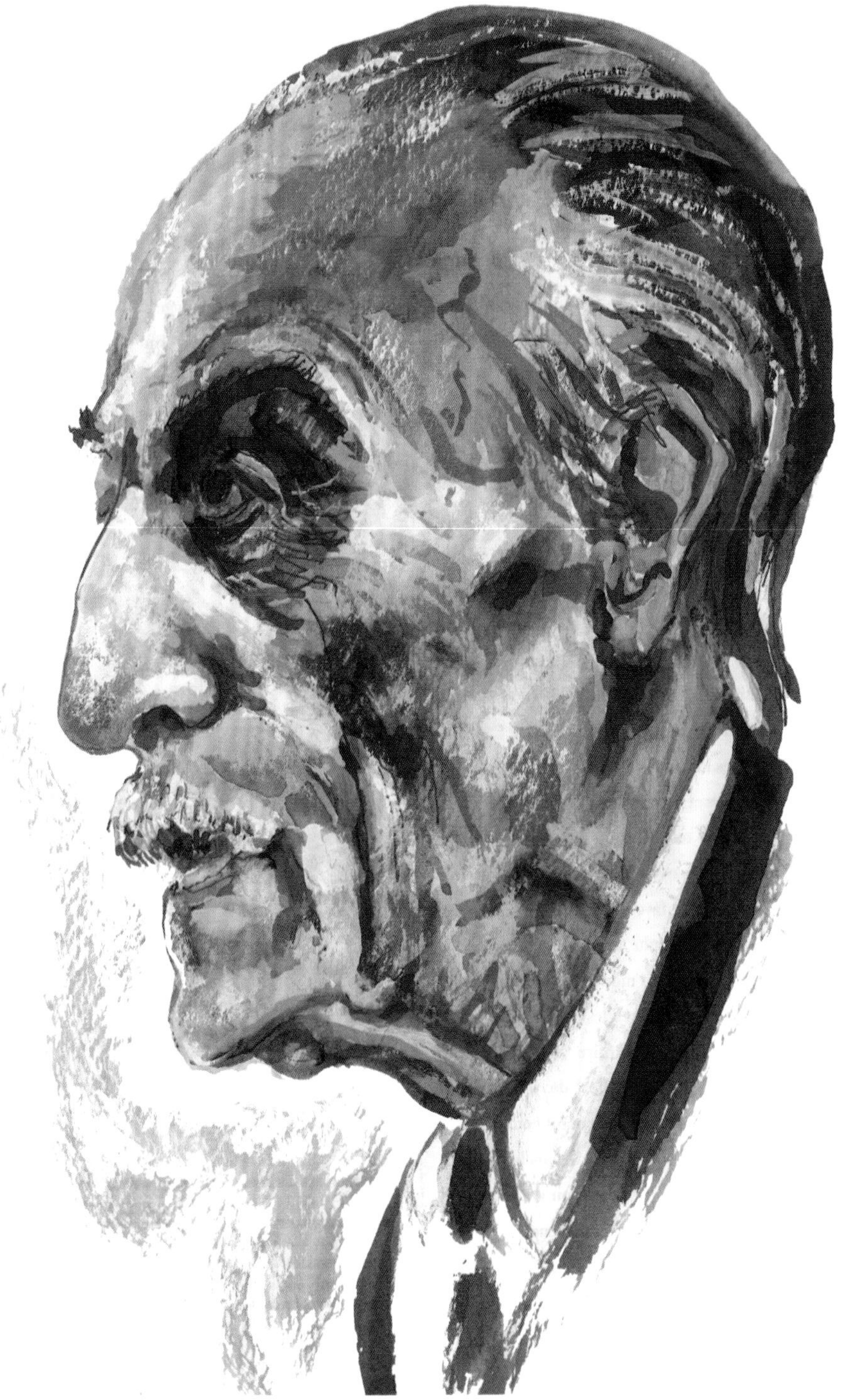

Elsewhere, Welles takes full scattershot advantage of his allotted space. There is a short cautionary tale inspired by the legend of Pygmalion; a reflection on the life and work of Danish author Isak Dinesen (pen-name of Baroness Karen Christenze von Blixen-Finecke); and a piece on Croatian artist Oja Kodar, his partner in the last years of his life.

The article 'My Father Wore Black Spats' – with an asterisk indicating that this is the first chapter of an unpublished autobiography Orson Welles is currently writing – is a lyrical tribute to his parents that is no less moving for its reliance on magical realism as much as reminiscence.

The striking black and white portrait accompanies a profile of Eduardo De Filippo, who Welles proclaims 'the greatest actor in the world.' Little known outside his native Italy, De Filippo (known simply as Eduardo) was also an acclaimed playwright, poet, filmmaker and theater director. A man very much after Welles's heart, although they never worked together. The painting is a rather somber depiction of someone renowned for their genius at light comedy, but typical of Welles to mine the pathos in that. It is terrifically expressive, and further evidence of Welles's versatility. Worlds away stylistically from the witty 'King of the World' illustrations, it is still unmistakably Welles.

ABOVE: Watercolor painting; *Vogue Paris* No 632 scanned for publication

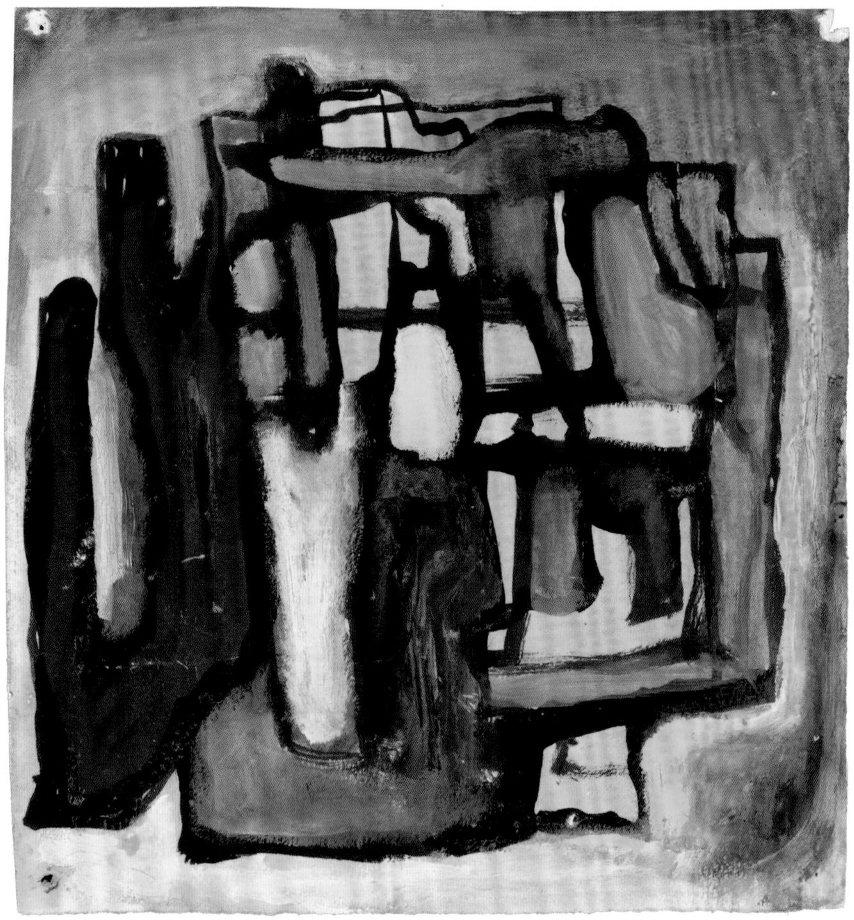

ABOLISHMENT

Touch of Evil was going to be Welles's kiss-and-make-up reconciliation with Hollywood, his triumphant all-is-forgiven return to the fold. Things didn't work out quite like that. And this painting, unambiguously titled Abolishment, is what Welles poured his creative energy into in its immediate aftermath. A stark, tangled abstract dominated by black lines and fiery orange hues, it has none of the wistful melancholy of his Don Quixote painting, another work inspired by artistic ambition thwarted. There is no regret here, only rage.

How Welles landed *Touch of Evil* is in some dispute. One version has him offering to direct producer Albert Zugsmith's worst script and being handed a trashy potboiler called *Badge of Evil*, an adaptation of Whit Masterson's 1956 crime novel. Another is that when Charlton Heston was told Welles was attached as an actor (Welles played corrupt police chief Hank Quinlan), he suggested him as director. Universal would probably have preferred Howdy Doody, but offered Welles the job to keep Heston happy.

At first, all looked hunky-dory. Welles filmed most of *Touch of Evil*, including its famous opening crane shot, on location in Venice, California, then a run-down beachside suburb of LA. The perfect surrogate for the film's seedy border town, it was also remote enough to keep prying studio execs at bay. Not that he needed to worry unduly about that; the suits loved the rushes he was sending them, and the whole shoot sailed by without major incident.

Post-production was a different story. Welles's first cut was met with stunned disbelief by Universal. They were expecting a conventional noir thriller and instead got a master class in non-linear narrative, one reveling in betrayal, corruption, sexual obsession and racial prejudice. When Welles went to New York to appear on *The Steve Allen Show*, Universal replaced his editor Virgil Vogel with Aaron Stell, whose previous experience had been limited to TV.

When Stell's cut, unsupervised by Welles, was shown to the studio brass, they went into fresh conniptions. Fearing for the project's commercial viability, they brought in Universal's head of post-production, Ernest Nims, to fix things. This was the writing on the wall for Welles, who already feared that *Touch of Evil* was slipping from his grasp. Nims had been editor on his 1946 film *The Stranger* and, Welles firmly believed, had butchered it by cutting a crucial twenty minutes of footage.

What followed was protracted and murky, a series of events – re-shoots, re-edits and Welles's infamous fifty-eight-page memo – that ended ultimately with Welles being removed from the film. The simple fact was, Universal wanted a saleable product; Welles wanted to make art. Which is a neat summation of why he found it impossible to work inside the studio machine.

On its initial release in 1958, *Touch of Evil* filled the bottom half of a double bill with *The Female Animal*, a forgettable star vehicle for Hedy Lamarr. A number of leading publications didn't bother to review it. Those that did almost universally loathed it. It was not seen in any form that honored Welles's vision until Walter Murch's superb restoration in 1998.

It must have been some consolation to Welles that the film was widely acclaimed in Europe, where the auteur theory held sway. Otherwise, it was heartbreaking: the film he had hoped would herald a triumphant return instead marked his irreversible exile.

ABOVE: Oil painting; photo supplied for publication

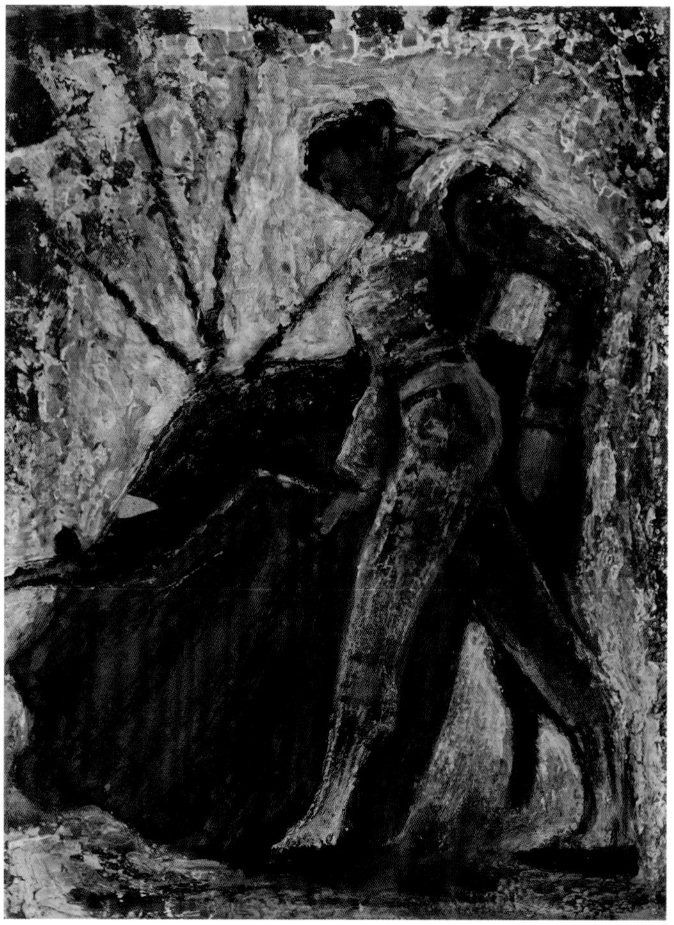

MATADOR

Death in the Afternoon, Ernest Hemingway's ode to the ceremony and tradition of Spanish bullfighting, had been on the shelves a matter of weeks when the seventeen-year-old Welles pitched up in Seville.

Welles arrived in southern Spain fresh from his adventures in Morocco, and would have found Andalusia scarcely less exotic than North Africa. Officially classified as a 'historical nationality', it has always been proudly separate from the rest of Spain, and, since the fifteenth century, bullfighting has been central to its cultural identity.

There is no doubt that Welles had read Hemingway's book, and even if he hadn't, he'd have found the drama of the bullring impossible to resist. And like Hemingway, he was not content to be a mere spectator.

Tempting though it is to imagine Welles striding across the killing floor in a glittering suit of lights, the reality was a little more mundane. His machismo, like Hemingway's before him, would have been tested at the amateur fights, held each morning before a smattering of locals. That the bulls were babies compared to the monsters of the *corrida*, and their horns were padded, detracts nothing from Welles's courage. The crowds swelled whenever 'The American,' as he was known, turned up to show his prowess. Whether they were there to assess his skill or to witness his gory comeuppance is a matter for conjecture. According to Welles, he actually did sustain an injury, albeit one that mysteriously shifted position from his lip to his thigh, depending on who he was describing it to.

Welles's time in Seville sparked a lifelong passion for bullfighting, one fully expressed in his dazzling painting of a matador in mid pass. The paint is thickly applied with a palate knife and the details are blurred, the bull and the matador caught in a blaze of sunlight.

During a television interview with Michael Parkinson in 1974, Welles explained, 'there are two kinds of people who follow the bulls, as they say in Spanish. There are those people who follow because they love the bullfighters, and there is a very small minority who are interested in the bulls. And I was always most interested in the bulls.' In fact, he was considered a true aficionado with a shrewd eye for the bulls – 'These noble creatures…' as he described them.

The matador in the painting is not a portrait, although Welles knew many fighters and counted Antonio Ordóñez, the most lionized matador of his day, among his closest friends. (Ordóñez's legendary rivalry with Luis Miguel Dominguin, the one-time lover of Ava Gardner who wore a suit of lights designed by Picasso, was chronicled by Hemingway in his book *The Dangerous Summer*.)

When Welles died in 1985 his ashes were buried at El Recreo de San Cayetano, Ordóñez's ranch in Ronda, Andalusia. Although Welles had never expressed a preference for his final resting place, Ronda was chosen by his wife Paola Mori Welles and his daughter Beatrice after careful deliberation. 'He was buried among people who really, really loved him for who he was,' said Beatrice at the time. 'He truly loved southern Spain. He was at his happiest there.'

Fourteen years later, when Ordóñez died, his ashes were interred next to Welles's. Even today, many shops and cafes in Ronda – home of the oldest bullring in the world – display photographs of Welles and Ordóñez together.

ABOVE: Oil painting; photo supplied for publication

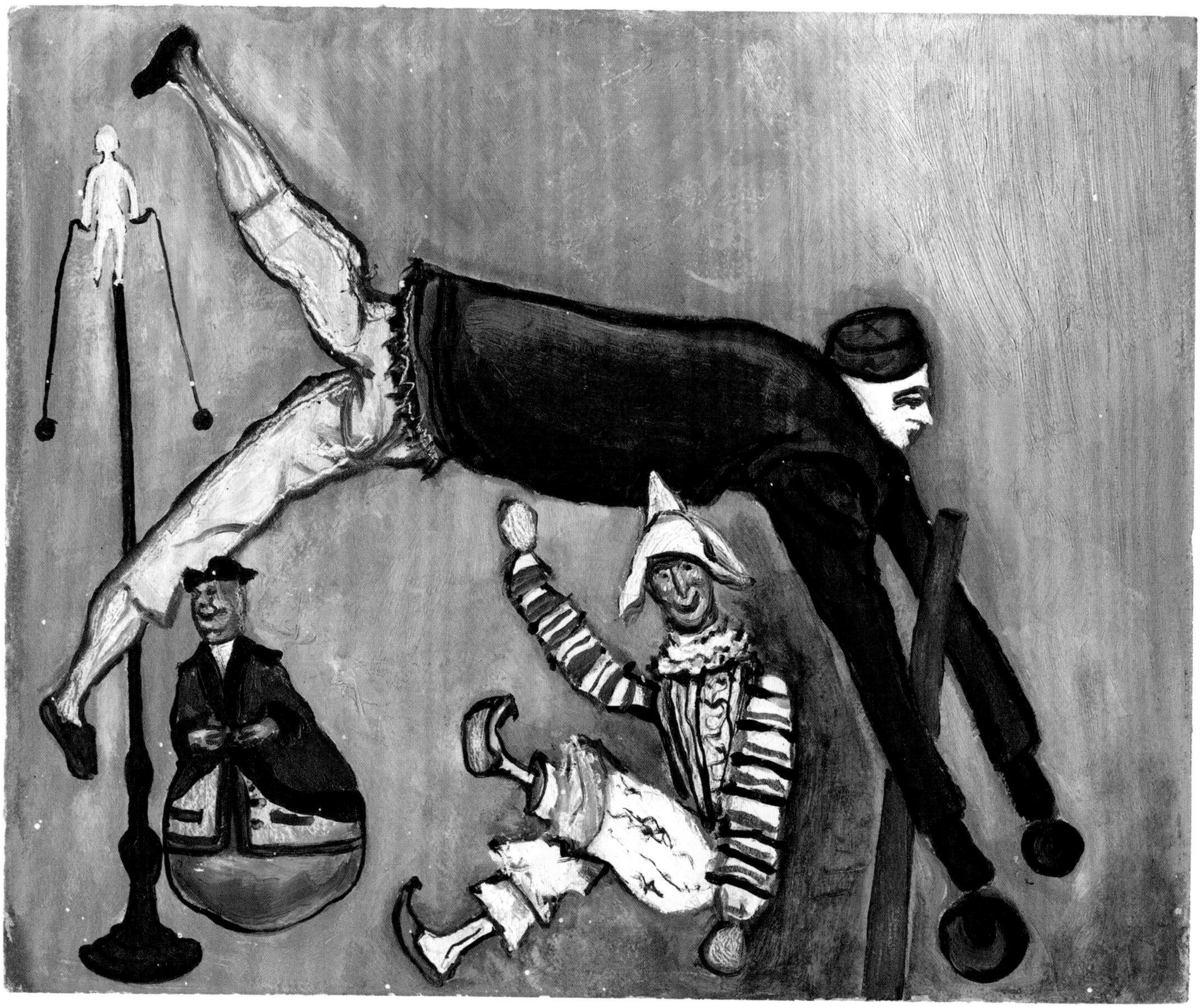

CIRCUS

This outwardly merry, but actually slightly sinister painting has been identified as Welles's tribute to Picasso. And there's some justification for that. Picasso painted circus scenes a number of times – as did many other modern artists – though his images were never surreal, as this one is. Even so, there is a faint echo here of Picasso's 1905 depiction of Circus Family The Tumblers, especially in the odd Weeble-like figure in the bottom left corner.

But Beatrice Welles has her doubts. 'I can't really say yes or no. I'd say it's highly unlikely that it's a tribute to Picasso, but that's just my gut feeling. I don't think he ever did anything in tribute to another artist. It just wasn't his style; everything he did was his. I remember seeing the painting when I was a little girl, but I'm not certain where or when he did it. I think it was while we were in Spain, which would put it around 1963.'

ABOVE: Oil painting; photo supplied for publication

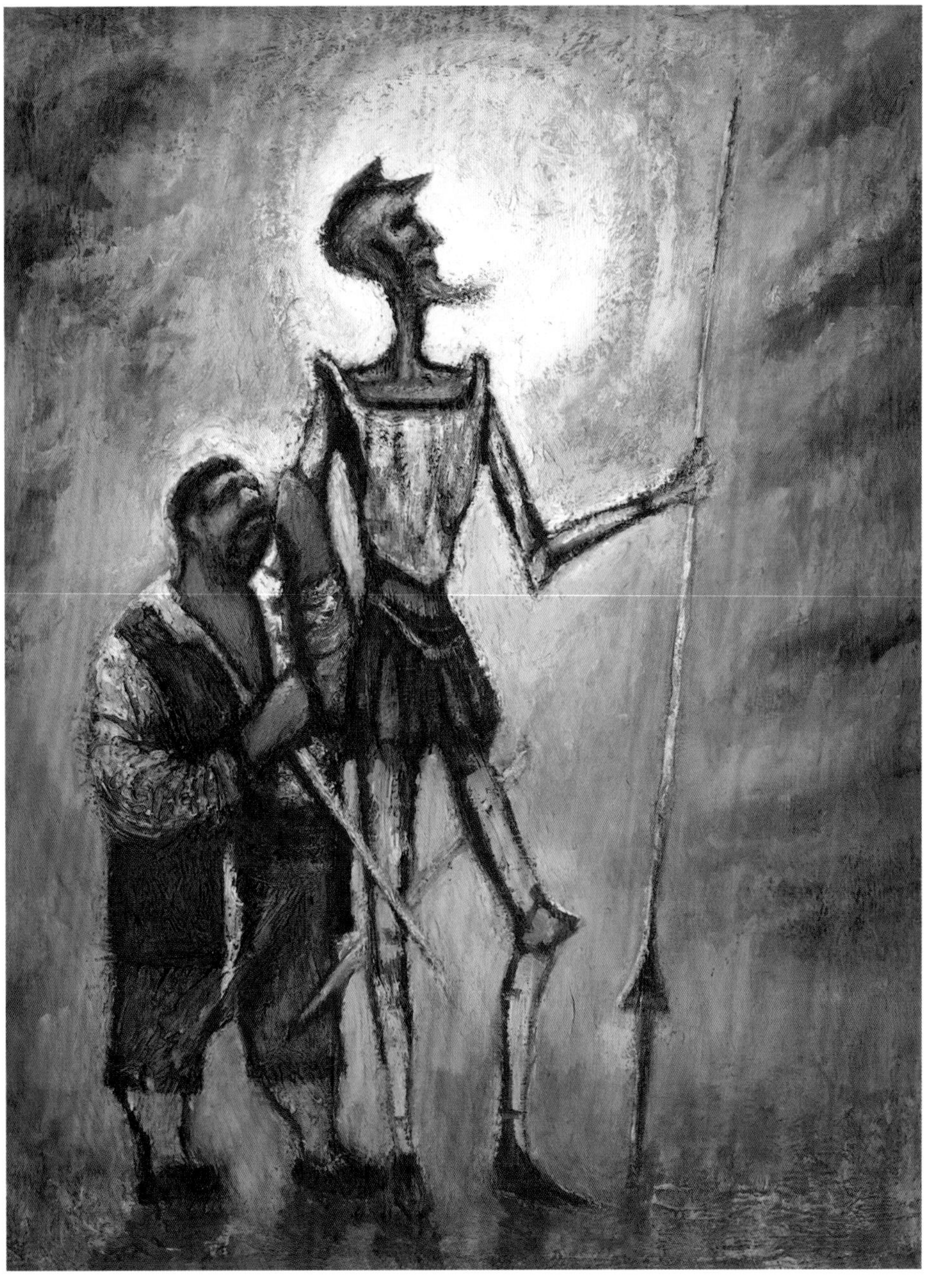

DON QUIXOTE

'You know what the fellow said – in Italy, for thirty years under the Borgias, they had warfare, terror, murder and bloodshed, but they produced Michelangelo, Leonardo da Vinci and the Renaissance. In Switzerland, they had brotherly love, they had five hundred years of democracy and peace – and what did that produce?'

Well, it wasn't the cuckoo clock; that was invented in Germany. Still, Harry Lime's speech from *The Third Man* makes its point. In fact, the speech was Welles's own, an after-dinner chestnut he delivered often and which he cleverly sneaked into Graham Greene's script. But if Welles truly believed that art flourishes in adversity, that belief must have been tested to breaking point by *Don Quixote*.

It was a longstanding ambition of Welles's to update the Cervantes novel to the twentieth century – or, at least, to place Quixote and Sancho Panza in a modern setting to better emphasize their anachronism. That ambition began to take shape first in 1955 as a doomed 30-minute TV movie and then – thanks to a $25,000 boost from Welles's friend Frank Sinatra and financing from Mexico – a full-length feature. Welles put up a substantial amount of his own money, too.

It says much about the project's subsequent fortunes that principal photography took from 1957 to 1969. Longer if you count test footage and second unit work, which progressed well into the 1970s.

When the financing ran out, Welles carried on filming on a tortuously haphazard basis, shooting scenes often without a script, guerilla-style in Mexico and Spain, with a silent 16mm camera (his plan was to dub sound later) whenever his cast could be mustered and funds from his acting work allowed. He described this labor of love, the Quixotic nature of which was lost on no one, as 'My own personal project, to be completed in my own time, as one might a novel.'

A novel, of course, is a solitary endeavor; a movie is not. And, although Welles continued to work on *Don Quixote* until almost the end of his life, his grand vision ultimately eluded him.

ABOVE: Oil painting; photo supplied for publication

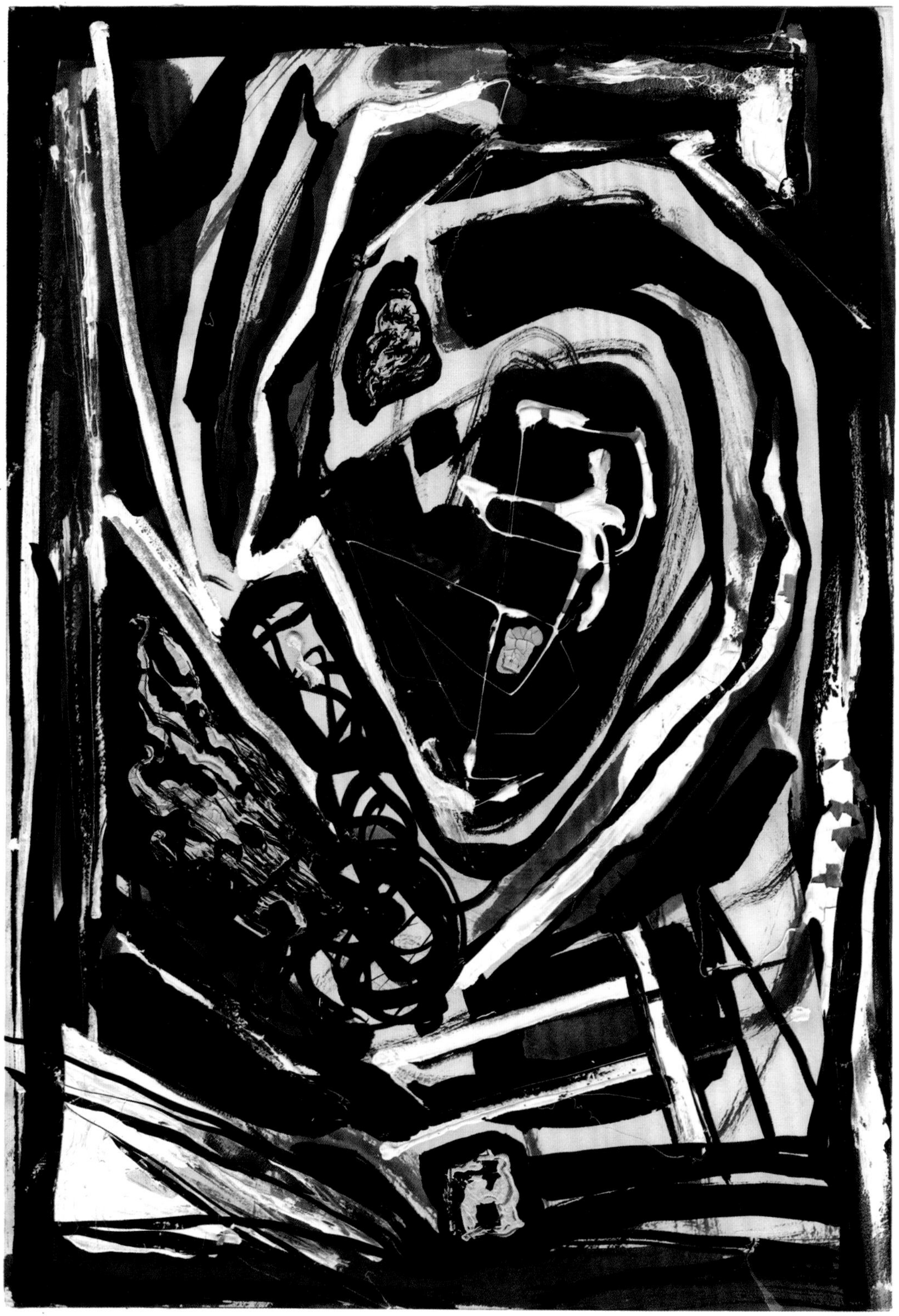

ABOVE: Oil painting; original scanned for publication

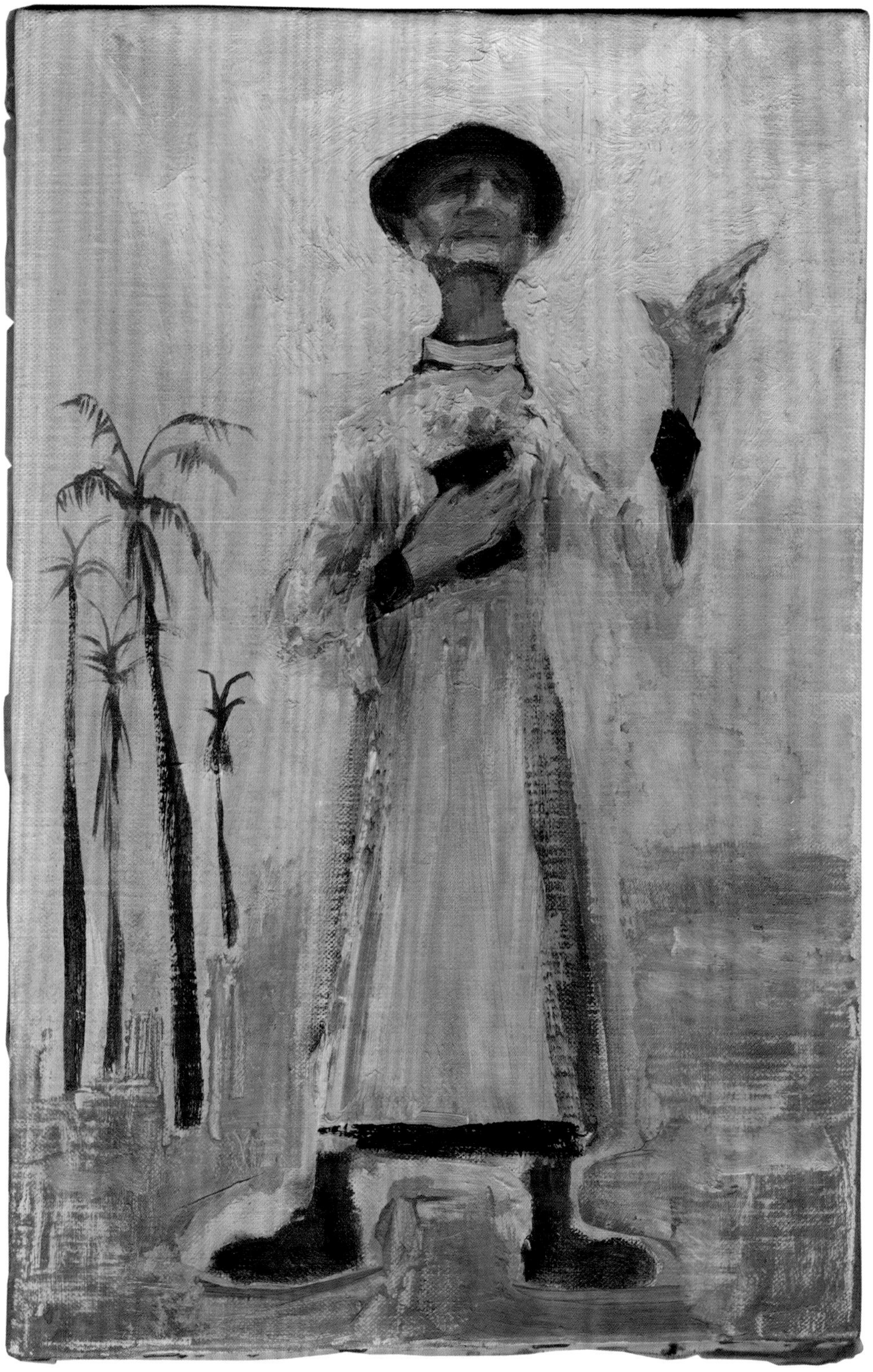

PRIEST

This entertaining little number is not so much evidence of Welles's skill as a painter as it is his brilliance as an illustrator. What inspired it is hard to tell. The juxtaposition of palm trees and a Catholic priest, with no other background detail, surely has some significance, but what it is only Welles could tell us.

It might have a connection to Welles's 1951 play *The Unthinking Lobster*, a snarky send-up of Hollywood religious epics, in which a wide-eyed ingénue lands a role as a saint and begins performing miracles in real life. That would explain the palm trees. But it seems too elaborate for a costume design, and entirely different from the swift lines of Welles's production sketches. It's also overly comical for a working drawing – note the contrast between the Father's beatific expression and his oversized, Chaplinesque boots. Perhaps we're over-thinking it. Perhaps it is simply Welles having fun with his paint box rather than looking for solace in it.

ABOVE: Oil painting; original scanned for publication

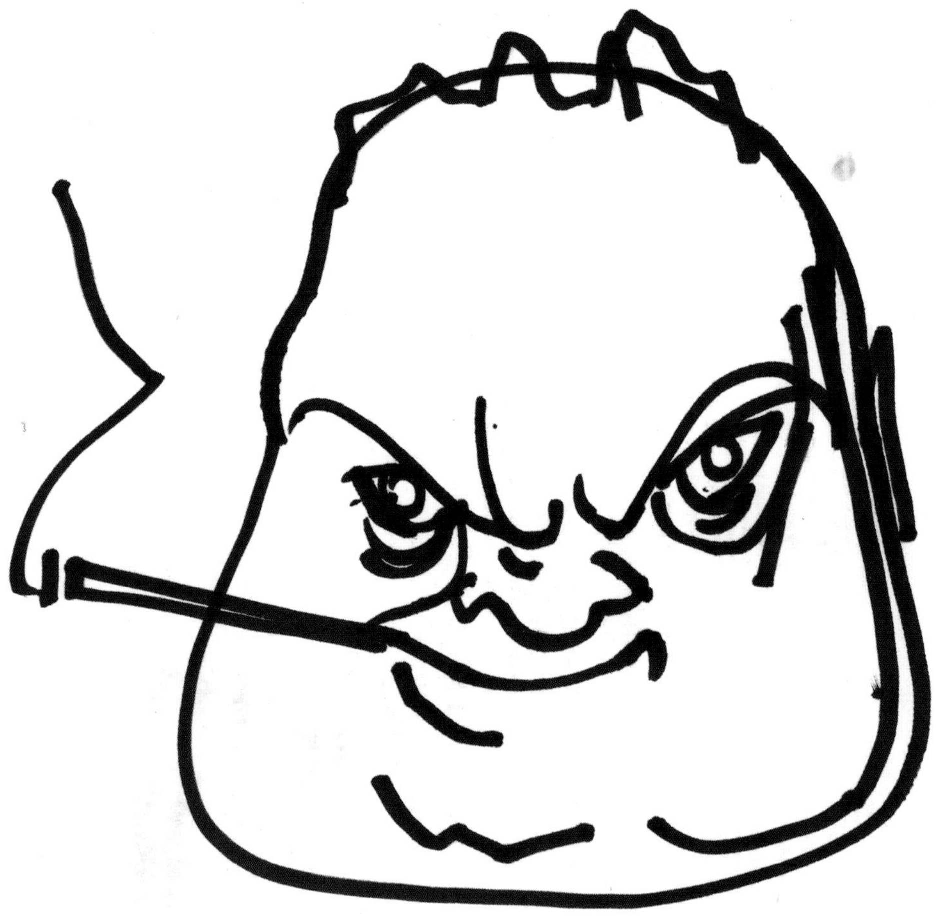

ABOVE: Self-portrait caricature sketch; original scanned for publication

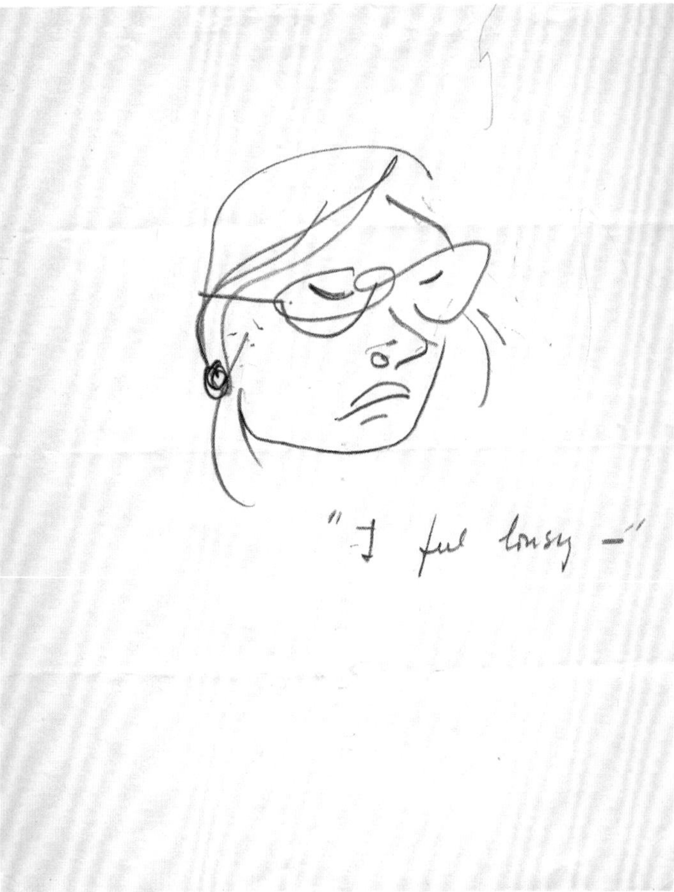

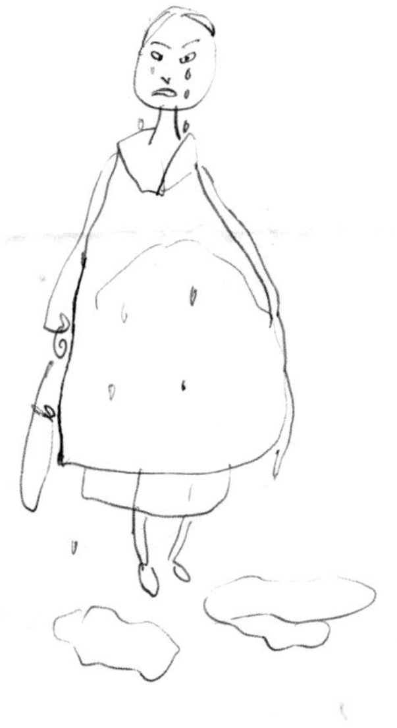

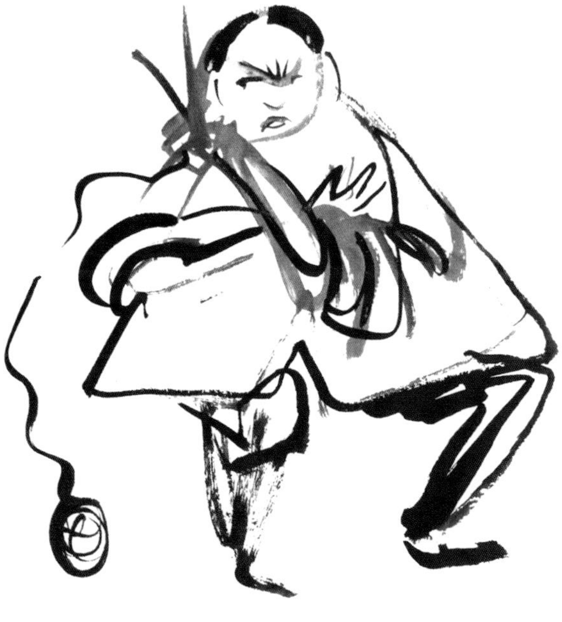

PAOLA

Beatrice Welles recalls these sketches very well. 'My mother had a very uncomfortable pregnancy,' she explains. 'I know because they used to talk and laugh about it. Her hormones were blowing up and she was in tears all the time. He would draw them for her to try to cheer her up.

'The one that makes me laugh, and he sent it to me, was the one of her with her glasses on where she's brandishing her knitting at him!' Beatrice continues with a laugh. 'A friend of mine, an artist, saw that for the first time years ago and he said, "Oh my god. He drew a Samurai!" I said, "No, you idiot. That's my mother!"'

TOP: Sketches; originals scanned for publication

ABOVE: Sketch; scan supplied for publication

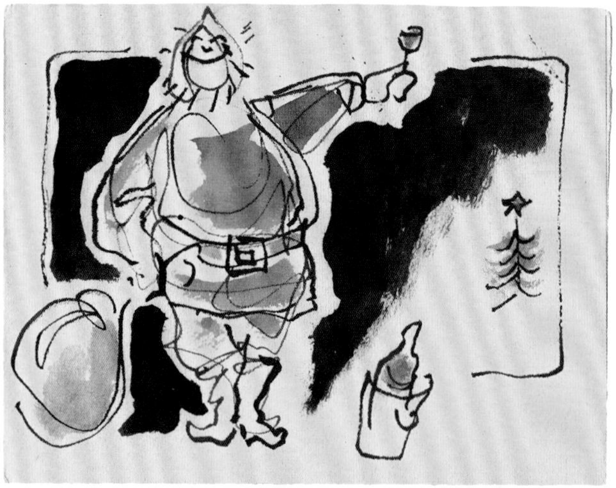

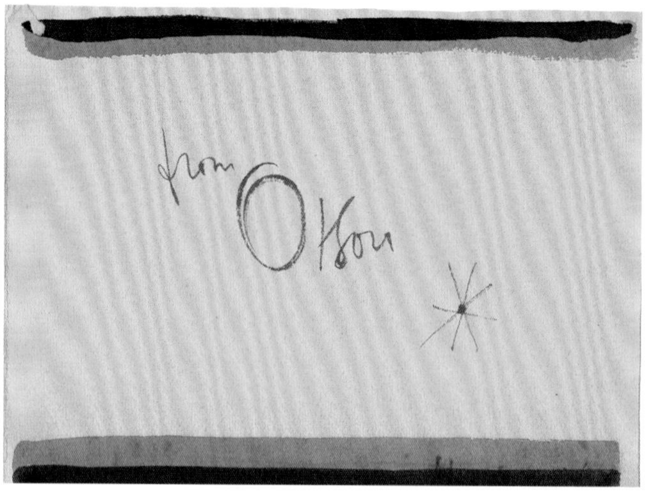

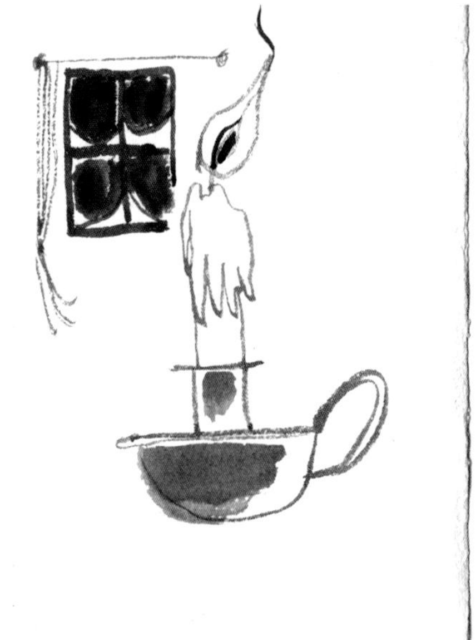

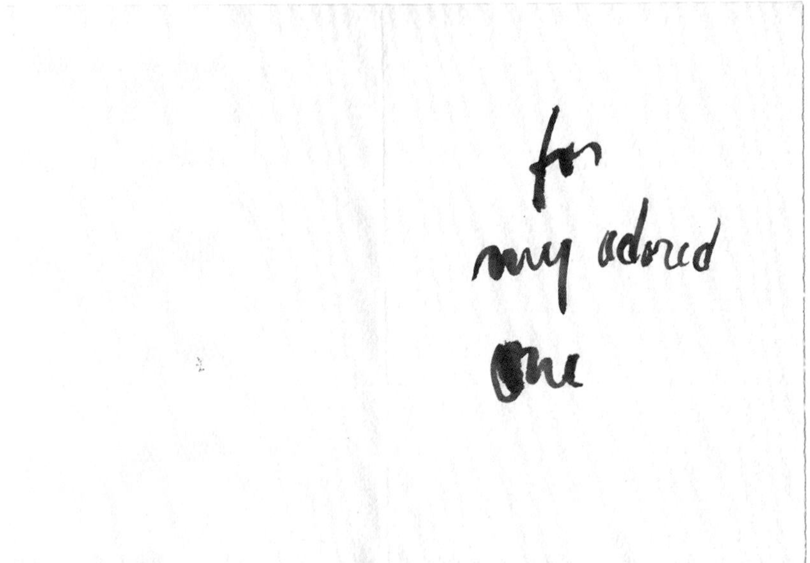

ABOVE: Christmas cards front and corresponding interior; originals scanned and scans supplied for publication

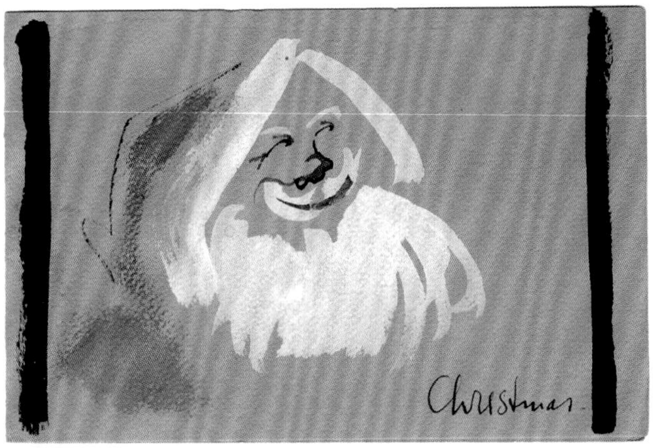

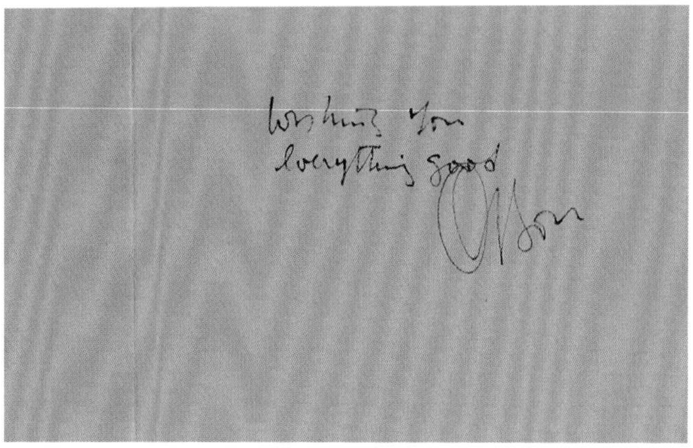

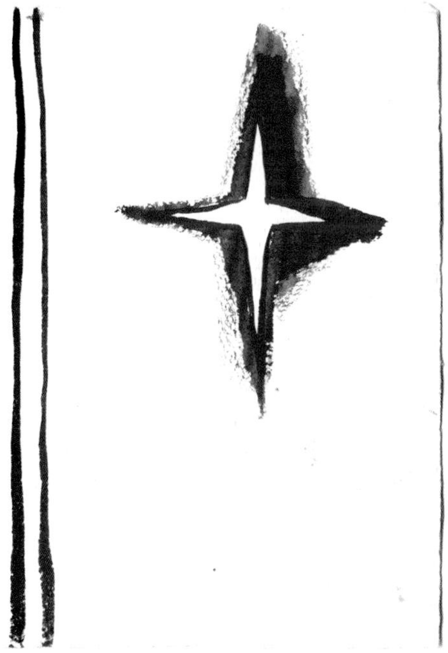

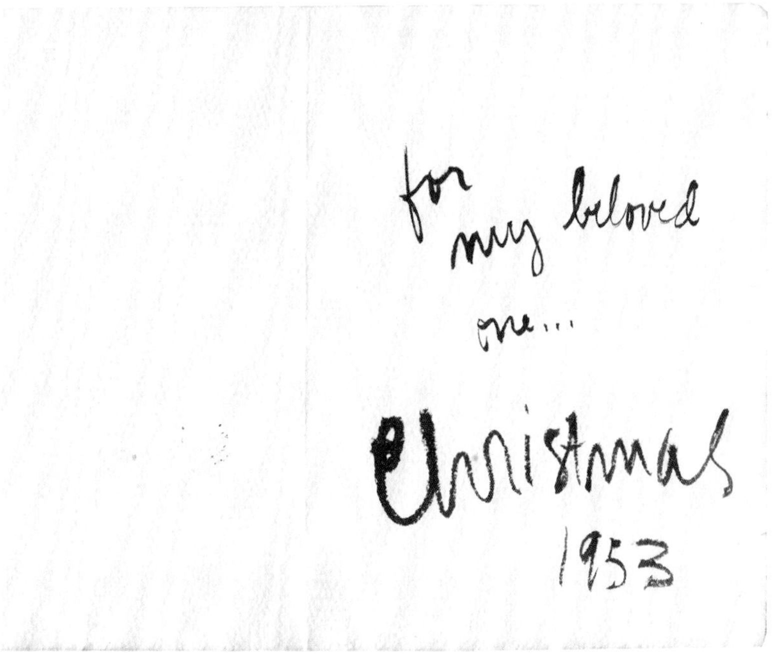

ABOVE: Christmas cards front and corresponding interior; originals scanned and scans supplied for publication

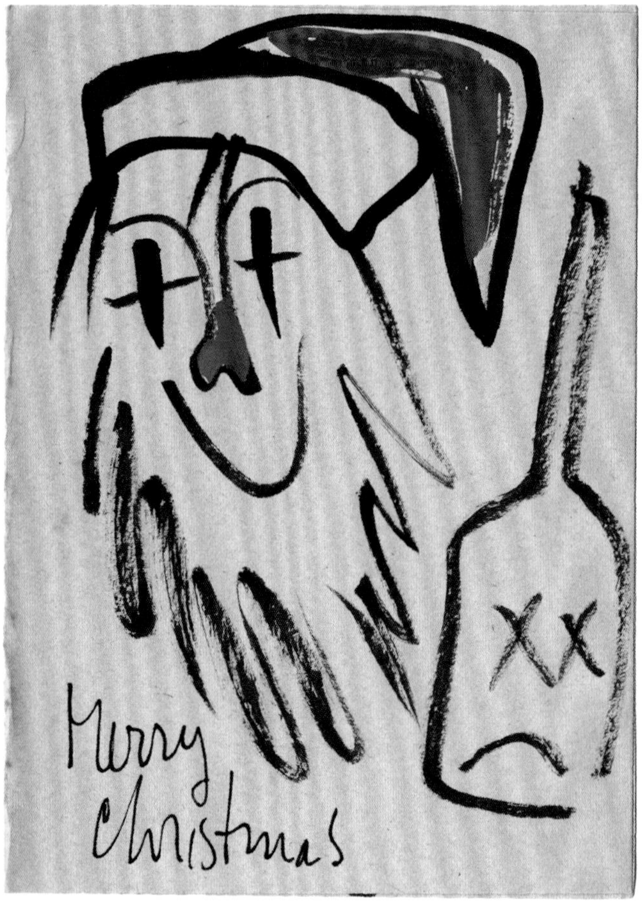

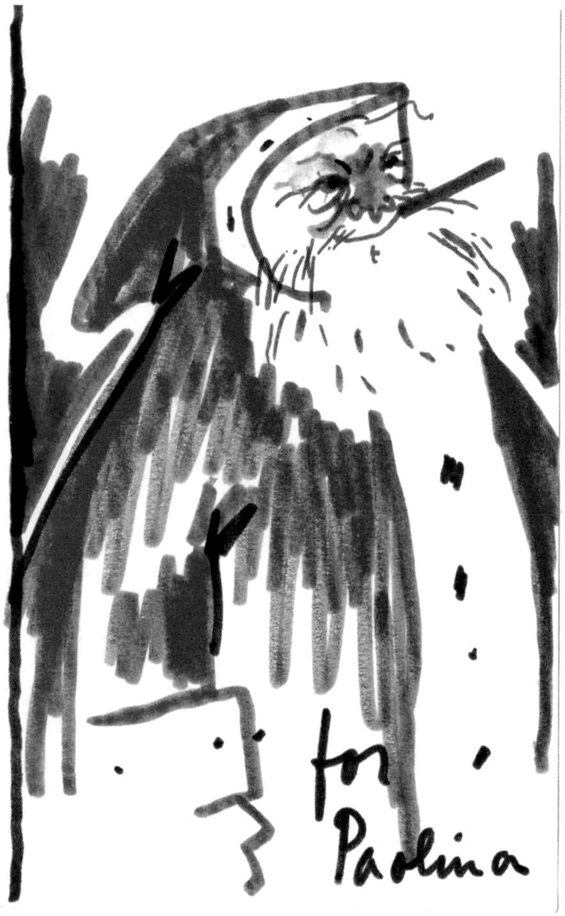

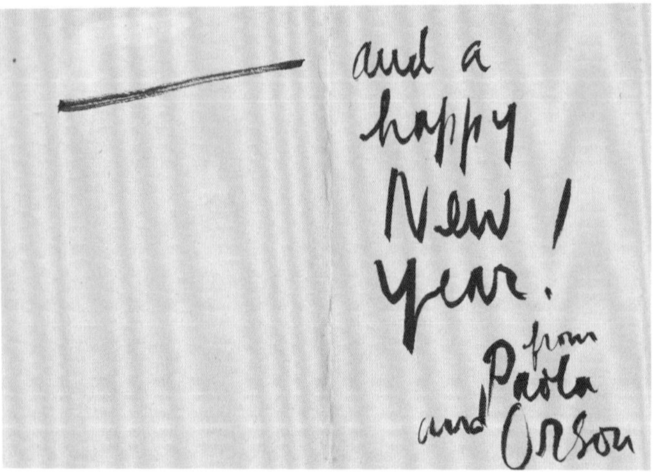

ABOVE: Christmas cards front and corresponding interior; originals scanned and scans supplied for publication

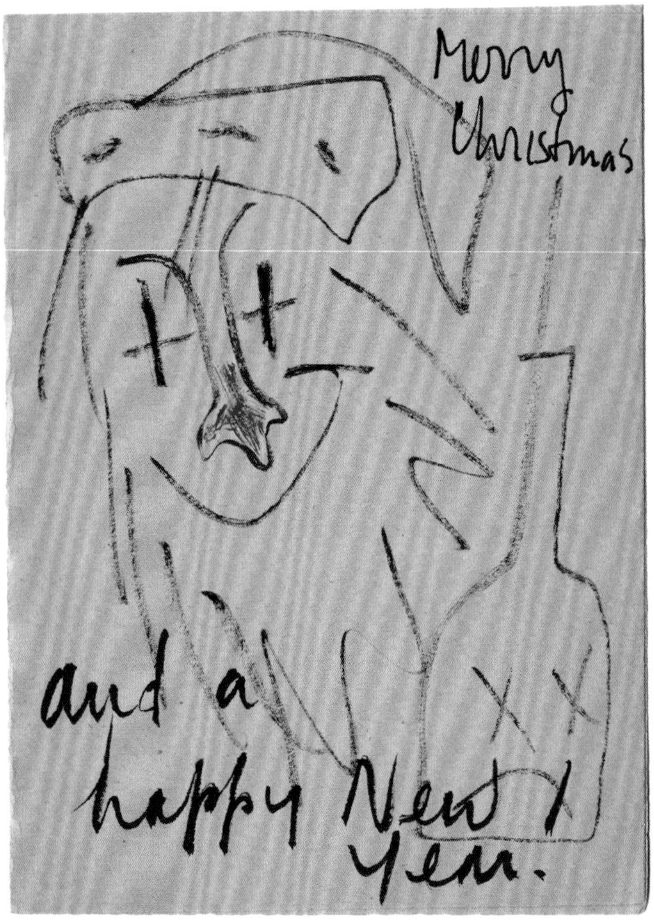

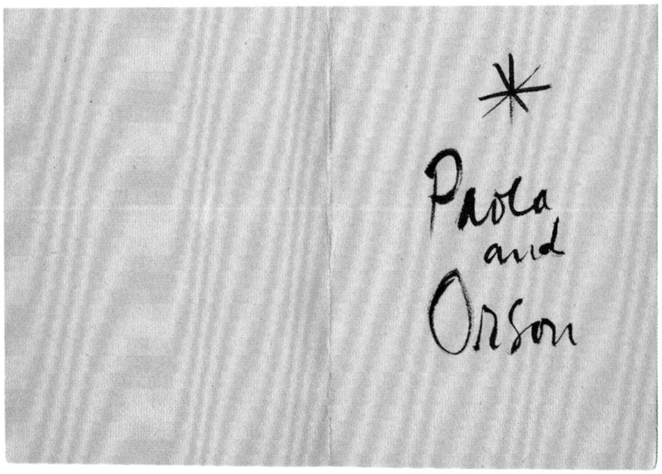

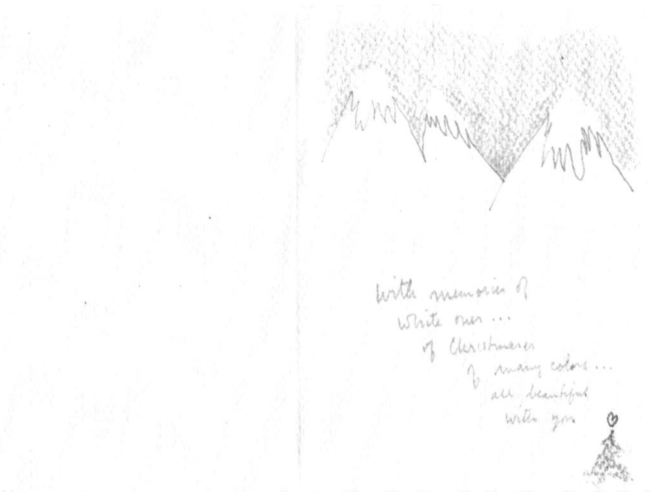

ABOVE: Christmas cards front and corresponding interior; originals scanned and scans supplied for publication

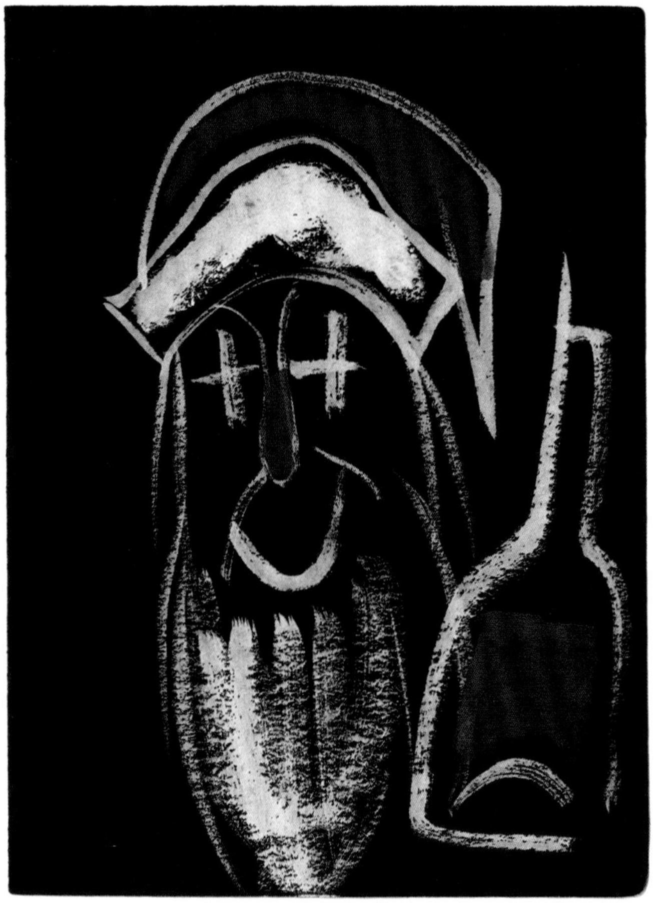

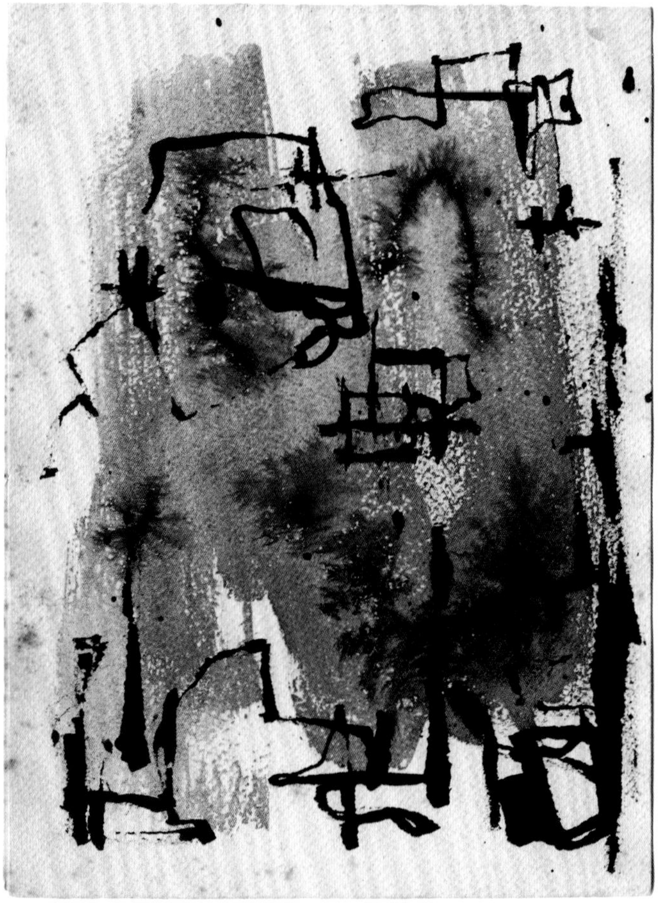

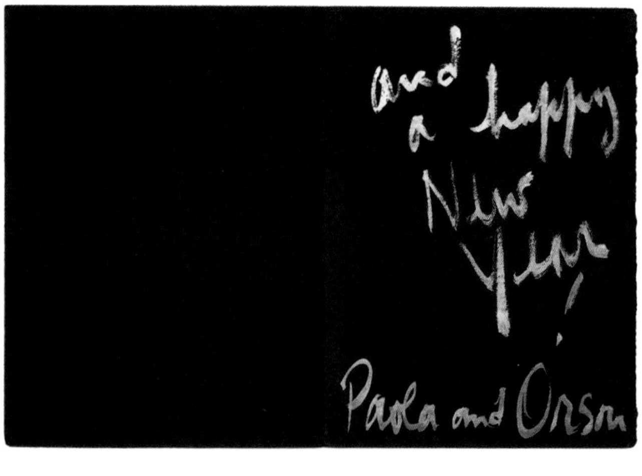

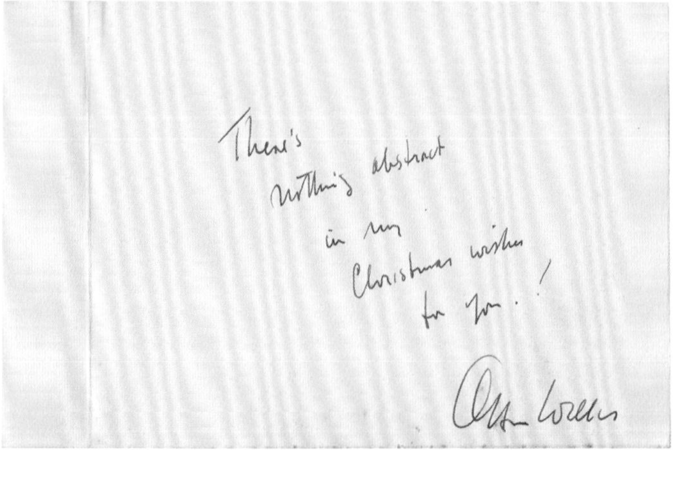

ABOVE: Christmas cards front and corresponding interior; originals scanned and scans supplied for publication

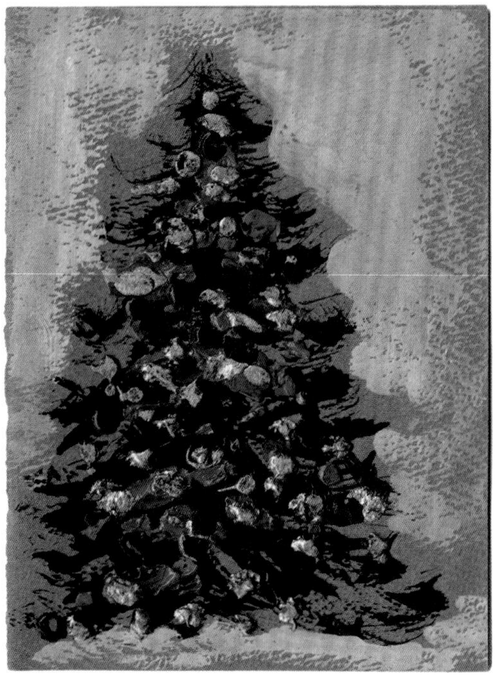

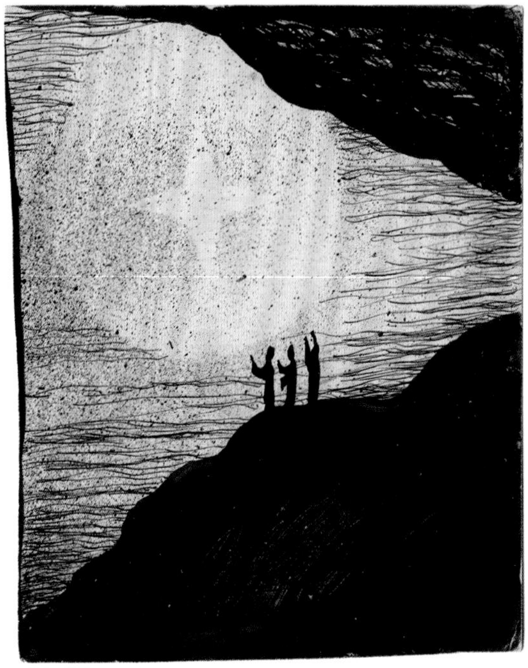

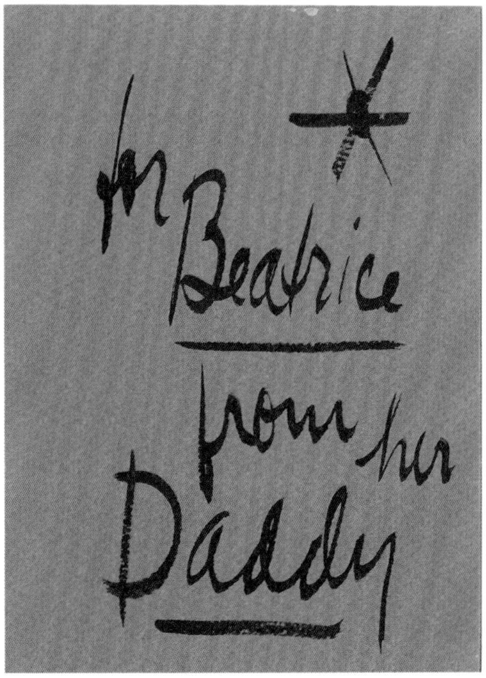

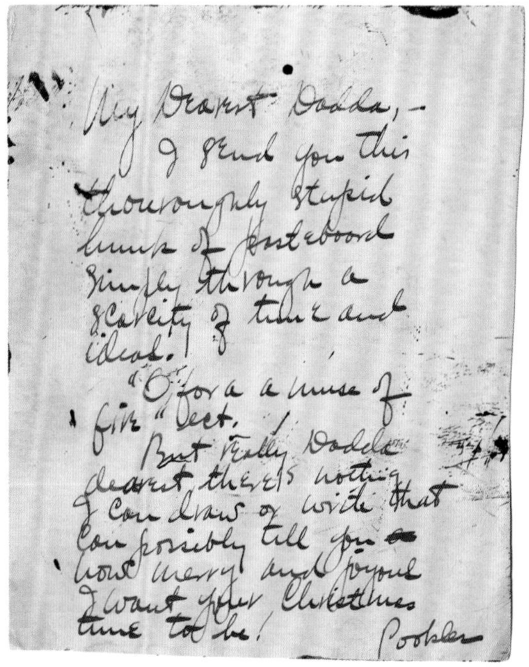
My Dearest Dadda,—
I send you this
thoroughly stupid
lump of pasteboard
simply through a
scarcity of time and
ideas.
"O for a muse of
fire" etc.
But really Dadda
dearest there's nothing
I can draw or write that
can possibly tell you
how merry and joyous
I want your Christmas
time to be!
Pookles

ABOVE: Christmas cards front and corresponding interior; originals scanned and scans supplied for publication

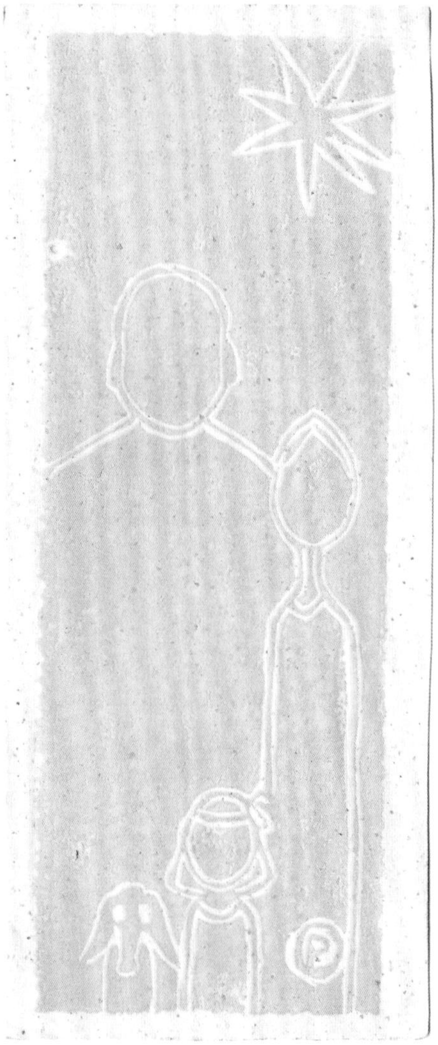

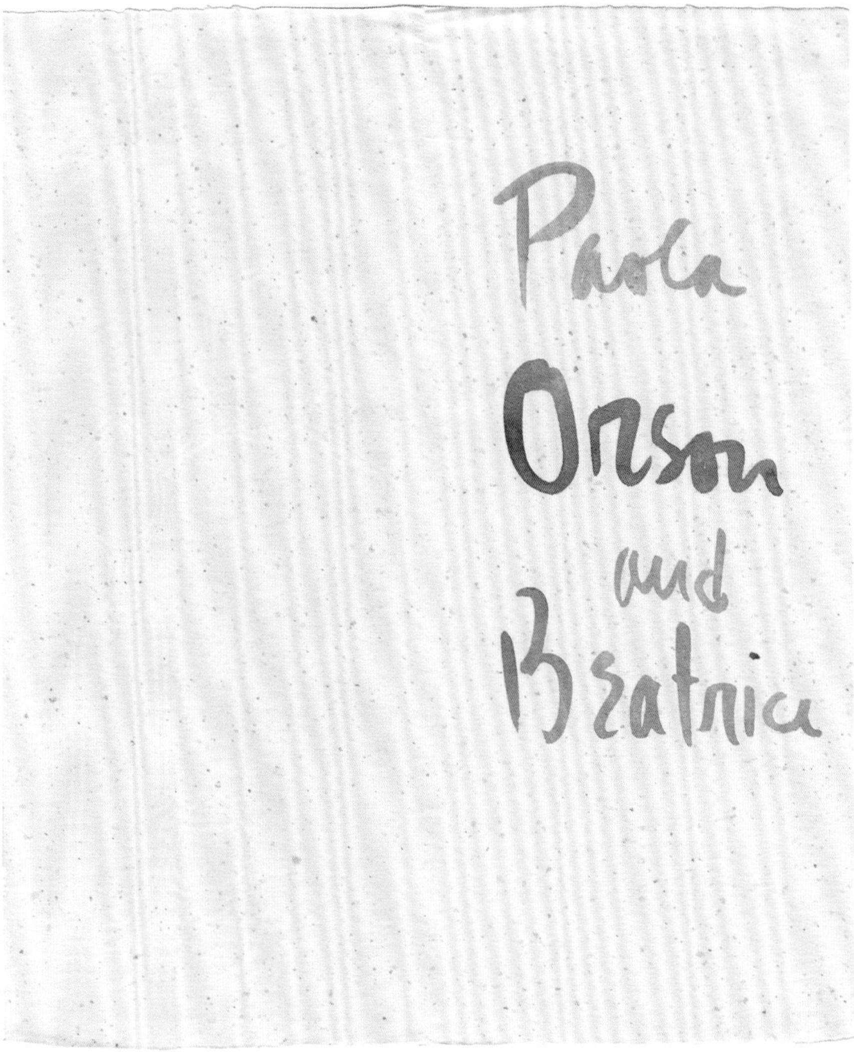

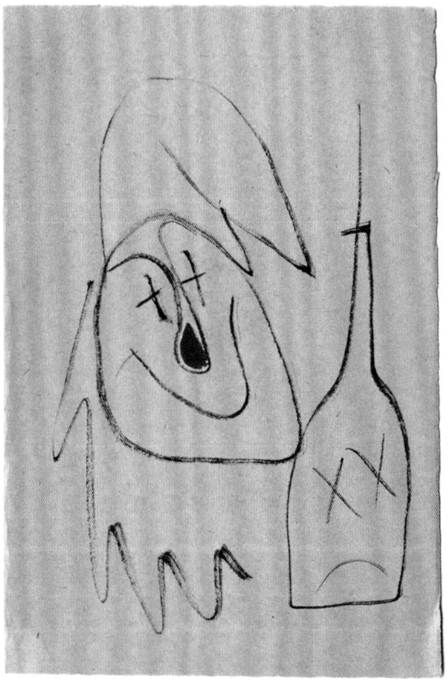

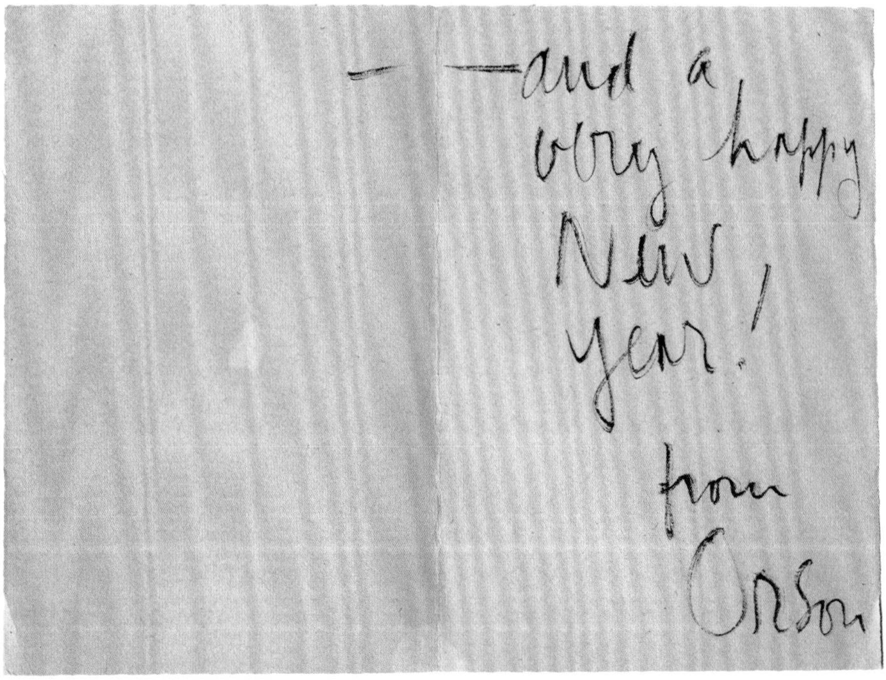

ABOVE: Christmas cards front and corresponding interior; originals scanned and scans supplied for publication

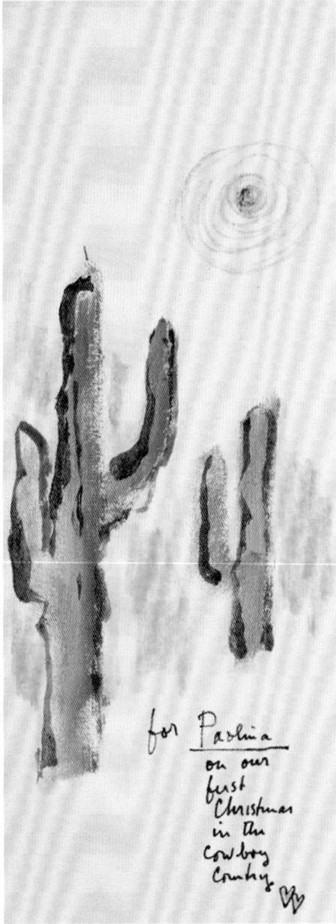

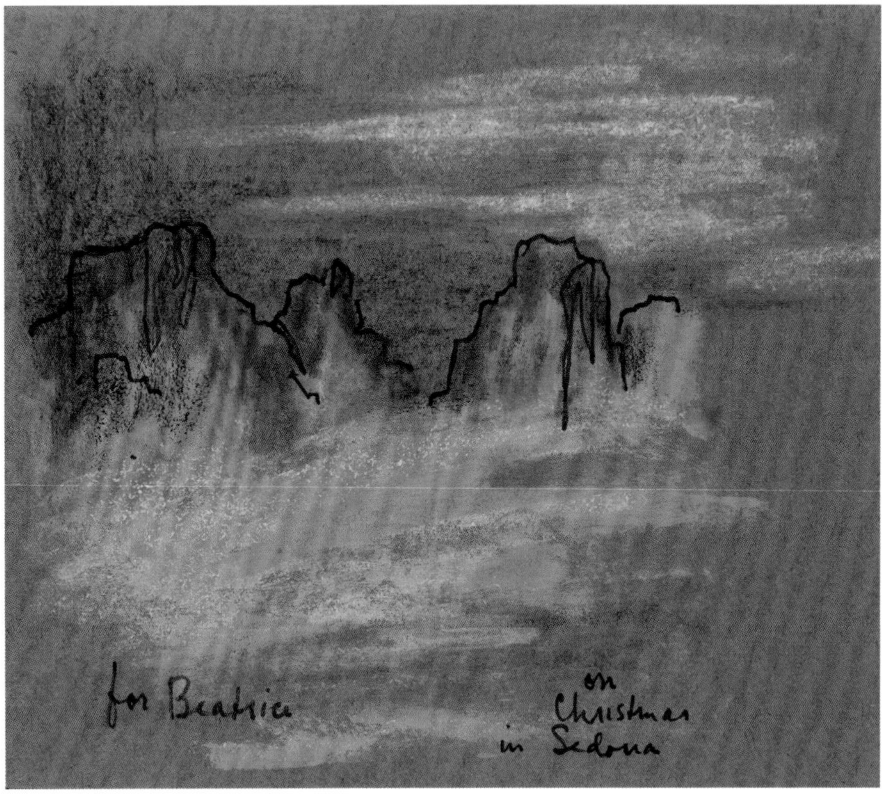

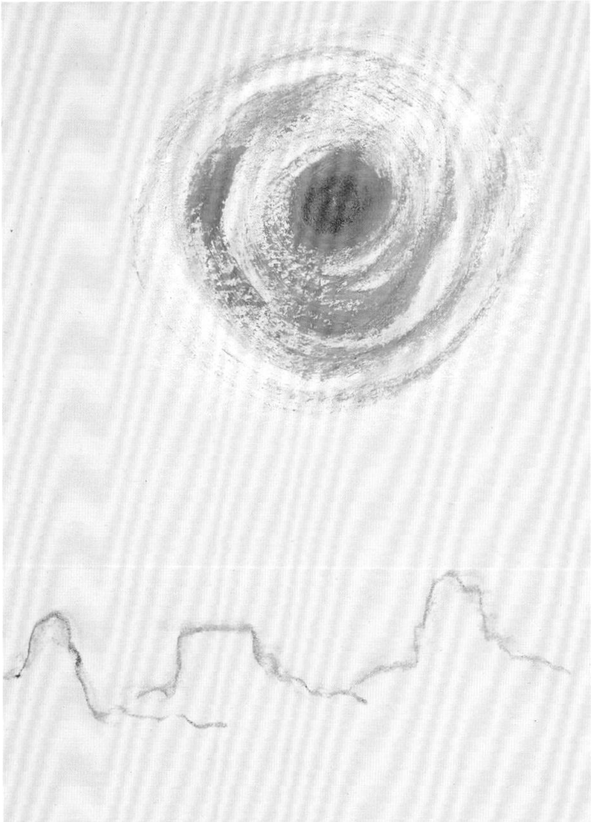

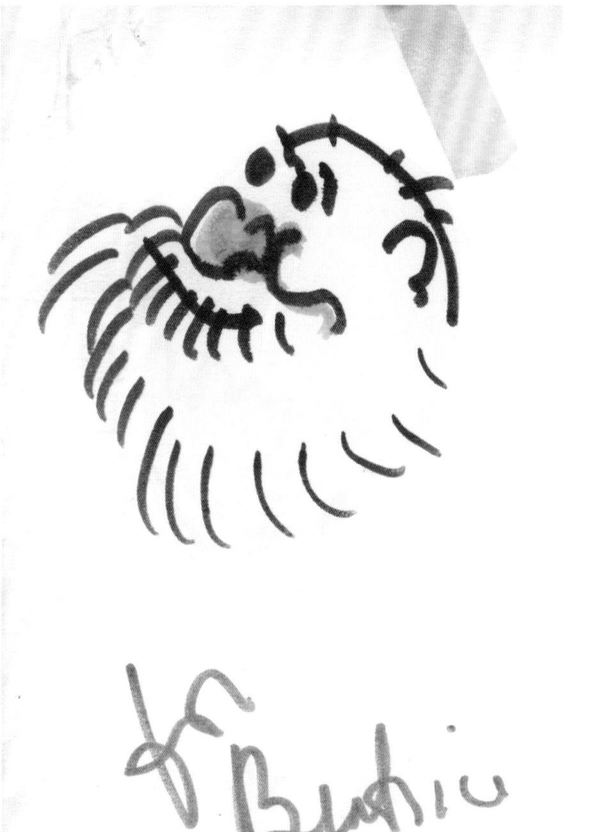

ABOVE: Christmas cards front; scans supplied for publication

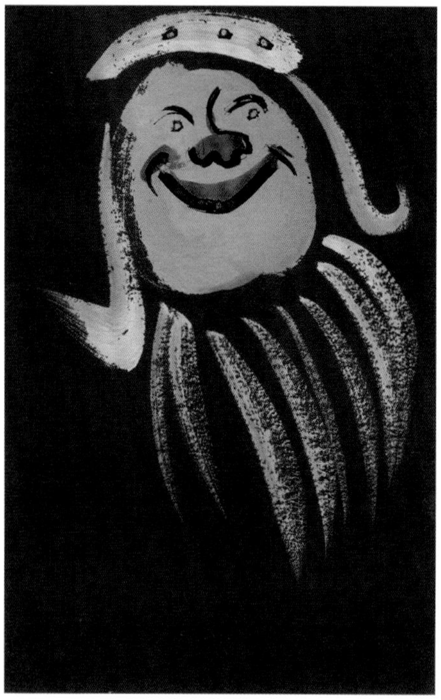

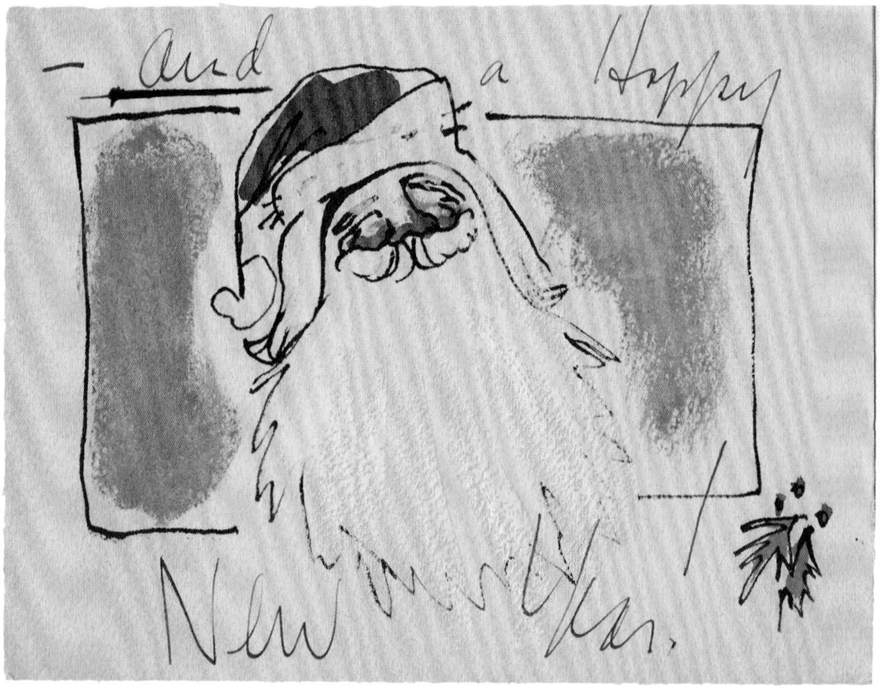

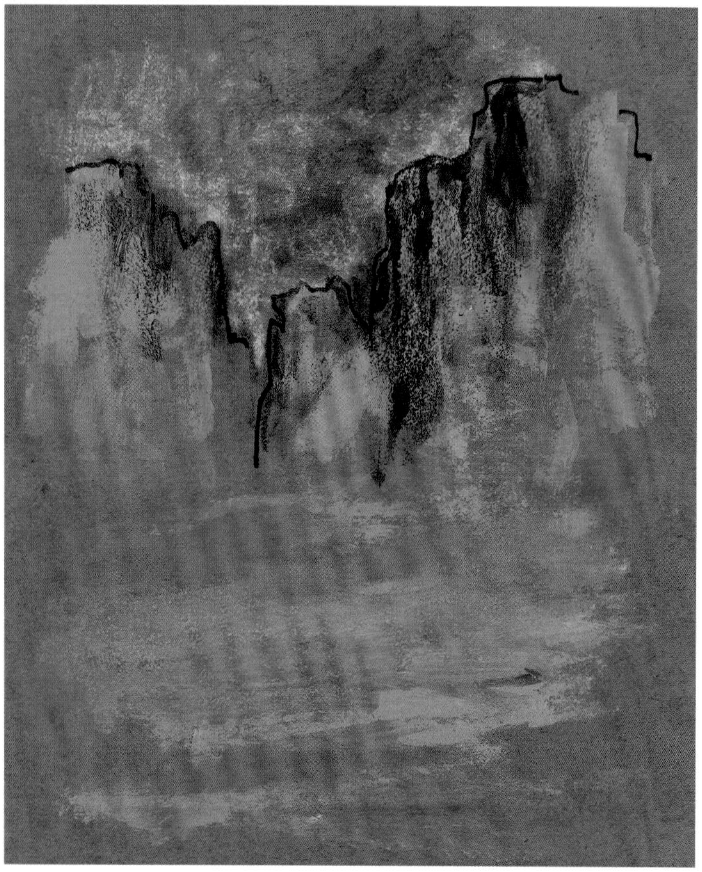

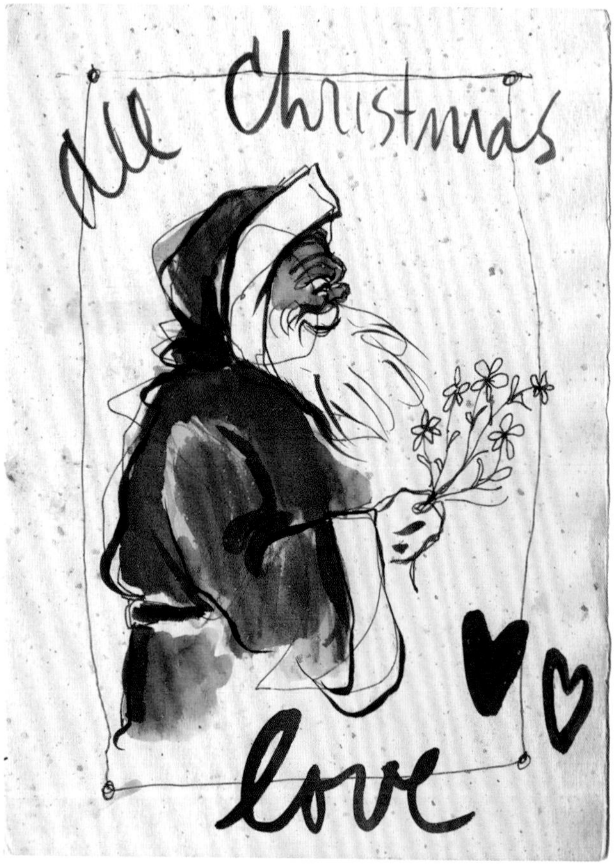

ABOVE: Christmas cards front; originals scanned and scans supplied for publication

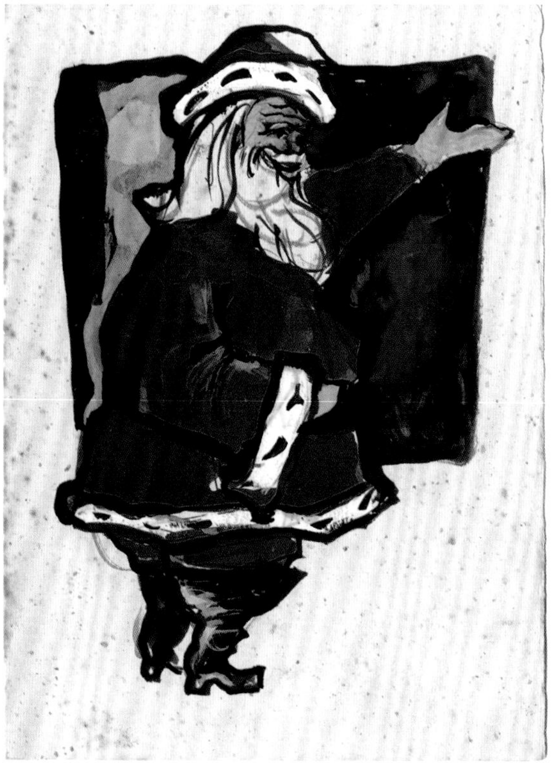

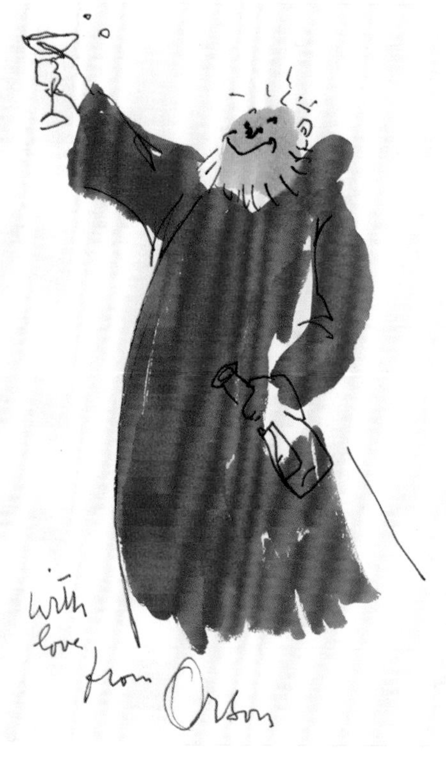

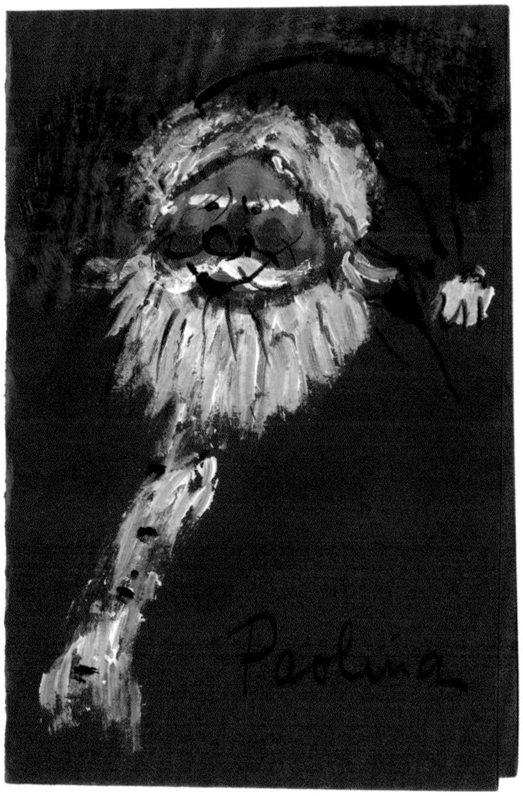

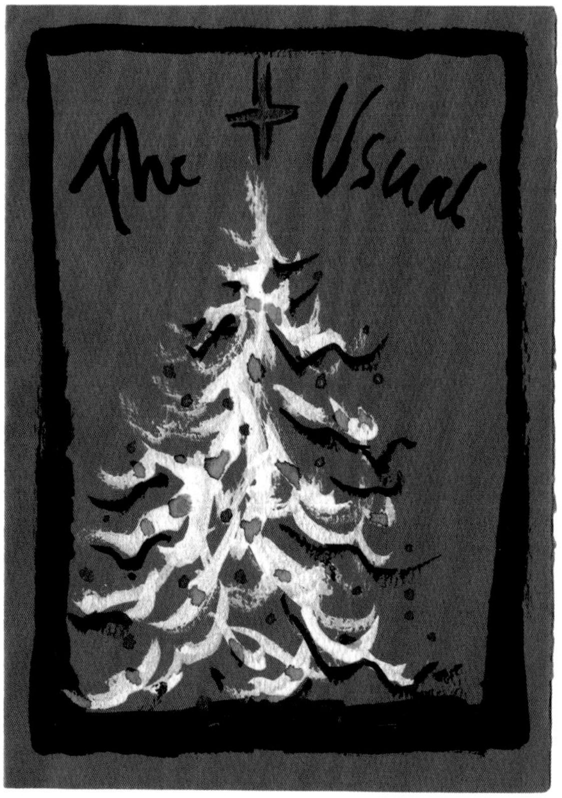

ABOVE: Christmas cards front; originals scanned for publication

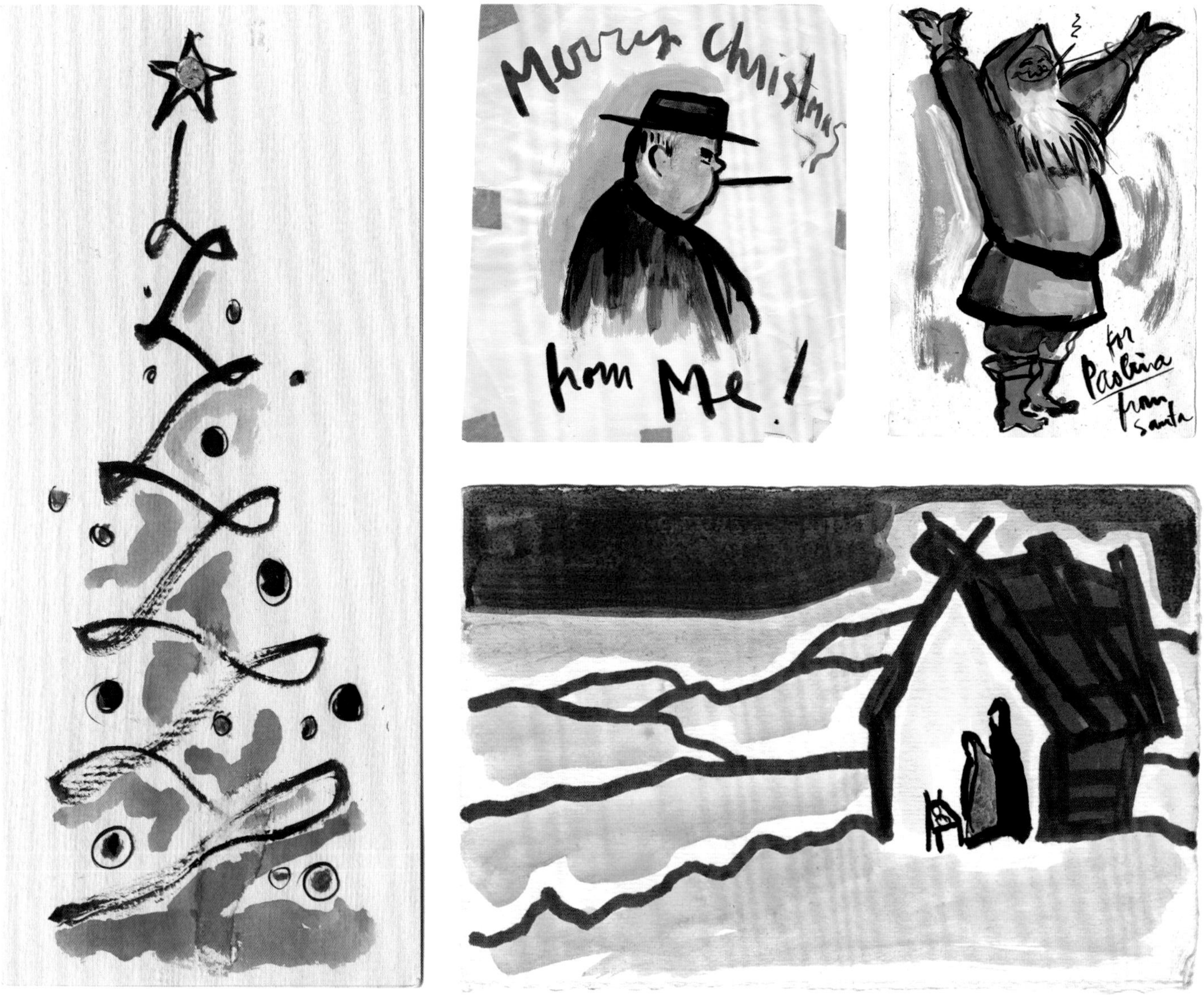

ABOVE: Christmas cards front; originals scanned for publication

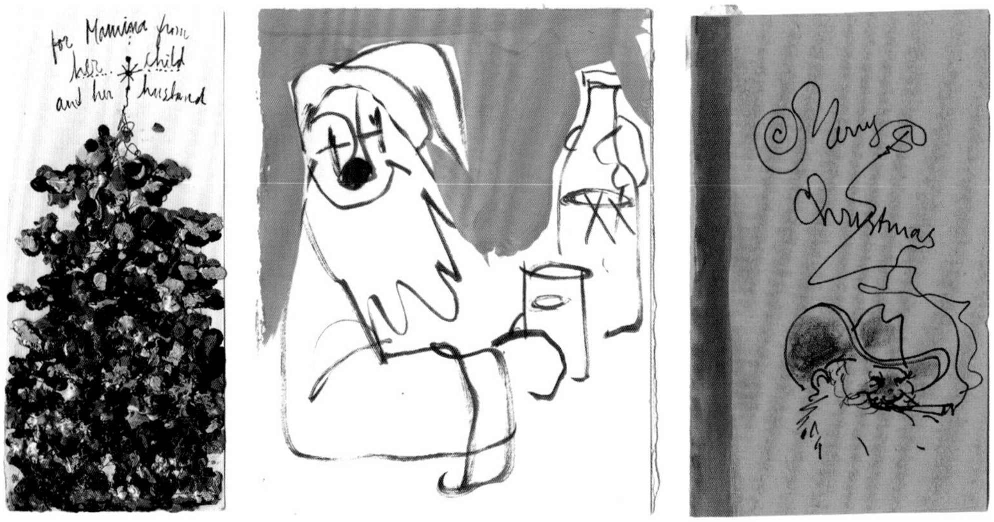

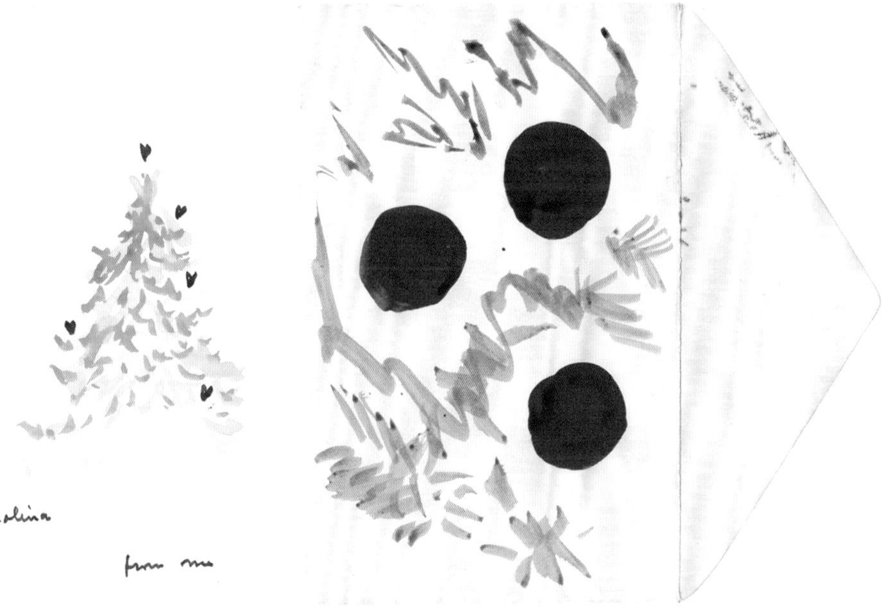

TOP: Christmas cards front; originals scanned for publication

ABOVE: Christmas card front and corresponding envelope; originals scanned for publication

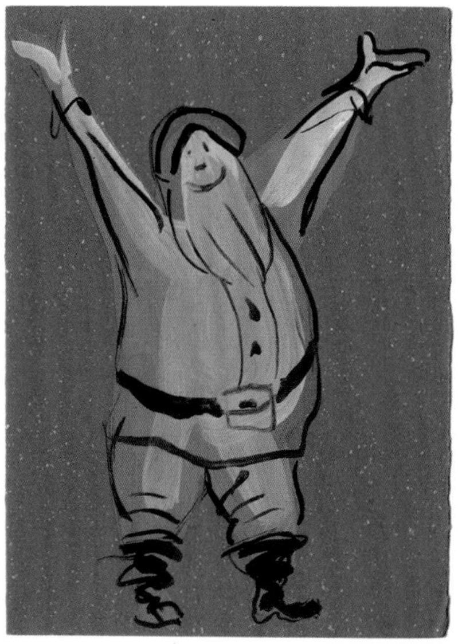

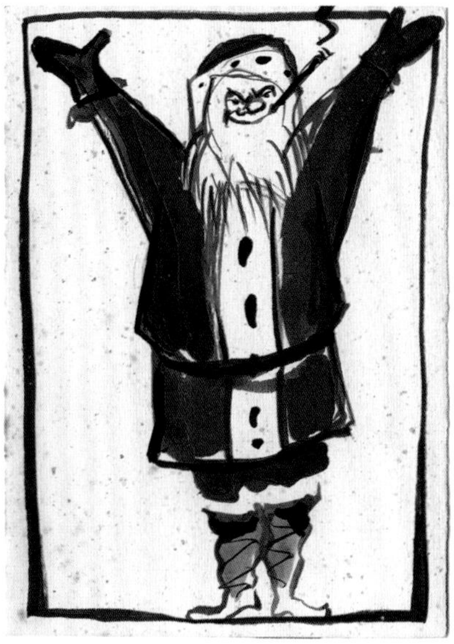

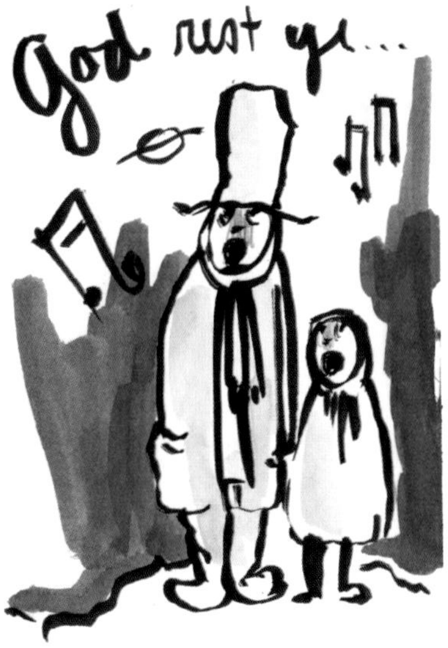

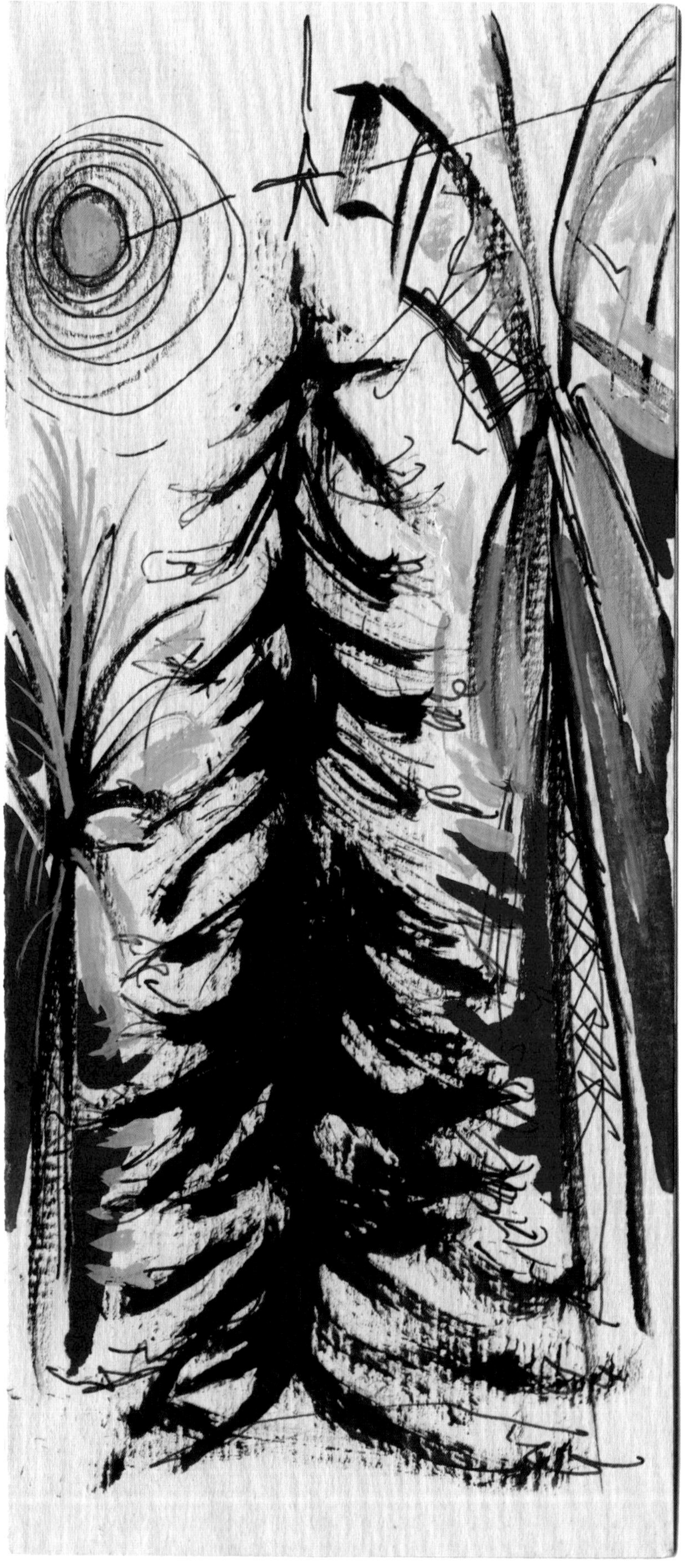

ABOVE: Christmas cards front; originals scanned for publication

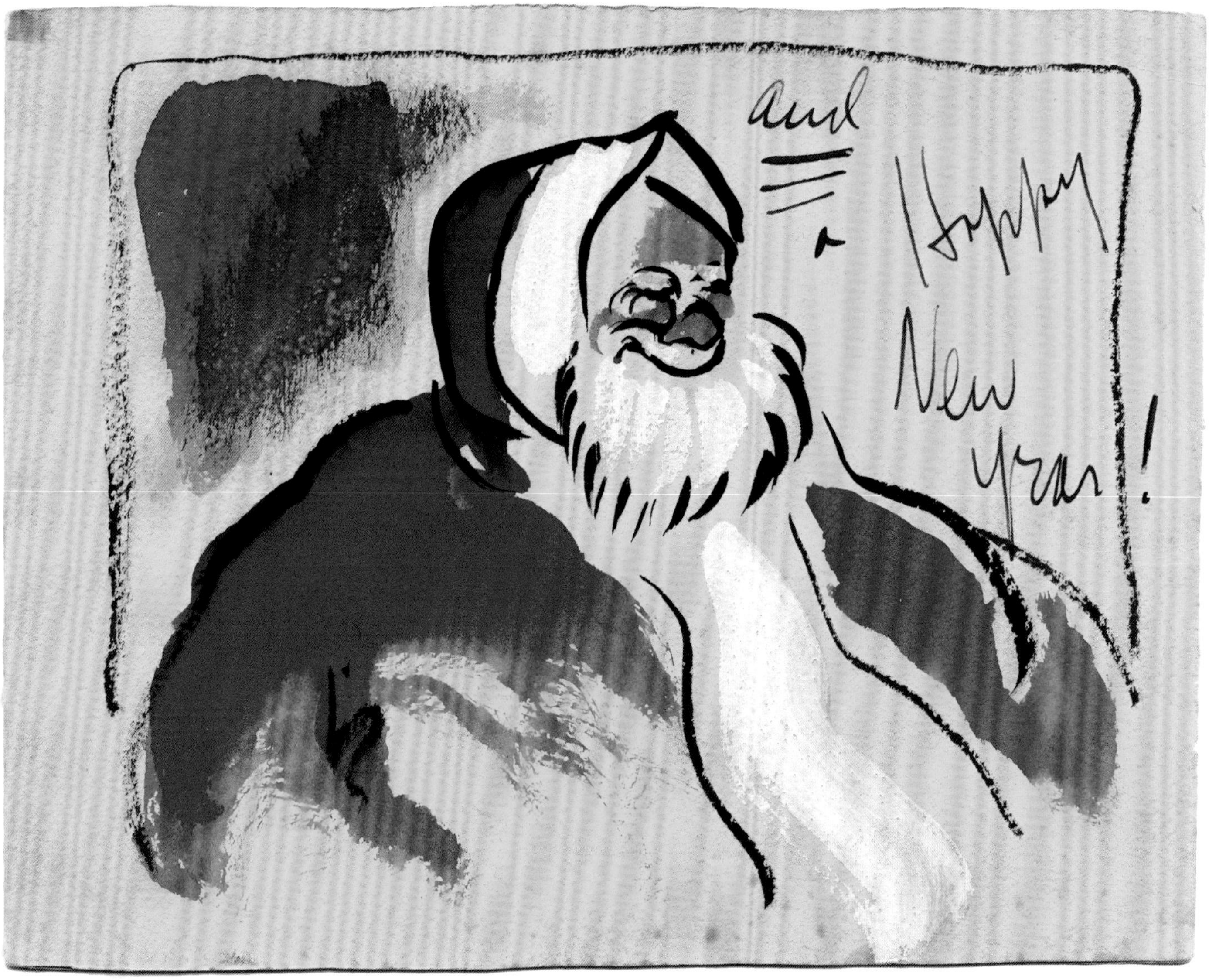

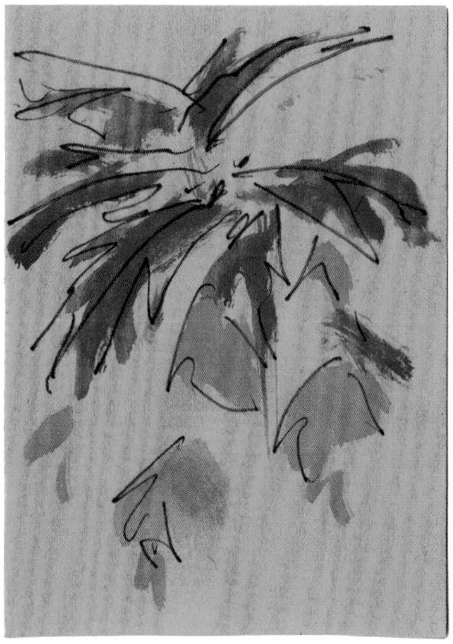

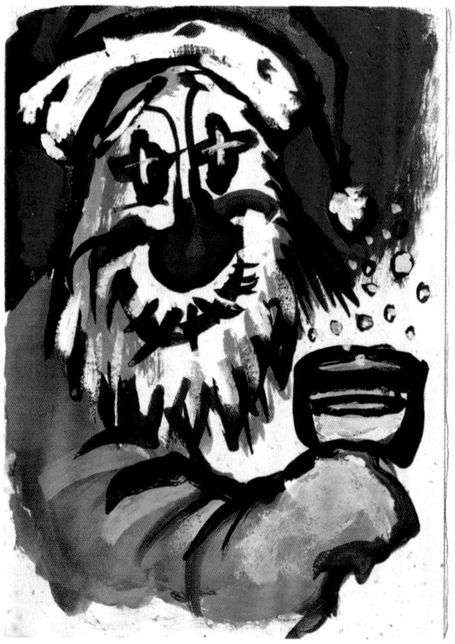

ABOVE: Christmas cards front; originals scanned for publication

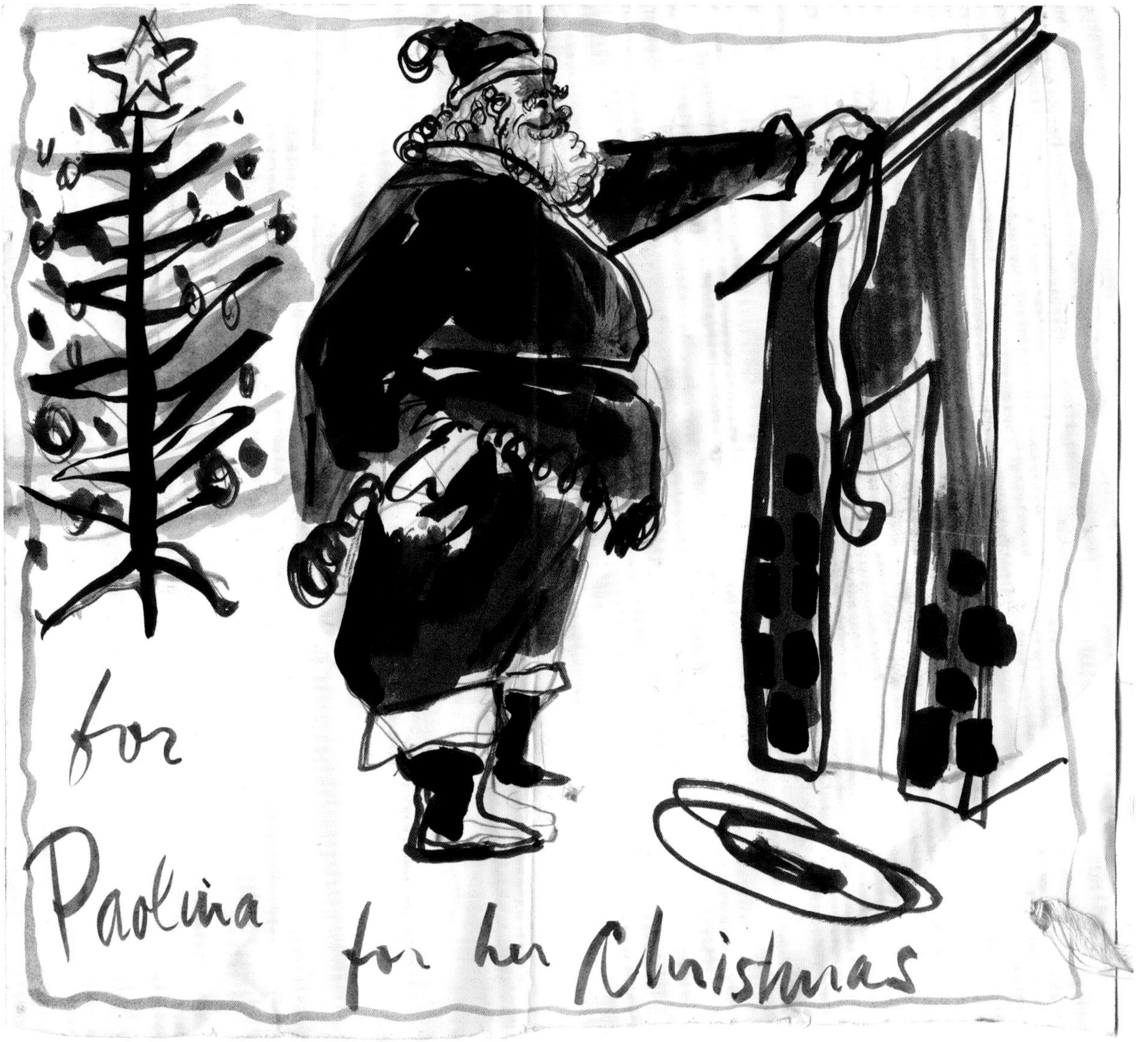

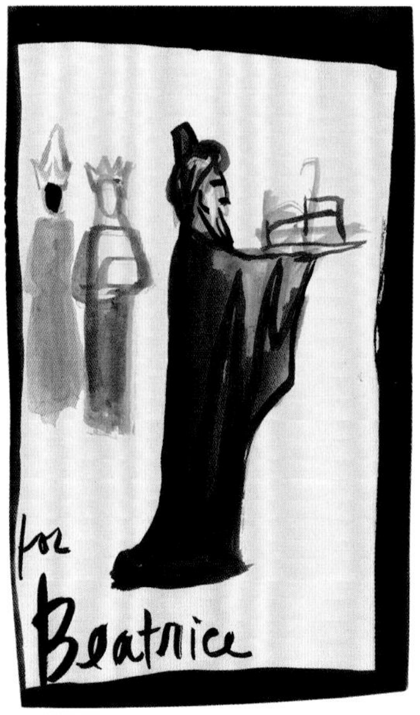

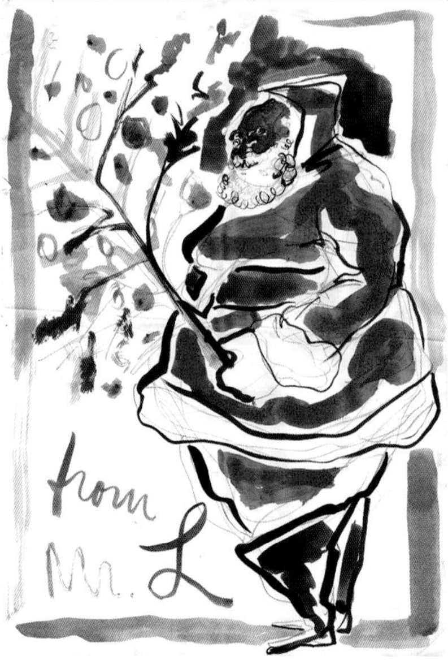

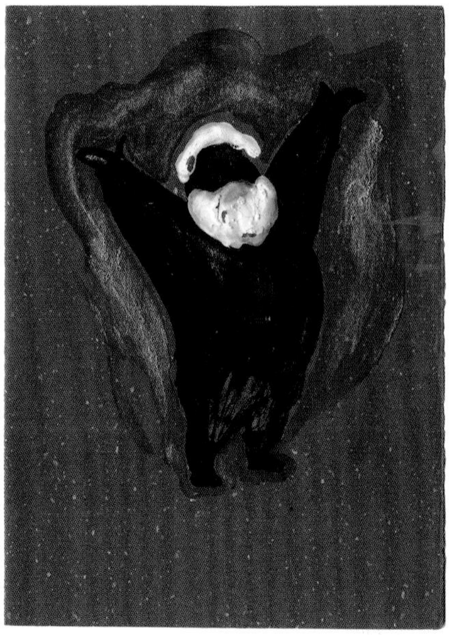

ABOVE: Christmas cards front; originals scanned for publication

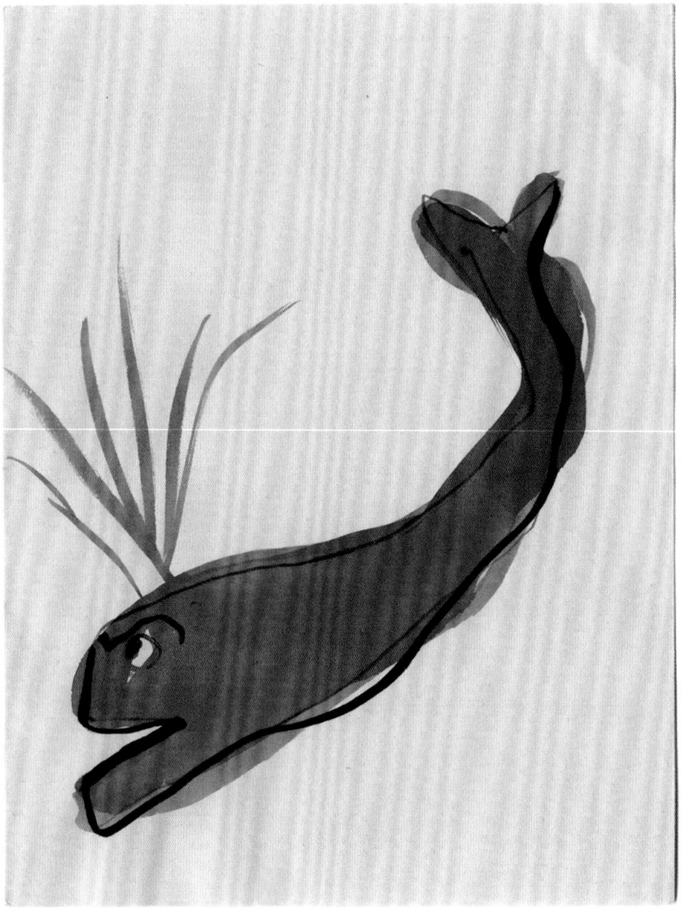

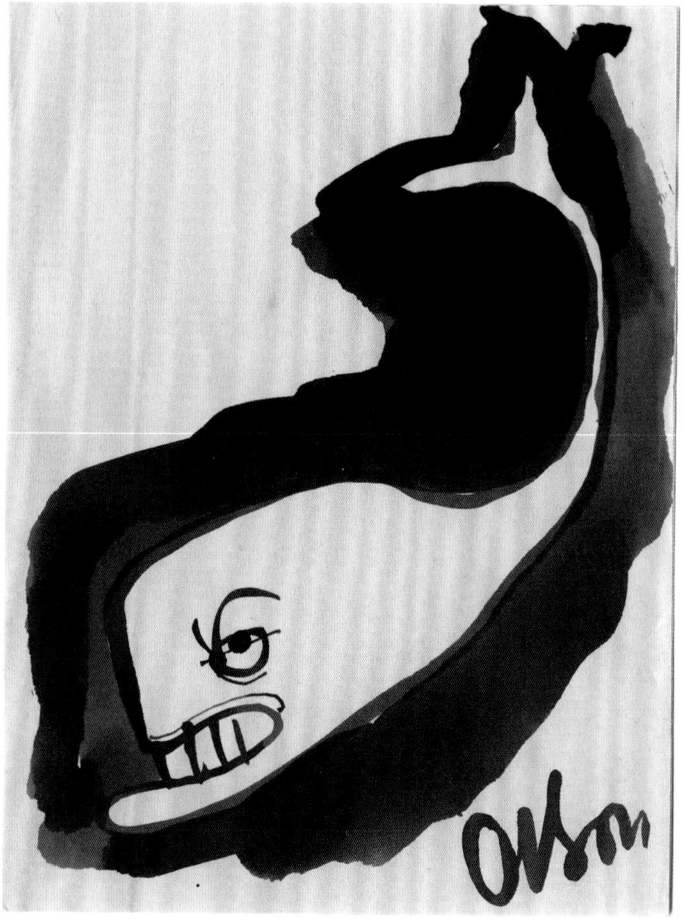

MOBY DICK

It's doubtful that these lively notecard daubs were preparation for any proposed production of *Moby Dick*, but Welles obviously had whales on his mind – the one on the right is also undeniably white and obviously in the mood for another helping of obsessive seafarer leg meat.

Welles had a long-term relationship with Melville's monolithic, infuriating novel. In 1955, he staged a heavily stylized version of it titled *Moby Dick – Rehearsed* in London with a cast that boasted Christopher Lee, Joan Plowright, Kenneth Williams, Patrick McGoohan and Peter Sallis. Its meta conceit was a troupe of actors portraying a troupe of actors improvising *Moby Dick* on a bare stage with minimalist props. Welles filmed 75 minutes of the play, hoping to sell it to American television. Instead, unhappy with the results, he abandoned it and the footage is now lost.

The following year, Welles played the minor role of Father Mapple in a big-screen adaptation directed by John Huston (from a script by Ray Bradbury) and starring Gregory Peck as Ahab.

In 1971, he took a final stab at it, filming himself reading from the book against a blue screen squirming with optical effects to simulate the ocean. The film remained unfinished until 1999 when a 22-minute cut assembled by the Munich Film Museum popped up on the festival circuit.

ABOVE: Notecards front; originals scanned for publication

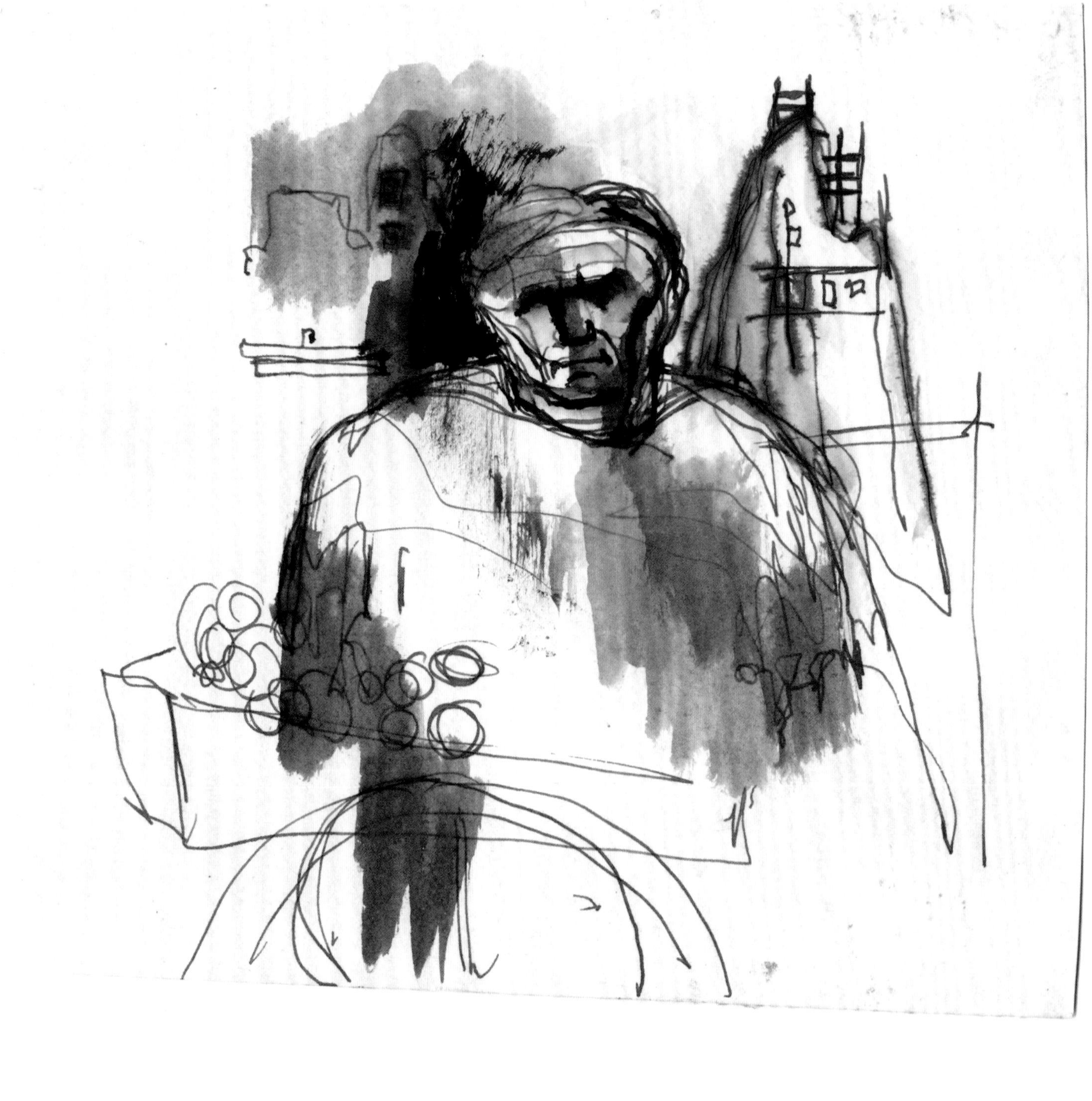

ABOVE: Watercolor sketch; original scanned for publication

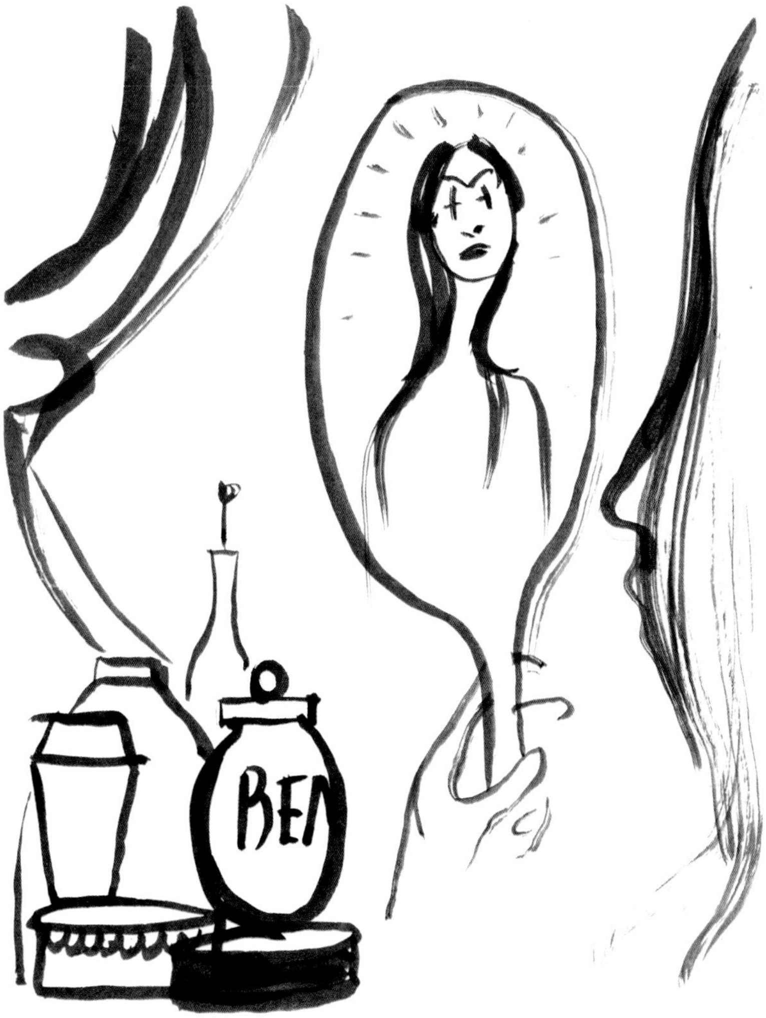

ABOVE: Sketch; original scanned for publication

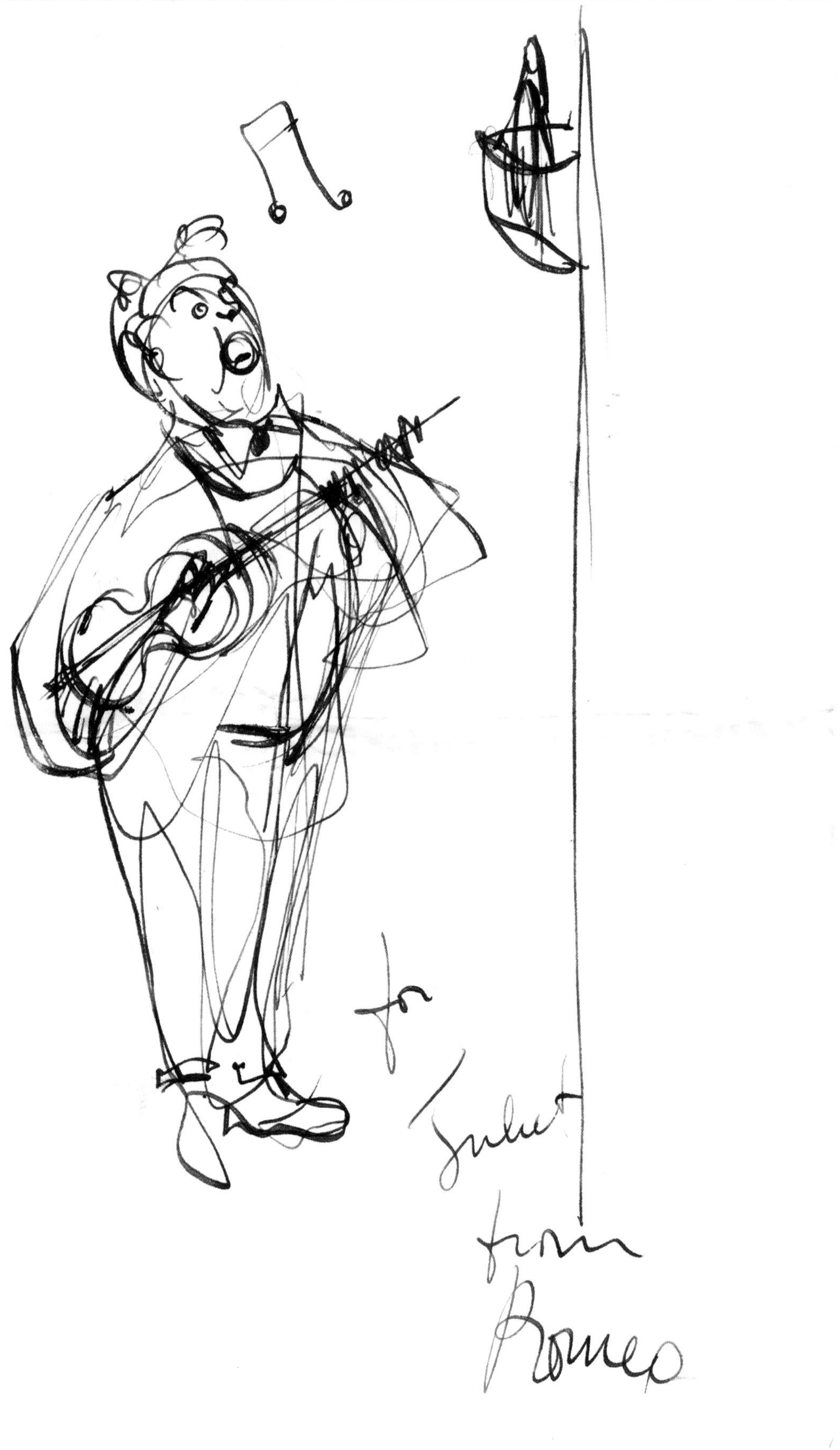

ABOVE: Sketch; original scanned for publication

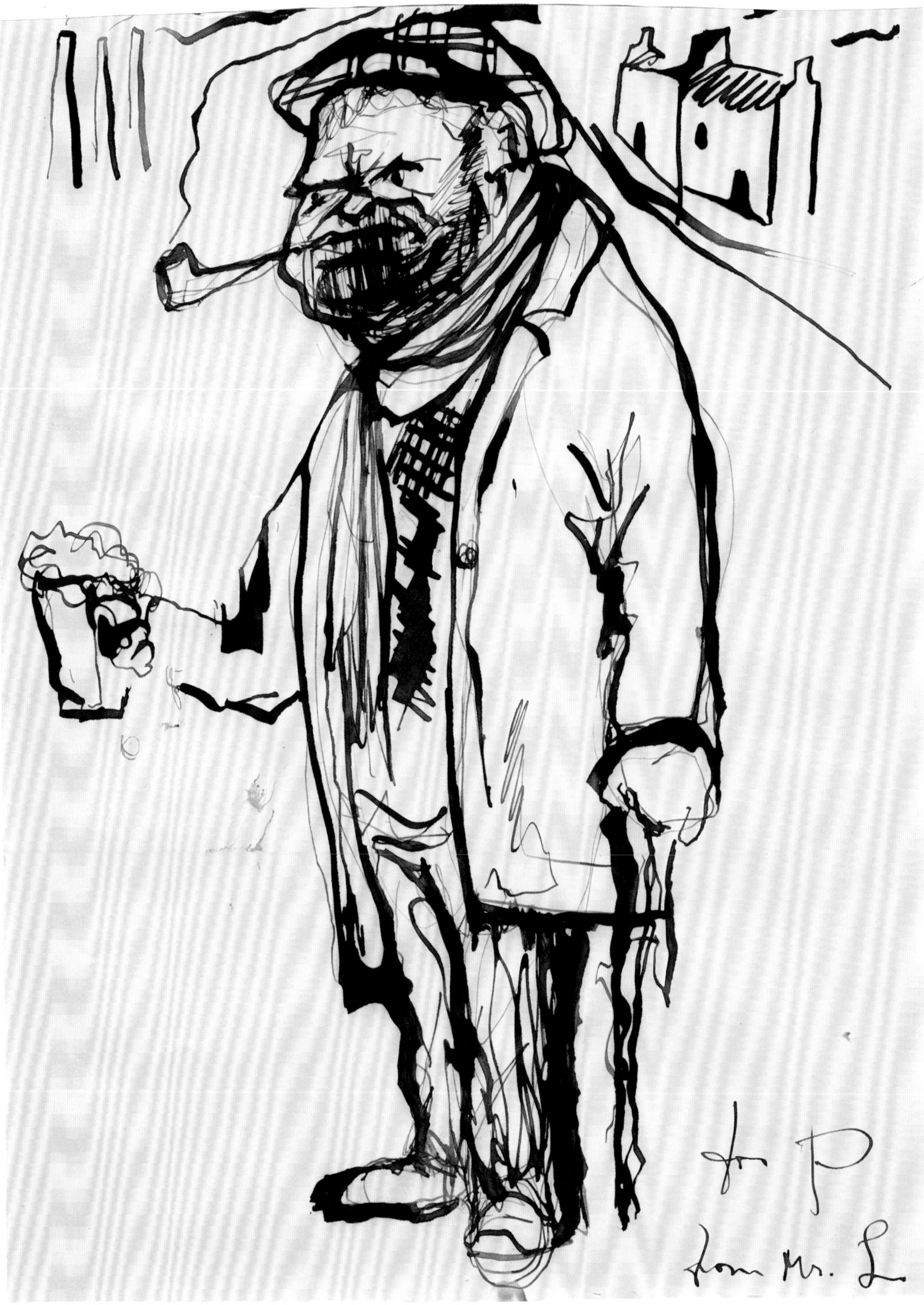

ABOVE: Sketch; original scanned for publication

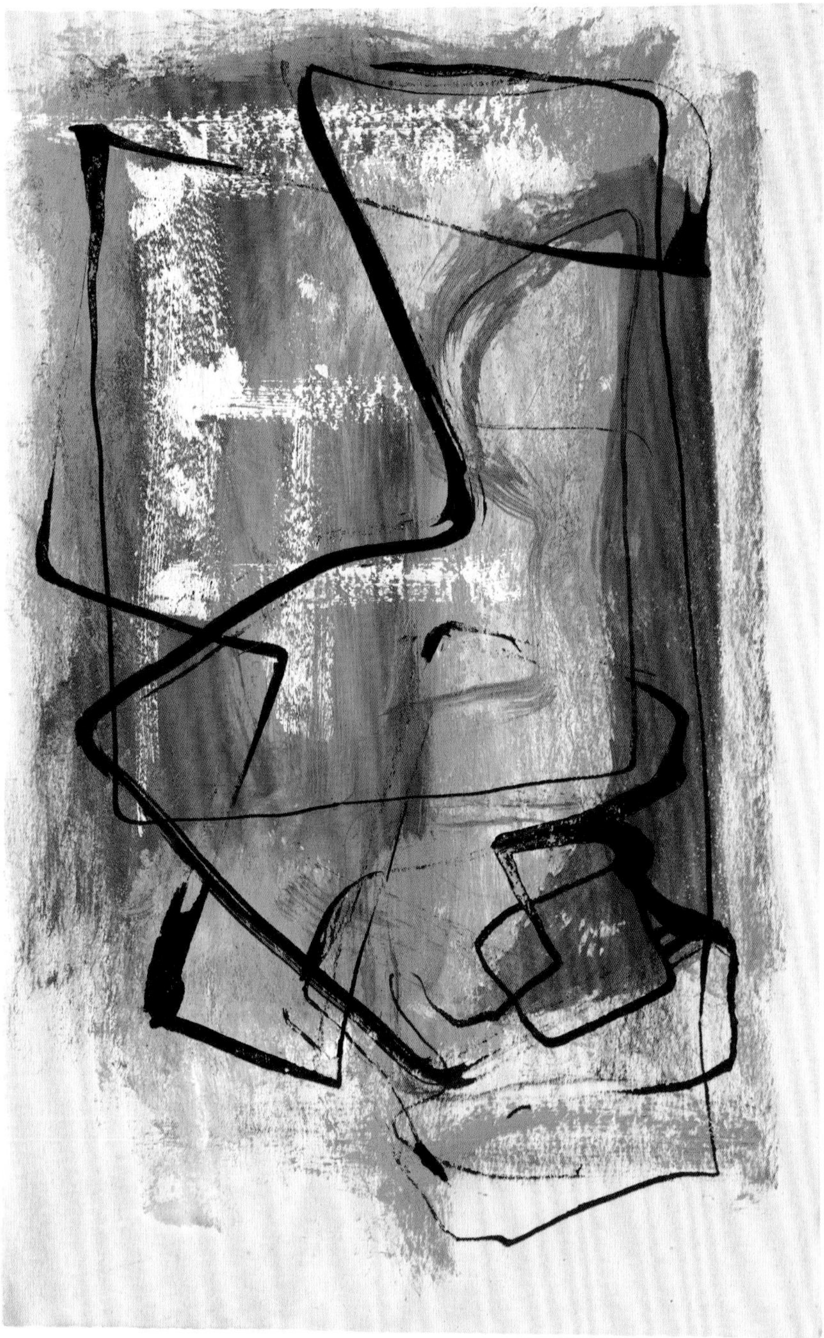

ABOVE: Watercolor notecard; original scanned for publication

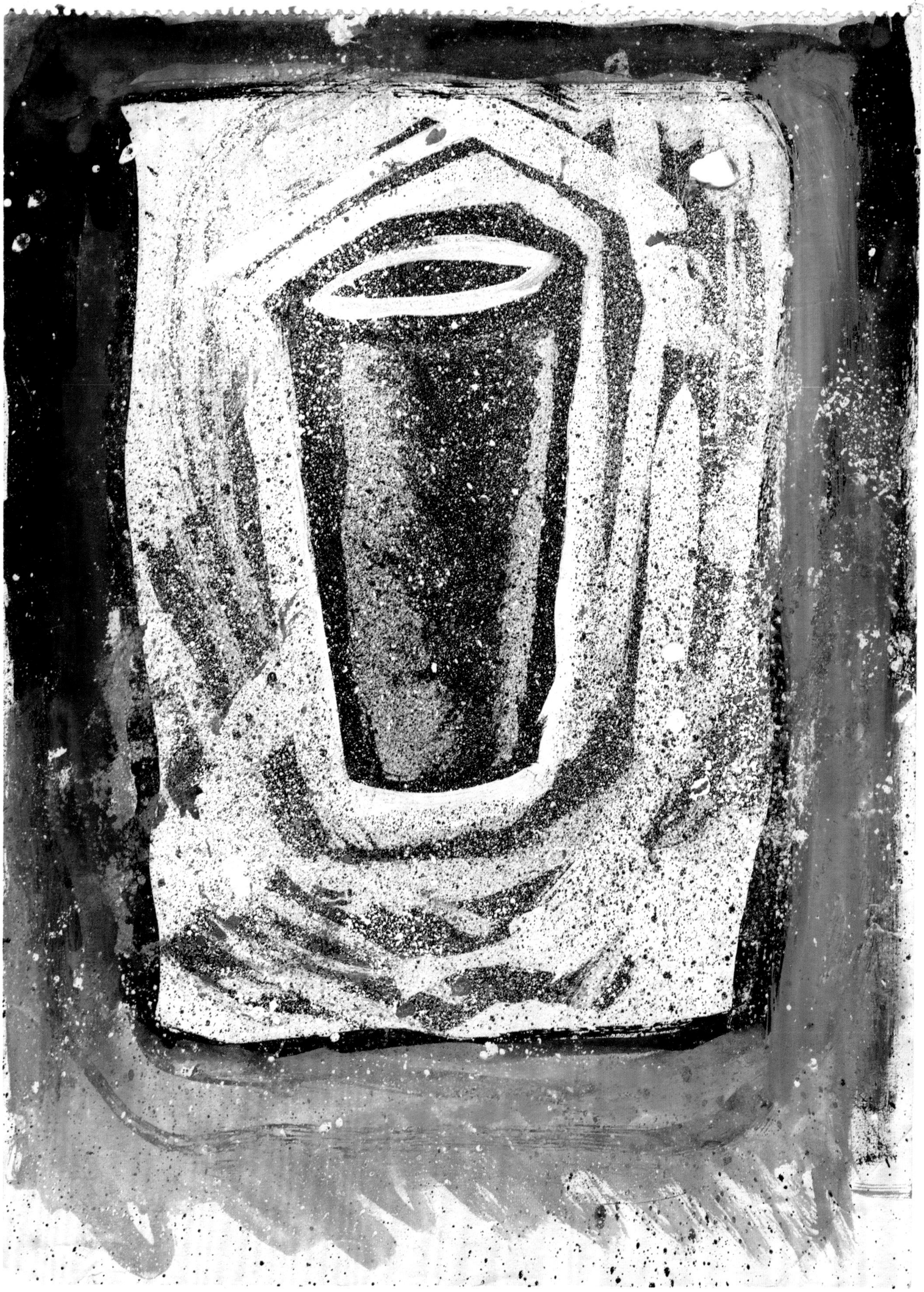

ABOVE: Painting; original scanned for publication

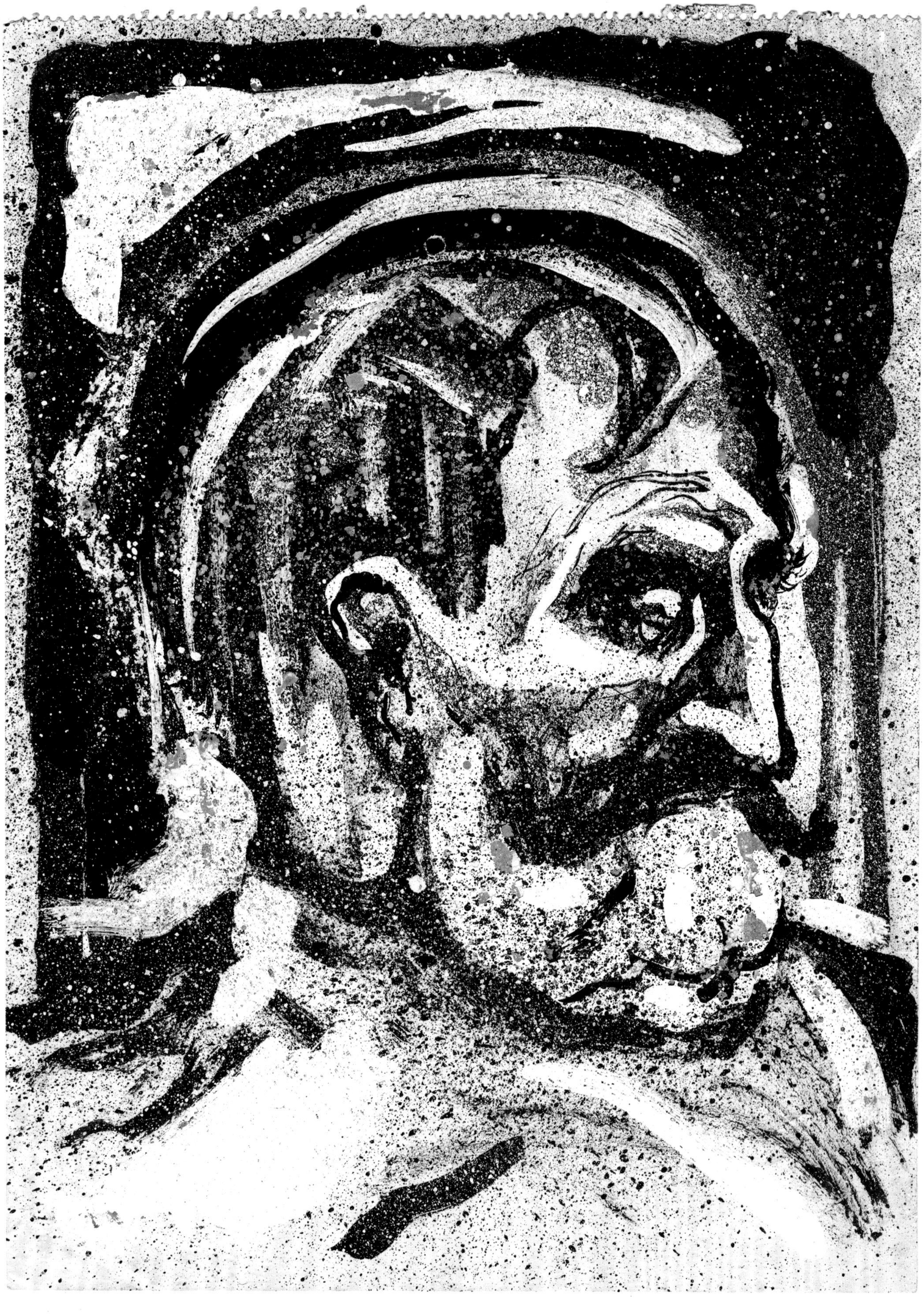

ABOVE: Painting; original scanned for publication

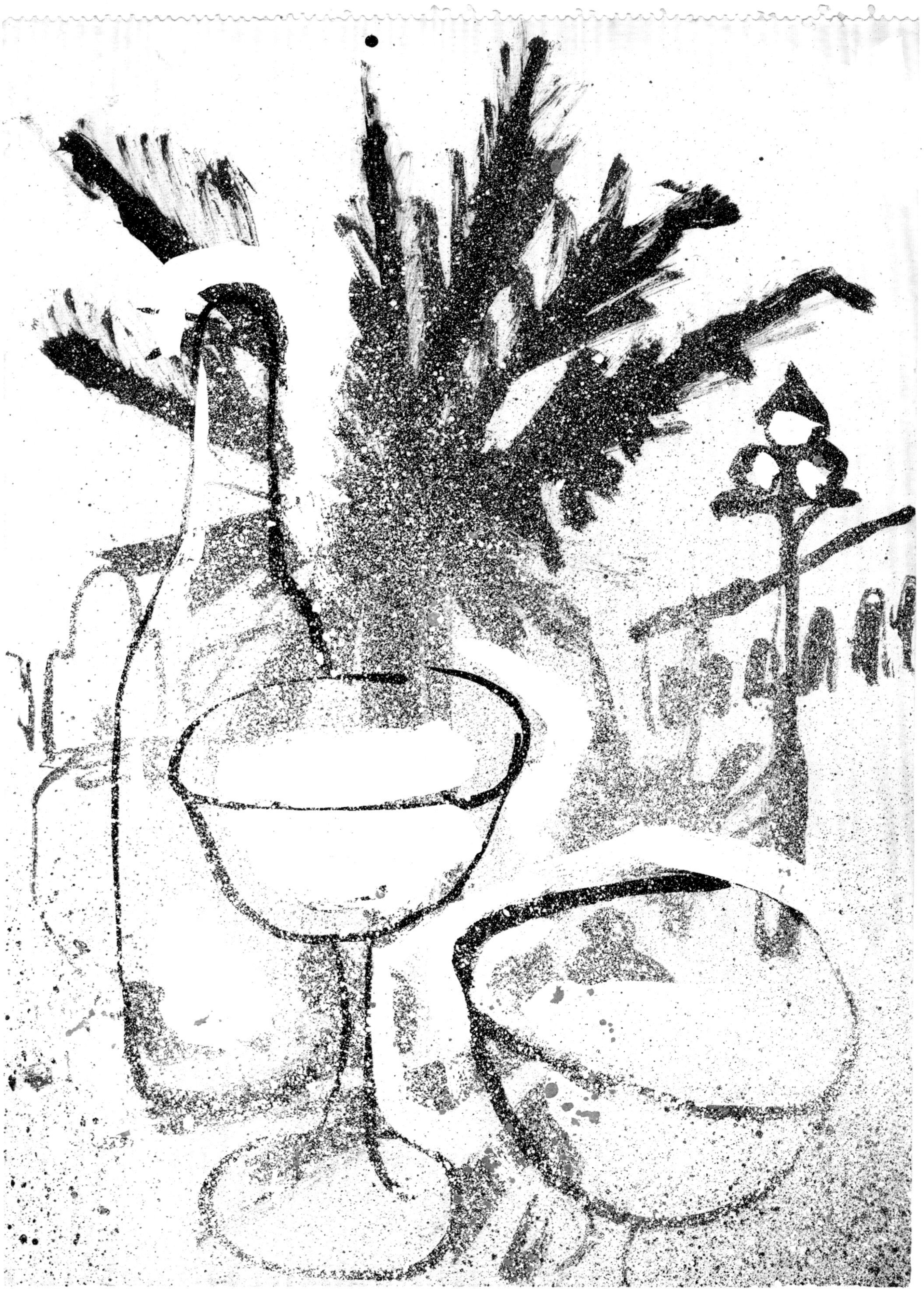

ABOVE: Painting; original scanned for publication

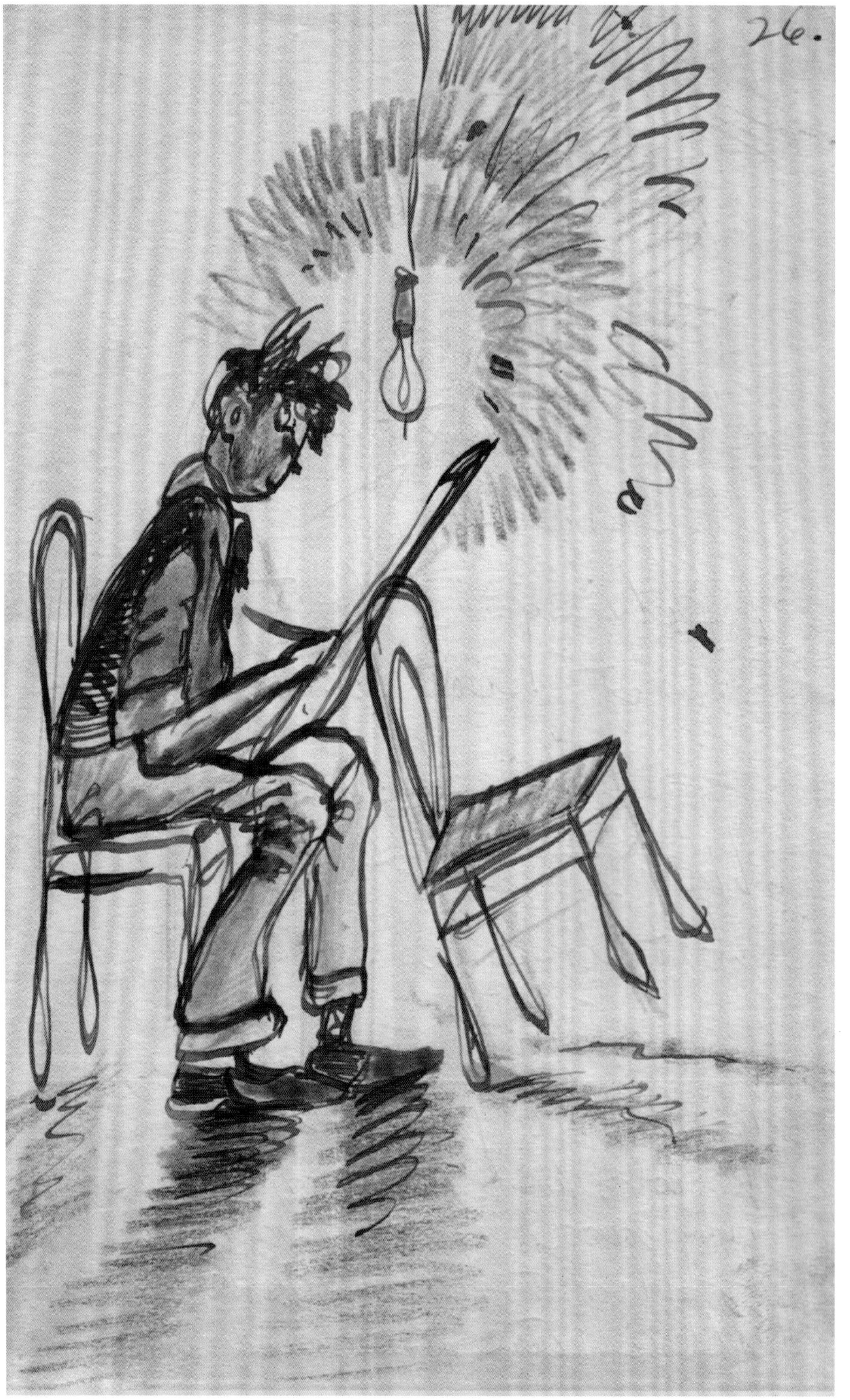

ABOVE: Pencil drawing, likely self-portrait; scan supplied for publication